The Life of ibn Ḥanbal

Letter from the General Editor

The Library of Arabic Literature series offers Arabic editions and English translations of significant works of Arabic literature, with an emphasis on the seventh to nineteenth centuries. The Library of Arabic Literature thus includes texts from the pre-Islamic era to the cusp of the modern period, and encompasses a wide range of genres, including poetry, poetics, fiction, religion, philosophy, law, science, history, and historiography.

Books in the series are edited and translated by internationally recognized scholars and are published in parallel-text format with Arabic and English on facing pages, and are also made available as English-only paperbacks.

The Library encourages scholars to produce authoritative, though not necessarily critical, Arabic editions, accompanied by modern, lucid English translations. Its ultimate goal is to introduce the rich, largely untapped Arabic literary heritage to both a general audience of readers as well as to scholars and students.

The Library of Arabic Literature is supported by a grant from the New York University Abu Dhabi Institute and is published by NYU Press.

Philip F. Kennedy
General Editor, Library of Arabic Literature

About this Paperback

This paperback edition differs in a few respects from its dual-language hardcover predecessor. Because of the compact trim size the pagination has changed, but paragraph numbering has been retained to facilitate cross-referencing with the hardcover. Material that referred to the Arabic edition has been updated to reflect the English-only format, and other material has been corrected and updated where appropriate. For information about the Arabic edition on which this English translation is based and about how the LAL Arabic text was established, readers are referred to the hardcover.

The Life of ibn Ḥanbal

by

Ibn al-Jawzī

translated by
Michael Cooperson

foreword by
Garth Fowden

volume editor
Tahera Qutbuddin

NEW YORK UNIVERSITY PRESS
New York

NEW YORK UNIVERSITY PRESS
New York

Library of Congress Cataloging-in-Publication Data
Names: Ibn al-Jawzi, Abu al-Faraj Abd al-Rahman ibn Ali, approximately 1116–1201 author. | Cooperson, Michael translator.
Title: The life of Ibn Hanbal / by Ibn al-Jawzi ; translated by Michael Cooperson ; foreword by Garth Fowden.
Other titles: Manaqib al-Imam Ahmad ibn Hanbal. English
Description: New York : New York University Press, 2016. | Includes bibliographical references and index.
Identifiers: LCCN 2016028108 (print) | LCCN 2016029914 (ebook) | ISBN 9781479805303 (pb : alk. paper) | ISBN 9781479886241 (e-book) | ISBN 9781479870394 (e-book)
Subjects: LCSH: Ibn Hanbal, Ahmad ibn Muòhammad, 780–855. | Islamic law—Biography.
Classification: LCC KBP310.I2653 I26513 2016 (print) | LCC KBP310.I2653 (ebook) | DDC 297.1/4092 [B]—dc23
LC record available at https://lccn.loc.gov/2016028108

New York University Press books are printed on acid-free paper, and their binding materials are chosen for strength and durability.

Series design and composition by Nicole Hayward
Typeset in Adobe Text

Manufactured in the United States of America

10 9 8 7 6 5 4 3 2 1

MIX
Paper | Supporting responsible forestry
FSC® C013604

Contents

Foreword

GARTH FOWDEN

During the first half of the ninth century, most of the Abbasid Caliphate's subjects were Christians, Jews, Zoroastrians or even pagans. The ruling minority of Muslims faced, at almost every turn, the threat—or allure—of other ways of life and thought, deeply rooted in landscape, history and custom. No wonder they often felt embattled, or succumbed to temptation: it might come in the form of an invitation to a neighbor's house, a casual romantic or sexual encounter, or the need to bury a non-Muslim parent. There was, in any event, a need for detailed instruction about everyday deportment. Guidance might be sought in the Qur'an, but much in it was ambiguous or left unsaid. Traditions about the Prophet's sayings and doings (hadiths) proliferated to fill the gap. The eminent legal thinker, al-Shāfiʿī (d. 204H/820AD), strongly advocated the authority of hadiths in his epoch-making *Epistle on Legal Theory* (recently translated for the Library of Arabic Literature).

In the next generation, Aḥmad ibn Ḥanbal (d. 241H/855AD) made a reputation that has never faded, not just as an indefatigable collector of hadiths, but also as one of the greatest exemplars, after the Prophet himself, of the conduct the hadiths prescribed. The numerous responses Ibn Ḥanbal offered to enquiries from pious fellow Muslims present a lively picture of daily life in ninth-century Baghdad. In the eyes of ordinary people, however, Ibn Ḥanbal's reputation rested chiefly on his unflinching endurance of a severe flogging at the command of the Caliph al-Maʾmūn (r. 198–218H/813–833AD). This was Ibn Ḥanbal's recompense for insisting on the doctrine of the uncreatedness of the Qur'an as God's living word, for which al-Maʾmūn sought to substitute a view of scripture that left room for human interpretation based on reason. Al-Maʾmūn had his own distinctive ideas about interpreting scripture and in general about the sources of authority in Islam; but Ibn Ḥanbal's resistance contributed decisively to the triumph of scholarly research over caliphal will in determining Muslim doctrine. Increasingly, an attachment to Qur'anic scholarship was construed as excluding resort to ratiocination or speculation—these were the sins of the philosophers. Whereas al-Maʾmūn was closely associated with the translation of Greek philosophy into Arabic, Ibn Ḥanbal would have no truck with such writings, which were neither Arabic nor Muslim.

The Ḥanbalī school—named for Ibn Ḥanbal—was already flourishing by the tenth century, despite competition from other schools of legal thought. It continued to renew itself during the centuries that followed, first in Baghdad, then in Damascus. It prospered less after the conquest of the Arab lands in the early sixteenth century by the Ottomans, who favored the Ḥanafī school of legal thought. By one of those symmetries of history that Ibn Ḥanbal himself would perhaps have appreciated, it was a little outside the Ottoman domains, in eighteenth-century Central Arabia, that his school experienced its most memorable revival, just as the Prophet himself had arisen in the relative obscurity of the seventh-century Hijaz, to address and resolve the political and theological tensions that were tormenting the neighboring empires of Sasanid Iran and—especially—East Rome (Byzantium).

Given the global reach of the Saudi version of Islam today, and its debt to Ibn Ḥanbal, much of the significance of Michael Cooperson's painstaking work on Ibn al-Jawzī's *Life of Ibn Ḥanbal* is in danger of being lost on those who fail to see it in the context, not just of Abbasid Baghdad, but also of Wahhabism in the Arabian Peninsula. In his erudite and elegantly written guide to the history of Hanbalism, the monumental *Commanding Right and Forbidding Wrong in Islamic Thought* (2001), Michael Cook draws a striking contrast. On the one hand there is a quietist Ibn Ḥanbal who reproved wrongdoing but discouraged aggression towards its perpetrators, keeping a firm distance from the repressive apparatus of the state and eschewing political activism. On the other hand there is the Ḥanbalī scholar Muḥammad ibn ʿAbd al-Wahhāb (d. 1206H/1792AD), who in alliance with the Emir Muḥammad ibn Saʿūd (d. 1179H/1765AD) launched an all-out assault on what he saw as "polytheistic" practices in the scattered oases of Central Arabia. As Cook puts it, "Hanbalism was now cast in the unfamiliar role of a doctrine of state-formation in a near-stateless tribal society." But the doctrine, as distinct from its possible political applications, remained the same.

As for the duty incumbent on every Muslim, and exemplified by Ibn Ḥanbal, of "commanding right and forbidding wrong," the Saudi state progressively institutionalized it by having local emirs conduct active investigations (Ibn Ḥanbal had preferred to avert his gaze where possible, and reprove only when he had no choice). Cook argues that as the Saudis ran out of opportunities for further expansion and jihad against the infidel, they turned their righteous aggression on the enemy within. But when in 1924–25 they finally conquered the Hijaz and the Holy Places, "the juxtaposition of Wahhābī Puritanism and the laxer attitudes of the wider Muslim world was a prescription for trouble" (182). Hence the setting up in 1926 of a "Committee for Commanding Right and Forbidding Wrong," populated by scholars and notables, to control the thuggish behavior of Bedouin enforcers towards the lucrative foreign pilgrims. Prayer-discipline, alcohol, smoking and segregation of women were major preoccupations. Similar committees were established throughout the kingdom, and their influence has endured. Cook concludes by reflecting on the effective strangulation, by bureaucratization, of what began as "a strongly apolitical and individual doctrine" (192).

In the pages that follow, readers will encounter for themselves the most convincing exemplar of that tradition, who has done as much as any other human, after the Prophet and his Companions, to shape the central characteristics of Sunni Islam as we see it lived today.

Garth Fowden
Sultan Qaboos Professor of Abrahamic Faiths,
University of Cambridge

Acknowledgments

My greatest debt of gratitude is to Dr. ʿAbd Allāh ibn ʿAbd al-Muḥsin al-Turkī, who has produced two annotated critical editions of this work. In the course of preparing this edition, I have had recourse to several manuscripts of the *Manāqib*, but found only a few places where I think the best reading may be different from the one Dr. al-Turkī has adopted. On every page I have benefited from his careful lists of variants, his voweling of unusual names, and his explanatory notes and references. I have also been impressed with his scholarly integrity and self-restraint, as proven—among other things—by his inclusion of reports that advocate positions he disagrees with.

A full account of the manuscript tradition appears in the note on the text. I am very grateful to Jeremy Farrell, who obtained a copy of the Dār al-Kutub manuscript and solved the technical problems associated with sending me a digital copy. It is a pleasure to thank Saud AlSarhan for obtaining a copy of the Ẓāhiriyyah manuscript from Imam Muḥammad ibn Saʿūd Islamic University, and to thank Bernard Haykel for mailing it to me. I would also like to thank Sinéad Ward and Frances Narkiewicz of the Chester Beatty Library for sending me their manuscript of the *Manāqib*.

I am also indebted to Mr. Farrell and to Albert Johns for kindly agreeing to take on the job of translating almost all of the *isnād*s. Though busy with their own work, Jeremy and Albert cheerfully and speedily produced an enormous amount of remarkably accurate English text just when I needed it most. Emily Selove did equally good work with one of the long lists of names. I could never have finished this project without their help.

As always when I translate, I learn once again to appreciate my friends for how much my friends know and how generous they are in sharing it. My project editor, Tahera Qutbuddin, made many suggestions and corrections, all of them judicious and kindly conveyed. It is not general practice to thank project editors for their help in particular instances, and most of Tahera's emendations have indeed been incorporated silently, but in several cases her astuteness in solving an utterly vexing conundrum so merits recognition that I have credited her in defiance of custom. Our colleagues at the Library—notably Joseph Lowry, James Montgomery, Devin Stewart, and Shawkat Toorawa—also solved a number of seemingly intractable problems, and our managing editor, Chip Rossetti, was also an unfailing source of good counsel. I am grateful to Stuart Brown for his inspired typography, and to Allison Brown and Alia Soliman for carefully proofreading the text. Jamal Ali, Muhammad Habib, Stefan Heidemann, Nuha Khoury, Peter Pormann, Nasser Rabbat, and Dwight Reynolds all responded to queries in their various areas of expertise. Charles Perry supplied generous answers to many questions about food and cookery. I am equally grateful to master chef Brigitte Caland, whose Abbasid-inspired luncheons allowed me to taste the dishes that Ibn Ḥanbal ate (or more usually, did not eat).

I am delighted to acknowledge the help of Christopher Melchert, who answered many queries, and made several helpful comments in his review of the first edition; Faisal Abdallah, who carefully read through the first volume of the first edition and brought a number of errors to my attention; and Kyle Gamble, who brilliantly corrected a bad mistake in 61.2. I also thank Marcia Lynx Qualey for the insightful questions she posed in two interviews published in her blog. I thank my friends in Malta, especially Annabel Mallia, David Mallia, Olvin Vella, and the people of Senglea, for showing me that some of Ibn Ḥanbal's language still survives in the most unexpected of places. I am grateful to my wife, Mahsa Maleki, not only for putting up with my many late nights at the office, but also for her help with the name-lists (which proved that pre-modern people were quite right about the helpfulness of reading aloud). Finally, I am indebted to our general editor, Philip Kennedy, for envisioning a project as ambitious as the Library of Arabic Literature, and for generously allowing me to take part in it.

Introduction

Aḥmad ibn Ḥanbal, who died in the 241st year of the Muslim calendar, 855 according to the Christian one, is probably one of the most famous Muslims in history. Thanks to him, many came to believe that the only right religion was the one practiced at the time of the Prophet Muḥammad. To keep their community together in this world and gain salvation in the next, Muslims needed to live as the Prophet and his Companions had lived: to eat what they ate, wear what they wore, buy and sell only as they had done. "Is there anything I'm doing wrong?" one of Ibn Ḥanbal's wives asked him a few days after they were married. "No," he answered, "except that those sandals you're wearing didn't exist at the time of the Prophet" (62.7).

To live as the first Muslims had lived, it was necessary to know as much as possible about them. Reports of their words and deeds were repeated by one believer to another, along with the names of those who had passed these reports on. By Ibn Ḥanbal's time, a proper report—called a Hadith—was expected to include a list of names beginning with the speaker's source and ending with the person who had seen the Prophet or a Companion doing or saying whatever it was that one wished to know. After Ibn Ḥanbal was arrested during the Abbasid Inquisition, a well-wisher counseled him by citing the following Hadith:

> We heard al-Layth ibn Sa'd report, citing Muḥammad ibn 'Ajlān, citing Abū l-Zinād, citing al-A'raj, citing Abū Hurayrah,

> that the Prophet, God bless and keep him, said: "If any ask you to disobey God, heed him not" (68.4).

What if a seeker could find no Hadith report about a particular question? In that case he might apply his own reasoning to the problem. Yet the scope for undisciplined individual effort was small and growing smaller. In Ibn Ḥanbal's time, most Muslims no longer believed that they could simply judge as they thought best. For many, it was necessary to take into consideration all related Qur'anic verses and Hadith reports, and then—using an increasingly complex system of legal reasoning—come up with a rule that seemed best to approximate God's will. Yet Ibn Ḥanbal himself could not accept this approach. The solution, in his view, was to learn more Hadith reports, in the hope that one or another report would supply the information needed. In practice, however, this solution placed great demands on the learner. For one thing, the people who happened to know a particular report might be living anywhere in the lands settled by Muslims, and it was necessary to seek them out. On his return from a Hadith-gathering mission to the town of Kufa, Ibn Ḥanbal was accosted by a friend who reproached him for overdoing it:

> "Today it's Kufa; tomorrow it'll be Basra again! How much longer can you keep this up? You've already copied thirty thousand reports! Isn't that enough?"
>
> [Aḥmad] said nothing.
>
> "What if you reach sixty thousand?"
>
> He was still silent.
>
> "A hundred thousand?"
>
> "At that point," he replied, "a man might claim to know something" (4.20).

Another problem was keeping track of what one was learning. Premodern societies are often described as oral cultures, and premodern people as having extraordinary abilities to memorize vast amounts of material, but not everyone found rote learning easy. Ibn

Ḥanbal's older contemporary al-Shāfiʿī reportedly ingested frankincense to strengthen his memory, to the point that he suffered internal bleeding.[1] Ibn Ḥanbal himself insisted that one write down the Hadiths one learned (13.9). He is described as carrying his notes—organized by topic—into the mosque to teach (26.2) and rummaging through piles of papers to find the report he wanted (26.1).

Even if one learned many Hadith reports, one's task had only begun. Simply knowing many reports was not enough: it was also necessary to live in accordance with the teachings they contained. For Ibn Ḥanbal, this meant denying oneself the luxuries the Prophet scorned, or had never seen, like chairs decorated with silver (53.3). It was, furthermore, necessary to avoid objects and activities that might have been acceptable in themselves but which were tainted by association with something forbidden or merely suspicious. For example, Ibn Ḥanbal had no way of knowing whether the taxes collected by the government were fairly levied and properly spent. He therefore refused to eat anything offered to him during his visits to the palace, whether as a prisoner or a guest (69.13, 69.25, 73.19–21). He also refused to eat bread or gourds baked in an oven that belonged to his son Ṣāliḥ, who had accepted a gift from the caliph (49.13, 49.20). This horror of ritual pollution was called *waraʿ*, which seems to have no precise English translation; it is often called "scrupulousness" or "scrupulosity." In practice, *waraʿ* meant renouncing luxury, and Baghdad—a famously wealthy and self-indulgent place at the time—had many luxuries to offer. Unlike some of his associates, Ibn Ḥanbal did not believe in interfering with the pleasures of others. Yet he refused to partake in them himself. Instead, he spent his days in a shabby room, sometimes wondering whether keeping a few coins wrapped in a rag was wrong because it implied doubt that God would provide for him (35.7, 41.17, 79.6).

For Ibn Ḥanbal's contemporaries, this spectacle was an especially moving one because his austerity was a matter of choice. To judge by their names, many of his fellow Hadith scholars were descendants of *mawālī*, that is, of non-Arabs who had adopted Islam.

Their fathers were traders and craftsmen, with names such as "the leather-worker," "the draper," "the maker of vinegar," and so on. Ibn Ḥanbal, by contrast, was an Arab: he belonged to the people who had given the world the Prophet Muḥammad and the language of the Revelation. Moreover, his family was a prominent one that had helped to bring the Abbasid regime to power. His grandfather had served as governor of Sarakhs, a town that now lies on the border between Turkmenistan and Iran (1.7). Presumably, Ibn Ḥanbal could have used his family connections to obtain a government job (3.5–7). Instead, he chose to seek Hadith. Admittedly, he did accept one of the benefits of inherited wealth: a number of rental properties that supplied enough income to support him and his family (40.1). But he is also described as giving his tenants breaks on their rent on the slightest pretext (42.1). When prices were high, he seems not to have collected rent at all, living instead from the sale of cloth woven by his wife Umm Ṣāliḥ (44.6).

With the benefit of hindsight, we see that Ibn Ḥanbal played a formative role in the movement later called Sunnism. For his followers, being a Muslim meant taking the practice (*sunnah*) of the Prophet, along with the Qur'an, as the basis for living one's life. It meant looking to Hadith—and not, for example, to the words of a living religious guide—as the source of right practice. It meant accepting the succession of caliphs after Muḥammad rather than claiming, as the Shiʿa did, that ʿAlī was the worthiest of the Prophet's Companions. Finally, it meant rejecting speculation in matters of religion and refusing to discuss matters not spelled out in the Qur'an or the Hadith.

Ironically, however, Ibn Ḥanbal seems hardly to have been laid to rest before his followers felt compelled to defend their position using the weapons of their adversaries, including theological disputation. Even while he was alive, a rapprochement had begun to take place between Hadith-minded Muslims and the Abbasid regime, which had tried to impose its own top-down, Shiʿa-style guidance on the mass of believers. And Ibn Ḥanbal's associates had already begun collecting the reports and opinions that would become fundamental texts for those who wished to follow his lead in matters of law (which included belief and ritual as well as the areas covered by Western legal systems). From all this activity emerged the so-called Ḥanbalī legal school, of which Ibn Ḥanbal was not the founder, but certainly the inspiration, or at least the figurehead. By taking a stand against Shiʿism, rationalism, and theological speculation, Ibn Ḥanbal helped articulate the positions now held, at least nominally, by the majority of the Muslims now living on the planet.

For someone who does not share Ibn Ḥanbal's view of the world, his positions may seem stifling, if not frankly repressive. Moreover, the adoration his followers felt for him can seem cloying. Indeed, many of today's Muslims—including the editor of two prior Arabic editions of this biography—take pains to condemn the cult of sanctity to which Ibn Ḥanbal was subjected. According to the reports in this book, Ibn Ḥanbal could cure nosebleeds (61.2) and drive ants from his house by uttering a prayer (61.1). On the battlefront against the Byzantines, soldiers would pray for his well-being so that God would guide their shots to their targets (19.1). After his death, a light spread from his grave to all the tombs nearby (95.1), and droves of dead men appeared in dreams to say that they had seen him in the Garden (that is, in Paradise) (93.14, 93.16ff.). It is not clear how much of this was actually believed in Ibn Ḥanbal's own time, but he certainly seems to have been the object of more attention than he wanted. "I wish for something I'll never have," he is supposed to have said, "a place with no one in it at all" (54.4).

For many modern readers, it is this element that vindicates Ibn Ḥanbal, at least as a subject of biography. If he is a saint (to use what is, strictly speaking, an inapposite Christian term), he is one who finds his own sainthood exasperating. Unlike the ethereal creatures of hagiography, Ibn Ḥanbal is not only a man of God but also a husband, a father, and a landlord—possibly the only saintly landlord in world literature. Instead of wrestling with demons, he struggles with the problems of daily life: where to find the money for a cupping (49.18), whether his daughter should be allowed to put clips in her hair (65.9), whether the law permits him to keep butter when the grocer sends it wrapped in leaves of chard (49.24). And, no matter how harsh the choices he eventually makes, he remains convinced that his efforts are never good enough. On one occasion, asked how he was, he launched into a tirade: "How can a man be," he answered, "with his Lord imposing obligations, his Prophet demanding that he follow the *sunnah*, his two angels waiting for good deeds, his soul clamoring for what it wants, the Devil goading him to lust, the Angel of Death seeking his life, and his family asking for money?" (56.6). It is this human frailty, finally, that heightens the effect of the most dramatic episodes in this biography—his imprisonment, trial, and flogging at the hands of the Abbasid Inquisition.

Ibn Ḥanbal did not believe in speculating about matters of religion. For him, if the first Muslims had not addressed a particular question of faith or practice, it was wrong to discuss it. The Abbasid caliph al-Maʾmūn (d. 218/833), on the other hand, not only embraced speculation, he believed himself the best-qualified person to engage in it, and furthermore that his subjects were obliged to accept whatever he might decide. To test the point, the caliph decided to take a position on a problem that could only be decided by the use of reason. That problem was the createdness of the Qurʾan. Al-Maʾmūn's position was that God had created everything, including the Qurʾan. To claim instead, as many Hadith-men did, that the Word of God was part of Him and therefore eternal too was in effect to be a Christian, or so the caliph insisted. But Ibn Ḥanbal was not one to be persuaded by mere argument. Asked to affirm that the Qurʾan is created, he refused to do so unless his interrogators could give him a verse from the Book itself or a statement by the Prophet saying this was so (69.7ff.).

As Ibn Ḥanbal doubtless knew, to rely on Qurʾan and Hadith alone was to deny the caliph any special interpretive authority. Predictably, al-Maʾmūn threatened to kill Ibn Ḥanbal if he did not recant.

What happened next is best read as it is told in the biography; what matters for the purpose of introduction is that the account depicts him as poignantly human and afraid. "I don't care if they keep me in prison," he is supposed to have told his friends. "My house is already a prison. And I don't care if they kill me by the sword. The only thing I'm afraid of is being flogged: I'm afraid I won't be able to take it" (68.1). Even readers who have little sympathy for his beliefs will, I hope, be able to admire Ibn Ḥanbal—or at least, his literary counterpart—for practicing principled nonviolent resistance to coercive state authority.

In the introduction to his wonderfully informative life of Ibn Ḥanbal, Christopher Melchert explains why he wrote a new biography instead of translating an old one. A medieval biography, he writes, "inevitably presents a medieval point of view":

> A full time scholar has had the chance to develop a taste for such literature, but most readers would find it grotesque. For example, one chapter of Ibn al-Jawzi's biography is simply a list of the more than four hundred persons from whom Ahmad collected Hadith. A proper analysis would easily exceed the limits of a normal biography. . . . I doubt it would interest any but specialists.

Moreover, says Melchert, the translation of a premodern work would be too long. For example, al-Dhahabī's life of Ibn Ḥanbal "would require a good 60,000 [words] and Ibn al-Jawzi's over 150,000."[2]

The latter work is the one edited and translated here: the *Virtues of the Imām Aḥmad ibn Ḥanbal* by the Baghdadi Hadith scholar, jurist, historian, biographer, and preacher Ibn al-Jawzī (d. 597/1201).[3] Melchert's estimate of length is remarkably accurate: the present translation of Ibn al-Jawzī's text comes to about 173,500 words. He is also quite right about the long lists of names. And he does not even mention the chains of transmitters. Like collections of Hadith reports, Arabic chronicles and biographies generally cite their sources by listing all the individuals who transmitted the original account of the event in question. As a Hadith scholar writing about another Hadith scholar, Ibn al-Jawzī seems to have been especially careful to cite all his sources. The result is a book approximately half of which is taken up with *isnād*s, as the lists of sources are called.

In the bilingual edition of this book, all of the original material, including the *isnād*s, was retained. This paperback edition, by contrast, drops almost all of Chapters 2, 11–14, 20, 90, and 100, keeping only a representative section, usually the first, intended to give the reader an idea of what has been left out. To maintain consistency with the hardcovers, however, the section numbers in the margins have been left unchanged in this paperback edition, even though that has led to some non-consecutive numbering in some places. This new edition also omits all the *isnād*s except for the first (1.1). As in the bilingual edition, the name given in brackets at the beginning of each report is the name of the narrator. When it appears in brackets, "Aḥmad" means "Ibn Ḥanbal" and the following report is in effect autobiographical. Other commonly cited narrators are Ibn Ḥanbal's sons Ṣāliḥ and ʿAbd Allāh, and his disciple al-Marrūdhī. More information on these figures may be found in the Glossary.

In his insightful review of the bilingual edition, Tasi Perkins asked why I did not have more to say about the author of this book.[4] There are several reasons why. First, the external facts of Ibn al-Jawzī's life are readily found in several sources both in print and on line. More importantly, Ibn al-Jawzī was less an author in the modern sense than a compiler. As the literary critic Abdelfattah Kilito has argued, pre-modern Arabic literature has distinct genres (praise poetry, love poetry, biography, etc.) but few distinct authors.[5] As Ibn al-Jawzī himself tells us, this book speaks for the whole Ḥanbalī tradition, not for him as an individual (see, e.g., 100.1). Of course, the book as we have it reflects the preoccupations of his time and place. As it happens, one chapter of my 2001 book *Classical Arabic Biography* deals with this topic, and for the most part I have preferred not to repeat myself here. Even so, points that help make sense of the text are included in the notes to this edition (see, for example, notes 335, 337, 342, 371, 379, 385, 386, and 422).

Leaving aside the matter of length, this book was not particularly difficult to translate. Unlike some of the other works published in this series, it is not a collection of arguments about a once-burning issue, a guide for specialists in a technical field, or a monument to verbal cleverness. It is a book by and about people who believed in simple truths expressed in simple language—even if some of that simplicity has been lost to us with the passage of time. In a sense, the difficult parts were also the most enjoyable to work on. These include the references to daily life and material culture: everything from "a dried-whey stew full of meat and chard" (38.11) to the galoshes a Turkish general wears as he splashes his way through the mud to Ibn Ḥanbal's door (73.41). The book is a trove of information on the physical and social world of the third/ninth century, and I hope some readers, at least, will mine its riches.

What I most wish the tradition had preserved for us is the voices. Ibn Ḥanbal's life is told as a series of reports, each narrated by an eyewitness, or by Ibn Ḥanbal himself. If the words on the page really are transcriptions of speech, each report should represent a distinct voice. In practice, though, there does not seem to be much variation in register, possibly because reports originally narrated in informal Arabic, and perhaps even other languages, have been put into literary Arabic of a more or less uniform kind by one or another of the transmitters (see, e.g., 38.10). Beyond the voices of the eyewitnesses, we also have the voices of all the people they quote. These include everyone from caliphs, judges, and jailors to doctors, grocers, and bandits. Unusually, if all too briefly, we also hear the voices of women (e.g., 61.7) and children (65.9). Here again, though, all of these people seem to be speaking the same sort of Arabic, making it difficult to give them distinctive voices in English.

Another problem was names. As in nineteenth-century Russian novels, all of the important characters seem to have several names, and authors seem to use them indiscriminately. In fact (as in Russian novels) there are reasons why one name might be used rather than another. In Ibn Ḥanbal's case, those who write about him usually call him Aḥmad ibn Ḥanbal ("Aḥmad the descendant of Ḥanbal"), or Aḥmad for short. But his friends, associates, and students called him 'Abū 'Abd Allāh, "father of 'Abd Allāh." This form conveys both intimacy and respect. Unfortunately, it is easily confused with 'Abd Allāh, the name of Ibn Ḥanbal's son. Also, Abū 'Abd Allāh happens to be the form of address for at least two other figures in the book. After much reflection, I decided to call him Ibn Ḥanbal in the introduction and notes, where it was necessary to refer to him as unambiguously as possible, but in the translation to call him Aḥmad wherever it was necessary to convey warmth or admiration.

Notes to the Introduction

1 Al-Dhahabī, *Siyar*, 10:15.

2 Melchert, *Ibn Hanbal*, viii.

3 On his life see Laoust, "Ibn al-Jawzī," which erroneously gives his birthdate as 510/1126 instead of 510/1116.

4 Perkins, "Hagiography."

5 Kilito, *Author*, esp. pp. 17–23.

The Life of ibn Ḥanbal

IN THE NAME OF GOD, FULL OF COMPASSION, EVER COMPASSIONATE 0.1

The Virtues of Abū ʿAbd Allāh Aḥmad ibn Muḥammad ibn Ḥanbal, of the tribe of Shaybān—God be pleased with him!—by the great religious authority Abū l-Faraj ʿAbd al-Raḥmān ibn ʿAlī ibn Muḥammad ibn al-Jawzī, God be pleased with him!

IN THE NAME OF GOD, FULL OF COMPASSION, EVER COMPASSIONATE 0.2

Praise God, Who did all things create with skill unmatch'd and chose of men who would come first and who behind. From humankind He raised His prophets and His seers, and of them both did make the righteous scholars heirs. Then of those knowing men did He a lesser number find, and to those few with gen'rous hand a special virtue give. May God bless and keep Muḥammad, of those who alight in desert lands the noblest rider of his race; and bless and save the ones who in joining him touched greatness, and those who followed him in faith, until the Day when He shall set this tott'ring world aright.

I pray, my brothers, that God crown your efforts with success; and 0.3
I ask you to recall that He, mighty and glorious, made Muḥammad—God bless him and keep him—the most virtuous being in creation,

and likewise placed his community above the rest. The reason for this precedence was knowledge: knowing, and acting on what one knows. Examine the life of our Prophet and you will realize that his superiority to other prophets arises from what he knew and how he put that knowledge into practice. Consider, likewise, the sciences of our learned men, and you will readily see how they elude the powers of the rabbis. Note, too, how the devotions of our worshippers put even monks to shame, for devotion restrained by the Law and undertaken against the grain of one's desires is more arduous—and worthier—than monasticism, which merits no regard. By the grace of God, our community suffers no dearth of knowledge or of action. Even so, when I set out to find people of the Successors' generation or later who had reached perfection in both respects—in what they knew and how they lived—I found only three whose achievement is perfect and uncompromised: al-Ḥasan al-Baṣrī, Sufyān ibn Saʿīd al-Thawrī, and Aḥmad ibn Ḥanbal.

0.4 After compiling one volume on the merits of al-Ḥasan and another on Sufyān, I realized that Aḥmad deserves more attention than either. He gathered more knowledge than they did and suffered more for telling the truth. Several authors, admittedly, have already collected reports of his attainments. Some, however, collected too little material, while others made no effort to organize what they had amassed. I therefore resolved to devote some time to making a proper collection of reports about his manners and merits, so that those who emulate him may know the man whose example they have set out to follow.[1] May God grant success!

Contents

0.5 I have divided this book into one hundred chapters, as follows—and may God help me choose aright!

Chapter 1
Ibn Ḥanbal's Birth and Family Background

We cite ʿAbd al-Malik ibn Abī l-Qāsim al-Karūkhī, who cites ʿAbd Allāh ibn Muḥammad al-Anṣārī, who cites Abū Yaʿqūb al-Ḥāfiẓ, who cites Abū Bakr ibn Abī l-Faḍl al-Muʿaddal,[2] *who learned it from Muḥammad ibn Ibrāhīm al-Ṣarrām; and*[3] *we cite ʿAbd al-Malik, who cites ʿAbd Allāh ibn Muḥammad, who cites Aḥmad ibn Muḥammad ibn Ismāʿīl al-Mihrawī,*[4] *who learned it from Muḥammad ibn Muḥammad ibn Yaʿqūb, the notary-witness of Būshanj, who learned it from Muḥammad ibn al-Ṭayyib ibn al-ʿAbbās, who [along with al-Ṣarrām] cites Ibrāhīm ibn Isḥāq al-Ghasīlī as saying:* 1.1

[Al-Ghasīlī:] I heard Aḥmad's son Ṣāliḥ say that he—meaning his father—was born in Rabīʿ I 164 [November–December 780], having left Marv[5] carried in his mother's womb.

[Aḥmad:] I was born in Rabīʿ I 164. 1.2

[Aḥmad:] I was born in the year 164. 1.3

[Al-ʿIjlī:] Aḥmad son of Muḥammad son of Ḥanbal, called Abū ʿAbd Allāh (the father of ʿAbd Allāh), was a full-blooded member of the clan of Sadūs.[6] The family had settled first in Basra and later in Khurasan,[7] but Aḥmad was born and raised in Baghdad. He was trustworthy and reliable as a transmitter of Hadith reports, and was skilled in using them as a source of law. He sought out reports about the early Muslims and lived according to their example. He was a good and honorable man. 1.4

[Aḥmad:] My mother was pregnant with me when she came from Khurasan.[8] I was born in 164. 1.5

[Abū Zurʿah:] Aḥmad ibn Ḥanbal's family came from Basra but their district of settlement was Marv. 1.6

[Ṣāliḥ:] I heard my father say that he was born in 164, toward the beginning of the year, in Rabīʿ I. He was brought from Marv in his mother's womb. His father died when he was thirty and the task of caring for him fell upon his mother.

[The author:] By this Ṣāliḥ means that Aḥmad's father died at the age of thirty, when Aḥmad was a child. So much is clear from the following report:

[Aḥmad:] I was brought from Khurasan as an unborn child, and I was born here in Baghdad. I never knew my father or my grandfather.

1.7 [Ibn Ḥātim:] Aḥmad ibn Muḥammad ibn Ḥanbal was from Marv. He left Marv as a child in his mother's womb. His grandfather, Ḥanbal ibn Hilāl, was governor of Sarakhs[9] and a descendant of the men who fought for the Abbasids during the revolution.[10]

1.8 [Aḥmad:] Al-Ḥasan ibn Yaḥyā, who was from Marv, reported to me that he heard Aws ibn ʿAbd Allāh ibn Buraydah report that his brother Sahl ibn ʿAbd Allāh ibn Buraydah reported, citing his father, who reported it citing the grandfather, Buraydah: "I heard the Emissary, God bless and keep him, say, 'After I die many expeditions will be sent forth. Join the one sent to Khurasan and settle in the city of Marv. It was built by Dhū l-Qarnayn, who asked God to bless it, and no harm befalls its inhabitants.'"[11]

Chapter 2

His Lineage[12]

2.1 [ʿAbd Allāh:] We heard reports from my father, Aḥmad son of Muḥammad son of Ḥanbal son of Hilāl son of Asad son of Idrīs son of ʿAbd Allāh son of Ḥayyān son of ʿAbd Allāh son of Anas son of ʿAwf son of Qāsiṭ son of Māzin son of Shaybān son of Dhuhl son of Thaʿlabah son of ʿUkābah son of Ṣaʿb son of ʿAlī son of Bakr son of Wāʾil son of Qāsiṭ son of Hinb son of Afṣā son of Duʿmī son of Jadīlah son of Asad son of Rabīʿah son of Nizār son of Maʿadd son of ʿAdnān son of Udd son of Udad son of al-Hamaysaʿ son of Ḥamal son of al-Nabt son of Qaydhār son of Ismāʿīl son of Ibrāhīm the Friend of God,[13] on whom eternal peace.

2.14 [Ibn Baṭṭah:] Aḥmad's mother was of Shaybān. Her name was Ṣafiyyah, daughter of Maymūnah, daughter of ʿAbd al-Malik al-Shaybānī of the clan of ʿĀmir. Aḥmad's father had come to stay as a guest of her clan and then married her. Her grandfather, ʿAbd al-Malik ibn Sawādah ibn Hind al-Shaybānī, was a leader among his people. The Arab tribesmen would camp nearby and she would offer them hospitality.[14]

Chapter 3
His Childhood

3.1 Our exemplar Aḥmad was born in Baghdad, as we have mentioned, and grew up there. After studying with the teachers and Hadith scholars of the city, he set out to seek learning elsewhere as well.

3.2 [Ibn Kurdī:] Aḥmad ibn Ḥanbal's house had the One-Eyed Tigris[15] directly behind it.

3.3 [Abū ʿAfīf:] Aḥmad was with us in Qurʾan school when he was just a little boy. Even then he stood out. At that time, the caliph was living in al-Raqqah and the courtiers who joined him there began writing letters to their families in Baghdad. When they wanted to reply to a letter, their womenfolk would ask our schoolmaster to send Aḥmad ibn Ḥanbal to their homes. The teacher would send him out and off he'd go, looking carefully at the ground. The women often dictated obscene words but he wouldn't write them down.

[Abū Sirāj:] When we were in Qurʾan school with Aḥmad, women would send messages to the schoolmaster saying, "Send Ibn Ḥanbal to write for us so we can reply to the letters we've received." Whenever he went in to where the women were, he would keep his head down so as not to look at them.

3.4 [Al-Marrūdhī:] Abū Sirāj also said that his father, whose name he gave, was impressed by how well Aḥmad conducted himself: "One day my father said to us, 'I spend money to hire tutors for my children hoping they'll learn to behave properly, but it doesn't seem to do any good. Then take Aḥmad ibn Ḥanbal: he's an orphan, but look how well he's turned out!'[16] He went on marveling for some time."

3.5 [Al-Marrūdhī:] Aḥmad told me, "When I was a boy, I would go to the Qur'an school, and then when I was fourteen I took up duties."[17]

3.6 [Abū l-Munabbih:] The first we heard of Aḥmad ibn Ḥanbal was when his uncle received a letter from the authorities. He wrote a reply which he gave to Aḥmad, who was supposed to pass it on to a courier who was waiting for it. But instead of handing it over, Aḥmad put it inside an alcove[18] they had in the house. When the courier asked for it, the uncle replied that he had already sent it out. He then asked Aḥmad, "Where's the letter I asked you to give the man at the door?"

"He was wearing a long-sleeved gown,"[19] he replied. "You'll find your letter in the alcove."[20]

3.7 [Al-ʿAbbās:] Dāwūd ibn Bisṭām told me: "Once when the briefing from Baghdad was delayed, I sent word to Aḥmad's uncle telling him I was hoping to write up all the dispatches to forward to the caliph but his still hadn't arrived. He replied that he had sent his nephew to deliver it. Then he sent for Aḥmad, who was only a boy at the time.

"'Didn't I tell you to deliver my report?' he asked.

"'Yes,' replied Aḥmad.

"'Why didn't you, then?'

"'I used to carry those reports but not any more.[21] I threw it into the water.'"

Ibn Bisṭām then recited «We are of God, and to Him we return!»[22] adding: "When a boy has such scruples, where does that leave us?"[23]

3.8 [Yūnus al-Muʾaddib:] I saw Aḥmad ibn Ḥanbal while Hushaym was still alive, and even then he was already well respected.

[Al-Marrūdhī:] I heard Aḥmad say, "When Hushaym died I was twenty years old."[24]

[A fellow Hadith-seeker:] Aḥmad always stood out. One day, I was waiting for him at Ismāʿīl ibn ʿUlayyah's. At the time, Aḥmad was not yet thirty. But when he came in, everyone tried to clear a space for him, calling out, "Come sit over here!" 3.9

Chapter 4

The Beginning of His Search for Knowledge and the Journey He Undertook for That Purpose[25]

Aḥmad began his studies with the learned men of Baghdad. He then traveled to Kufa, Basra, Mecca, Medina, Yemen, Syria, and northern Iraq, writing down what he acquired from the men of learning in each region he visited. 4.1

[Aḥmad:] The first teacher whose Hadith I wrote down was Abū Yūsuf.[26] 4.2

[Aḥmad:] I started learning Hadith when I was sixteen. When Hushaym died, I was twenty. I first heard Hadith from him in 179 [795–96]. 4.3

[Aḥmad:] I started in '79 [795–96], when I was sixteen.[27] That was my first year studying Hadith. I remember someone coming up to us and saying that Ḥammād ibn Zayd was dead. That was also the year we lost Mālik ibn Anas. In 198 [813–14], when we were studying with ʿAbd al-Razzāq in Yemen, we heard that Sufyān ibn ʿUyaynah, ʿAbd al-Raḥmān ibn Mahdī, and Yaḥyā ibn Saʿīd were gone, too.[28] 4.4

[Aḥmad:] I heard Hadith from Sulaymān ibn Ḥarb in Basra in '94 [809–10], and from Abū l-Nuʿmān ʿĀrim in the same year, and from ʿUmar al-Ḥawḍī too.

[Aḥmad:] I started studying Hadith in '79. 4.5

[Aḥmad:] I started studying Hadith in '79. I remember going to Ibn al-Mubārak's circle but missing him. He'd come to us first in '79. 4.6

4.7 [Aḥmad:] I studied with ʿAlī ibn Hāshim ibn al-Barīd in ’79, my first year studying Hadith. Then I went back to him for another session but he had died in the meantime. Mālik ibn Anas died that year too.

4.8 [ʿAbd Allāh:] My father said, “Khālid ibn ʿAbd Allāh, meaning al-Ṭaḥḥān (the miller), and Abū l-Aḥwaṣ, Mālik ibn Anas, and Ḥammād ibn Zayd all died in ’79. Mālik died shortly before Ḥammād. That was the year I started studying Hadith. I remember we were gathered at the door of Hushaym’s house and he was dictating either *Funerals* or *Rites*”[29]—I can’t recall which he said—“when a man coming from Basra said that Ḥammād ibn Zayd was dead.”

4.9 [Ṣāliḥ:] I heard my father say: “I began learning when I was sixteen. The first teacher I heard was Hushaym, in ’79. In that same year, Ibn al-Mubārak came to Baghdad for the last time. I went to his circle but they told me that he had left for Tarsus.[30] He died in ’81. I spent ’79 writing down the Hadith reports that Hushaym was teaching us. We continued with him in ’80, ’81, and ’83, when he died, after dictating the *Book on Pilgrimage*, which had about a thousand Hadith reports, some interpretation of the Qur’an, the *Book on Judgeship*, and some smaller things.”[31]

I said I supposed that he had written three thousand reports in all.

“More,” he said. He continued: “I remember we were gathered at Hu-shaym’s door and he was dictating *Funerals* when we heard that Ḥammād ibn Zayd had died.

“I also heard Hadith from ʿAbd al-Mu’min ʿAbd Allāh ibn Khālid Abī l-Ḥasan al-ʿAbsī in ’82, before Hushaym died.

“I also heard Hadith from ʿAlī ibn Mujāhid al-Kābulī, who was from Rey and was called Abū Mujāhid. That was the year I made my first trip. ʿĪsā ibn Yūnus reached Kufa a few days after I left. That was in ’82.

“My first trip to Basra was in ’86. In ’87 I went to find Sufyān ibn ʿUyaynah. We were too late to see Fuḍayl ibn ʿIyāḍ before he died. That was the year I went on pilgrimage for the first time. I wrote down Hadith from Ibrāhīm ibn Saʿd and prayed behind him several times. At the end of the prayer, he would say the *taslīm* only once.[32] If I had had fifty dirhams, I would have gone out to Rey to see Jarīr ibn ʿAbd al-Ḥamīd. Some of the other students went but I couldn't."

He added: "When I went to Kufa, I stayed in a room where I slept with my head resting on a brick. I came down with fever and went back to my mother, God show her mercy!"

[Aḥmad:] If I had had fifty dirhams I would have gone out to Rey 4.10
to see Jarīr ibn ʿAbd al-Ḥamīd. Some of my fellow students went but I couldn't because I had nothing to spend.

[Aḥmad:] When I went to Kufa, I stayed in a room where I slept 4.11
with my head resting on a brick. I came down with fever and went back to my mother. I had never asked her permission to leave.

[Al-ʿAbbādānī:] I heard Ibn Ḥanbal say, "I reached ʿAbbādān in 4.12
'86 sometime during the last ten days of Rajab. I had gone that year to see al-Muʿtamir. There was a man there involved in Disputation."[33]

"You mean Haddāb?"[34]

"Right! Abū l-Rabīʿ was there too, and I wrote down some of his reports."

[Aḥmad:] Some days I tried to leave for Hadith sessions as early 4.13
as I could but my mother would grab me by the clothes and pull me back, saying, "Wait until the call to prayer!" or "Wait until people wake up!"

I used to go early to hear Abū Bakr ibn ʿAyyāsh and others.

[Aḥmad:] I was studying with Yaḥyā ibn Saʿīd al-Qaṭṭān (the 4.14
cotton merchant) and then left for Wāsiṭ. Yaḥyā ibn Saʿīd came asking for me and they told him where I'd gone.

"What's he doing in Wāsiṭ?" he asked.

"Studying with Yazīd ibn Hārūn."

"What for?" asked Yaḥyā.

[Abū ʿAbd al-Raḥmān:] By that Yaḥyā meant that Aḥmad knew more than the man he'd gone to study with.

[Aḥmad:] I've visited Basra five times. The first was at the begin- 4.15
ning of Rajab 186. That's when I heard Hadith from al-Muʿtamir ibn Sulaymān. The second time was in '90. The third was in '94, after

Ghundar died.[35] I studied with Yaḥyā ibn Saʿīd for six months. In 200 I went again.[36]

4.16 [Ibrāhīm ibn Hāshim:] When Jarīr ibn ʿAbd al-Ḥamīd came to Baghdad he went to stay with the family of Musayyab. After Jarīr had crossed over to the East Side, the Tigris rose. I asked Aḥmad ibn Ḥanbal if he wanted to cross with me.

"My mother won't let me," he said. So I crossed alone and joined Jarīr's circle.

[The author:] Aḥmad ibn Ḥanbal did hear Hadith from Jarīr, though he did not have the chance to hear very much.

The flooding mentioned here took place in 186, during the reign of al-Rashīd. The Tigris rose visibly in its banks and reached a point higher than anyone had ever seen before. Al-Rashīd had his family, his womenfolk, and his property put aboard ships.

Abū ʿAlī l-Baradānī reported: "The governor of Baghdad at the time was al-Sindī ibn Shāhak, called 'son of Shāhak' after his mother. To keep people safe, he forbade them to cross the river."

4.17 [Aḥmad:] I wrote down Hadith dictated for us by Sulaymān ibn Ḥarb while Ibn ʿUyaynah was still alive.

4.18 [ʿAbd Allāh:] My father walked all the way to Tarsus on foot.[37]

4.19 [Ḥanbal:] I heard Aḥmad say, "ʿAbd al-Raḥmān ibn Mahdī arrived in '80 [796–97], while Abū Bakr"—meaning Ibn ʿAyyāsh—"was here. ʿAbd al-Raḥmān was forty-five and had dyed his beard with henna. I used to see him in the Friday mosque. Then he came to Baghdad. We joined him there, and he dictated six or seven hundred of his reports for us. It was in '80 that he used to attend Abū Bakr's circle."

4.20 [Ibn Manīʿ:] I heard my grandfather talk about seeing Aḥmad ibn Ḥanbal coming back from Kufa.

"He was carrying a satchel with some documents in it. I took his hand and said, 'Today it's Kufa; tomorrow it'll be Basra again! How much longer can you keep this up? You've already copied thirty thousand Hadith; isn't that enough?'

"He said nothing. I asked, 'What if you reach sixty thousand?'

"He was still silent.

"'A hundred thousand?'

"'At that point,' he replied, 'a man might claim to know something.'"

We checked and found that Aḥmad had written down 300,000 reports transmitted by Bahz ibn Asad and ʿAffān alone.

[Aḥmad ibn Muḥammad ibn Yāsīn:] I think Ibn Manīʿ may have added "and Rawḥ ibn ʿUbādah."

[Aḥmad:] I went to Yemen to find Ibrāhīm ibn ʿAqīl, who was bad-tempered and refused to see anyone. By waiting at his door for a day or two, I managed to see him and he recited two Hadith reports for me. He also knew the reports that Wahb had gotten from Jābir, but I never got to hear them because of his bad temper. Ismāʿīl ibn ʿAbd al-Karīm knew those reports too, but he refused to recite them because Ibrāhīm ibn ʿAqīl was still alive. So I never heard them from anyone. 4.21

[Yaʿqūb ibn Isḥāq:] My father was traveling with Aḥmad ibn Ḥanbal in search of Hadith when their ship was wrecked and they washed up on an island. There they found the following written on a stone: "Soon enough, all men will find themselves in riches or in want. After they are gathered before God Almighty, He will send some to the Garden and some to the Fire."[38] 4.22

[Khushnām:] I asked Aḥmad ibn Ḥanbal whether Yaḥyā ibn Yaḥyā had been a reliable source of *sunnah.* 4.23

"*I* certainly thought so," replied Ibn Ḥanbal. "If I'd been able to afford it, I'd have gone to see him."

[Ṣāliḥ:] After resolving to make the pilgrimage to Mecca, my father set out in the company of Yaḥyā ibn Maʿīn. After the pilgrimage, said my father, he would go to Sanaa to hear Hadith from ʿAbd al-Razzāq. 4.24

"When we reached Mecca," he told me later, "we began to walk around the Kaʿbah, the way you do as soon as you arrive. Then who does Yaḥyā recognize but ʿAbd al-Razzāq? When we finished the walk, all of us prayed two cycles[39] behind the Maqām[40] and sat down. Then Yaḥyā got up, went over to ʿAbd al-Razzāq, and greeted him.

"'This is your brother Aḥmad ibn Ḥanbal,' he said, introducing me.

"'God keep him, and strengthen his resolve!' said ʿAbd al-Razzāq. 'I've heard so many good things about him.'

"'God willing,' said Yaḥyā, 'we'll come see you tomorrow and copy down your reports.'"

After ʿAbd al-Razzāq left, my father turned to Yaḥyā and asked why he had said that.

"So we can hear his Hadith right here," said Yaḥyā. "God's just saved you a month of travel back and forth, not to mention the cost of the journey."

"God would never approve," said my father, "of my seeing him here when I've already resolved to see him somewhere else."[41]

In the end, to hear ʿAbd al-Razzāq, my father traveled all the way to Sanaa.

4.25 [Aḥmad:] I missed hearing Hadith from Mālik ibn Anas, but God sent me Sufyān ibn ʿUyaynah to take his place. I also missed Ḥammād ibn Zayd, but God sent me Ismāʿīl ibn ʿUlayyah.

4.26 [Aḥmad ibn Sinān:] A group of Baghdadi students, among them Aḥmad ibn Ḥanbal, came to see Yazīd ibn Hārūn. All of them borrowed money from me and paid it back—except for Aḥmad ibn Ḥanbal. Instead of borrowing, he gave me his fur and I sold it for seven dirhams.[42]

4.27 [Aḥmad:] In al-Raqqah the best transmitter I found was Fayyāḍ ibn Muḥammad ibn Sinān, a client of Quraysh.[43] His house was built against the Friday mosque. He died in al-Raqqah sometime after 200 [815–16].

4.28 [Ṣāliḥ:] A man once noticed my father carrying an inkpot and said to him, "What do you still need that for? You're the imam of the Muslims!"

"I'll need it until they bury me," he answered.

4.29 [Aḥmad:] "I'll stop seeking knowledge when I'm dead and buried."

[Muḥammad ibn Ismāʿīl:] My father was a goldsmith in Baghdad. One day I was working with him when Aḥmad ibn Ḥanbal came running by with his sandals in his hand. My father took hold of his clothing—like *this*—and said, "Aḥmad! Aren't you ashamed still to be racing around like a schoolboy?" 4.30

"I'll keep at it until I'm dead," he replied.

['Abd Allāh:] Once when I went to Mecca, I stayed in a house where an elderly man, a Meccan called Abū Bakr ibn Samāʿah, told me, "Your father stayed with us here when I was a boy. My mother told me: 'Stick close to that man and look after him because he's a righteous man,' so I used to look after him. 4.31

"One day, while he was out studying Hadith, his bedclothes and belongings were stolen. When he came home, my mother said to him, 'Some thieves broke in and took your things.'

"'What about my slates?' he asked. When she told him they were safe in the alcove, he asked no more questions."

['Abd Allāh:] My father walked all the way to Tarsus on foot, and to Yemen as well. 4.32

['Abd Allāh:] My father said, "'Abd al-Razzāq never taught us anything from memory except the first time we sat with him. We arrived at night and found him sitting somewhere, and he dictated seventy Hadith reports for us. Then he turned to the group and said, 'The only reason I've taught you Hadith tonight is because of who our guest is.'" 4.33

By this he meant my father.

[Al-Dawraqī:] I saw Ibn Ḥanbal right after he came back from seeing 'Abd al-Razzāq in Yemen. He looked pale and weary. I told him that he had pushed himself too hard by going to see 'Abd al-Razzāq. 4.34

"It was nothing," he said, "compared to what I gained. He dictated for us all the Hadith reports that al-Zuhrī got from Sālim ibn 'Abd Allāh, going back to his father, and the ones al-Zuhrī got from Saʿīd ibn al-Musayyab, going back to Abū Hurayrah."

[Aḥmad:] I tried to learn the Qur'an by heart, but then I got too busy with Hadith. I was so afraid I'd never learn that I asked God 4.35

to help me. It didn't occur to me to ask Him to make it easy. When I finally did learn it, I was chained up in prison. So if you ask God for anything make sure to say: "Let me have it without misery or suffering."

Chapter 5

The Major Men of Learning Whom He Met and on Whose Authority He Recited Hadith

5.1 I have listed them alphabetically by first name.

Names Beginning with *Alif*

5.2 *Men named Aḥmad* Aḥmad ibn Ibrāhīm ibn Khālid. Aḥmad ibn Ibrāhīm ibn Kathīr al-Dawraqī, called Abū ʿAbd Allāh. Aḥmad ibn Jamīl, called Abū Yūsuf. He was from Marv but settled in Baghdad. He sold wheat in Qaṭīʿat al-Rabīʿ. Aḥmad ibn Janāb ibn al-Mughīrah, called Abū l-Walīd al-Ḥadīthī and al-Miṣṣīṣī. Aḥmad ibn Janāḥ, called Abū Ṣāliḥ. Aḥmad ibn Ḥātim ibn Yazīd the Tall, called Abū Jaʿfar al-Khayyāṭ. Aḥmad ibn al-Ḥajjāj, called Abū l-ʿAbbās al-Dhuhlī, from Marv. Aḥmad ibn Dāwūd, called Abū Saʿīd al-Ḥaddād al-Wāsiṭī. Aḥmad ibn Abī Shuʿayb (whose name was ʿAbd Allāh ibn Muslim), Abū l-Ḥasan al-Ḥarrānī, client of ʿUmar ibn ʿAbd al-ʿAzīz. Aḥmad ibn ʿAbd al-Malik ibn Wāqid, called Abū Yaḥyā l-Jazarī l-Ḥarrānī, and often referred to using his grandfather's name, that is, as Aḥmad ibn Wāqid. Aḥmad ibn Ṣāliḥ, Abū Jaʿfar al-Miṣrī. Aḥmad ibn Muḥammad ibn Ayyūb al-Warrāq, called Abū Jaʿfar.

[The list continues down through names beginning with *yāʾ*, the last letter of the Arabic alphabet.]

Women from Whom Aḥmad Transmitted Hadith

5.84 Umm ʿAmr bint Ḥassān ibn Yazīd al-Thaqafī.

NOTE

Aḥmad encountered a number of righteous ascetics, some of whom we have listed among his sources of Hadith. Others, of whom some were too busy with reverential practices to transmit Hadith, he met but did not hear any reports from. In the course of this book, we will, God willing, have occasion to mention many of the ascetics he encountered. 5.87

[Aḥmad:] To my mind, nothing comes close to being poor. Do you know what it means to suffer poverty without complaint? I've seen so many upright men: men like ʿAbd Allāh ibn Idrīs, as old as he was, wearing a tunic of felt.[44] I've seen Abū Dāwūd al-Ḥafarī wearing a ripped tunic with the cotton coming out of it, praying from sunset to nighttime while swaying on his feet from hunger. I've seen Ayyūb ibn al-Najjār in Mecca after he gave up all his property, walking around the city carrying a rope and pail to draw water from the wells. He gave up everything he owned; he was a true worshipper. He had lived with the things of this world, but left them all in the hands of Yaḥyā l-Qaṭṭān. I've seen Ibn Bajālah the Worshipper; I used to hear the sound of his shoes as he circled the Kaʿbah at night. In the mosque there was also someone called al-ʿArfī[45] who would stay up from nightfall to dawn, weeping the whole time. When I went to see what he looked like, he turned out to be a pale young man. I've seen Ḥusayn al-Juʿfī, who was like a monk. In Kufa I met no one better than Ḥusayn al-Juʿfī. In Basra the best was Saʿīd ibn ʿĀmir. 5.88

CHAPTER 6

HIS DEFERENCE TO HIS TEACHERS AND HIS RESPECT FOR LEARNING

[Ismāʿīl al-Daylamī:] ʿAmr al-Nāqid said, "We were studying with Wakīʿ when Aḥmad ibn Ḥanbal came in and sat down." He began describing how deferential Aḥmad was to Wakīʿ. Then he said: "I told Aḥmad how highly our teacher thought of him and asked him 6.1

why he wouldn't speak in his presence. He said, 'So what if he thinks highly of me? I still have to treat him with reverence.'"

6.2 ['Abd Allāh:] I heard Muhanna' ibn Yaḥyā l-Shāmī report, "I saw Aḥmad ibn Ḥanbal in Sufyān's study circle with 'Abd al-Razzāq sitting in front of him. I remember thinking, 'I wonder if they have any idea who they're sitting with.'" By this he meant: Did they know how learned Ibn Ḥanbal was?

6.3 [Qutaybah ibn Sa'īd:] I came to Baghdad with one purpose: to meet Aḥmad ibn Ḥanbal. In the event, he came to me, along with Yaḥyā ibn Ma'īn. We exchanged Hadith reports[46] and then he stood up, came over, and sat down in front of me.

"Dictate that one to me," he said. Then [he returned to his seat and] we went back to exchanging reports. After a time, he again rose and came over to me.

"Aḥmad," I said, "you don't have to get up!"

"Don't worry about me," he replied. "All I care about is getting the learning right."

6.4 [Al-Shahīdī:] I remember seeing Yaḥyā l-Qaṭṭān pray the afternoon prayer and then lean against the pillar of the mosque where he prayed. 'Alī ibn al-Madīnī, al-Shādhakūnī,[47] 'Amr ibn 'Alī, Aḥmad ibn Ḥanbal, Yaḥyā ibn Ma'īn, and others would stand before him and ask about Hadith. They would stay on their feet until it was time for sunset prayer. Al-Qaṭṭān would never invite any of them to sit down, and they were too much in awe of him to sit down by themselves.

6.5 [Khalaf:] Ibn Ḥanbal came to me to hear the Hadith of Abū 'Awānah. I tried as hard as I could to persuade him to take a higher seat, but he refused. "The only place I'll sit is in front of you," he said. "We Muslims ought to show deference to our teachers."[48]

Chapter 7

His Eagerness to Learn and His Single-Minded Pursuit of Knowledge

Ibn Ḥanbal, may God be pleased with him, traveled great distances in search of Hadith and spent a long time acquiring it, and did not permit himself to be distracted by earning a living or seeking a wife until he had achieved what he set out to do. 7.1

[Aḥmad:] I didn't marry until I was past forty. 7.2

[Aḥmad al-Dawraqī:] I heard Aḥmad ibn Ḥanbal say, "We've written down six or seven versions of a Hadith and even then didn't feel sure of its provenance. So how can someone feel sure of a report they've written only once?" or words to that effect. 7.3

[Ṣāliḥ:] I heard my father say, "I've written down a million Hadith reports in my own writing, not counting the ones written down for me." 7.4

Chapter 8

His Powers of Retention and the Number of Reports He Knew by Heart

[ʿAbd Allāh:] I heard Abū Zurʿah say that Aḥmad ibn Ḥanbal knew a million Hadith reports. 8.1

"How would you know?" he was asked.

"He and I recited them to each other, and we went through the different topics."[49]

[Ṣāliḥ:] My father told me that a man once came to Ibn ʿUlayyah's door with Hushaym's Hadith books. 8.2

"He started reading the reports out to me, and I would say the chain of transmitters for each one. Al-Muʿayṭī also used to memorize Hadith, and when he arrived I asked him to take over, but he wouldn't."[50]

My father said, "I even knew of reports [transmitted by Hushaym] that I had never heard directly from him."

8.3 [Aḥmad:] I memorized everything I heard from Hushaym while he was still alive.

8.4 [Ibn Abī Ḥātim:] Saʿīd ibn ʿAmr al-Bardhaʿī once asked Abū Zurʿah who had memorized more, he or Aḥmad ibn Ḥanbal.

"Aḥmad ibn Ḥanbal, of course."

"How do you know that?"

"When I looked at his papers," said Abū Zurʿah, "I saw that at the front of each quire,[51] he didn't list the names of the transmitters he heard reports from. Instead, for every quire, he knew the names of the transmitters by heart. I could never do that."

8.5 [Al-Tustarī:] Abū Zurʿah was asked which of the senior transmitters had the best memory.

"Aḥmad ibn Ḥanbal," he said. "The day he died, they made an estimate of the number of papers he left behind. It came to twelve and a half loads.[52] Nowhere on any of the outside pages had he written 'the Hadith of So-and-So,' or 'So-and-So reported to us' on any of the inside pages. All of that he knew by heart."

8.6 [Abū Zurʿah:] I went to see Aḥmad ibn Ḥanbal and asked him to find Sufyān's Hadith for me. He brought out quires all labeled *Sufyān*, just *Sufyān*, without marking a single report as "Transmitted by So-and-So." I thought they must all have been transmitted by the same person. But when I picked some out for him to read back, he would say for each Hadith, "Wakīʿ," or "Yaḥyā," or whoever, "reported to us . . ." I was amazed. More than once I've tried to do something like that, but I've never been able to.

8.7 [Aḥmad:] I used to challenge Wakīʿ to recite al-Thawrī's Hadith reports from memory. Whenever Wakīʿ finished the last prayer of the night, he would leave the mosque and head for home. I would challenge him and he would often reply by citing nine or ten reports, which I would then memorize. After he left, the Hadith scholars would ask me to dictate the reports to them, and I would.

8.8 [Ibn Saʿīd:] Whenever Wakīʿ would leave the Hadith-circle to pray the evening prayer, Aḥmad ibn Ḥanbal would go with him and stand by the door while Wakīʿ kept quizzing him about reports. One night, Wakīʿ stopped in the doorway with his hands on the jamb and said, "I'm going to test you on the Hadith of Sufyān."

"Go ahead," said Ibn Ḥanbal.

"Have you memorized what Sufyān transmitted citing Salamah ibn Kuhayl . . . ?" asked Wakīʿ, reciting the Hadith.

"Yes," said Aḥmad. "We heard Yaḥyā report," giving the transmitter.

"What about Salamah on such-and-such?"

"We heard ʿAbd al-Raḥmān report," said Aḥmad.

"What about Sufyān from Salamah on such and-such?"

"We heard that from you."

And so they continued until they had covered all of the reports transmitted by Salamah. Then Aḥmad asked: "Do you know Salamah's report about . . . ?" giving the Hadith.

"No," said Wakīʿ.

Aḥmad then began asking about one report after another. Each time, Wakīʿ was stumped. Aḥmad went through the reports of the other major transmitters one by one. He was still standing there when the servant girl appeared and said, "The morning star"—or "Venus"—"is up!"

8.9 [Aḥmad:] Wakīʿ used to recite reports that all had the same chain of transmitters, as if he had memorized them all that way. At night I used to commit ten or fifteen of them to memory.[53]

8.10 [ʿAbd Allāh:] My father used to tell me, "Take any of the books of Wakīʿ's collection and tell me what any report says and I'll tell you the chain of transmitters. Or tell me the chain and I'll tell you what the report says."[54]

Chapter 9

His Learning, His Intelligence, and His Religious Understanding

9.1 [Abū l-Qāsim al-Jabbulī:] Most people think that Aḥmad ibn Ḥanbal became famous largely because of what he did during the Inquisition, but that's not so. It was because you could ask him about any issue and he would answer as if he had all the learning in the world laid out before him.

9.2 [Al-Ḥarbī]: I lived to see three men like no other: men unlike any of woman born. The first was Abū ʿUbayd al-Qāsim ibn Sallām. The only thing I can compare him to is a mountain filled with the breath of life. The second was Bishr ibn al-Ḥārith. The only way to describe him is to say that all of him, from the crown of his head down to the soles of his feet, seemed to have been kneaded from the clay of self-restraint. The third was Aḥmad ibn Ḥanbal. To me he seemed to have gathered the learning of ancient times and latter days alike, of whatever kind, so that he could say as much as he wanted or keep back whatever he wished.

9.3 [Al-Dārimī:] I never saw a dark-headed man[55] learn more Hadith reports of God's Emissary (God bless and keep him) by heart, nor reach a better understanding of everything they meant, than Aḥmad did.

9.4 [Ibn Rāhawayh:] In Iraq I used to study with Aḥmad ibn Ḥanbal, Yaḥyā ibn Maʿīn, and my own cohort. We used to test each other on Hadith by asking about the chain of transmitters—or the two or three different chains—that might exist for a single report. Then Yaḥyā ibn Maʿīn would speak up and offer yet another chain. "We all agree on that one, don't we?" I would ask, and they would all say they did. Then I would ask, "What does the report mean? How would you explain it? And what implications can we draw from it?"

At that, everyone would fall silent except for Aḥmad ibn Ḥanbal.

[Ibn Yūnus:] I heard Abū ʿĀṣim say, when the topic of religious understanding was raised, "There's no one there"—in Baghdad—"except that man," meaning Aḥmad. "No one's ever come to us from there who understands as well as he does." 9.5

Someone then mentioned ʿAlī ibn al-Madīnī, but Abū ʿĀṣim waved his hand dismissively.

[Al-Kūfī:] Yaḥyā ibn Maʿīn was once asked a question about living in a shop. "I don't deal with that," he replied. "Ask Aḥmad ibn Ḥanbal." 9.6

Al-Khallāl said that Aḥmad copied down the books of rationalist jurisprudence and memorized them, but then stopped consulting them. Whenever he spoke about religious understanding, he did so with the air of a man who had tested all the forms of knowledge and could speak from experience. 9.7

Ḥubaysh ibn Mubashshir and a number of other jurists said, "When we debate, we're willing to challenge anyone except Ibn Ḥanbal. With him, all we can do is keep quiet." 9.8

[Al-Ḥarbī:] Aḥmad [ibn Ḥanbal] was asked whether a Muslim should say "May God grace you!" to a Christian. 9.9

"Yes," he said. "He should say it, and mean by it 'May God grace you by making you Muslim!'"[56]

He was also asked whether a man who has sworn three binding oaths to have intercourse with his wife that night, or divorce her, discovers that she is menstruating.

"He must divorce her and not have intercourse," he replied. "God has permitted divorce but forbidden intercourse with a menstruating woman."[57]

Abū l-Wafāʾ ʿAlī ibn ʿAqīl (may God be pleased with him) said:[58] 9.10

One of the surprising things you hear ignorant young men say is that Aḥmad was no good at religious understanding, only Hadith transmission. That claim is as ignorant as any they could make, and they make it because they don't understand his method of using Hadith to reach decisions about the preferable course of action. Certainly, his rulings are more nuanced than any we have seen them produce. This is not even to mention his superior mastery of Hadith itself, which they themselves concede. More than once he joined them for Hadith sessions and outdid the best of them.

9.11 A particularly intricate ruling of his concerns the fact that his views differed about the division of a debt that is the liability of two persons. They did not differ in regard to the rejection of the validity of the division of a debt that is the liability of one person. The point seems to be that, if it is a single liability, it is not subject to division. This is because the one who incurred the indebtedness is one person, and one of the two partners who are owed the debt has only the right to demand payment according to his rights under the partnership—he may do nothing else, so how could the liability be subject to division? But that is not the case when the debt is the obligation of two persons. That is because one of the two partners who are owed the debt may, on his own, seek recourse against the liability of one of the two who owe the debt. In such a case the division is valid, because one of the two sources of payment is distinguishable from the other. As for his view according to which such a division is precluded, that would be because division of a debt owed by two persons is precluded due to the fact that the liabilities usually differ, and are not equivalent.[59]

9.12 Another example of Aḥmad's religious understanding and the subtlety of his reasoning is the time when he was asked about a man who had vowed to circle the Kaʿbah on all fours. He answered that the man should perform two circumambulations but not crawl. Note the religious understanding: Aḥmad seems to have contemplated the act of falling on one's face and concluded that it provokes ridicule and reduces a sentient creature to the level of a beast. Accordingly, he moved to protect the man from becoming a spectacle and bringing dishonor to God's House and the Mosque. But instead of invalidating the wording of the man's vow to crawl, he substituted the feet—the proper instrument of motion—for the hands.[60]

On another occasion Aḥmad was asked about a man who had died and left a singing slave to his son, who needed to sell her. Aḥmad said that she could only be sold as if untrained. 9.13

"A singer is worth 30,000 dinars," he was told, "but an untrained slave is worth only twenty!"

"She can only be sold as if untrained," he repeated.

This is an admirable bit of religious understanding on his part, because the ability to sing in a slave is like the construction of an instrument of idle diversion and it is not to be assigned a value in cases of usurpation. If a man usurps a singing female slave who then forgets how to sing, he is not liable.[61]

On another occasion, Aḥmad was asked what to do when a dead mouse was found in a quantity of sesame seeds that had been left to soak. He ruled that the seeds should be used as fodder for livestock. 9.14

"What about rinsing them repeatedly and then draining them?" he was asked.

"Not after they've been soaked," he said.

This is another example of careful reasoning on his part. The water that had already been absorbed by the seeds would not be removed by pouring additional liquid over them, since water cannot displace water. Note the man's acumen and his mastery of detail.

On another occasion he was asked about exposing silkworms to the sun to kill them in their cocoons and prevent them from consuming the filaments they had produced. "If there is no other way," he said, "and if the purpose is something other than making them suffer, then it's allowed." 9.15

This verdict is evidence of his great discernment. He permitted an act that causes suffering only because the act had a purpose other than causing that suffering.

Ibn ʿAqīl added: Aḥmad's striking feats of reasoning attest to the presence of a mind that had reached the highest level of understanding. On one occasion, for example, he received a visit from Abū ʿUbaydah and rose from his seat. 9.16

"Hasn't it been reported," asked Abū ʿUbaydah, "that 'a man's place is his own'?"

"That's right," said Aḥmad. "It means he can take the place if he wants, or offer it to someone else."

This degree of understanding, here joined with quick thinking, is unsurpassable.

9.17 Faced with this degree of insight and sound judgment, any fair observer can only avert his eyes in modesty.[62] The only people who do find fault with Aḥmad are purveyors of reprehensible innovations who burn with resentment when they see how often his judgments are adopted and theirs forgotten. So well known are his verdicts that most scholars say, "My ruling in particular cases follows that of So-and-So, but the basis for my reasoning is Aḥmad's." To see a man's judgments adopted as foundational should be enough to convince anyone of his merits.

Chapter 10

Praise of Him by His Teachers

10.1 As you doubtless know, a person's character is manifest even in youth; the way a life begins gives a good idea of how it is likely to end. In Aḥmad's case, piety and love of learning were evident in him from the beginning. As a result, his teachers praised him and granted him precedence.

10.2 [Al-Nasāʾī:] When Aḥmad ibn Ḥanbal would approach a Hadith transmitter, he would ask the men of learning who were present for their permission to gather Hadith, since they would be hearing the reports because of him.

Among the teachers who praised him are the following.

Yazīd ibn Hārūn

10.3 [Ibn Zanjuwayh:] I remember seeing Aḥmad ibn Ḥanbal come to visit Yazīd ibn Hārūn, who was performing the ritual prayer. After finishing his prayer, Yazīd turned to Aḥmad and asked, "What's your position on things lent for use?"

"The borrower is liable for them."

"We cite Ḥajjāj," said Yazīd, "citing al-Ḥakam: 'Not liable.'"

Aḥmad replied by reciting: "The Prophet, God bless and keep him, borrowed some suits of armor from Ṣafwān ibn Umayyah. Ṣafwan asked, 'Are you liable for them?' and the Prophet, God bless and keep him, said, 'The borrower is liable for what he borrows.'"[63]

Having nothing to say in reply, Yazīd adopted Aḥmad ibn Ḥanbal's view.

[Ibn Sālim:] We were sitting in Yazīd ibn Hārūn's Hadith-circle 10.4
and Yazīd made a teasing remark to his amanuensis. From Aḥmad ibn Ḥanbal came a clearing of the throat, and Yazīd, striking himself on the forehead, cried, "Why didn't you tell me Aḥmad was here so I wouldn't joke?"

[Ibn Sinān:] I never saw Yazīd ibn Hārūn regard anyone with 10.5
as much reverence or show anyone as much honor as he did Ibn Ḥanbal. He used to seat Aḥmad beside him when we gathered for Hadith. He maintained a dignified bearing in his presence and wouldn't tease him. Once when Aḥmad fell ill Yazīd even rode to his house to visit him.

[Al-Marrūdhī:] I asked Aḥmad how it happened that Yazīd ibn 10.6
Hārūn visited him when he was ill. He replied:

[Aḥmad:] It was in Wāsiṭ. I used to sit near him while he taught Hadith, and he knew who I was. One day he recited, "Yaḥyā ibn Saʿīd said, 'I heard Sālim ibn ʿAbd Allāh say . . .'"

"It doesn't say 'I heard Sālim say,'" I told him. "It says, 'I heard that Sālim said . . .'"

Yazīd went inside and brought out his notes, and sure enough the text read "that Sālim said." He asked who had corrected him and the others told him it was me.

"Correct what you've written," he told us. After that, whenever he would take his seat he would say, "Ibn Ḥanbal! Come over here."

Once when I got sick Yazīd came to visit me. I had guinea worm.[64] I wasn't staying in this house we're in now—at that time it was my uncles who lived here. I had moved out. The house we moved to was outside.[65]

Ismāʿīl ibn ʿUlayyah

10.7 [Ibn Abī ʿAwn and Ibn Hishām:] Once when the ritual prayer was starting we heard Ibn ʿUlayyah saying, "Is Aḥmad ibn Ḥanbal here anywhere? Tell him to come forward!"

10.8 [Ibn al-Mubārak:] Once when I was at Ismāʿīl ibn ʿUlayyah's someone made a remark that made some of us laugh. Ibn Ḥanbal was there too. Later we went to Ismāʿīl and found him looking angry.

"How could you laugh," he asked, "with Aḥmad ibn Ḥanbal there?"

ʿAbd al-Razzāq ibn Hammām

10.9 [ʿAbd al-Razzāq:] I never saw anyone more astute or more scrupulous[66] than Aḥmad ibn Ḥanbal.

10.10 [Muḥammad ibn ʿAlī:] Abū Bakr Muḥammad ibn Abān said, "Aḥmad, Isḥāq, and I studied with ʿAbd al-Razzāq. If anyone else asked him a question, he would say, 'I'm not reciting Hadith for you. I'm reciting only for the sake of these three.'"

By "these three" he meant Aḥmad, Isḥāq, and Ibn Abān.

10.11 [ʿAbd al-Razzāq:] I have never taught anyone like Aḥmad ibn Ḥanbal.

10.12 [ʿAbd al-Razzāq:] I never taught anyone the like of Aḥmad ibn Ḥanbal.

10.13 [ʿAbd al-Razzāq:] Four of the great scholars of Hadith came to us from Iraq. There was al-Shādhakūnī, who had the most tenacious memory for Hadith. There was Ibn al-Madīnī, who had mastered the differences between reports. There was Yaḥyā ibn Maʿīn, who had the most thorough knowledge of the transmitters. And then there was Aḥmad ibn Ḥanbal, who was the best at putting all three kinds of learning together.

Abū Ya'qūb added: "After the Emissary, no one had more people travel to learn from him than did 'Abd al-Razzāq."

['Abd al-Razzāq:] I've taught Hadith to three men so worthy that I don't care if I never teach anyone else. There was Ibn al-Shādhakūnī, who had such a retentive memory; Yaḥyā ibn Ma'īn, who knew the transmitters so well; and Aḥmad ibn Ḥanbal, who renounced so much. 10.14

['Abd al-Razzāq:] If that man—meaning Aḥmad—survives, it won't matter that the rest of us are gone. 10.15

['Abd al-Razzāq:] I never saw anyone like Aḥmad ibn Ḥanbal. 10.16

[Ibn Zanjawayh:] I told 'Abd al-Razzāq that I was Aḥmad ibn Ḥanbal's neighbor. 10.17

"If that's so," he said, "I'll come visit you."

[Aḥmad:] 'Abd al-Razzāq taught us some Hadith reports on the Mahdī[67] and when he was done, looked over at me and said, "If not for this fellow here"—or "if not for him" (meaning me)—"I would never have taught you those reports." 10.18

Wakī' ibn al-Jarrāḥ

[Wakī':] Of all those who ever came to Kufa, that young man—meaning Aḥmad ibn Ḥanbal—was the best. 10.19

[Ibn Shammās:] I asked Wakī' to teach us the Hadith he had learned from Khārijah ibn Muṣ'ab. 10.20

"I won't," he said. "Aḥmad ibn Ḥanbal told me not to."

Ḥafṣ ibn Ghiyāth al-Nakha'ī

[Ibn Ghiyāth:] Of all those who ever came to Kufa, that young man—meaning Aḥmad ibn Ḥanbal—was the best. 10.21

Abū l-Walīd Hishām ibn 'Abd al-Malik al-Ṭayālisī

[Al-Bukhārī:] I was in Basra when the news came that Aḥmad ibn Ḥanbal had been flogged. Abū l-Walīd exclaimed, "If that man had lived in the days of the Children of Israel, they would have made him a legend." 10.22

10.23 [Ibn Makhlad:] I was at Abū l-Walīd al-Ṭayālisī's when a letter came from Aḥmad ibn Ḥanbal. "There's no one in the two towns"—meaning Basra and Kufa—"dearer to me than Aḥmad ibn Ḥanbal," I heard him say, "or anyone I admire more."

10.24 [Ḥamdān ibn ʿAlī:] Abū l-ʿAwāmm al-Bazzāz (the draper) told me, "Once we were at Abū l-Walīd's when we heard them saying, 'Aḥmad ibn Ḥanbal's here!'

"Abū l-Walīd, who had been sitting at ease, sprang up and then said nothing at all until Aḥmad had sat down. Aḥmad asked him to recite some Hadith, and he did."

I think [al-Bazzāz] added that Abū l-Walīd turned to face Aḥmad.

"I remember," continued al-Bazzāz, "saying"—to himself, that is—"that all of us are senior men of learning, but the only one that Abū l-Walīd treats with deference is Aḥmad!"

Ḥusayn al-Juʿfī

10.25 [Ibn Samāʿah:] We were at Ibn Abī ʿUmar al-ʿAdanī's in Mecca. All of us except for him were talking about Aḥmad ibn Ḥanbal. After we had gone on for a while he broke his silence and said, "Those who could give Aḥmad his due are no longer with us. When he went to study Hadith with Ḥusayn al-Juʿfī, he brought a letter"—that is, a letter of recommendation. "But al-Juʿfī said, 'Aḥmad, there's no need to put a patron between us. You can appeal to me using whatever name you want, but you're a better man than anyone you name.'"

ʿAbd al-Raḥmān ibn Mahdī

10.26 [Ibn Abī Ḥātim:] I heard Aḥmad ibn Sinān al-Qaṭṭān (the cotton merchant) report that he saw Aḥmad ibn Ḥanbal approaching ʿAbd al-Raḥmān ibn Mahdī—or perhaps it was when Aḥmad had gotten up and left the circle—and heard Ibn Mahdī say, "No one knows the Hadith transmitted by Sufyān al-Thawrī better than that man there."

[Ibn Mahdī:] Every time I look at Ibn Ḥanbal I can't help thinking of Sufyān al-Thawrī. 10.27

[Ibn Shammās:] We were at ʿAbd al-Raḥmān ibn Mahdī's when Aḥmad ibn Ḥanbal had just left—or was approaching—and ʿAbd al-Raḥmān said, "Anyone who wants to know what al-Thawrī carried in his head should ask that man there." 10.28

[Ibn Mahdī:] "That boy"—meaning Aḥmad ibn Ḥanbal—"was almost an exemplar while still in his mother's womb." 10.29

Yaḥyā ibn Saʿīd al-Qaṭṭān

[Al-Qaṭṭān:] "I never had another student as good as Aḥmad ibn Ḥanbal." 10.30

[Al-Qaṭṭān:] My two best students were Aḥmad ibn Ḥanbal and Yaḥyā ibn Maʿīn. 10.31

[Al-Qaṭṭān:] "I never had another student as good as Aḥmad ibn Ḥanbal and Yaḥyā ibn Maʿīn." 10.32

[Al-Karābīsī:] When Aḥmad ibn Ḥanbal went to Basra, Ibn al-Shādhakūnī came to resent him, and made some remark about him to Yaḥyā ibn Saʿīd al-Qaṭṭān, who said, "Let me have a look at him." 10.33

After he had seen him, al-Qaṭṭān said to Ibn al-Shādhakūnī, "Shame on you, Sulaymān! Have you no fear of God? That's one of our sages you're talking about."

[Al-Qaṭṭān:] Of the ones who came from Baghdad, no one was dearer to me than Aḥmad ibn Ḥanbal. 10.34

[Ibn al-Madīnī:] Yaḥyā, Aḥmad, and Khalaf came to study with Ibn Saʿīd al-Qaṭṭān. He asked me who Yaḥyā was. 10.35

"That's Yaḥyā ibn Maʿīn," I told him.

"What about that one?"

"That's Khalaf."

"What about that one?"

"Aḥmad ibn Ḥanbal."

"If any of them is the one," he said, "it's him."

[Aḥmad:] I never met anyone else like Yaḥyā ibn Saʿīd. 10.36

Abū ʿĀṣim al-Nabīl, Whose Proper Name Was al-Ḍaḥḥāk ibn Makhlad

10.37 [ʿAbd Allāh:] A group of Hadith-men once gathered at the circle of Abū ʿĀṣim al-Daḥḥāk ibn Makhlad.

"All of you claim to have religious understanding," he said, "but do any of you have it?" With that he began to rebuke them.

"One of us does," they said.

"Who?"

"He's on his way."

When my father arrived, they said, "That's him!"

Abū ʿĀṣim looked at him and said, "Come up front."

"I don't like to step over people," he said.

"Now there's a man who understands!" said Abū ʿĀṣim. "Make room for him!"

They moved aside and he came in. Abū ʿĀṣim asked him to sit in front of him. Then he asked him a question, which he answered. He asked him another question, and he answered that one too, and then a third, and then many, and he answered them all.

"This is a sea creature," said Abū ʿĀṣim, "not a land animal!" Or he may have said, "This is a sea creature that walks on land!"[68]

10.38 [Abū ʿĀṣim:] Aḥmad ibn Ḥanbal came to see me. I heard people saying "Ibn Ḥanbal's here! Ibn Ḥanbal's here!"

"Show me this Ibn Ḥanbal," I said, and they pointed him out.

"You there!" I said. "I have a bone to pick with you. You came to my town and didn't present yourself so we could show you the welcome you deserve."

"Abū ʿĀṣim," he said, "you'll be doing more than enough if I can trouble you to teach some Hadith."

I could see that he was modest, earnest, and well-mannered, and would go as far as any man.

10.39 [ʿAbbās:] I heard Abū ʿĀṣim al-Nabīl say, at the mention of Ibn Ḥanbal, that he had met him. Then he turned around and asked, "Who do you consider the leading Hadith-men in Baghdad today?"

They listed Yaḥyā ibn Maʿīn, Aḥmad ibn Ḥanbal, Abū Khaythamah, al-Muʿayṭī, al-Suwaydī, and other Hadith-men.

"What about here in Basra?"

We named ʿAlī ibn al-Madīnī, Ibn al-Shādhakūnī, Ibn ʿArʿarah, Ibn Abī Khadduwayh, and so on.

"What about Kufa?"

We named the two sons of Abū Shaybah, Ibn Numayr, and some others.

Abū ʿĀsim heaved several sighs—making a sound like "ah, ah, ah"—and said, "Every one you mentioned has come here to see me, and I've met them all. None of them is a match for that young fellow Aḥmad ibn Ḥanbal."

ʿAbbās added that Abū ʿĀṣim was saying this even before Aḥmad ibn Ḥanbal was tried by the Inquisition.

[Aḥmad ibn Manṣūr:] When I took my leave of Abū ʿĀṣim al-Nabīl, he said to me, "Convey my greetings to that righteous man Aḥmad ibn Ḥanbal." 10.40

Abū l-Yamān al-Ḥakam ibn Nāfiʿ

[Abū l-Yamān:] I used to think Aḥmad ibn Ḥanbal resembled Arṭaʾah ibn al-Mundhir.[69] 10.41

Yaḥyā ibn Ādam

[Yaḥyā ibn Ādam:] Aḥmad ibn Ḥanbal is our exemplar. 10.42

Sulaymān ibn Ḥarb

[A man:] Sulaymān ibn Ḥarb once said to me, "Ask Aḥmad ibn Ḥanbal what he says about this problem, because he's our exemplar." 10.43

ʿAffān ibn Muslim al-Ṣaffār (the Coppersmith)

[Al-Mukharrimī:] I heard ʿĪsā ibn ʿAffān say: "Yaḥyā ibn Maʿīn and Abū Khaythamah"—and others he mentioned—"all used to come and hear Hadith from my father. Then Aḥmad ibn Ḥanbal came and 10.44

heard Hadith from him. After he left, my father said to me, 'He was worth the lot of them,' referring to how much Aḥmad knew."

Al-Haytham ibn Jamīl, Abū Sahl al-Baghdādī

10.45 [Abū 'Uthmān:] I heard al-Haytham ibn Jamīl say: "If that young man"—meaning Aḥmad ibn Ḥanbal—"lives long enough, he'll be God's proof of Islam for a whole generation."

10.46 [Ibn Abī l-Ḥawārī:] I heard al-Haytham ibn Jamīl say, "Every age has a man who serves as a proof of Islam to his generation. Fuḍayl ibn 'Iyāḍ is the proof for his time, and I think that if that young man"—meaning Aḥmad ibn Ḥanbal—"lives long enough, he'll be the proof for his."

10.47 [Yūsuf ibn Muslim:] Haytham ibn Jamīl once made an error while reciting a Hadith citing Hushaym.

"Some people recite that report differently," he was told.

"Like who?"

"Aḥmad ibn Ḥanbal."

"I wish my life could be shorter," said al-Haytham, "and his longer."

10.48 [Asad al-Khashshāb:] I heard al-Haytham ibn Jamīl say, "I wish God would make Aḥmad ibn Ḥanbal's life longer and mine shorter."

Then he turned to a man who was present and said, "Tell me: Why did you say that I had anything useful to impart to Muslims?"

Abū Nu'aym al-Faḍl ibn Dukayn

10.49 [Al-Ramādī:] I remember one occasion when we were at Abū Nu'aym's studying with Aḥmad ibn Ḥanbal and Yaḥyā ibn Ma'īn. In those days, when Abū Nu'aym held Hadith sessions, Aḥmad used to sit on his right and Yaḥyā on his left. One day Yaḥyā came to me with a piece of paper on which he had written some of Abū Nu'aym's reports and then, in the spaces between them, copied out reports transmitted by others. "When it's us there," he said, "Give Abū Nu'aym the paper and have him read it."

When the session ended and people were leaving, he handed him the paper.[70] Abū Nuʿaym read the whole thing, then stared at me for a while, and finally looked at Aḥmad ibn Ḥanbal and Yaḥyā ibn Maʿīn.

"This fellow here," he said, gesturing toward Aḥmad, "takes his religion too seriously to do something like this. As for you," he said, looking at me, "you don't do this sort of thing. The one who did it," he continued, "must be this one," and gave Yaḥyā a kick that knocked him off the stoop. "Who are you trying to fool?" he cried.

Yaḥyā picked himself up and kissed Abū Nuʿaym. "May God reward you on behalf of Islam!" he said. "You are just the sort of man who should teach Hadith. I was only testing you."

[Ibn Manṣūr:] When Aḥmad ibn Ḥanbal and Yaḥyā ibn Maʿīn 10.50
went to study with ʿAbd al-Razzāq, I went along with them as their servant. After we returned to Kufa, Yaḥyā said to Aḥmad, "I want to test Abū Nuʿaym."

"No you don't," said Aḥmad. "The man can be trusted."

"This is something I have to do," said Yaḥyā. Taking a piece of paper, he wrote out thirty reports he had heard from Abū Nuʿaym. After every ten, he slipped in a report he had heard from someone else. Then they went to see Abū Nuʿaym.

When they knocked, Abū Nuʿaym came out and sat down on an earthen stoop next to the door. Taking hold of Aḥmad, he seated him to his right, then took hold of Yaḥyā and seated him to his left. I sat down on the ground next to the stoop. Then Yaḥyā took out his sheaf of papers[71] and began reading out the reports. Abū Nuʿaym said nothing about the first ten, but when Yaḥyā read the eleventh, he said, "That's not one of mine. Cross it out!"

Then Yaḥyā read the next ten. Abū Nuʿaym said nothing until Yaḥyā read the second of the reports he had slipped in. When he heard it he said, "That's not one of mine. Cross it out!"

Then Yaḥyā read the next set, including the third report he had slipped in. When he heard it, Abū Nuʿaym's expression changed. Turning to Yaḥyā, he said, "This fellow here"—meaning Aḥmad, whose arm he was still holding—"has too many scruples to do what you've done. And this one"—meaning me—"doesn't know enough. So that leaves you, smart-ass!" With that, he lifted his leg and kicked Yaḥyā off the stoop. Then he got up and went back inside his house.

"Didn't I tell you to leave the man be?" said Aḥmad to Yaḥyā. "Didn't I tell you he was reliable?"

"By God," replied Yaḥyā, "that kick was worth the trip we took."

Qutaybah ibn Saʿīd

10.51 [Al-Marwazī:] I heard Qutaybah ibn Saʿīd say, "In our generation the best men are Ibn al-Mubārak and that young fellow."

"Which young fellow?" asked Abū Bakr al-Rāzī.

"Ibn Ḥanbal."

"He's the senior man of learning in Iraq, and you're calling him a young fellow?"

"He was young when I met him," said Qutaybah.

10.52 [Qutaybah:] Aḥmad ibn Ḥanbal and Isḥāq ibn Rāhawayh are the only two exemplars in the world.

10.53 [Qutaybah:] If you find that someone admires Ibn Ḥanbal, you can be sure that he upholds the *sunnah.*

10.54 [Qutaybah:] If you find that someone admires Ibn Ḥanbal, you can be sure that he upholds the *sunnah* and stands with the community.[72]

10.55 [Qutaybah:] If you find that someone admires Ibn Ḥanbal, you can be sure that he's on the path.

10.56 [Qutaybah:] If Aḥmad had lived in the time of al-Thawrī, Mālik, al-Awzāʿī, and al-Layth ibn Saʿd, he would have been the foremost among them.

10.57 [Ibn Shabbuwayh:] I heard Qutaybah say, "If Aḥmad had lived in the time of al-Thawrī, Mālik, al-Awzāʿī, and al-Layth ibn Saʿd, he would have been the foremost among them."

"You'd rank Aḥmad with the Successors?" I asked.

"With the greatest of them," said Qutaybah.

[Al-Naysābūrī:] I was once talking with Qutaybah ibn Saʿīd and mentioned Yaḥyā ibn Yaḥyā, Isḥāq ibn Rāhawayh, and Aḥmad ibn Ḥanbal. 10.58

"Of the ones you named," he said, "Aḥmad ibn Ḥanbal is the greatest."

[Ibn Shabbuwayh:] I heard Qutaybah say, "If not for al-Thawrī, being scrupulous would have died out, and if not for Ibn Ḥanbal, people would have added things to our religion." 10.59

"You'd rank Aḥmad with the Successors?" I asked.

"With the greatest of them," said Qutaybah.

[Ibn Ṭarkhān:] I heard Qutaybah say, "If not for al-Thawrī, being scrupulous would have died out; and if not for Ibn Ḥanbal, people would have added whatever they wanted to our religion." 10.60

Somebody said, "Abū Rajāʾ, you'd count Aḥmad with the Successors?"

"With the greatest of them," said Qutaybah.

[Al-Rāzī:] I heard Qutaybah say, "As soon as Aḥmad ibn Ḥanbal dies, the reprehensible innovations will start." 10.61

Addendum

Aḥmad ibn Ḥanbal was also praised by many men of learning, equal in rank to his teachers, with whom he did not study. One was Abū Mushir al-Dimashqī. 10.62

[Ibn al-ʿAbbās:] I asked Abū Mushir if he knew anyone who could keep our community's religion safe.

"I can't think of anyone," he replied, "except one young man out east," meaning Aḥmad ibn Ḥanbal.

[The author:] A good many more reports like this will appear—God willing—in the course of this book.

Chapter 11

Teachers and Senior Men of Learning Who Cite Him[73]

11.1 These include:

Maʿrūf al-Karkhī

11.8 [Ibn Aktham:] I once heard Maʿrūf say, when Aḥmad ibn Ḥanbal was mentioned: "To me, Ibn Ḥanbal seemed a young man marked by devotion—one who could convey a great deal in a few words. Once I heard him say: 'If you remember that you'll be forgotten when you die, you'll do good deeds and harm no one.'"

Aswad ibn ʿĀmir, Known as Shādhān

11.9 [Shādhān:] I sent a message to Abū ʿAbd Allāh—meaning Aḥmad ibn Ḥanbal—asking his permission to transmit the Hadith reported by Ḥammād, citing Qatādah, citing ʿIkrimah, citing Ibn ʿAbbās, citing the Prophet, God bless and keep him: "I saw my Lord, mighty and glorious . . ."[74]

Aḥmad told the messenger, "Tell him to go ahead. That report has been transmitted by learned men."

ʿAlī ibn al-Madīnī

11.16 [ʿAlī ibn al-Madīnī:] My master Aḥmad ibn Ḥanbal told me not to recite Hadith except from a written document.

Chapter 12

All the Men of Learning Who Cite Him[75]

Women Who Transmitted on His Authority

Aḥmad ibn Ḥanbal's slave Ḥusn. Khadījah, Umm Muḥammad. Aḥmad ibn Ḥanbal's cousin and wife Rayḥānah, the mother of his son ʿAbd Allāh. Aḥmad ibn Ḥanbal's wife ʿAbbāsah bint al-Faḍl, the mother of his son Ṣāliḥ. Mukhkhah, sister of Bishr al-Ḥāfī. 12.57

Chapter 13

Praise of Him by His Peers, His Contemporaries, and Those Close to Him in Age

Muḥammad ibn Idrīs al-Shāfiʿī (God Be Pleased with Him)

[Ḥarmalah ibn Yaḥyā:] I heard al-Shāfiʿī say: "I left behind me in Baghdad no one more scrupulous, more God-fearing,[76] or more insightful in matters of law"—and I think he added "or more learned"—"than Aḥmad ibn Ḥanbal." 13.1

[Al-Shāfiʿī:] Three men of learning never cease to amaze me. One is Abū Thawr: even though he's an Arab, he never uses grammatical inflections. The second is al-Ḥasan al-Zaʿfarānī: even though Arabic is not his first language, he never makes a mistake. The third is Ibn Ḥanbal: whatever he says, his elders believe. 13.2

[Al-Shāfiʿī:] No one I met back in Iraq was like Ibn Ḥanbal. 13.3

[Al-Shāfiʿī:] I have never seen anyone more self-restrained than Aḥmad ibn Ḥanbal and Sulaymān ibn Dāwūd al-Hāshimī. 13.4

Abū Bakr ʿAbd Allāh ibn al-Zubayr al-Ḥumaydī

13.5 [Al-Ḥumaydī:] So long as I'm in the Hijaz, Aḥmad's in Iraq, and Isḥāq's in Khurasan, we will never be defeated.

Ibn Abī Uways

13.6 [Al-Baladī:] Once at Ibn Abī Uways's house I heard him reply to a Hadith scholar who had remarked that there were no Hadith scholars left.

"As long as God spares Ibn Ḥanbal," he said, "there will still be Hadith scholars."

ʿAlī ibn al-Madīnī

13.7 [ʿAlī ibn al-Madīnī:] I have taken Aḥmad ibn Ḥanbal as a guide in all my dealings with God. Who else is strong enough to do what he does?

13.8 [ʿAlī ibn al-Madīnī:] Aḥmad ibn Ḥanbal is our leader.

13.9 [Ibrāhīm ibn Ismāʿīl:] ʿAlī ibn al-Madīnī came to us and we gathered around him and asked him to teach us some Hadith.

"My master," he said, "is Aḥmad ibn Ḥanbal, and he told me never to recite Hadith except from a written text."[77]

13.10 [Muḥammad ibn ʿAbduwayh:] I heard ʿAlī ibn al-Madīnī say, at the mention of Aḥmad ibn Ḥanbal: "I think he is greater than Saʿīd ibn Jubayr was in his time, since Saʿīd had peers but Aḥmad doesn't," or words to that effect.

13.11 [ʿAlī ibn al-Madīnī:] No one I know has a better memory than Aḥmad ibn Ḥanbal, but I've heard that even he won't recite Hadith without a written text, and that's the good example I intend to follow.

13.12 [ʿAlī ibn al-Madīnī:] When I have a question, I'd rather ask Aḥmad ibn Ḥanbal than Abū ʿĀṣim or ʿAbd Allāh ibn Dāwūd. Age doesn't always make a man more learned.

13.13 [Muḥammad ibn al-ʿAbbās ibn Khālid:] I heard ʿAlī ibn al-Madīnī say, when someone mentioned Aḥmad ibn Ḥanbal, "May God protect Aḥmad! He's God's living proof to His creatures of the truth of Islam."

['Alī ibn al-Madīnī:] God, mighty and glorious, has exalted this religion of ours through two men who have no equal: Abū Bakr al-Ṣiddīq, for what he did during the Apostasy, and Aḥmad ibn Ḥanbal, for what he did during the Inquisition.[78] 13.14

[Al-Maymūnī:] I heard 'Alī ibn al-Madīnī say, "No one after God's Emissary, God bless and keep him, has done for Islam what Aḥmad ibn Ḥanbal did." 13.15

"What about Abū Bakr al-Ṣiddīq?" I asked.

"No," he answered. "Abū Bakr had friends and allies, but Aḥmad ibn Ḥanbal didn't."

[Abū Ya'lā l-Mawṣilī:] I heard 'Alī ibn al-Madīnī say, "God, mighty and glorious, has exalted this religion of ours through two men who will have no equal until Judgment Day: Abū Bakr al-Ṣiddīq, for what he did during the Apostasy, and Aḥmad ibn Ḥanbal, for what he did during the Inquisition." According to another report of his words, he added, "Abū Bakr had friends and allies, but Aḥmad ibn Ḥanbal didn't." 13.16

[Al-Madīni:] I've known Aḥmad for fifty years and he keeps getting better. 13.17

[Yaḥyā ibn Sa'īd:] "How can you reproach me for admiring 'Alī ibn al-Madīnī when he's my teacher?"[79] 13.18

[Yaḥyā ibn Sa'īd:] "People reproach me for sitting with 'Alī [ibn al-Madīnī], but I learn more from him than he does from me." 13.19

Abū 'Ubayd al-Qāsim ibn Sallām

[Al-Qāsim ibn Sallām:] Knowledge of Hadith has come down to four men: Aḥmad ibn Ḥanbal, who understood it best; Ibn Abī Shaybah, who had the most retentive memory; 'Alī ibn al-Madīnī, who knew the most; and Yaḥyā ibn Ma'īn, who wrote down more of it than the others. 13.20

[Al-Qāsim ibn Sallām:] Knowledge of Hadith has come down to four men: Aḥmad ibn Ḥanbal, 'Alī ibn al-Madīnī, Yaḥyā ibn Ma'īn, and Abū Bakr ibn Abī Shaybah. Of the four, Aḥmad understood it best. 13.21

13.22 [Al-Qāsim ibn Sallām:] Aḥmad ibn Ḥanbal is our guide; it's an honor for me to speak of him.

13.23 [Abū Bakr al-Athram:] We were at Abū ʿUbayd's and I was debating with someone there. At one point the man asked me to name my authority for a report.

"The one who has no equal, east or west," I replied.

"Who's that?"

"Aḥmad ibn Ḥanbal."

"He's right," interjected Abū ʿUbayd. "There's no one like him, east or west. I never met anyone who knew the *sunnah* better than he did."

13.24 [Al-Maymūnī:] Abū ʿUbayd al-Qāsim ibn Sallām said, "I've sat opposite Abū Yūsuf, the judge; Muḥammad ibn al-Ḥasan"—as best I can remember, he added, "Yaḥyā ibn Saʿīd and ʿAbd al-Raḥmān ibn al-Mahdī"—"but I was never more intimidated when discussing a question than I was with Aḥmad ibn Ḥanbal."

13.25 [Al-Qāsim ibn Sallām:] One day I went to Aḥmad Ibn Ḥanbal's. He seated me in the place of honor and took a lower seat for himself.

"Aḥmad," I protested, "don't they say the host should take the best seat?"

"What they mean," he answered, "is that he can seat himself and his guests anywhere he wants."

"That's worth remembering," I told myself.

Then I said, "If I were to visit you as much as you deserve, I would come every day."

"Don't say that," he warned. "I have close friends I see only once a year, but I trust them more than the people I see every day."

"Another point to remember," I thought.

When it was time to leave he rose with me. When I protested, he recited, "Al-Shaʿbī said: 'A perfect host accompanies his guest to the door and holds his stirrups.'"

"Another lesson!" I thought.

He walked me all the way to the door and held my stirrups.

[Muḥammad ibn Abī Bishr:] I went to Aḥmad ibn Ḥanbal to ask him a question, and he told me, "Go ask Abū ʿUbayd; he has an explanation you won't hear from anyone else." 13.26

So I took the question to Abū ʿUbayd, who answered it to my satisfaction. Then I told him what Aḥmad had said about him.

"Cousin," he replied, "there you see a man doing God's work. I pray to God to spread the news of his good works far and wide in this world, and reward him with closeness to Him in the next! Have you seen how people are drawn to him? And how he makes them feel welcome and sets them at ease? No one else in Iraq brings together all the fine qualities he does. He is patient, knowledgeable, and perceptive. May God bless him in the use of the virtues He has given him!"

Then he said, "The poet who praised him put it well: 13.27

A joy it is to see his face, and proud
　Is he who calls a man like him a friend.
Let learning barricade itself away:
　Fear not, for he will draw it out again.
And when he sees injustice done, he speaks
　Without a qualm, for God and all that's right
And for his friends, the favored ones who know
　The Law of God, and rise to scale the heights."

Yaḥyā ibn Maʿīn

[Yaḥyā ibn Maʿīn:] I've only seen three men teach Hadith expecting no reward but God's good pleasure: Yaʿlā ibn ʿUbayd, al-Qaʿnabī, and Aḥmad ibn Ḥanbal. 13.28

[ʿAbd Allāh ibn Ibrāhīm:] I heard Yaḥyā ibn Maʿīn say that there are only four scholars you can trust—or only four true Hadith scholars—namely Wakīʿ, Yaʿlā ibn ʿUbayd, al-Qaʿnabī, and Aḥmad ibn Ḥanbal. 13.29

[ʿAbbās ibn Muḥammad:] Once when someone mentioned Aḥmad ibn Ḥanbal, I heard Yaḥyā ibn Maʿīn say, "By God, I can't do what Aḥmad does; I'm not strong enough." 13.30

13.31 [Yaḥyā ibn Maʿīn:] People wanted me to be like Aḥmad ibn Ḥanbal, but that's impossible: I'll never be like him.

13.32 [Al-Anmāṭī:] I was once sitting with Yaḥyā ibn Maʿīn, Abū Khaythamah, Zuhayr ibn Ḥarb, and other senior men of learning. When they began praising Aḥmad ibn Ḥanbal and describing his virtues, someone said, "Enough already! Don't get carried away," to which Yaḥyā ibn Maʿīn replied, "As if one could go too far in praising Aḥmad! Even if we'd come here to do nothing but speak of his merits, we would still fail to recount them all."

Abū Khaythamah Zuhayr ibn Ḥarb

13.33 [Abū Zurʿah:] I heard Zuhayr ibn Ḥarb say, "I've never seen anyone like Ibn Ḥanbal, or anyone tougher—to stand up the way he did, with people being flogged and executed." He added, "No one stood up the way he did. He was persecuted and hounded all those years, but he stayed the course."

Isḥāq ibn Rāhawayh

13.34 [Aḥmad ibn Muḥammad ibn Yāsīn:] I heard Muḥammad ibn ʿAbd al-Raḥīm say that he heard Isḥāq ibn Ibrāhīm al-Ḥanẓalī say, at the mention of Ibn Ḥanbal, "No one comes close."

13.35 [Muḥammad ibn Isḥāq:] I heard my father say, "Aḥmad ibn Ḥanbal is God's sign to His worshippers on earth."

13.36 [Muḥammad ibn Isḥāq:] I heard my father say, "If Aḥmad hadn't laid his life on the line the way he did, Islam would have disappeared."

Bishr ibn al-Ḥārith the Barefoot

13.37 [Ibn Khashram:] Someone asked Bishr about Aḥmad ibn Ḥanbal, and I heard him reply, "Why should you care what someone like me has to say about Aḥmad? He went into the bellows and came out red gold."[80]

13.38 [Bishr ibn al-Ḥārith:] Aḥmad ibn Ḥanbal was put into the bellows and came out like a chunk of red gold.

[Ibn Khashram:] I heard Bishr ibn al-Ḥārith say "Aḥmad ibn Ḥanbal was put into the bellows and came out like a chunk of red gold." When Aḥmad learned of this, he said, "Thank God Bishr approves of what I did!" 13.39

[Al-Tammār:] When Aḥmad ibn Ḥanbal was flogged during the Inquisition, Bishr came to see me. "Abū Naṣr," he said, "today that man has done what everyone else has failed to do. I hope God counts his learning in his favor." 13.40

[Muḥammad ibn al-Shāh:] After the Inquisition was over, Bishr ibn al-Ḥārith was asked about Aḥmad ibn Ḥanbal and said, "He's one of the exemplary leaders of Islam." 13.41

[Ibrāhīm ibn al-Ḥārith:] When Aḥmad ibn Ḥanbal was flogged, Bishr's associates said, "If only you had gone out and said, 'I stand with Ibn Ḥanbal!'" 13.42

"Do you want me to do what the prophets did?"[81] replied Bishr. "That's what Aḥmad ibn Ḥanbal's doing."

[Al-Asadī:] When Aḥmad ibn Ḥanbal was taken away to be flogged, people went to Bishr ibn al-Ḥārith and said, "They've taken Aḥmad and they've brought out the whips. You need to speak out." 13.43

"Do you want me to do what the prophets did?" said Bishr. "I can't. May God keep Ibn Ḥanbal safe from every danger!"

[ʿAbd Allāh:] Bishr was asked—when they were flogging Aḥmad ibn Ḥanbal—to say something, and he replied, "You're asking me to stand where the prophets stood? That's what Aḥmad ibn Ḥanbal is doing." 13.44

[Al-Ṭabbāʿ:] I heard Abū ʿAbd Allāh al-Baynūnī, who was a Worshipper,[82] say, "I asked Bishr why he wouldn't do what Ibn Ḥanbal had done. He said, 'Do you want me to stand on a level with the prophets?' or '. . . to lift me up to where the prophets are? My body's too weak for that. May God guard Aḥmad ibn Ḥanbal from every danger before him or behind, above or below, and from either side.'" 13.45

[Ḥanbal ibn Isḥāq:] Al-Haytham the Worshipper said, "I was at Bishr's and someone came in saying, 'Aḥmad ibn Ḥanbal's been struck seventeen lashes so far.' At that, Bishr stuck out his foot and 13.46

said, 'How ugly my leg looks without a fetter on it in defense of that man!'"

Ḥanbal added: One of my teachers, who was himself a Worshipper, told me, "When they took Aḥmad ibn Ḥanbal, I went to Bishr ibn al-Ḥārith and said, 'Come on, let's go help the man.' He replied, 'That's what a prophet does; I can't.'"

13.47 [Ibrāhīm ibn Hāni' al-Naysābūrī:] Once when I was praying with Bishr ibn al-Ḥārith, I lifted my hands. After the prayer leader had signaled the end of the ritual prayer, Bishr said, "Abū Isḥāq, I'm surprised that you and your teacher Aḥmad ibn Ḥanbal lift your hands. I heard Hushaym report, citing Mughīrah, that Ibrāhīm used to tell people to let their hands drop when they pray."[83]

I went to Aḥmad and told him what Bishr had said. He replied, "Seventeen of the Emissary's Companions used to lift their hands." Then he recited, «Let those who go against his order beware»[84] and remarked, "Lifting one's hands makes the ritual prayer more beautiful."

So I went back to Bishr and told him what Aḥmad had said. "Who am I compared to him?" he exclaimed. "Who am I compared to him? He knows better. He knows better!"

13.48 [Muḥammad ibn Jaʿfar:] I heard Ibrāhīm report, citing his uncle al-Jahm al-ʿUkbarī, who used to attend both Aḥmad ibn Ḥanbal and Bishr ibn al-Ḥārith, the following: "One day I went to see Aḥmad ibn Ḥanbal. He had draped his breechclout[85] over one shoulder but it had slipped down, revealing his scars." He may have added, "My eyes filled with tears." He continued: "Aḥmad ibn Ḥanbal saw me looking and pulled the garment back up.

"Later I went to see Bishr ibn al-Ḥārith and told him the story. 'If only you knew!' he exclaimed. 'With the hurt and pain they brought him,[86] Aḥmad ibn Ḥanbal has flown high in Islam.'"

I repeated this story to Abū Bakr al-Marrūdhī, who liked it and wrote it down.

13.49 [Ibrāhīm ibn Isḥāq al-Ḥarbi:] I heard Bishr ibn al-Ḥārith say that he heard al-Muʿāfā ibn ʿImrān say that Sufyān al-Thawrī was asked to explain what *futuwwah* is. Sufyān replied as follows: "*Futuwwah* is mindfulness and modesty. It starts with self-discipline, and it gains luster by the cultivation of forbearance and good manners. In its highest form, it demands religious knowledge and the scrupulous avoidance of dubious activities. A man of *futuwwah* prays regularly, treats his parents and relatives kindly, spends freely, and cares for his neighbor. He is not overbearing, nor does he diverge from common practice; he maintains his dignity and avoids looking at things he shouldn't. He speaks gently, greets others cheerfully, and supports any other right-thinking *fityān* who know what God wants them to do and not to do. He speaks the truth and avoids swearing oaths. He is friendly, cheerful, convivial, and a good listener. He knows how to keep a secret, to conceal the shortcomings of others, and to take good care of whatever is entrusted to him. He stabs no one in the back and he keeps his word. He keeps silent in company, though he can hold his own if he must, and walks humbly even when he need not do so. He respects his elders, treats younger people kindly, and does whatever he can to help his fellow Muslims. When things go badly, he suffers patiently; when things go well, he remembers to be grateful. The full perfection of *futuwwah* is fear of God, mighty and glorious, and anyone who posesses these virtues is a true *fatā*."

Bishr ibn al-Ḥārith then said, "According to Sufyān, then, Aḥmad ibn Ḥanbal was a *fatā*, since he did have all those virtues. Not only that: he wore a breechclout of twisted cloth."[87]

Al-Ḥārith al-Muḥāsibī[88]

['Abd Allāh:] Al-Fatḥ ibn Shakhraf wrote to me in his own hand, saying that when someone mentioned Aḥmad ibn Ḥanbal in the presence of al-Ḥārith ibn Asad al-Muḥāsibī, he—that is, al-Fatḥ—had cited 'Abd al-Razzāq, who heard Sufyān ibn 'Uyaynah say that Ibn 'Abbās was the greatest scholar of his age, al-Sha'bī of his, and al-Thawrī of his. Then al-Fatḥ added, "And, in his age, Aḥmad ibn Ḥanbal," to which al-Ḥārith replied, "He suffered more than al-Thawrī or al-Awzā'ī ever did." 13.50

Dhū l-Nūn al-Miṣrī (of Egypt)

13.51 [Al-Marrūdhī:] When we were in Samarra,[89] I went to see Dhū l-Nūn, who was in prison. He asked me, "How is our master?" meaning Aḥmad ibn Ḥanbal.

Abū Zurʿah al-Rāzī

13.52 [Al-Ḥasan ibn al-Layth:] I once heard someone say to Aḥmad ibn Ḥanbal, "There's a man called Abū Zurʿah who recites Hadith in Rey. Should we write down what he says?"

"You're asking about Abū Zurʿah?" said Aḥmad ibn Ḥanbal, incredulous. "May God guard Abū Zurʿah, and protect him, and ennoble him! May He grant him victory over his enemies!" He went on to recite a lengthy prayer for him.

Some time later, after I had joined Abū Zurʿah, I mentioned this incident to him. "Every time I'm in trouble," he said, "I remember that prayer and I say, 'God, now that Aḥmad has prayed for me, keep me safe, and keep those people from harming me!'"[90]

13.53 [Abū Zurʿah:] I've never seen anyone match Aḥmad ibn Ḥanbal in the different branches of Hadith-learning, nor seen anyone stand up the way he did.

13.54 [ʿAbd Allāh ibn Muḥammad ibn ʿAbd al-Karīm:] I heard Abū Zurʿah say, "I never saw anyone like Aḥmad ibn Ḥanbal."

"You mean you never saw anyone who knew more?"

"Not just that. I'm talking about learning, and renouncing the world, and understanding the law, and having real knowledge, and every other good thing you can think of."[91]

13.55 [Ibn Abī Ḥātim:] I heard Abū Zurʿah say, "People still talk about Aḥmad ibn Ḥanbal. They say he's better than Yaḥyā ibn Maʿīn, ʿAlī l-Madīnī, and Abū Khaythamah. And it's true: I can't think of anyone his age who has more insight into the law, or anyone who knows more different things than he does."

"What about Isḥāq ibn Rāhawayh?"

"Aḥmad knows more and understands it better. I knew the scholars of old, and none of them brought together all the qualities he has—self-denial, learning, insight, and so many other things—as fully as he does."

Abū Ḥātim Muḥammad ibn Idrīs al-Rāzī

['Abd al-Raḥmān ibn Abī Ḥātim:] I asked my father whether 'Alī l-Madīnī or Aḥmad ibn Ḥanbal had memorized more Hadith. 13.56

"They had memorized more or less the same number of reports," he said, "but Aḥmad understood them better."

I also heard my father say, "If a man loves Ibn Ḥanbal, you can be sure that he knows the *sunnah*."

I also heard him say, "I used to see Qutaybah ibn Sa'īd going about his business in Mecca with no one writing down his reports. So I said to the Hadith-men, 'How can you ignore Qutaybah after Aḥmad ibn Ḥanbal sat in his circle?'

"When they heard that, they made a beeline for him and copied down his reports."

[Abū Ḥātim al-Rāzī:] "If a man loves Ibn Ḥanbal, you can be sure 13.57 that he knows the *sunnah*. He's the test that marks us off from the purveyors of reprehensible innovations."

Abū Ibrāhīm Ismā'īl ibn Yaḥyā l-Muzanī, the Associate of al-Shāfi'ī

[Al-Muzanī:] Aḥmad ibn Ḥanbal was like[92] Abū Bakr during the 13.58 Apostasy; 'Umar, on the day of the Porch; 'Uthmān, on the day they attacked his house; and 'Alī at the Battle of Ṣiffīn.[93]

Abū Ya'qūb al-Buwayṭī

[Al-Rabī' ibn Sulaymān:] In a letter al-Buwayṭī wrote to me from 13.59 prison in Baghdad, he said, "Instead of rewarding all of us who defied the Inquisition, I sorely wish God would transfer our rewards to Aḥmad ibn Ḥanbal, our leader in Baghdad."

Abū Thawr

13.60 [Al-Marrūdhī:] I was present when someone asked Abū Thawr about something and he answered, "Our teacher and authority, Aḥmad ibn Ḥanbal, has addressed that question as follows . . ."

13.61 [Abū Thawr:] "Aḥmad ibn Ḥanbal is more learned and more understanding of the law than al-Thawrī."

13.62 [Abū Thawr:] If you were to say that Aḥmad ibn Ḥanbal is among the saved, no one would rebuke you. Why not? If you go to Khurasan and the regions around, you'll hear people saying that Aḥmad ibn Ḥanbal is a good man. If you go to Syria and those parts, or Iraq, you'll hear the same thing. So this is a matter of consensus, which wouldn't be the case if even one person were to take issue with it.

13.63 [Abū Thawr:] Aḥmad ibn Ḥanbal always looked as if he could see the Law written on a tablet in front of him.

Abū ʿAbd Allāh Muḥammad ibn Yaḥyā l-Dhuhlī

13.64 [Al-Dhuhlī:] I have chosen Aḥmad ibn Ḥanbal as my exemplar in all my dealings with God.

13.65 [Al-Dhuhlī:] My exemplar is Aḥmad ibn Ḥanbal.

Sufyān ibn Wakīʿ

13.66 [Ibn Wakīʿ:] Aḥmad ibn Ḥanbal is the test: as far as we're concerned, anyone who says anything against him is a sinner.[94]

Aḥmad ibn Ṣāliḥ al-Miṣrī

13.67 [Aḥmad ibn Ṣāliḥ:] Nowhere in Iraq did I meet anyone to compare with Aḥmad ibn Ḥanbal in Baghdad, or with Muḥammad ibn ʿAbd Allāh ibn Numayr in Kufa. Both of them brought together more virtues than anyone else I saw.

13.68 [Abū Bakr ibn Zanjuwayh:] When I went to Egypt, I met Aḥmad ibn Ṣāliḥ, who asked me where I was from. I told him I was from Baghdad.

"Do you live anywhere near Aḥmad ibn Ḥanbal?" he asked.

"I'm with him all the time," I said.

"Write down for me where your house is," he said. "I want to come to Iraq so you can introduce me to him."

I wrote down what he asked, and he came and stayed with ʿAffān, and I introduced him to Aḥmad. The two of them exchanged Hadith, and Aḥmad recited a report that Ibn Ṣāliḥ insisted on copying down.

"Let me get it from the book," said Aḥmad. He went inside, came out with the book, and dictated the report.

"If this is all I get out of coming to Iraq, it'll be more than worth the trip," said Ibn Ṣāliḥ. With that, he bid Aḥmad farewell and departed.

Abū ʿUmar Hilāl ibn al-ʿAlāʾ al-Raqqī

[Al-Tirmidhī, al-Ṣābbāḥ, and al-Baghdādī:] We heard Hilāl ibn al-ʿAlāʾ al-Raqqī say, "There are four men who deserve to be recognized as blessings from God upon our community: Abū ʿUbayd, for explaining difficult Hadith reports; al-Shāfiʿī, for discerning the law in the Hadith; Yaḥyā ibn Maʿīn, for casting out false reports; and Aḥmad ibn Ḥanbal, for standing firm during the Inquisition." 13.69

If not for Aḥmad, we'd all be Ingrates. (This remark was added by Ismāʿīl ibn al-ʿAbbās.)

Abū ʿAbd al-Raḥmān Aḥmad ibn Shuʿayb al-Nasāʾī

[Al-Nasāʾī:] The four greatest figures of Aḥmad ibn Ḥanbal's time were ʿAlī ibn al-Madīnī, Yaḥyā ibn Maʿīn, Aḥmad himself, and Isḥāq ibn Rāhawayh. The one who knew the most about defects in transmission was ʿAlī ibn al-Madīnī. The one who knew the transmitters best, and knew the most reports, was Yaḥyā ibn Maʿīn. The one who most readily memorized reports and their legal implications was Isḥāq ibn Rāhawayh. In my view, though, Aḥmad ibn Ḥanbal knew more about defects in transmission than Isḥāq did. Besides his knowledge of Hadith, Aḥmad also had all the virtues of legal insight, scrupulosity, and renunciation, and he could suffer without complaint. 13.70

Naṣr ibn ʿAlī

13.71 [Naṣr ibn ʿAlī:] Aḥmad ibn Ḥanbal was the greatest man of his time.

Abū Maʿmar Ismāʿīl ibn Ibrāhīm al-Hudhalī l-Qaṭīʿī

13.72 [Bakr ibn Muḥammad:] It was thirty-four years ago, or even more, that I heard Abū Maʿmar say, "In the last fifty years, I never saw anyone like Aḥmad ibn Ḥanbal. Even as a boy he kept going from strength to strength."

ʿAmr ibn Muḥammad al-Nāqid

13.73 [ʿAmr ibn Muḥammad al-Nāqid:] So long as Aḥmad ibn Ḥanbal agrees with me on a Hadith report, I don't care who disagrees.

Aḥmad ibn al-Ḥajjāj

13.74 [Aḥmad ibn al-Ḥajjāj:] I never met anyone like Aḥmad ibn Ḥanbal. Even if he had lived at the same time as Ibn al-Mubārak, I would still give him precedence.

Muḥammad ibn Mihrān al-Jammāl

13.75 [Al-Faḍl ibn Ziyād:] I once heard Muḥammad ibn Mihrān al-Jammāl say, at the mention of Aḥmad ibn Ḥanbal: "He's the only one, really. Whenever I cast my mind over the transmitters working in Mecca and Medina, he's the one who stands out. If I think about Basra and Kufa, I come back to him. If I turn to Syria and northern Mesopotamia, again it's him; and the same with Khurasan."

Muḥammad ibn Muslim Wārah al-Qūmisī

13.76 [Muḥammad ibn Muslim Wārah al-Qūmisī:] The pillars of our religion are Aḥmad ibn Ṣāliḥ in Egypt; in Baghdad, Aḥmad ibn Ḥanbal; in Ḥarrān, al-Nufaylī; and in Kufa, ʿAbd Allāh ibn Numayr.

13.77 [ʿAbd al-Raḥmān ibn Abī Ḥātim:] I heard someone ask Muḥammad ibn Muslim ibn Wārah whether ʿAlī ibn al-Madīnī or Yaḥyā ibn Maʿīn had retained more Hadith. He replied, "ʿAlī could recite more fluently and accurately, while Yaḥyā had a better grasp of what was correct and what was doubtful. But better than both was Aḥmad ibn Ḥanbal, with his insight, his memory, and his knowledge."

Abū Jaʿfar ʿAbd Allāh ibn Muḥammad ibn ʿAlī ibn Nufayl al-Nufaylī

[Al-Nufaylī:] Aḥmad ibn Ḥanbal was a waymark of our religion. 13.78

Muḥammad ibn Muṣʿab

[Muḥammad ibn Muṣʿab:] Any of the lashes that Aḥmad ibn Ḥanbal 13.79 bore for the sake of God is worth all the days of Bishr ibn al-Ḥārith.

Al-Ḥasan ibn Muḥammad ibn al-Ṣabbāḥ al-Bazzār

[Abū Muḥammad ibn Abī Ḥātim:] I heard my father say that when- 13.80 ever al-Ḥasan ibn Muḥammad ibn al-Ṣabbāḥ heard that anyone had criticized Aḥmad ibn Ḥanbal, he would gather the senior men of learning and confront the offender. "He would turn people against him," he said.[95]

[Al-Ḥasan ibn al-Ṣabbāḥ al-Bazzār:] Aḥmad ibn Ḥanbal is our 13.81 elder and our master.

Yaʿqūb ibn Sufyān

[Abū ʿAbd al-Raḥmān al-Nihāwandī:] I heard Yaʿqūb ibn Sufyān say 13.82 that he had written down reports recited for him by a thousand different teachers but counted only two as authorities in his dealings with God.

I asked him who his authorities were, recalling that he had copied reports from prominent authorities, such as al-Anṣārī and Ḥabbān[96] ibn Hilāl.

"Aḥmad ibn Ḥanbal," he said, "and Aḥmad ibn Ṣāliḥ al-Miṣrī."

Muḥammad ibn Yaḥyā l-Azdī al-Baṣrī

[Muḥammad ibn Yaḥyā l-Azdī:] We stand by the creed of Aḥmad 13.83 ibn Ḥanbal. He is our exemplar, the last one left to the believers. We accept him as our guide and will not go against him. He is the remnant of the learned men of old. We declare ourselves quit of anyone who opposes him; anyone who opposes him is a misdirected purveyor of reprehensible innovations.

Abū Hammām al-Walīd ibn Shujāʿ al-Sakūnī

13.84 [Abū Hammām:] I've never seen anyone like Aḥmad ibn Ḥanbal, nor has Aḥmad met anyone like himself.

Abū ʿUmayr ibn al-Naḥḥās al-Ramlī al-Falastinī (of Palestine)

13.85 [Abū ʿUmayr, at the mention of Aḥmad ibn Ḥanbal:] May God have mercy on him! How long he suffered in silence, and how greatly did he resemble the first Muslims and approach the pious men of old! The world's riches came within his reach, and he returned them; he was asked to embrace heresies, but he spurned them.

13.86 [Abū Ḥātim:] Abū ʿUmayr ibn al-Naḥḥās al-Ramlī was a Muslim worshipper. One day I went to see him and he asked if I had anything copied from Ibn Ḥanbal.

When I said I did, he asked me to dictate it. So I dictated to him the Hadith reports I had memorized after learning them from Aḥmad. Then he asked me to read them for him, and I did.[97]

Muḥammad ibn Ibrāhīm al-Būshanjī

13.87 [Al-Būshanjī:] I never met anyone so complete in his merits, or as self-restrained, as Aḥmad ibn Ḥanbal.

13.88 [Al-Būshanjī:] In my view, he was worthier and more discerning than Sufyān al-Thawrī, who never suffered the same trials and hardships, and whose learning, like the learning of the earlier jurists of various regions, could not match Aḥmad's. His learning was more comprehensive, and he knew more than Sufyān did about which transmitters were accurate and truthful and which ones were sloppy or mendacious. I was told that Bishr ibn al-Ḥārith said, "Aḥmad has done the work of a prophet." The way I see it, Aḥmad endured two distinct ordeals. Four caliphs took their turn with him, some testing him by tormenting him, and others by tempting him, but he took strength in God, mighty and glorious, and prevailed. Al-Maʾmūn, al-Muʿtaṣim, and al-Wāthiq tried everything from flogging and imprisonment to threats and intimidation, but Aḥmad never wavered from true religion, nor did the lash or the dungeon sway his faith. Then came al-Mutawakkil, who showered him with tokens of esteem, and offered him the world, but he spurned it, remaining as he had always been, unmoved by ambition and unswayed by greed. Sufyān was never subjected to trials like these. Someone quoted al-Mutawakkil as saying, "Aḥmad won't even let me send gifts to his sons!"

Ḥajjāj ibn al-Shāʿir

[Ḥajjāj ibn al-Shāʿir:] I didn't want to die in the path of God and I didn't join the funeral prayer for Aḥmad ibn Ḥanbal.[98] 13.89

[Ḥajjāj ibn al-Shāʿir:] Aḥmad ibn Ḥanbal was God's blessing to this community: he stood firm on the Qur'an. If he hadn't, all of us would have perished. 13.90

[Ḥajjāj ibn al-Shāʿir:] I once kissed Aḥmad on the forehead and told him that God had put him on a par with Sufyān and Mālik. I don't think I could have said more, as Aḥmad surely outdid both of them as an exemplar of Islam. 13.91

[Al-Qāsim ibn Naṣr:] Al-Marrūdhī once passed Ḥajjāj ibn al-Shāʿir, who rose respectfully and said, "Peace be upon you, servant of the righteous!" 13.92

[Ḥajjāj ibn al-Shāʿir:] I never saw a living, breathing human being worthier than Aḥmad ibn Ḥanbal. 13.93

[Abū Bakr ibn al-Muṭṭawwiʿī:] I heard Ḥajjāj ibn al-Shāʿir say, "I used to stay at Aḥmad ibn Ḥanbal's until late at night, and on the way home, I would weep"—or "I would start crying"—"because I couldn't bear to be parted from him." 13.94

Ibrāhīm ibn ʿArʿarah

[Abū Yaḥyā l-Nāqid:] We were at Ibrāhīm ibn ʿArʿarah's and ʿAlī ibn ʿĀṣim's name came up. Someone noted that Aḥmad ibn Ḥanbal 13.95

called him a weak transmitter. Someone else responded, "But if he's reliable, so what?"

"By God," interjected Ibrāhīm ibn ʿArʿarah, "if Aḥmad had criticized ʿAlqamah and al-Aswad, no one would trust them any more."

Ismāʿīl ibn Khalīl

13.96 [Ismāʿīl ibn Khalīl:] "If Aḥmad had lived among the Children of Israel, they would have taken him for a sign from God."

ʿAlī ibn Shuʿayb al-Ṭūsī

13.97 [Al-Ṭūsī:] We think of Ibn Ḥanbal as being like the ones God's Emissary meant when he said, "In my community are men like those who lived among the Children of Israel. Nothing, not even the blade of a saw placed on the crown of their heads, could turn them from their religion." If Aḥmad ibn Ḥanbal hadn't done what he did, then not a single man of those put into the crucible would have emerged from it, and the shame would remain until the Day of Resurrection.

Muḥammad ibn Naṣr al-Marwazī

13.98 [Abū l-ʿAbbās ibn ʿUthmān ibn Salm:] I asked Muḥammad ibn Naṣr al-Marwazī whether he had met Aḥmad ibn Ḥanbal.

"I went to see him many times," he answered, "and asked him questions."

"Who knew more Hadith?" someone asked. "Aḥmad or Isḥāq ibn Rāhawayh?"

"Aḥmad."

"Who was more accurate?" I asked.

"Aḥmad."

Someone asked who had more legal insight.

"Aḥmad."

"Who was more scrupulous?"

"What kind of question is that?" cried Muḥammad ibn Naṣr. "Aḥmad was the most scrupulous man of his day."

Abū ʿUmayr al-Ṭālqānī, Citing His Teachers

[Al-Jaḥḥāf:] I heard Abū ʿUmayr al-Ṭālqānī say, "I used to hear them saying that Ibn Ḥanbal was a balm and a delight to the Muslims and their religion." 13.99

Addendum

Aḥmad's teachers, peers, contemporaries, and followers are all credited with statements praising him. By the grace of God, he was the sort of man whose merits were acknowledged even by his enemies. 13.100

[Idrīs ibn ʿAbd al-Karīm al-Muqriʾ:] More Hadith scholars and jurists than I can count praise and honor Aḥmad ibn Ḥanbal, speaking of him with reverence and esteem, and seeking him out in order to pay their respects. Among his admirers I recall al-Haytham ibn Khārijah; Muṣʿab al-Zubayrī; Yaḥyā ibn Maʿīn; Abū Bakr ibn Abī Shaybah; ʿUthmān ibn Abī Shaybah; ʿAbd al-Aʿlā ibn Ḥammād al-Narsī; Muḥammad ibn ʿAbd al-Malik ibn Abī l-Shawārib; ʿAlī ibn al-Madīnī; ʿUbayd Allāh ibn ʿUmar al-Qawārīrī; Abū Khaythamah Zuhayr ibn Ḥarb; Abū Maʿmar al-Qaṭīʿī; Muḥammad ibn Jaʿfar al-Warkānī; Aḥmad ibn Muḥammad ibn Ayyūb, author of the *Campaigns*; Muḥammad ibn Bakkār ibn al-Rayyān; ʿAmr ibn Muḥammad al-Nāqid; Yaḥyā ibn Ayyūb al-Maqābirī the Worshipper; Shurayḥ ibn Yūnus; Khalaf ibn Hishām al-Bazzāz; and Abū l-Rabīʿ al-Zahrānī.

[ʿAbd ibn Ḥumayd:] I remember one day when the Hadith-men were comparing reports in a mosque. Aḥmad was still a young man at the time, but everyone was already looking to him. 13.101

[Ibn Abī Ḥātim:] We heard Muḥammad ibn Muslim report: "I was leaving al-Haytham ibn Jamīl's and heading for Muḥammad ibn al-Mubārak al-Ṣūrī's when I heard that Abū l-Mughīrah ʿAbd 13.102

al-Qaddūs ibn al-Ḥajjāj had died. They said that Aḥmad ibn Ḥanbal had been the one to pray over him."

There was no lack of scholars in Homs at the time, but they asked Aḥmad ibn Ḥanbal to do the honors because, despite his youth, they all respected him.

13.103 [Muḥammad ibn Shaddād:] A group of us, including Aswad ibn Sālim and certain disciples of al-Thawrī, were gathered at Ismāʿīl ibn ʿUlayyah's door. Aḥmad ibn Ḥanbal appeared and greeted us. He was asked a question, and he answered it. After he left, everyone agreed that Ismāʿīl had no visitor more learned than he.

Chapter 14

Praise of Him by Prominent Successors Who Knew Him Well

Abū Dāwūd al-Sijistānī

14.1 [Abū Dāwūd al-Sijistānī:] If a man loves Ibn Ḥanbal, you can be sure that he knows the *sunnah*.

14.2 [Abū Dāwūd al-Sijistānī:] I've met two hundred teachers of Hadith but none like Aḥmad ibn Ḥanbal.

He never bothered with the things most people care about, but whenever Hadith was mentioned he would speak.

Ibrāhīm al-Ḥarbī

14.3 [Ibrāhīm al-Ḥarbī:] Aḥmad ibn Ḥanbal was the greatest man of his time, just as Saʿīd ibn al-Musayyab was in his own time, and Sufyān al-Thawrī in his.

14.4 [Ibrāhīm al-Ḥarbī:] The Hadith transmitted by the people of Medina, Kufa, Basra, and Damascus ended up in the hands of four men: Aḥmad ibn Ḥanbal, Yaḥyā ibn Maʿīn, Zuhayr ibn Ḥarb, and Abū Bakr ibn Abī Shaybah. Of the four, Aḥmad understood it best.

14.5 [Muḥammad ibn ʿAbd Allāh al-Shāfiʿī:] When Aḥmad ibn Ḥanbal's son Saʿīd died, Ibrāhīm al-Ḥarbī went to see ʿAbd Allāh ibn Aḥmad, who rose to greet him. When Ibrāhīm protested, ʿAbd Allāh said, "Why shouldn't I get up? By God, if my father were here, he would too."

"If Ibn ʿUyaynah had met your father," replied Ibrāhīm, "he would have gotten up to greet *him*."

[Ibrāhīm al-Ḥarbī:] I've heard it said that people praise Aḥmad ibn Ḥanbal without knowing what they're talking about. But by God, I can't think of a single Successor who has anything over him, nor do I know of anyone who can be the kind of Muslim he was. I knew him for twenty years; I was with him night and day, summer and winter, in the heat and in the cold, and every day he outdid what he had done the day before. The leading scholars of Islam and the learned men of every town and region used to come to see him. As long as they were outside his mosque, they carried themselves proudly, but when they went in, they became pupils all over again. 14.6

[Al-ʿUkbarī:] I heard Ibrāhīm al-Ḥarbī say, "The way I see it, the opinions of all the Successors have equal weight, and the last man to count as a Successor is Aḥmad ibn Ḥanbal, who in my view is the greatest of them all. Regarding a man who swears to divorce his wife if he does such-and-such an act and then forgets his oath and performs the act, the Successors all say that he must divorce his wife."[99] 14.7

Ibrāhīm was also asked about what should happen if a group of people are shipwrecked and have to pray without proper clothing. He said, "The Successors—including Aḥmad, who is the greatest of them—say that the leader should stand with them[100] and that the group should make gestures instead of kneeling and prostrating themselves. Some people may disagree with Aḥmad and the Successors about this, but I don't care." 14.8

[Abū l-Ḥasan Dulayl:] I heard Ibrāhīm al-Ḥarbī say, "Of the great men of this world, I've met three like no other. The first was Aḥmad ibn Ḥanbal. I don't think another like him will ever be born. The second was Bishr ibn al-Ḥārith, who was filled with self-restraint from the crown of his head down to the soles of his feet. The third 14.9

was Abū ʿUbayd al-Qāsim ibn Sallām, who was like a mountain filled with learning."

Of the three, Aḥmad was the only one Ibrāhīm would cite as a source for Hadith.

Abū Bakr al-Athram

14.10 [Al-Athram:] I once debated a man who asked me whose opinion I was citing. I replied: "Someone who has no equal anywhere."

"Who's that?" he asked.

"Aḥmad ibn Ḥanbal," I said.

ʿAbd al-Wahhāb al-Warrāq

14.11 [ʿAbd al-Wahhāb al-Warrāq:] The Prophet, God bless and keep him, said "Ask someone who knows," and so we would ask Ibn Ḥanbal. He was the most learned man of his time.

14.12 [ʿAbd al-Wahhāb al-Warrāq:] Aḥmad is our guide and one of those firmly grounded in knowledge.[101] When I stand before God tomorrow and He asks me who my examplar was, I'll say "Aḥmad." The man suffered for twenty years:[102] What could there be about Islam that he wouldn't know?

14.13 [Muḥammad ibn Jaʿfar al-Rāshidī:] I once heard ʿAbd al-Wahhāb al-Warrāq say, "I never met anyone like Aḥmad ibn Ḥanbal."

Those present asked: "So what did he know that made him different from the other scholars you met?"

"This was a man," he replied, "who could cite an authority for sixty thousand different questions."

Muhanna' ibn Yaḥyā al-Shāmī

14.14 [Muhanna' ibn Yaḥyā l-Shāmī:] I never met anyone with as much merit in all respects as Aḥmad ibn Ḥanbal, and I've met Sufyān ibn ʿUyaynah, Wakīʿ, ʿAbd al-Razzāq, Baqiyyah ibn al-Walīd, Ḍamrah ibn Rabīʿah, and many other men of learning. But none could match Aḥmad in knowledge, understanding, renunciation, and scrupulosity.

[The author:] I have cited only these few sources, who have only a little to say about Aḥmad's piety, and left out those who have much more to say, as their testimony will appear later in this book, God willing. «God is sufficient for us; He is the best guardian.»[103] 14.15

Chapter 15

A Report That the Prophet Elijah Sent Him Greetings

[Abū Ḥafṣ al-Qāḍī:] Aḥmad ibn Ḥanbal was once visited by a man from the Indian Ocean who said, "I come from the Indian Ocean. I was on my way to China when we were shipwrecked. Two men came riding toward me on a wave. One of them asked, 'If you wish, God will save you, on condition that you greet Aḥmad ibn Ḥanbal for us.' 15.1

"'Who's Aḥmad?' I asked. 'And who on earth are you?'

"'I'm Elijah, and this is the angel who watches over the islands in the sea. You'll find Aḥmad in Iraq.'

"'I agreed, and the sea spat me out onto the shore by Ubullah. So here I am with a greeting to you from the two of them.'"[104]

Chapter 16

Reports That al-Khaḍir Spoke in His Praise

[Bilāl al-Khawwāṣ:] I was in the desert of the Israelites when suddenly I found a man walking beside me. I was surprised, but then I was given to realize that he was al-Khaḍir. 16.1

"I ask you by God," I said. "Who are you?"

"Your brother al-Khaḍir."

"I want to ask you something."

"Go ahead."

"What do you think of al-Shāfiʿī?"

"He's one of the Pegs."[105]

"What about Aḥmad ibn Ḥanbal?"

"A truth-teller."[106]

"What about Bishr ibn al-Ḥārith?"

"He's the last of his kind."

"So how is it that I'm able to see you?"

"Because you were kind to your mother."

16.2 [A man of Baghdad:] I was traveling on a ship and we landed on an island. There was an elderly white-haired man sitting there. I greeted him and he asked me where I was from.

"From Baghdad," I said.

"When you get there," he said, "give Ibn Ḥanbal my regards, and tell him, «Have patience! God's promise is true; let not those who will not be convinced make you discouraged.»"[107]

Then he disappeared, and we realized that he was al-Khaḍir.

Chapter 17

Praise of Him by Pious Strangers and Allies of God

17.1 [Aḥmad ibn al-ʿAbbās al-Shāmī:] I left Baghdad to make the pilgrimage. On the way I met a man who bore the stamp of piety. He asked me where I was from.

"From Baghdad," I replied, "which has gotten so corrupt that God is likely to wipe it off the face of the earth along with everyone who lives there. I was afraid, so I ran."

"Go back," he said, "and don't be afraid. In the city are the graves of four allies of God who will protect Baghdad from harm."

"Who are they?"

"The exemplar Aḥmad ibn Ḥanbal, Maʿrūf al-Karkhī, Bishr ibn al-Ḥārith, and Manṣūr ibn ʿAmmār."

So I went back and visited the graves.

[The author:] Both reports agree up to this point. Abū Yaʿqūb adds:

I asked him, "Where are you headed?"

"To visit the graves," he replied.

"Where are you from?"

"Look behind you."

I looked but there was nothing to see. When I turned around, he was gone.

Chapter 18

Allies of God Who Visited Him to Seek His Blessing

[Ṣāliḥ:] One day I came home and heard that my father had sent for me the day before. When I found him, he said, "There was someone here yesterday I wanted you to meet. It was around noon; I was sitting here and I heard a man at the door. Somehow I felt drawn to him. I got up and opened the door. Standing there was a sunburned man wearing a cloak of fur and a ragged piece of cloth on his head. He had no shirt on under the cloak, and he wasn't carrying a leather water bottle or a staff. I invited him in and he came into the anteroom. 18.1

"'Where are you coming from?' I asked.

"'From the east,' he said, 'and I'm heading for the coast. If not for you, I wouldn't have come into the city, but I wanted to pay my respects.'

"'Do you travel dressed like that?'

"'I do.' Then he asked me: 'What do you understand by renunciation of the world?'

"'Not taking anything for granted,' I answered, surprised.

"Then I thought to myself, 'I have no silver or gold to give him.' So I went into the house, found four loaves of bread, and brought them out.

"'I have no silver or gold,' I told him, 'but this is what I eat.'

"'Would it make you happy if I took them?'

"'Yes,' I said. So he took them and put them under his arm and said, 'I think now I'll have enough food to get me TO al-Raqqah. Good-bye!'

"I couldn't stop staring at him until he left the house."

Afterward my father spoke of him often.

18.2 [Ibn Sāfirī:] When we were young, we used to pray and practice austerities at the Perfumer's Mosque. Some of us would weave palm fibers, others would make spindles, and so on. One member of the group was a strapping young man who told us this story. "We used to fish around Dujayl," he said. "One day, as it was getting dark, a man dressed in rags walked by. I ran after him but couldn't catch him. So I called him over.

"'Hey you!' I said. 'Are you one of the Substitutes?'[108]

"'Yes.'

"'Where are you going?'

"'Syria.'

"'Where are you coming from?'

"'Aḥmad ibn Ḥanbal's.'

"'What were you doing there?'

"'Asking him a question,' he said. 'Aḥmad is one of us, but he knows more than any of us.'

"It was time to pray the sunset prayer, so we did, and then prayed the evening prayer. When he finished, I said, 'Have some of this fish; we catch it ourselves.'[109]

"'We don't eat,' he replied, and then vanished as if the earth had swallowed him up."

18.3 [Al-Marrūdhī:] One day a renunciant approached us, and I took him in to see Aḥmad. He was wearing a ragged cloak of fur and a scrap of cloth on his head, and wore no shoes despite the bitter cold. Ibn Ḥanbal greeted him and he replied, "I've come a long way, but all I want to do is pay my respects. I'm heading for ʿAbbādān, and if I return from there, I'd like to come and see you again."

"If you return, then," said Ibn Ḥanbal.

The man rose and said good-bye to Aḥmad who was sitting down.

It was the only time I ever saw anyone get up and leave before Aḥmad had stood up.

"He looks like one of the Substitutes, doesn't he?" said Aḥmad; or perhaps, "He makes me think of the Substitutes."

Then he brought some food—four loaves split and filled with fermented grain paste[110]—out to him. "If I had anything more to give you," he said, "I would."

[Ismāʿīl al-Daylamī:] I was at Aḥmad ibn Ḥanbal's when someone knocked on the door. I went out to see who it was and found a young man wearing a ragged hair shirt. 18.4

"What do you want?" I asked.

"I want Aḥmad ibn Ḥanbal," he said.

When I told Aḥmad that there was a young man in a ragged hair shirt asking for him, he went out and greeted him.

"Aḥmad," the man said, "tell me what renunciation of the world means."

"I heard Sufyān report, citing al-Zuhrī, that renunciation of the world means not taking anything for granted."

"Tell me more," said the young man, who was standing in the sun even though there was a patch of shade directly in front of him.

"It means never being sure that if you leave the sun you'll live long enough to reach the shade."

The man turned to leave, but Aḥmad said, "Wait!" He went into the house and came back holding out a little bundle.

"I don't count on living long enough to reach the shade," said the man. "What would I need that for?"

Then he turned and walked away.

[Aḥmad:] Early one morning I went out and came across a man with a cloth over his face. He handed me a slip of paper. When the light had grown strong enough to see by, I took it out and read what was written on it: 18.5

For each delight, the world brings a grief
To the pauper's hut and the rich man's gate;
While those who study
Seek not to learn,
But to vaunt, and vex their peers with vain debate.[111]

I thought it must have been Muḥammad ibn Yaḥyā l-Dhuhlī who had handed me the paper. Later, though, I found Muḥammad and asked him about it, and he said, "I never saw you and I never gave you a piece of paper."

It was then that I realized that the poem had been an admonition.

Chapter 19

His Fame

19.1 In the chapter about his childhood, we noted that Aḥmad ibn Ḥanbal was highly regarded even as a youth.

[Al-Marrūdhī:] I once said to Aḥmad, "There are a lot of people praying for you."

"That frightens me," he said. "It could be a temptation to think highly of myself. Why do they do it?"

I once told him that I had met a man from Tarsus who said that he had been fighting the Byzantines. In the still of the night, he told me, the men would call out "Pray to God for Abū ʿAbd Allāh!" He went on: "We would pull back the arm of the mangonel[112] and then release it. Once we shot a stone at a barbarian[113] standing on a rampart behind his shield, and the stone knocked off his head and the shield both."[114]

Aḥmad's face fell, and he said, "If only it weren't a temptation!"

Then he said, "Do you think it's a temptation?"

"Of course not," I answered.

19.2 [Al-Abbār:] We'd been marching along the Balkh River for several days when our provisions ran out, so two of us headed off toward Bukhārā to buy something to eat. On the way we met a blond-haired,

red-faced man who asked us where we were from. When we told him we were from Baghdad, he asked, "How is Aḥmad ibn Ḥanbal?"

"When we left, he was alive and well."

The man raised his head and prayed to God for Aḥmad's well-being.

"Now I've seen it all," I said to my companion. "Even here, on the frontier of Islam, among the Turks!"

[Al-Marrūdhī:] I once told Aḥmad that someone had said that 19.3
from here as far as the land of the Turks, people were praying for his well-being. I asked him how he showed his gratitude for the popularity God had blessed him with.

"I pray to God that I do nothing for the sake of appearances," he said.

[ʿAbd Allāh:] Bilāl and I went to see Muḥammad ibn Saʿīd 19.4
al-Tirmidhī, who told us, "A group of us were at Wahb ibn Jarīr's. Aḥmad was there too. He asked me to read,[115] but I didn't."

We asked him why not.

"I didn't want to read because Aḥmad might say something, or show some kind of reaction, and people would start talking about it."

[Aḥmad ibn al-Ḥusayn:] I heard a man from Khurasan say, "Back 19.5
home people think Aḥmad ibn Ḥanbal isn't human. They think he's some kind of angel."

I also heard from a man who had been at the frontier that people there were saying, "One look from Aḥmad ibn Ḥanbal is better than"—or "equal to"—"a year's worth of ritual devotion."

[ʿAlī ibn al-Jahm:] Once when I was young I saw crowds of people 19.6
rushing by and asked where they were going. They told me, "There's a man here who saw Aḥmad ibn Ḥanbal!"

I asked the man if he had really seen Aḥmad.

"I prayed in his mosque," he replied.

[Al-Qūmisī:] Two Zoroastrian women had a dispute over an 19.7
inheritance and went to a scholar for arbitration. The scholar ruled against one woman, who said, "If you've judged according to what Aḥmad ibn Ḥanbal would say, I accept; otherwise I don't."

The scholar replied that he had ruled as Ibn Ḥanbal would have, and the woman accepted the judgment.[116]

19.8 Al-Marrūdhī said: "I once saw a Christian doctor coming out of Aḥmad's house with a priest or maybe a monk. I heard the doctor tell someone, 'He asked to come with me so he could get a look at Aḥmad.'"

Al-Marrūdhī said: "I once brought a Christian to Aḥmad's house to treat him. 'Aḥmad,' he told him, 'I've been hoping to meet you for years. Your well-being concerns not only the Muslims but everyone else as well. You've never given any of us cause for complaint.'"

I said to Aḥmad, "If only everyone everywhere would pray for you."

"So long as a man knows himself," he replied, "it makes no difference what people say."

19.9 [ʿAbd Allāh ibn ʿAdī:] I heard Muḥammad ibn ʿAbd Allāh al-Ṣayrafī addressing students of the Shāfiʿī system as follows: "Take careful note of what happened to Ḥusayn al-Karābīsī and Abū Thawr. Ḥusayn was famous for his learning and his powers of retention, which were ten times greater than Abū Thawr's. But when Aḥmad ibn Ḥanbal objected to Ḥusayn's view of utterance[117] Ḥusayn lost his reputation, and when Aḥmad praised Abū Thawr for sticking to the *sunnah*, his reputation grew."

19.10 [Ibn Rāhawayh:] I once went to see ʿAbd Allāh ibn Ṭāhir, who said, "I've never seen anything like these Postponers![118] They'll say, 'My faith is as strong as Gabriel's,' but by God I don't think it's right even to say, 'My faith is as strong as Yaḥyā ibn Yaḥyā's, or Aḥmad ibn Ḥanbal's.'"

19.11 [Muḥammad ibn Yaḥyā:] I've never seen generousity as meaningful as Aḥmad ibn Ḥanbal's. I used to hear Hadith from him in the morning and dictate it to my students that same evening.

19.12 [Aḥmad:] I traveled to Sanaa in Yemen with Yaḥyā ibn Maʿīn. We arrived around the time of the afternoon prayer and asked where ʿAbd al-Razzāq's house was. They told us he lived in a village called al-Ramādah. I was so eager to meet him that I went on ahead, but Yaḥyā stayed behind. It wasn't that far from Sanaa. As soon as I asked, they pointed out the house. But then when I went to knock on the door, a grocer across the street said, "Don't knock; the shaykh is a terror."

So I sat down to wait until it was almost time for the sunset prayer. When ʿAbd al-Razzāq came out to pray, I jumped up, holding out some Hadith I had chosen.

"Peace be upon you!" I said. "Will you recite these for me, please? I've come a long way."

"Who are you?" he asked.

"Aḥmad ibn Ḥanbal."

When he heard that, he stopped and drew his shoulders together as if to make himself smaller. Then he turned back and embraced me. "Are you really Aḥmad?" he asked. He took the Hadith reports and started reading them, not stopping until it got too dark for him to see. He asked the grocer for a lamp and kept going until the time for the sunset prayer—which he usually performed at the last possible time—had passed.

[ʿAbd Allāh:] Whenever my father recalled learning that he had been praised in the presence of ʿAbd al-Razzāq, he would weep.

[Abū l-ʿAbbās al-Ḥaṭṭāb:] Back when many of the great men 19.13
were still with us, I took some slips of paper and wrote down their names, one on each slip: Aswad ibn Sālim, Bishr ibn al-Ḥārith, Aḥmad ibn Ḥanbal, and so on. Then I prayed two cycles and asked God, mighty and glorious, to choose one for me as an exemplar. I shuffled the slips and put them out of sight, then picked one. To my delight, it turned out to be Aḥmad ibn Ḥanbal. I prayed two more cycles, invoked God, and reshuffled the slips, and again it came out Aḥmad. When I tried it a third time the same thing happened.

Chapter 20
His Creed

His Position on the Fundamentals of Belief

20.1 [Aḥmad:] Belief consists of what you say and what you do. It can increase or decrease. It is the only source of piety, and disobedience to God lessens it.

His Position on the Qur'an

20.2 [Isḥāq ibn Ibrāhīm:] When asked about people who say that the Qur'an is created, Aḥmad ibn Ḥanbal replied, "Anyone who says that is an Ingrate."[119]

20.3 [Isḥāq ibn Ibrāhīm:] Asked about anyone who says that the Qur'an is created, Aḥmad ibn Ḥanbal replied, "He's an unbeliever," using the participle.[120]

20.4 [Salamah ibn Shabīb:] I heard Aḥmad ibn Ḥanbal say that whoever says that the Qur'an is created is an Ingrate.

20.5 [Al-Sarrāj:] I asked Aḥmad ibn Ḥanbal about someone who says that the Qur'an is created.

"He's an Ingrate."

"What about someone who says that the text of the Qur'an spoken aloud is a created thing?"

"He's a follower of Jahm."[121]

20.6 [Al-Kawsaj:] I asked Aḥmad ibn Ḥanbal what he thought of someone who called the Qur'an created.

"He's committed UN-BE-LIEF," he answered, stressing each syllable.

20.7 [Al-ʿUkbarī:] I asked Aḥmad ibn Ḥanbal whether it was true that the Qur'an is the speech of God, uncreated, and that it came from Him and goes back to Him.

He answered: "From Him came the knowledge of it, and to Him belongs the judgment concerning it."[122]

[Ṣāliḥ:] I found out that Abū Ṭālib had been quoting my father as saying "The text of the Qur'an, spoken aloud, is uncreated." I told my father about this, and he asked how I knew. I told him I had heard it from So-and-So. 20.8

"Send for Abū Ṭālib," he said.

I sent for him and he came, along with Fūrān.[123]

"Did I ever say to you that the text of the Qur'an spoken aloud is uncreated?" said my father, shaking with anger.

"I read «Say, He is God, the one»[124] out loud and you said, 'That's not created.'"

"But why did you quote me as saying 'The text of the Qur'an spoken aloud is uncreated'? Not only that: I hear you wrote this down and sent it to people. If you wrote it down, rub it out as hard as you can, and write to the people you wrote to and tell them I never said that."

Fūrān began apologizing, and finally left looking terrified. Abū Ṭālib came back to say that he had rubbed the words out of his notes and written a letter explaining that he had misquoted my father.

On Reports of God's Attributes[125]

[Aḥmad:] We transmit these reports as we find them. 20.9

[Aḥmad:] A believer who belongs to the people of *sunnah* and 20.10
community should defer what he doesn't understand to God. If he hears a Hadith report like "The people in the Garden will see their Lord,"[126] he should believe it without trying to explain it. All men of learning everywhere are agreed on this.

His Position against Disputation[127] and Those Who Engage in It

['Abd Allāh:] My father once wrote the following to 'Ubayd Allāh 20.11
ibn Yaḥyā ibn Khāqān: "I don't engage in Disputation, and I don't think one should talk about any of that unless it appears in Scripture or the Hadith of the Prophet, God bless and keep him. Talking about anything else is no good."

20.12 [Aḥmad:] Don't sit with Disputationists, even if they're defending the *sunnah*.[128]

His Position on the Heresies of the Followers of Jahm, the Proponents of Created Utterance, the Stoppers, and the Proponents of Free Will[129]

20.13 [Aḥmad:] The Proponents of Created Utterance are worse than the followers of Jahm.

20.14 Ibn al-Layth added: "I once heard someone ask Aḥmad ibn Ḥanbal about the Stoppers, and he said: 'As far as I'm concerned, the Stoppers, the followers of Jahm, and the Proponents of Created Utterance are all equally bad.'"

20.15 [Aḥmad:] If you do the ritual prayer and the man next to you turns out to be a follower of Jahm, do it over.

20.16 [Salamah ibn Shabīb:] I went to see Aḥmad ibn Ḥanbal to ask him what he thought of someone who says, "The Qur'an is the speech of God."[130]

"If he doesn't say, 'The Qur'an is the speech of God, uncreated,' then he's an Ingrate." He went on: "Have no doubt about it. If he doesn't say, 'The Qur'an is the speech of God, uncreated,' then he's saying it's created. And anyone who says it's created has sinned against God, mighty and glorious."

I asked him if the Stoppers were Ingrates.

"They are."

20.17 [Aḥmad:] Anyone who says that the text of the Qur'an spoken aloud is a created thing[131] is a follower of Jahm.

20.18 ['Abd Allāh:] I told my father that al-Karābīsī was saying that the Qur'anic text spoken aloud is a created thing.

"He's lying, the tricky bastard," he said. "May God expose him! He's taken up where Bishr al-Marīsī[132] left off."

20.19 [Aḥmad:] Have no doubt that a Stopper is an Ingrate.

20.20 [Isḥāq ibn Ibrāhīm ibn Hāni':] Someone asked Aḥmad ibn Ḥanbal whether it was allowed to perform the ritual prayer behind a leader who believes that the text of the Qur'an spoken aloud is a created thing.

"No praying behind him, no sitting with him, no talking to him, and no praying over him when he dies."

[Aḥmad:] Scholars who are Secessionists[133] are heretics.[134] 20.21

[Ṣāliḥ:] My father was asked whether it was permissible to pray 20.22
behind a Proponent of Free Will.

"If he says that God doesn't know what human beings are going to do until they do it, then no praying behind him; or behind a Rejectionist,[135] either, if he criticizes the Prophet's Companions."

I also heard my father say: "The followers of Jahm have spilt into three groups. One says that the Qur'an is a created thing. One says that it's the speech of God, and stops there. And one says that the text of the Qur'an read aloud is a created thing."

"So we're not allowed to talk to the Stoppers?"

"No."

"But what if someone does talk to them?"

"Tell him not to. If he listens, then you can talk to him; but if he doesn't, then you can't."

My father also said: "No praying behind anyone who says, 'The Qur'an is a created thing.' If you've prayed behind someone like that, pray again. The same goes for Stoppers and Proponents of the Created Utterance."

[Al-Balkhī:] I was once at Aḥmad ibn Ḥanbal's when a messenger 20.23
came from the caliph to ask whether it was permissible to employ Muslim sectarians in state service. He replied that it was not.

"But we employ Jews and Christians! Why not sectarians?"

"The Jews and Christians don't try to win people over, but the sectarians do."

His Position on the Relative Merits of the Prophet's Companions[136]

[Al-Muṭṭawwiʿī:] I once heard someone ask Aḥmad ibn Ḥanbal 20.24
about the relative merits of the Prophet's Companions, and he

answered, "They should be ranked according to the Hadith of Ibn 'Umar.[137] As far as the caliphate is concerned, the order is the one given in the Hadith of Safīnah: first Abū Bakr, then 'Umar, then 'Uthmān, then 'Alī."

"Was that report transmitted by Ḥashraj?"

"No, by Ḥammād ibn Salamah."

[The author:] This question arose because both Ḥammād ibn Salamah and Ḥashraj ibn Nubātah transmitted the Hadith of Safīnah, but Ḥashraj is of dubious reliability while Ḥammād ibn Salamah is an exemplar.

20.25 ['Abd Allāh:] I asked my father about the testimony that Abū Bakr and 'Umar are in the Garden. He said, "It's true. I follow the Hadith of Sa'īd ibn Zayd, which says, 'I testify that the Prophet is in the Garden, and so are his nine Companions.' And the Prophet, God bless and keep him, said, 'The people in the Garden stand in a hundred and twenty rows, of which eighty are filled by members of my community.' If his Companions aren't included, then who would be?"

20.26 [Al-Maymūnī:] Aḥmad ibn Ḥanbal said to me, "Abū l-Ḥasan, if you hear anyone saying anything bad about the Companions of the Prophet, God bless and keep him, then you should doubt his Islam."

20.27 [Aḥmad:] When God's Emissary, God bless and keep him, fell ill, he sent Abū Bakr to lead the ritual prayer even though there were others who were better readers. The point was to show who the caliph should be.

20.28 [Aḥmad:] The best member of this community, after the Prophet, was Abū Bakr the Righteous, then 'Umar ibn al-Khaṭṭāb, then 'Uthmān ibn 'Affān. We put those three first, as the Companions of God's Emissary did, with no difference of opinion. Next come the five members of the Shūrā Council: 'Alī, al-Zubayr, Ṭalḥah, 'Abd al-Raḥmān ibn 'Awf, and Sa'd. Any one of them could have been caliph, and all of them are exemplars. This follows the report where Ibn 'Umar says, "While God's Emissary, God bless and keep him, was alive, and his Companions were numerous, we used to list them by saying Abū Bakr, ʿUmar, and ʿUthmān, and then stopping."

20.29 After the Council members come the Emigrants who fought at Badr, then the Helpers who fought there, in order of their emigration or acceptance of Islam. After these come the Companions—that is, of the generation the Emissary was sent to. Anyone who was in his company for a year, or a month, or a day, or an hour, or saw him, counts as a Companion, to be honored according to the length of time he spent with him and how soon he started, or how often he heard him speak, or looked at him. The least distinguished member of that generation is more distinguished than any member of the generation that never saw him. When they meet God, those who joined the Prophet, saw him, and heard him speak will have greater merit by virtue of their being his Companions than any member of the next generation, even if the latter should have done all manner of good deeds. Anyone who disparages a Companion, or dislikes him for something he may have done, or lists his faults, remains a supporter of dangerous novelties[138] until he blesses them all, without any ill feeling.

His Position on Giving ʿUthmān Precedence over ʿAlī

20.30 [Ṣāliḥ:] Someone asked my father—with me present—whether someone who says that ʿAlī was better than ʿUthmān is doing something new and bad.

"Anyone who does that deserves to be denounced," said my father. "The Companions of the Emissary put ʿUthmān—God be pleased with him—first."

20.31 [ʿAmr ibn ʿUthmān al-Ḥimṣī:] When Aḥmad ibn Ḥanbal was transported from Samarra to the Byzantine frontier, they stopped here in Homs. I found him and asked him his position on ʿAlī and ʿUthmān.

"First ʿUthmān, then ʿAlī," he said. "Listen, Abū Ḥafṣ," he continued. "Anyone who puts ʿAlī before ʿUthmān is scoffing at the Council."[139]

20.32 [Muḥammad ibn ʿAwf:] I asked Aḥmad ibn Ḥanbal about putting some Companions before others. He said, "Anyone who puts ʿAlī ahead of Abū Bakr is questioning the judgment of God's Emissary. Anyone who puts ʿAlī ahead of ʿUmar has questioned the judgment of God's Emissary and Abū Bakr both. Anyone who puts ʿAlī ahead of ʿUthmān has questioned the judgment of God's Emissary, Abū Bakr, ʿUmar, *and* the Emigrants, and I can't imagine that someone who does that will benefit from any good works he does."

His Position on ʿAlī, on Whom Eternal Peace, and the Members of the Prophet's Household[140]

20.33 [ʿAbd Allāh:] One day I was sitting with my father when some people from al-Karkh came in. They spoke for a good long while about the caliphates of Abū Bakr, ʿUmar, and ʿUthmān. Then they turned to the caliphate of ʿAlī and went on and on about it. After a while my father looked up at them and said, "You've said a lot about ʿAlī and the caliphate, but it wasn't holding the office that made ʿAlī great. It was having ʿAlī as caliph that made the office great."

Al-Sayyārī added, "I told this story to a Shiʿi, and he said, 'You've just taken away half the resentment I had against Aḥmad ibn Ḥanbal.'"

20.34 [ʿAbd Allāh:] After hearing my father recite the Hadith of Safīnah,[141] I asked him, "Dad, what do you say about putting some Companions before others?"

"As far as the succession goes, it's Abū Bakr, then ʿUmar, then ʿUthmān."

"What about ʿAlī ibn Abī Ṭālib?"

"Son, ʿAlī was a member of the Prophet's household. No one compares with them."

20.35 [Aḥmad:] None of the Companions has as many well-attested virtues as ʿAlī ibn Abī Ṭālib.

20.36 [Aḥmad:] Anyone who denies that ʿAlī was an exemplar is even worse at finding his way than the family donkey.

20.37 [Ḥanbal:] I asked Aḥmad ibn Ḥanbal whether ʿAlī's caliphate was valid.

"God help us!" he cried. "'Alī upheld the law and cut off the hands of thieves; he collected the alms-tax and distributed it without taking his own share. How for God's sake could anyone object to his being caliph? He was a good one, too: the Companions of God's Emissary, God bless and keep him, supported him, prayed behind him, joined his expeditions, fought for him, went on pilgrimage with him, and called him Commander of Believers, willingly and without reservation. Who are we to do otherwise?"

His Position on the Disputes That Broke Out among the Companions

[Abū Bakr al-Marrūdhī:] When we were in Samarra, one of the caliph's messengers asked Aḥmad ibn Ḥanbal what he thought about the dispute between ʿAlī and Muʿāwiyah. 20.38

"I have nothing but good to say about them."

I also heard Ibn Ḥanbal say, after someone mentioned the Companions of God's Emissary: "God have mercy on them all! Muʿāwiyah, ʿAmr ibn al-ʿĀṣ, Abū Mūsā l-Ashʿarī, and al-Mughīrah are all described in the Book of God, where it says, «Their marks are on their faces, the traces of their prostrations.»"[142]

[Ibrāhīm ibn Āzir:] I was once at Ibn Ḥanbal's when a man asked him about what had happened between ʿAlī and Muʿāwiyah. Ibn Ḥanbal ignored him. Then, when he was told that the man was from the house of Hāshim, he turned to him and recited: "«Those were a people that have passed away; theirs is what they did and yours what you have done. You shall not be answerable for their deeds.»"[143] 20.39

His Position on the Rejectionists[144]

[ʿAbd Allāh:] I asked my father what a Rejectionist is. 20.40

"Anyone who curses and reviles Abū Bakr and ʿUmar."

I also asked him about cursing any of the Companions of the Emissary of God.

"I wouldn't call him a Muslim."[145]

Chapter 21

His Insistence on Maintaining the Practices of the Early Muslims

21.1 Aḥmad ibn Ḥanbal, God be pleased with him, strove to emulate the practices of the early Muslims to the point that—as we learned from al-Ḥusayn ibn al-Munādī—he asked his wife's permission to have a concubine in emulation of them. With his wife's consent, he bought a woman for a trifling price and named her Rayḥānah, following the example set by the Prophet, God bless and keep him.

21.2 [Al-Baghdādī:] Someone once greeted Aḥmad ibn Ḥanbal by saying, "May you live long in Islam!"

"And in the *sunnah*," he replied.

21.3 [Al-Maymūnī:] Never have I laid eyes on anyone with more merit than Aḥmad ibn Ḥanbal, nor any latter-day Muslim[146] more wary of transgressing God's law, or more devoted to the *sunnah* of the Prophet, God bless and keep him. If a report proved reliable, no one was more rigorous than he in living by it.

21.4 [Al-Athram:] I heard Aḥmad ibn Ḥanbal say, "It's nothing more than knowing the *sunnah* and following it. Reasoning by analogy works only if you have a place to start from. But you can't work your way to the starting point, demolish it, and then call what you've done 'reasoning by analogy.' Analogy based on what?"

Someone once said to Aḥmad: "No one should attempt to reason by analogy unless he's very learned and knows how to compare things properly."

"Right," he replied.

21.5 In dealing with legal problems, Aḥmad, in my experience, would follow Hadith reports citing the Prophet, if there were any, and ignore divergent opinions attributed to the Companions or members of later generations. If the Companions had disagreed among themselves, he would choose among their opinions; he would not consult later opinions. If there was no Prophetic Hadith and no

Companion reports to draw on, he would go to the Successors. Sometimes there would be a problem with the transmission of a Prophetic Hadith, but he would accept the report so long as no stronger contrary report existed. This was the case, for example, with the Hadith narrated by ʿAmr ibn Shuʿayb and Ibrāhīm al-Hajarī. Sometimes he would cite a report with a link missing at the Companion level if there was nothing to contradict it.

[Muḥammad ibn Dāwūd:] Abū Bakr al-Marrūdhī told us, "I once went to the mosque with Aḥmad ibn Ḥanbal. After we went in he got up to pray, and I saw him extend his hand out of his sleeve and go like this." Here al-Marrūdhī made a gesture by waving two fingers. "When the prayer was over, I asked him why he had gestured with his fingers while praying. He said, 'Satan came to me and said that I hadn't washed my feet, and I was showing him that I had two witnesses to the contrary.'" 21.6

[Al-Maymūnī:] Aḥmad ibn Ḥanbal once said to me, "Abū l-Ḥasan! Make sure never to speak on a question unless you have an exemplar to cite." 21.7

[ʿAbd al-Raḥmān the physician:] Aḥmad ibn Ḥanbal and Bishr ibn al-Ḥārith both fell ill. Whenever I went to see Bishr, I would ask how he was feeling, and he would praise God and then tell me, saying "Praise God! I feel such-and-such." But whenever I went to see Aḥmad ibn Ḥanbal and ask him how he was feeling, he would say "Fine." 21.8

One day I said to Aḥmad, "Your brother Bishr is ill too, and whenever I ask him how he is, he begins by praising God."

"Ask him who he got that from."

"I'm afraid to ask him that."

"Tell him that his brother Abū ʿAbd Allāh wants to know."

The next time I saw Bishr, I told him what Aḥmad had said. He replied, "Aḥmad won't take anything without a list of transmitters! It's Abū ʿAwn citing Ibn Sīrīn, 'If you praise God before complaining, then it's not a complaint.' So I'm telling you that I feel such-and-such, to acknowledge God's power over me."

I left Bishr's house and went to Aḥmad to report what he had said. After that, every time I went to see Aḥmad he would say, "Praise God" and then tell me what was wrong.

21.9 [Al-Marrūdhī:] Aḥmad told me, "I have never written down a Hadith of the Prophet, God bless and keep him, without putting it into practice. So when I came across a report that the Prophet paid Abū Ṭaybah a dinar to perform a cupping on him, when I next had myself cupped I gave the cupper a dinar."[147]

21.10 [Al-Aʿmash:] I heard someone ask Aḥmad ibn Ḥanbal about obsessive and distracting thoughts. He said, "Neither the Companions nor the Successors had anything to say about them."

Chapter 22

His Reverence for Hadith Transmitters and Adherents of the *Sunnah*

22.1 [Muḥammad ibn Ismāʿīl:] Aḥmad ibn al-Ḥasan al-Tirmidhī and I were once at Aḥmad ibn Ḥanbal's and al-Tirmidhī said, "Someone mentioned Hadith scholars to Ibn Abī Qutaybah in Mecca and he called them a bad lot."

"Heretic!" exclaimed Aḥmad, rising and shaking out his garment. "Heretic! Heretic!" Then he disappeared into his house.

22.2 [Ṣāliḥ:] I heard my father say: "Anyone who reveres Hadith scholars will acquire standing in the eyes of the Prophet, God bless and keep him, and anyone who treats them with contempt will lose his favor, since Hadith scholars are the Prophet's own rabbis."

22.3 [Al-Marrūdhī:] I said to Aḥmad: "Whoever dies a Muslim and a follower of the *sunnah* dies well."

"I should say so!" he retorted. "Whoever dies a Muslim and a follower of the *sunnah* dies as well as anyone could."

22.4 [Al-Bazzāz:] Someone asked Aḥmad ibn Ḥanbal where to find the Substitutes. He remained silent so long we thought he wasn't going to respond. Then he said, "If not among the Hadith scholars, I don't know where."

[Al-Zabīdī:] Once, seeing the Hadith scholars approaching, Aḥmad ibn Ḥanbal pointed at the inkpots in their hands and said, "Those are the lamps of Islam." 22.5

[Al-Makkī:] Once, seeing the Hadith scholars emerging from a session with their teacher, inkpots in their hands, Aḥmad ibn Ḥanbal said, "If these people aren't the best we have, I don't know who would be." 22.6

[Al-Qāflānī:] I heard Aḥmad ibn Ḥanbal say, "If the Hadith scholars are not the Substitutes, I don't know who would be." 22.7

[Abū l-Thalj:] I asked Aḥmad ibn Ḥanbal whether it was better to write down Hadith or to pray and fast. 22.8

"It's better to write down Hadith," he said.

"Why?"

"Because with praying and fasting, someone can always say, 'I saw others doing it so I did it too.'"

[Al-Faḍl ibn Ziyād:] I heard Aḥmad ibn Ḥanbal say: "Anyone who rejects a Hadith of the Prophet, God bless and keep him, stands on the brink of ruin." 22.9

Chapter 23

His Shunning and Reviling of Innovators and His Forbidding Others to Listen to Them

[Ṣāliḥ:] Al-Ḥizāmī visited Ibn Abī Du'ād[148] and then came to call on my father. When my father came out and saw him coming, he shut the door in his face and went back inside. 23.1

[Al-Sijistānī:] I once asked Aḥmad whether, if I see a man I know to be an adherent of the *sunnah* in the company of a reprehensible innovator, I should stop speaking to him. 23.2

"No," he replied. "First tell him that the man you saw him with is an innovator. If he stops talking with him, fine. If not, consider him an innovator too. As Ibn Masʿūd said, 'Judge a man by his friends.'"

23.3 [Al-Ḥasan ibn Thawwāb:] Aḥmad ibn Ḥanbal once told me, "People have never needed Hadith more than they need it now."

"Why?"

"Reprehensible innovations have appeared," he answered. "Without Hadith, you'll be caught up in them."

23.4 [Abū Muzāḥim:] My uncle, Abū ʿAlī ʿAbd al-Raḥmān ibn Yaḥyā ibn Khāqān, told me that al-Mutawakkil ordered him to ask Aḥmad ibn Ḥanbal who was qualified to serve as a judge. I asked my uncle to show me Ibn Ḥanbal's response and he sent me a copy of it. I made my own copy and then went back to him to check that what I had written was correct. The text ran as follows:

23.5 In the name of God, full of compassion, ever compassionate

This is a copy of the document I presented to Aḥmad ibn Ḥanbal after requesting that he confirm its contents, which he did. I asked him to sign it, and he asked his son ʿAbd Allāh to sign for him at the bottom.

I asked Aḥmad ibn Ḥanbal about Aḥmad ibn Rabāḥ. He replied that he was a well-known follower of Jahm who had held a position of authority where he had brought harm to Muslims because of his sectarian beliefs.

I asked him about Ibn Khalanjī. He replied as he had in the case of Ibn Abī Rabāḥ, saying that he was a well-known follower of Jahm—in fact, an especially bad and dangerous one.

I asked him about Shuʿayb ibn Sahl, and he replied that he was a well-known follower of Jahm.

I asked him about ʿUbayd Allāh ibn Aḥmad, and he replied that he was a well-known follower of Jahm.

I asked him about the man called Abū Shuʿayb, and he replied that he was a well-known follower of Jahm.

I asked him about Muḥammad ibn Manṣūr, judge in al-Ahwāz. "He was involved with Ibn Abī Du'ād and worked for him, though he was one of the better ones, and I don't know where he stands."

I asked him about Ibn ʿAlī ibn al-Jaʿd and he said, "He was well-known for being a follower of Jahm, but then I heard that he's recanted."

I asked him about al-Fatḥ ibn Sahl, who had run Muḥammad ibn ʿAbd Allāh's grievance court in Baghdad. He replied that he was a well-known follower of Jahm and an associate of Bishr al-Marīsī, and that it was dangerous to allow anyone like him to hold authority over Muslims.

I asked him about Ibn al-Thaljī and he said, "A reprehensible innovator and a sectarian."

I asked him about Ibrāhīm ibn ʿAttāb and he said, "I don't know him, but he was an associate of Bishr al-Marīsī, so I would steer clear of him, and keep him out of any position of authority. In general, heretics and sectarians should not be employed in positions of authority, since giving them power is extremely dangerous to Islam, as the Commander of Believers—God grant him long life—well knows, given his insistence on upholding the *sunnah* and combating heresy."

I, Aḥmad ibn Ḥanbal, declare that ʿAbd al-Raḥmān ibn Yaḥyā ibn Khāqān has asked me about everything on this document and what I said is what he wrote down. As I am too ill to move or see clearly, I could not write anything myself. At my request and in my presence, my son ʿAbd Allāh has signed at the bottom of this document. I pray to God to give the Commander of Believers long life and good health and bless him with help and guidance, by His grace and power.

[Aḥmad:] Any grave where lies a follower of the *sunnah*, even 23.6
one who has sinned, is a flowerbed in the Garden. Any grave where lies a follower of innovation, even one who renounced the world, is a pit inside the Fire.

23.7 Our exemplar Aḥmad ibn Ḥanbal was so fervent in his attachment to the *sunnah* and his rejection of innovation that he would criticize many virtuous persons for actions that went against the *sunnah*. Such criticisms are to be understood as good counsel in a matter of religion.

23.8 [Al-Sarrāj:] One day Aḥmad ibn Ḥanbal said to me, "I hear that you see a lot of al-Ḥārith," meaning al-Muḥāsibī. "Next time he comes to your house, could you hide me somewhere so I can hear what he has to say?"

I was glad that he had come to me, and I told him that I would be happy to do as he asked. Then I went to see al-Ḥārith and asked him to come over that night and to bring his associates as well.

"Ismāʿīl," he told me, "they're a large group. Give them all the dregs of oil and dates as you can, but nothing more."

I agreed to do as he asked. Then I went to Aḥmad and let him know. He arrived after the sunset prayer and went into a room upstairs, where he busied himself with his personal devotions.[149] After he finished, al-Ḥārith and his followers arrived. They ate and then got up to pray the evening prayer, which was the last prayer they performed that night. Then they sat down in front of al-Ḥārith without saying a word. No one said anything until it was almost midnight. Then one of them asked al-Ḥārith about a problem. He spoke and the others listened, as rapt as if they had birds nesting on their heads, with some weeping, others crying out, and others again sighing as he spoke. I went upstairs to check on Aḥmad and found that he had been weeping so hard that he had passed out. I went back to the group, which kept on until dawn came and they rose and left. I went back up to Aḥmad, who seemed to be in an altered state.

"What did you think of them?" I asked.

"I don't think I've ever seen anything like them," he said, "or heard anyone speak about direct knowledge[150] the way that man does. Having said that, though, I don't think you should join them any more."

Then he got up and left.[151]

[Al-Naṣrābādhī:] I heard that after al-Ḥārith al-Muḥāsibī engaged in some Disputation, Aḥmad ibn Ḥanbal stopped speaking to him. Al-Muḥāsibī disappeared into a house in Baghdad and died there, and only four people prayed at his funeral. 23.9

Chapter 24

His Seeking of Blessings and Cures Using the Qur'an and Water from the Well of Zamzam, as Well as Some Hair and a Bowl That Belonged to the Prophet

[Ṣāliḥ:] Whenever I got sick my father would take a cup of water and recite something over it, then tell me to drink some of it and wash my hands and face in it. 24.1

['Abd Allāh:] I saw my father take one of the Prophet's hairs, place it over his mouth, and kiss it. I may have seen him place it over his eyes, and dip it in water and then drink the water for a cure. Once I saw him take the Prophet's bowl, wash it in the water jar, and drink from it. And more than once I saw him drink water from the well of Zamzam[152] for a cure, and rub it on his hands and face. 24.2

Chapter 25

His Age When He Began Teaching Hadith and Giving Legal Opinions

It is noteworthy that Aḥmad—God be pleased with him—would sometimes give legal opinions even in his youth and would recite Hadith if asked, without being concerned about his age, as we learn from the following report. 25.1

[Al-Qūmisī:] In 198 [814], I saw Aḥmad ibn Ḥanbal leaning against the minaret at the mosque of al-Khayf.[153] When the Hadith scholars arrived, he began teaching them Hadith and legal implications and answering their questions about the pilgrimage rites.

25.2 [Al-Qūmisī:] In 198 [814], when Ibn ʿUyaynah was still alive, I saw Aḥmad ibn Ḥanbal at the mosque of al-Khayf, delivering legal opinions on all kinds of subjects. I had never seen him before, so I joined the group around him and asked someone who he was.

"You're not from here, are you?"

"No."

"That's Aḥmad ibn Ḥanbal."

I waited until the group had broken up, then took his hand and greeted him. We've known each other ever since then.

25.3 [The author:] It should nevertheless be noted that our exemplar Aḥmad—God be pleased with him—did not put himself forward to teach Hadith and give legal opinions until he was forty years old.

[Ibn al-Shāʿir:] I went to Aḥmad ibn Ḥanbal in 203 [818–19] and asked him to teach me Hadith, but he refused so I went out to study with ʿAbd al-Razzāq. Then, in '04, I came back and found that Aḥmad had turned forty and begun teaching, and people had accepted him as an authority.[154]

25.4 [Al-Ṣayrafī:] I was at Aḥmad ibn Ḥanbal's door and he mentioned a Hadith transmitted by ʿAbd al-Razzāq. I asked him to dictate it to me.

"What would you do with it, coming from me?" he asked. "ʿAbd al-Razzāq is still alive!"

"Can I tell you something?"

"Go ahead."

"I swear that if you taught it to me and then I left your door and found ʿAbd al-Razzāq himself at the gate of your alley, I wouldn't ask him about it."

25.5 [The author:] Even when he was teaching Hadith, Aḥmad would urge people to consult those senior transmitters who were still alive. For example:

[Ibn ʿAlī l-Warrāq:] In '13 [828–9] we went to see Aḥmad ibn Ḥanbal and I asked him to teach us Hadith.

"You'd hear it from me," he said, "when men like Abū ʿĀṣim are still alive? Go to him!"

Chapter 26

His Devotion to Learning and the Attitudes That Informed His Teaching

[Al-Būshanjī:] Once when Aḥmad ibn Ḥanbal was dictating for us, a man from Marv named Abū Yaʿqūb asked him about a Hadith. Aḥmad told his son ʿAbd Allāh to go inside and get the *Book of Useful Points.*[155] ʿAbd Allāh brought it out and Aḥmad looked through it, but he couldn't find the report he wanted. So he got up, left his mosque and went inside the house.[156] A short time later, he came back carrying a stack of quires, sat down, and started looking through them. After a while, the man who had asked the question said, "Never mind, Aḥmad! This is too much trouble." 26.1

"No it isn't," he replied. "It's me who needs to know."

We realized that he had gone into the house and looked at every quire where he thought the report might be, and then—because he didn't want to stay inside looking for the report—he had brought the papers out so that it wouldn't seem as if he were putting himself to a lot of trouble. It's hard to imagine a better example of courtesy.

[Abū Ḥātim al-Rāzī:] When I first met Aḥmad ibn Ḥanbal, in 213, I saw him go out to the ritual prayer carrying the *Book of Belief*[157] and the *Book of Drinks.*[158] He finished praying and waited, but no one asked him a question so he took the books back with him. Another day, I saw that he had taken them out again. I suspect that his reason for having those particular books with him was that the *Book of Belief* provides the basis of religion and the *Book of Drinks* is about turning people away from bad things—since drunkenness is the root of all evil.[159] 26.2

[Al-Marrūdhī:] Aḥmad once had a visit from Abū l-ʿAlāʾ the Servant,[160] who was a humble old man who went around with 26.3

his sleeves and pant legs rolled up[161] looking like a Qur'an-reader. When he arrived at the gate of the mosque, Aḥmad came out to welcome him.

It so happened that there was also a stranger in the mosque: a man dressed in rags and carrying a writing kit. As he sat down, Aḥmad happened to look around. As soon as he noticed the stranger, he said to Abū l-ʿAlāʾ, "I wouldn't want you to get caught outside in the heat," and Abū l-ʿAlāʾ got up and left.

Then Aḥmad began looking over at the stranger expecting him to ask a question, but the man said nothing. Finally Aḥmad asked, "Can I help you?"

"Teach me some of what God has taught you."

Aḥmad rose, went inside, and came back with some books. "Come over here," he said, then began dictating Hadith to the man, stopping to say, "Read back what you've written down."

Chapter 27

His Works[162]

27.1 Our exemplar Aḥmad—God be pleased with him—did not believe in writing books. He forbade anyone to write down what he said or to record his replies to legal questions.[163] Had he believed otherwise, he would have generated many compilations and had many had many writings to his credit. His works are therefore compilations of Hadith reports, such as the *Authenticated Reports Listed by Transmitter*, which contains thirty thousand reports.[164] He used to tell his son ʿAbd Allāh: "Take good care of that *Authenticated Reports* because people will need it." He also compiled the *Interpretation of the Qur'an*, which contains 120,000 reports,[165] *The Abrogating and Abrogated Verses of the Qur'an*,[166] *Fixing of Dates*,[167] *Hadith Reports Transmitted by Shuʿbah*,[168] *Transposed Elements in the Qur'an*, *Answers Regarding the Qur'an*, *The Greater Book on Pilgrimage Rites*, *The Lesser Book on Pilgrimage Rites*, and other titles.[169]

Although Aḥmad did not allow anyone to write down what he said, God nevertheless allowed him to fulfill his benevolent intentions by ensuring that his words were transmitted and preserved. Few indeed are the questions where he has not contributed a relevant text, whether on the principles of jurisprudence or on specific points of law. In many cases, his contribution has been preserved, whereas the work of jurists who did write and amass documents has been lost. 27.2

[Ḥanbal ibn Isḥāq:] Aḥmad ibn Ḥanbal gathered us together—me, Ṣāliḥ, and ʿAbd Allāh—and read his *Authenticated Reports* to us. We are the only ones to have heard it from him. He told us, "This is a book I put together by sorting through more than 750,000 reports. Whenever you find Muslims disagreeing about a Hadith of the Emissary, check to see if the report is in here. If it's not, it's doesn't count." 27.3

Chapter 28

His Aversion to Writing Books Containing Opinions Reached through the Exercise of Independent Judgment at the Expense of Transmitted Knowledge

Aḥmad ibn Ḥanbal—may God be pleased with him—deplored the writing of books that drew excessive legal implications and opinions reached through the exercise of independent judgment. What he cherished was firm adherence to transmitted reports. 28.1

[ʿUthmān ibn Saʿīd:] Ibn Ḥanbal once said to me, "Don't look at ʿUbayd's books, or whatever Isḥāq, Sufyān, al-Shāfiʿī, and Mālik have written. Go back to the source!" 28.2

[Ibrāhīm ibn Abī Ṭālib:] I heard Salamah ibn Shabīb tell Aḥmad ibn Ḥanbal that the Hadith scholars were copying the book of al-Shāfiʿī. 28.3

He said, "I don't think they should."

28.4 [Ibn Hāni':] I asked Aḥmad ibn Ḥanbal about what Abū Thawr had written, and he said: "It's a work where he comes up with bad novelties!"

He didn't approve of writing books. "Stick to Hadith!" he said.

28.5 [Al-Khāqānī:] My uncle ʿAbd al-Raḥmān ibn Yaḥyā ibn Khāqān reported to me that he heard it said of Aḥmad ibn Ḥanbal that he was telling people to copy *The Well-Trodden Path* by Mālik and saying that it was acceptable to consult it (or words to that effect), but not to read the *Compendium* of Sufyān.[170] My uncle told me that he asked Aḥmad which of the two he liked more.

"Neither one," he answered. "Stick to reports!"

According to another story, a man asked Aḥmad whether he should copy books containing opinions arrived at through the exercise of independent judgment.

"No," he answered.

"But Ibn al-Mubārak copied them."

"Ibn al-Mubārak didn't fall from heaven," said Aḥmad. "That's where we get our learning from."

Chapter 29

His Forbidding Others to Write Down or Transmit His Words[171]

29.1 [Ḥanbal ibn Isḥāq:] I remember that Aḥmad hated to have anyone write down his views or his judgments in matters of law.

29.2 [Aḥmad ibn al-Rabīʿ:] Aḥmad ibn Ḥanbal once said to us, "I heard that Isḥāq al-Kawsaj is teaching my answers to legal questions out in Khurasan. Bear witness, all of you: I renounce them all!"

29.3 [Al-Marrūdhī:] I once saw a man from Khurasan approach Aḥmad and give him a quire. He looked at it and when he saw that it had some of his own words in it, he grew angry and tossed the document away.

[Aḥmad al-Burjī:] Aḥmad ibn Ḥanbal once said, "Sometimes a tall cap falls from the sky, and you have to move your head like *this*," and he shook his head as if to keep a cap from settling on it. 29.4

What he meant was that certain people have leadership thrust upon them. He also seems to have meant that good people duck their heads modestly when that happens. Out of modesty, too, did Aḥmad forbid people to write his words down, but God decreed that they be recorded, put in order, and made known to all.[172]

Chapter 30

His Remarks on Sincerity, on Acting for the Sake of Appearances, and on Concealing One's Pious Austerities

[Ibn al-Sammāk:] I heard Aḥmad ibn Ḥanbal say, "Letting people see your inkwell is showing off."[173] 30.1

Al-Anṣārī said, "I think the Ibn al-Sammāk who reported this comment is Muḥammad ibn Bundār al-Sammāk al-Jarjarāʾī, who associated with Aḥmad."

[Al-Marrūdhī:] Someone once asked Ibn Ḥanbal what his people had done to become so well regarded. 30.2

"They've been truthful," he said.

[Al-Marrūdhī:] After someone mentioned being truthful and earnest, Aḥmad said, "That's what makes this group[174] better than others." 30.3

[Al-Marrūdhī:] I was with Aḥmad in Samarra for about four months. During that time he never stopped praying at night and reading the Qur'an by day, but even when he finished a reading of the whole Qur'an, he never let on. He did it all in secret. 30.4

[Abū Bakr ibn Muḥammad:] Aḥmad once ran into a man who had been dishonest with him. 30.5

"If you made things right," he told him, "you wouldn't have to be afraid of anyone."

I also heard him say, when he was asked what it meant to love others in God, that it meant loving them without thought of worldly gain.

Chapter 31

His Statements about Renunciation and Spiritual Weakness[175]

31.1 [Muḥammad ibn Naṣr the Worshipper:] I heard Aḥmad ibn Ḥanbal say, “If you have a chance to do something good, don’t wait!”

I asked him about going out to fight on the frontiers and he said, “Don’t wait: go!”

31.2 [Al-Ṭarasūsī:] I went with Yaḥyā l-Jallāʾ—who was supposed to be one of the Substitutes—to see Aḥmad. He was with Fūrān, Zuhayr, and Hārūn al-Ḥammāl (the porter).

“God bless you, Aḥmad!” I said. “Tell me: What softens a person’s heart?”

He turned to his companions and winked. Then he bowed his head for a time. Finally he looked up and said, “Son, it’s eating permitted foods.”

I left and went directly to Abū Naṣr Bishr ibn al-Ḥārith and asked him the same question. He recited: «Do hearts not find reassurance in the thought of God?»[176]

I told him that I had just come from Aḥmad ibn Ḥanbal’s.

“I see,” he said. “So what did Aḥmad tell you?”

“He said ‘eating permitted foods.’”

“He’s right,” said Bishr. “That’s the place to start!”

Then I went to see ʿAbd al-Wahhāb al-Warrāq and asked him the same question. He recited: «Do hearts not find reassurance in the thought of God?»

I told him that I had just come from Aḥmad ibn Ḥanbal’s. His face turned pink with delight and he asked what he had said.

“He said ‘eating permitted foods.’”

"He's right: that's the essence!" he exclaimed. "The place to start is where he told you."

[Al-Marrūdhī:] I heard Aḥmad say to his soul: "Suffer now or regret it later!" 31.3

[ʿAbd Allāh:] I once heard my father say, when someone mentioned the things of this world, that one can be satisfied with having little but never satisfied with having much. 31.4

On another occasion, when someone mentioned poverty, he said: "Poverty with virtue!"

[Al-Marrūdhī:] I once heard Aḥmad say: "Nothing has as much merit as being poor. Do you know that when your wife asks you for something and you can't afford it, what a reward you've earned?" 31.5

[Al-Khallāl:] ʿAbd al-Malik ibn ʿAbd al-Ḥamīd told us that Aḥmad once said to him, "How long does any of us live? Fifty years? Sixty? You're not that far behind us!" 31.6

[Al-Warrāq:] I once heard Aḥmad ibn Ḥanbal say, "Losing my youth seems no different to me than letting something drop out of my sleeve."[177] 31.7

[Al-Marrūdhī:] I once heard Aḥmad say, "The less of this world you take, the lighter your reckoning in the end." 31.8

[Yaʿqūb ibn Isḥāq:] Asked what it meant to be completely reliant on God, Aḥmad ibn Ḥanbal said, "Learning not to look around hoping for help from other people." 31.9

"What's your source for that?"

"What Abraham said when they put him on the mangonel."[178]

[Yaʿqūb ibn Isḥāq:] Asked what it meant to be completely reliant on God, Aḥmad ibn Ḥanbal said, "Learning not to look around for help from any other creature." 31.10

"What's your source for that?"

"The story about Abraham, the Friend of God, when he was put on the mangonel and said to Gabriel, 'From you, no.' Then, when Gabriel said, 'Ask the One who can help you, then,' he answered, 'I accept whatever He chooses for me.'"

31.11 ['Abd Allāh:] Aḥmad was asked what bravery meant and he said, "Renouncing what you crave and embracing what you fear."

31.12 [Muḥammad ibn Naṣr:] I heard Aḥmad ibn Ḥanbal say, "If there's anything good you intend to do, hurry up and do it before something gets in the way."

31.13 ['Abd al-Ṣamad ibn Sulaymān:] Once when I spent the night at Aḥmad ibn Ḥanbal's he put some water out for me. In the morning he saw I hadn't used it.

"You call yourself a Hadith scholar," he said, "and you didn't do a night prayer?"

I protested that I was traveling.

"So what?" he retorted. "When Masrūq performed the pilgrimage, he slept only one way: with his forehead on the ground."[179]

31.14 [Abū 'Iṣmah:] Once when I spent the night at Aḥmad ibn Ḥanbal's he brought some water and put it out for me. In the morning he saw it was untouched.

"God help us!" he cried. "A man who seeks Hadith but doesn't pray at night?"

31.15 [Ibn al-Madīnī:] Once, before a trip, as I was taking leave of Ibn Ḥanbal, I asked if he wanted me to do anything for him.

"Yes," he replied. "Carry the fear of God wherever you go, and keep your eyes on the next world."

31.16 [Yaḥyā l-Jallā':] I heard Aḥmad ibn Ḥanbal say, "I hate to see the things of this world weaken the resolve of men who know the Qur'an."

31.17 ['Abd Allāh:] One day I asked my father to give me some advice. He said, "Always intend to do the right thing. As long as your intention is sound, you'll be all right."

31.18 [Al-Marrūdhī:] Someone once asked Ibn Ḥanbal what his people had done to become so well regarded.

"They've been truthful," he said.

31.19 ['Abd Allāh:] I heard my father say, "You can't be rightly fearful unless you know what to fear."[180]

Chapter 32

His Remarks on Different Subjects

[Abū Yūsuf:] I once heard Aḥmad say, "There are three ways to eat: with friends for pleasure, with the poor in charity, and with worldly men out of duty." 32.1

[Al-Marrūdhī:] I heard Aḥmad ibn Ḥanbal say, "Anything can be noble. A person's heart is noble when it accepts God's will."[181] 32.2

[Ibn ʿAbd al-ʿAzīz:] I once saw al-Muṭīʿ li-Llāh[182] on the pulpit trying to win over a crowd of Ḥanbalīs—maybe thirty thousand—who were looking at him. He said, "I heard my teacher Ibn Bint Manīʿ say that he heard Aḥmad ibn Ḥanbal say, 'When a man's friends die he comes down in the world.'" 32.3

[Ismāʿīl ibn al-ʿAlāʾ:] I accepted an invitation from Rizq Allāh al-Kalawādhī, who served us a great deal of food. Aḥmad ibn Ḥanbal, Yaḥyā ibn Maʿīn, Abū Khaythmah, and some others were there as well. When our host presented an almond pastry roll[183] that had cost him eighty dirhams, Abū Khaythamah exclaimed, "That's an extravagance!" 32.4

"No it isn't," said Aḥmad ibn Ḥanbal. "If only the things of this world could be folded up into a little ball that one Muslim could feed to another, there would be no extravagance involved."[184]

"Well said, Aḥmad," said Yaḥyā.

[Jaʿfar al-Ṣāyigh:] One of Aḥmad ibn Ḥanbal's neighbors was a man who lived a life of sin and filth. One day he came over to where Aḥmad was sitting and greeted him. Aḥmad seemed to shrink away from the man and returned his greeting only half-heartedly. 32.5

"No need to turn away from me, Aḥmad," said the man. "I've given up those things you've seen me do—all because of a dream I had."

"What did you dream? Come over here!"

"I dreamed I saw the Prophet, God bless and keep him, standing on a sort of hill with a lot of people sitting at the bottom. One by one they got up and asked him to pray for them, and he did. Soon I was the only one left. I tried to get up, but I was too ashamed at the ugly things I had been doing.

"'You there!' said the Prophet. 'Why don't you get up and ask me to pray for you?'

"'Emissary of God,' I answered, 'I'm too ashamed.'

"'If you can feel shame,' he said, 'you can get up, and if you ask me I'll pray for you, since you've never cursed any of my Companions.'

"So I got up and he prayed for me. Then I woke up, feeling that God had made my past life hateful to me."

"Jaʿfar!" cried Aḥmad, calling out to me, and then to the others present. "You, and you! Go out and repeat this story, and don't forget it. It will do people good to hear it."

32.6 [ʿAmmār ibn Rajāʾ:] I heard Aḥmad ibn Ḥanbal say, "It's a good practice to seek the highest possible authority for your reports."[185]

32.7 [Ḥarb ibn Ismāʿīl:] Asked about seeking higher authority, Aḥmad ibn Ḥanbal said that it was a practice of previous generations of scholars. "Even the people who heard reports from ʿAbd Allāh, the son of ʿUmar, would travel all the way from Kufa back to Medina to study with ʿUmar and hear the same reports from him."

32.8 [Ḥanbal ibn Isḥāq:] Aḥmad ibn Ḥanbal once saw me writing in a very small hand and said, "Don't do that; when you most need to read what you've written, you might not be able to."

32.9 [Al-Maymūnī:] I asked Aḥmad which reading of the Qurʾan I should use.

"The reading of Abū ʿAmr ibn al-ʿAlāʾ," he replied. "It's in the speech of Quraysh and the Companions who had the clearest pronunciation."

32.10 Isḥāq ibn Ḥassān said: "I wrote to Aḥmad asking his advice on marriage. He wrote, 'Marry a virgin and make sure her mother is dead.'"

32.11 Abū Bakr ʿAbd al-ʿAzīz ibn Jaʿfar reported that Aḥmad ibn Ḥanbal told his two sons, "Make a list of everyone who came to say good-bye when they went on the pilgrimage. When they return, we'll go and welcome them back."

Ibn ʿAqil commented that Ibn Ḥanbal did this not out of pride but in order to keep up his scholarly connections.

Chapter 33

Poems He Recited or Had Attributed to Him

[Thaʿlab:] I wanted to meet Aḥmad ibn Ḥanbal, so I went looking for him. When I found him he asked me what my field was. "Grammar and Arabic," I told him. He then recited: 33.1

You may think yourself unnoticed
But One on high is watching you,
Never sleeping or forgetting
Every deed done here below.
Heedless do we let the days pass
Adding sin to grievous sin;
Pray God pardon all our evil
When we turn contrite to Him.[186]

[Thaʿlab:] The first thing I noticed about Ibn Ḥanbal was his gaze: he looked as if he could see Hell blazing before him.[187] I greeted him and he asked me who I was. 33.2

"Thaʿlab."

"What kind of learning are you after?"

"Rhymes and poems," I said, and immediately wished I had said something else.

"Write this down!" he said. Then he recited:

You may think yourself unnoticed
But One on high is watching you,
Never sleeping or forgetting
Every deed done here below.

Heedless do we let the days pass
Adding sin to grievous sin;
Pray God pardon all our evil
When we turn contrite to Him.
Once your generation passes
All those you knew are gone,
Leaving you amid new faces,
Abandoned, friendless, and alone.[188]

33.3 It was also reported to me that ʿAlī ibn Khashram heard Aḥmad ibn Ḥanbal recite:

How swiftly fly the joys of sin!
How long-abiding is the shame!
How dear the thrill of sinful pleasures
That damn you to eternal flame![189]

33.4 [Al-Khayyāṭ:] I recited part of what Aḥmad ibn Ḥanbal said about ʿAlī ibn al-Madīnī:

Why embrace a creed you once called damned?
Why barter faith for worldly gain?
Did a lying creed at once seem true,
Or did Mammon lead my friend astray?
I knew you once, when none could sway you
From proclaiming, fearless, where you stood.
Let riches go, and you lose nothing,[190]
But faith, once sold, is gone for good.[191]

Chapter 34
His Correspondence

34.1 [Al-Dārimī:] Aḥmad ibn Ḥanbal once addressed a letter to me as follows: "To Abū Jaʿfar—God grace you!—from Aḥmad ibn Ḥanbal."

34.2 [Al-Marrūdhī:] Aḥmad used to say that the word "to" in addresses should be *ilā* and not *li-*, and addressed his letters accordingly.[192]

[Saʿid ibn Yaʿqūb:] Aḥmad ibn Ḥanbal wrote me the following letter: 34.3

> In the name of God, full of compassion, ever compassionate
> From Aḥmad ibn Muḥammad to Saʿid ibn Yaʿqūb
> Now then: desire for the things of this world is one kind of sickness, and desire for earthly power is another. The man of learning, on the other hand, is a physician. But if you ever see a physician bringing sickness on himself, avoid him.
> Peace to you!

[Ḥanbal:] Aḥmad ibn Ḥanbal used to address letters by writing from So-and-So to So-and-So. When I asked him why, he said, "The Prophet, God bless and keep him, wrote to Chosroes and Caesar, and all his other letters, that way. So did his Companions, as when ʿUmar—God be pleased with him—wrote to ʿUtbah ibn Farqad. And today that's how I write to a Hadith scholar I don't know." 34.4

"So you mention yourself first?"

"If you're writing to your father, it's better to put his name first instead of yours, and the same if you're writing to someone old. Otherwise it's fine."

[Ibn Manīʿ:] I wanted to go study with Suwayd ibn Saʿīd and I asked Aḥmad ibn Ḥanbal if he would write to him for me. So he wrote a letter describing me as "a man who writes down Hadith." 34.5

"Aḥmad," I protested, "think how long I've served you. Couldn't you write that I'm a Hadith-man?"

"A Hadith-man," he said, "is what I call someone who puts Hadith into practice."

Chapter 35

His Appearance and Bearing

[Al-Walīd al-Naḥwī:] Aḥmad ibn Ḥanbal was a handsome man of medium height. He dyed his hair lightly with henna, leaving some 35.1

black hairs in his beard. His clothing was coarse but white. When I saw him he was wearing a turban and a breechclout.

35.2 [ʿAbd Allāh:] My father began dyeing his hair and beard with henna when he was sixty-three.

35.3 [Al-Sijistānī:] Aḥmad ibn Ḥanbal never joined people in talking about the things that most of them care about, but whenever Hadith was mentioned he would speak.

35.4 [Al-ʿUkbarī:] When I saw Aḥmad ibn Ḥanbal, he was a tall old man with dyed hair and very dark skin.

35.5 [Al-Marrūdhī:] When Aḥmad was at home, he usually sat knees to the chest with his head bowed humbly before God. When he was outside, though, the humility was not so easy to see as it was when he was inside. I would come in and find him reading from a quire he held in his hand. When I sat down, he would close it and put it down in front of him.

35.6 [Khaṭṭāb ibn Bishr:] I was sitting in Aḥmad's mosque with Abū Bakr al-Marrūdhī trading Hadith reports when Abū Bakr heard the door open and jumped up. There was Aḥmad, sticking his head out.

"Go look and see where Ḥasan's gotten to," he said, meaning his little boy.

"The boy's really got the poor man worried," I thought to myself. The time was midday, and it was summer.

Abū Bakr went into one of the houses where the weavers lived, found the boy, and brought him out. He told him where I was, and he told me to come in.[193]

I went into the entryway and found Aḥmad sitting on the dirt floor. The dye in his hair had run, and I could see the white roots of his hair. He was wearing a small, dirty breechclout of white cotton and a coarse shirt with a smudge on the shoulder and sweat stains on the collar.

I asked him a question about being scrupulous and the lawfulness of earning a living. No sooner had I asked the question than I saw his face fall and assume such a sorrowful expression of self-contempt that it pained me to look at him. As I left, I said to someone who was with me, "Some days he seems so dissatisfied with himself."

[Ismāʿīl:] Upwards of five thousand people used to come hear Aḥmad speak. Fewer than five hundred of them came to write down Hadith: the rest were there to study his manners and his bearing. 35.7

[Al-Muṭṭawwiʿī:] For twelve years I went to see Aḥmad read his *Authenticated Reports* to his children. I never wrote down a single report: I was there to follow his example, study his ethics, and observe his manners. 35.8

[Al-Būshanjī:] I saw Aḥmad ibn Ḥanbal sit only one way—knees to the chest—except when he was praying. That's the way of sitting that Qaylah describes in the Hadith report where she says, "I saw the Emissary of God sitting knees to the chest, like a man making himself humble before God." He used to perform his ablutions with sand while sitting in that position, which is the most timid before God. It means sitting on one's behind with the knees to the chest and feet flat on the floor. Sometimes he would put his arm around his legs. No posture is more timid than that. 35.9

[Muḥammad ibn Yūnus:] We heard al-Ruʾāsī report: "Of all the Emissary's Companions, none was closer to him in his example, his bearing, and his carriage than ʿAbd Allāh ibn Masʿūd. In the next generation, the one who most resembled Ibn Masʿūd was ʿAlqamah ibn Qays. After ʿAlqamah, the one who most resembled *him* was Ibrāhīm al-Nakhaʿī. After al-Nakhaʿī, the one who most resembled *him* was Manṣūr ibn al-Muʿtamir. After Manṣūr ibn al-Muʿtamir, the one who most resembled *him* was Sufyān al-Thawrī. After Sufyān, the one who most resembled *him* was Wakīʿ ibn al-Jarrāḥ." 35.10

And the one closest to Wakīʿ was Aḥmad ibn Ḥanbal.

[Al-Ḥasan ibn al-Rabīʿ:] In his example and his bearing, the only person I can compare Aḥmad ibn Ḥanbal to is Ibn al-Mubārak. 35.11

Chapter 36

His Imposing Presence

36.1 [Muḥammad ibn Muslim:] We were too much in awe of Aḥmad ibn Ḥanbal to disagree with him or argue with him about anything.

This was because of how imposing he was, and how intimidating the devotion to Islam he had been blessed with.[194]

36.2 [Al-Marrūdhī:] Al-Ḥasan ibn Aḥmad, the superintendent of the bridge, who lived in my neighborhood, told me, "I've met Isḥāq ibn Ibrāhīm, and So-and-So, and So-and-So"—all of them men of authority—"but I never saw anyone as overpowering as Aḥmad ibn Ḥanbal. I once went to talk to him about something, and the moment I saw him, I shuddered."

Al-Kalbī, the chief of intelligence, once came to see him at night, but he and his men were too intimidated to knock on his door and so knocked on his uncle's door instead. Aḥmad said that he heard them knocking and answered.

36.3 [ʿAbdūs:] Aḥmad once saw me laugh. I'm still embarrassed about it.

36.4 [Al-Qāsim ibn Sallām:] I've sat with Abū Yūsuf, Muḥammad ibn al-Ḥasan, Yaḥyā ibn Saʿīd, and ʿAbd al-Raḥmān ibn Mahdī, and I was never as intimidated as I was when I sat with Aḥmad ibn Ḥanbal. When he was in prison, I went to visit him. Someone asked me a question but with Aḥmad there I was afraid to answer it.

Ibn Makram added: "I told Yaʿqūb ibn Shaybah this story, and he said, 'He was probably afraid to make a mistake with Aḥmad there.'"

Chapter 37

His Cleanliness and Ritual Purity

37.1 [Al-Maymūnī:] I don't think I've ever seen anyone who kept his clothes as clean as Ibn Ḥanbal did, or took such good care of his hair, mustache, and body hair, or anyone whose clothing was as immaculately white as his.

[Al-Marrūdhī:] Aḥmad never went to the bathhouse. When he needed to depilate himself, he did it at home. I prepared the paste for him more than once. I also bought him a leather glove. He would put it on and remove the paste himself.[195] 37.2

[Abū l-ʿAbbās:] I once prepared a depilatory paste for Aḥmad and began removing his hair. When I reached the pubic area, he took over. 37.3

Chapter 38

His Kindness and His Consideration for Others

[Al-Būshanjī:] Of all the people I saw in Aḥmad's time, I never met anyone as mindful of religion, as careful, as self-controlled, or as abstinent as Aḥmad, nor anyone as learned or as discerning in matters of religion, nor anyone so generous in spirit, so firm of heart, so congenial in company, or so unmistakably sincere.[196] 38.1

[ʿAlī ibn al-Madīnī:] Aḥmad ibn Ḥanbal once said to me, "I wish I could accompany you to Mecca, but I'm afraid I'll get tired of your company, or you of mine." 38.2

When I came to say good-bye, I asked him if he wanted anything and he said, "I want you to remain fearful of God and mindful of the afterlife."

[Ḥanbal:] I remember that whenever Aḥmad ibn Ḥanbal wanted to get up, he would say to whoever was with him, "By your leave." 38.3

[Al-Sijistānī:] Sitting with Aḥmad ibn Ḥanbal meant talking about the next world; the things of this world were never mentioned. I never saw him talk about this world at all. 38.4

[Ibn al-Munādī:] I heard my grandfather say, "Aḥmad was extremely modest, but generous in spirit; he was one of the most thoughtful and considerate people I've ever seen. He would sit with 38.5

his head bowed and his eyes averted much of the time, and avoid talking about anything unseemly or frivolous. When he did talk, it was to exchange Hadith or recall the example set by righteous men and renunciants, which he did with quiet dignity and eloquence. When meeting people, he would smile and give them his full attention. He showed great deference to senior men of learning, who in turn respected him enormously. He displayed the greatest veneration for Yaḥyā ibn Maʿīn, who was seven or so years older than he."

38.6 [ʿAbd Allāh:] Whenever my father left the mosque to come into the house, he would slap his sandal against the ground so people could hear him coming. He would often clear his throat, too, to let people know he was coming in.

38.7 [Muhannaʾ:] I saw Aḥmad ibn Ḥanbal more than once or twice—more than three or four or five times, really—letting people kiss his face, his head, or his cheek. He wouldn't say anything, but he wouldn't stop them, either. I saw Sulaymān ibn Dāwūd al-Hāshimī kiss him on the head and forehead. He didn't stop him and he didn't seem to disapprove. I also saw Yaʿqūb ibn Ibrāhīm kissing him on the forehead and the face.

38.8 [Al-Khallāl:] I asked Zuhayr ibn Ṣāliḥ if he had ever seen his grandfather, Aḥmad ibn Ḥanbal.

"Yes," he said. "I was about eight years old the first time. I was ten when he died."[197]

"Do you remember what he was like?"

"My sisters and I used to visit him every Friday. The door between our house and his was left open. He used to write a note to a man he bought nuts and dried fruit from and tell him to give each of us two silver pennies' worth, and we would go and take two pennies' worth of nuts or fruit and bring something for our sisters too.[198]

"Many times I saw him sitting in the sun with his back exposed and the scars showing.

38.9 "I had a younger brother named ʿAlī, with the nickname Abū Ḥafs. My father wanted to have him circumcised. He prepared a lot of food and invited people to come over. When the time came, he sent someone to invite my grandfather too. Later my father told me what he said: 'I've heard about this new thing you're doing, and I've heard that you've been wasteful about it. You should start with the poor and ill and feed them first.'

"The next day, when the cupper and the family members had arrived, my father went in to tell my grandfather. My grandfather came out with him, sat down next to the little boy, and stayed there while the circumcision took place. Afterward he took out two knotted pieces of cloth and gave one to the cupper and the other to the boy. Then he went back into his house. The cupper looked into the little bag and found a single dirham. We looked into the boy's bag and found the same.

"We had removed most of the things we had spread on the floor and put the boy on a little platform resting on some dyed garments. My grandfather didn't seem to disapprove.

"Once my grandfather's maternal cousin, who had the *kunyah* 38.10
Abū Aḥmad, came from Khurasan and stayed with my father. One day after sunset prayers, my father told me to take Abū Aḥmad by the hand and show him in to my grandfather. I went into my grandfather's house and found him doing more prayers so I sat down. When he finished, he asked me if Abū Aḥmad had arrived.

"'Yes.'

"'Tell him to come in.'

"I went out, found Abū Aḥmad, and brought him back in. He sat down. My grandfather called out to an elderly woman—a tenant of his[199]—who used to work for him, and she brought out some bread, fresh herbs, vinegar, and salt on a wicker tray. Later she brought out one of those big platters and put it in front of us. It was a dried-whey stew[200] with lots of meat and chard. We started eating and he joined us. As we ate, he asked Abū Aḥmad about the members of the family who were still in Khurasan. Several times, Abū Aḥmad had trouble understanding things in Arabic and so my grandfather would speak to him in Persian. All the while, he would choose pieces of meat and serve them to Abū Aḥmad and me too. Afterward he picked up the platter himself and put it aside, then brought over a serving dish containing premium Barnī dates and shelled walnuts and put it in front of us on the tray. He ate and we did too, with him serving Abū Aḥmad. Then we washed our hands, with each of us taking care of himself."

38.11 [Al-ʿAṭṭār:] I sent my young son, along with a slave woman, to give my regards to Aḥmad. He welcomed the boy, held him in his lap, and asked him questions. He also sent out for a pudding,[201] which he brought in, put in front of the boy, and coaxed him to eat, inviting the woman to eat as well. Then he went out to a vendor of fruits, nuts, and sweets, and came back with some almonds and sugar wrapped up in his gown. He took everything out, wrapped it up in a handkerchief, and gave it to the servant. Then he said to the boy, "Tell Abū Muḥammad I said hello."

38.12 [Al-Marrūdhī:] I once saw Aḥmad toss two dirhams into a circumciser's basin.

38.13 [Al-Maymūnī:] I would often ask Aḥmad about something and he would say, "At your service!"

38.14 [Al-Marrūdhī:] Aḥmad was never abusive. If anyone was abusive to him, he would bear it patiently. Instead of getting angry, he would say, "May God suffice!"[202]

He didn't bear grudges or speak rashly. His uncle once quarreled with the neighbors. When they would come to see Aḥmad, he would receive them as courteously as he always had, without taking sides or arguing his uncle's part.

He was very humble and loved the poor. I never saw poor men treated as well as they were when sitting in his company. He would treat them with special consideration while disregarding the affluent. He was graced with a quiet dignity. Whenever, in the late afternoon, he would sit in his usual place and give legal opinions, he would not speak until someone asked him a question. If he went out to his mosque, he didn't go sit in the center of the gathering; instead, he sat wherever there was room. When he sat, he would never extend his leg, for fear of seeming disrespectful of others.

He was kind, cheerful, and accommodating, and never vulgar or coarse. What he loved, he loved for the sake of God, and likewise for the things he hated. When he liked someone, he would show as much regard for his well-being as he would for his own, making no distinction between his own wishes and aversions and those of his friend. Even so, friendship never prevented him from intervening when someone he cared for behaved badly or wronged anyone else. Whenever he learned that someone was righteous, or self-denying, or had stood up for justice, or furthered the cause, he would inquire about him, talk about wanting to meet him, and express curiosity about his circumstances.

He was a sensitive man: if he didn't like something, he showed it. He would become indignant, though only on behalf of God; he would never get angry on his own behalf or do anything to promote his own interests. Wherever a matter of religion was at stake, he would become so incensed that he seemed a different person altogether: one heedless of blame or reproach. All the same he was easy to live with because he would suffer without complaint. One of his neighbors—a man who shared a wall with him—told me this story.

"We had a dovecote, with pigeons in it, overlooking Aḥmad's house. As a boy, I would climb up there and look down at him. He put up with it and never told me to stop. Then one day my uncle went up there and saw that the dovecote overlooked Aḥmad's house.

"'Shame on you!' he said to me. 'Can't you see that you're disturbing Aḥmad?'

"'But he never said anything to me!'

"'You'd better give me those birds, or else!'

"He kept after me until I gave him the birds. Then he slaughtered them and tore down the dovecote."

[Hārūn ibn Sufyān:] When Aḥmad ibn Ḥanbal decided to give away the money that al-Mutawakkil had given him, I went to see him and he gave me two hundred dirhams. 38.15

"I need more," I told him.

"That's all there is," he said, "but I tell you what I'll do. I'll give you three hundred and you can give it away."

After I took the money I said, "Aḥmad, I'm not giving a single dirham away to anyone."

All he did was smile.

38.16 [Al-Anmāṭī:] Once I was at Aḥmad's and he mentioned a Hadith I wanted to write down. He had his inkwell in front of him, and I asked if I could use it.

"Of course," he said gruffly. "No need to stand on ceremony!"[203]

38.17 ['Abd Allāh:] Someone asked my father why he didn't spend more time with people.

"Because I hate saying good-bye," he said.

38.18 [Ibrāhīm al-Ḥarbī:] Aḥmad would attend marriages, weddings, and circumcisions if invited, and eat what he was served there.

I once heard him say to Aḥmad ibn Ḥafṣ al-Wakī'ī, "I'm very fond of you, Abū 'Abd al-Raḥmān." Then he recited, "We heard Yaḥyā report, citing Thawr, citing Ḥabīb ibn 'Ubayd, citing al-Miqdām, that the Prophet—God bless and keep him—said, 'When one of you feels affection for another, he should tell him.'"

38.19 [Hārūn:] One night Aḥmad ibn Ḥanbal came knocking on my door.

"Who is it?" I asked.

"It's Aḥmad," he said.

I rushed to the door. He wished me a good evening and I did likewise. Then I asked him if something was wrong.

"Yes," he said. "I've been worried about you."

"Why?"

"Today, when I walked by you, you were reciting Hadith sitting in the shade while the people holding the pens and notebooks were sitting in the sun. Don't do that again! When you teach, make sure to sit with the people who are listening to you."

38.20 [Al-Maṣṣīṣī:] I was once at Aḥmad ibn Ḥanbal's when they were reciting Hadith. Muḥammad ibn Yaḥyā l-Naysābūrī recited a weak report, and Aḥmad said, "Don't cite reports like that."

Muḥammad ibn Yaḥyā looked abashed, but then Aḥmad said, "I said that only out of respect for you."

[Aḥmad ibn al-Ḥakam:] Aḥmad ibn Ḥanbal came to Kufa to study Hadith. He came regularly to hear Wakīʿ ibn al-Jarrāḥ and heard a great many reports from him. 38.21

[Isḥāq ibn Hāniʾ:] We were once at Aḥmad's house with al-Marrūdhī and Muhannaʾ ibn Yaḥyā l-Shāmī. There was a knock on the door and someone called out, "Is al-Marrūdhī here?" 38.22

Since al-Marrūdhī didn't want anyone to know where he was, Muhannaʾ ibn Yaḥyā put his finger on the palm of his hand[204] and called back, "Al-Marrūdhī's not here. What would he be doing here anyway?"

Aḥmad laughed and did not seem to disapprove.

Chapter 39

His Forbearance and His Readiness to Forgive

[Al-Khiraqī:] I heard Aḥmad ibn Ḥanbal say, "I forgive al-Muʿtaṣim for flogging me." 39.1

[Al-Ṣarrām:] I heard Ibrāhīm ibn Isḥāq report that al-Mutawakkil took the partisan of ʿAlī who had denounced Aḥmad to the government and sent him to Aḥmad so he could recommend a punishment for him. But Aḥmad forgave him, saying, "He may have children who would be grieved if he were killed." 39.2

That was the gist of the story.[205]

[Ibn Hāniʾ:] I was once at Aḥmad ibn Ḥanbal's when a man said, "Aḥmad! I spoke against you behind your back. Will you forgive me?" 39.3

"Yes, if you don't do it again."

"How can you forgive him," I protested, "when he's slandered you?"

"But I've asked him not to do it again," he answered. "Didn't you see?"

39.4 [Ḥanbal:] Once, when I was performing the afternoon prayer with Aḥmad, a man named Muḥammad ibn Saʿīd al-Khuttalī joined us. Afterward he asked Aḥmad why he had told people not to talk to Zayd ibn Khalaf.

"The people at the frontier wrote asking about him," replied Aḥmad. "I told them about his opinions and about the unprecedented things he had said, and I asked them not to sit with him."

Al-Khuttalī flew into a rage. "As God is my witness," he shouted, "I'll have you thrown back in prison!" He kept on shouting, saying things like, "I'll break your ribs one by one!"

"Don't say anything," Aḥmad told me, "and don't bother answering him."

So no one said anything. Aḥmad picked up his sandals, rose, and went inside.

"Tell the tenants not to argue with him," he said.

Al-Khuttalī went on shouting for a while and finally left. He was made market inspector in Samarra and died there.

39.5 [Al-Ājurrī:] Aḥmad and I were once walking back from the Friday mosque when I mentioned Abū Ḥanīfah. He waved his hand dismissively.

"Abū Ḥanifah's piss," I said, "was worth more than a world full of people like you!"

He looked at me, then said, "Good-bye."[206]

Early the next morning, I went to him and said, "Aḥmad, I didn't mean to say what I said. Will you forgive me?"

"I forgave you while I was standing there," he replied.

39.6 [Al-Ḥarbī:] Aḥmad ibn Ḥanbal always seemed to know the right thing to do. He had an enormous reserve of patience and understanding. One day a man came to him and said, "Do you have any books with heresy in them?"[207]

Aḥmad sat silent for a time then said, "The only place a believer is safe is in the grave."

Another time someone said to him, "People say you never heard Hadith from Ibrāhīm ibn Saʿd," and he made no reply at all.

Ibrāhīm also reported: 39.7

"One day we were at Dāwūd ibn ʿAmr's and Dāwūd asked him, 'Aḥmad, how are you eating these days? And sleeping? And what about sex?'

"Aḥmad replied, 'I have no aversion to women, and I have a body as well as a spirit.'

"He refused to say any more."

Chapter 40
His Property and Means of Subsistence

Aḥmad—God be pleased with him—inherited from his father some 40.1
tenements and the house where he lived. He rented out the tenements and lived off the rents, without having to ask anyone for anything.[208]

[Muḥammad ibn ʿUbayd Allāh:] Aḥmad ibn Ḥanbal told me, "Every year I survey the house I live in and pay the alms-tax on it, following what ʿUmar ibn al-Khaṭṭāb said about the Black Land in Iraq."[209]

Aḥmad lived in one part of the property and rented part of it out to others. Aḥmad ibn Jaʿfar reported that someone asked him how he knew that he was the rightful owner.

"It's something I inherited from my father," he replied. "If anyone comes and proves it's his, I'd move out and give it to him."

[Al-Marrūdhī:] I heard Aḥmad say, "This property doesn't sup- 40.2
port us, but I'm staying with it until it yields something."[210]

I said, "I heard someone suggest that he'd like it better if you gave it up and let a friend manage it for you."

"That's an invitation to disaster," said Aḥmad, or perhaps what he said was, "That's no good." He continued: "Once you get used to that sort of arrangement you can't live without it." He added, "I'd rather have it this way than any other," referring to the property that generated the income. Finally he said to me, "You know the income doesn't support us. I only take it because I have to."

40.3 [Al-Baladī:] Once, when I was sitting with Aḥmad, one of his tenants brought him a dirham and a half. As soon as it fell into his hands, he got up, leaving me where I was, and went into his house looking pleased. I had the feeling he needed it for something important.

Addendum

40.4 Aḥmad was sometimes so needy that he had to glean from the fields.[211]

[Al-Ṭarasūsī:] The man who gave lodging to Aḥmad told me: "When he came to stay here he went out to glean. He came back having collected only a little. I said to him, 'You've eaten more than you gleaned!'

"He said, 'I saw them doing something I couldn't bring myself to do: when they gleaned, they would crawl on all fours. But I dragged myself along sitting down.'"

40.5 [Al-Marrūdhī:] Aḥmad told me, "I walked out to the frontier on foot and we went gleaning. I saw people tearing up the fields. But no one should cross onto another's land without permission."

He also told me, "I walked all the way to Tarsus. We used to go out and glean."

Addendum

40.6 Aḥmad was sometimes so poor that he had to copy manuscripts for a fee. To meet his expenses while traveling, he once hired himself out to some camel drivers. This episode will be described in the next chapter, God willing.

Chapter 41

His Refusal to Accept Help Even in Distress

[Isḥāq ibn Rāhawayh:] When Aḥmad ibn Ḥanbal made the journey to study with ʿAbd al-Razzāq, he ran out of money, so he hired himself out to a camel driver for the duration of the journey to Sanaa. His companions had offered help, but he refused to accept anything from anyone. 41.1

[ʿAbd ibn Ḥumayd:] ʿAbd al-Razzāq told us: "Aḥmad ibn Ḥanbal came and stayed here for almost two years. At one point I said to him, 'Aḥmad, there's no way for you to make any money in this part of the world, so take this'"—and here ʿAbd al-Razzāq put out a handful of dinars to show us what he meant—"'and spend it on yourself!' But Aḥmad said, 'I'm fine,' and refused to accept anything from me." 41.2

[Al-Wāsiṭī:] I heard that Aḥmad ibn Ḥanbal, as he was leaving Yemen, pawned his sandals to a baker in exchange for some food. He also hired himself out to some camel drivers when he left. ʿAbd al-Razzāq offered him some perfectly good dirhams,[212] but he wouldn't take them. 41.3

[Al-Ramādī:] Once, in the village where ʿAbd al-Razzāq lived, we mentioned Ibn Ḥanbal, and Baḥr the greengrocer said, "Whatever happened to him?" 41.4

"How do you know who Aḥmad is?" I asked him.

"He was living here for a while," said the grocer. "When his friends left, he stayed behind. He came to me and said, 'Baḥr, I owe you a dirham, so take these sandals. I'll try to send you the money from Sanaa, but if I can't, sandals are worth a dirham.[213] Agreed?'

"I said yes and he left. Later I told ʿAbd al-Razzāq's nephew Hammām and he said, 'Why on earth did you let him give you the sandals?'"

[Al-Ramādī:] I once heard ʿAbd al-Razzāq, tears in his eyes, say of Aḥmad ibn Ḥanbal: "He came to me one day and said that his 41.5

money had run out. I found ten dinars and took him aside—behind closed doors, with no one else there—and said, 'I don't save money, but I did find these ten dinars in the women's quarters, so take them and make them last until I can find something more.' He smiled and said, 'Abū Bakr, if I were going to accept help from anyone, it would be you.' But he wouldn't take it."

[The author:] The two versions of the report are largely the same.

41.6 ['Abd Allāh:] My father told me, "Yazīd ibn Hārūn once offered me five hundred dirhams—more or less—but I didn't take it. He also offered money to Yaḥyā ibn Ma'īn and Abū Muslim al-Mustamlī, and they did."

41.7 [Al-Wāsiṭī:] Aḥmad ibn Ḥanbal and several others came to study with me, but their money ran out. I offered them money and they took it, except for Aḥmad, who came to me with a fur and said, "Ask someone to sell this for me. That will give me enough to live on."

I bundled up some dirhams and offered them to him, but he refused to take anything. My wife said, "He's a righteous man. Maybe it wasn't enough. Give him twice that." So I doubled the amount but he still wouldn't take it. Finally he took his fur and left.

41.8 [Ibrāhīm ibn Ḥassān:] I heard this story from a man who had known Aḥmad ibn Ḥanbal in Wāsiṭ, where they were students at the door of Yazīd ibn Hārūn. Aḥmad came to him with a cloak he wanted to sell even though it was the coldest time of year. "It took a while, but I persuaded him not to sell it. Then I went to Yazīd and said, 'Aḥmad ibn Ḥanbal just asked me to sell off his cloak—in this weather!'

"Yazīd told his servant to weigh out a hundred dirhams and bring them in. Then he gave the money to me and told me to pass it on Aḥmad. So I brought him the money and said, 'This is for you, from Yazīd.'

"'I do need it,' he said, 'and I am on a journey. But I don't want to get used to accepting help. Take it back!'

"So I took it back. Then he gave me his cloak and I sold it."

[Ṣāliḥ:] One day Ḥusn[214] came to me and said, "A man just came and left a basket of dried fruit and a note." 41.9

I read the note, which said:

> Aḥmad, I sold some merchandise in Samarqand worth such-and-such on your behalf and made a profit of such-and-such. Herewith are four thousand dirhams, which I'm sending to you along with some fruit I picked from my orchard, which belonged to my father and grandfather before me.

When he came home, I gathered the boys and went in to see him. "Dad," I said, "doesn't it hurt you to see me live on charity?" Putting the children in front of him, I wept.

"How did you find out?" he asked. Then he said, "Leave it be for now. Tonight I'll ask God what to do."

The next day, he said, "Ṣāliḥ, don't tell anyone about this. I asked God and He told me not to accept."

He opened the basket and gave the fruit to the children. Then he sent the money back, along with a ten-cubit robe he had. Later I heard that the man set the robe aside to use as a shroud.

[ʿAlī ibn al-Jahm:] A neighbor of ours once showed us a document and asked if we recognized the handwriting. 41.10

"Yes," we said, "it's Aḥmad ibn Ḥanbal's. But why did he write this for you?"

"We were staying with Sufyān ibn ʿUyaynah in Mecca," said the neighbor. "Aḥmad disappeared for a few days so we went to look for him. The people at the house where he was staying pointed out his room. We found the door ajar and saw that he was there, but dressed in rags.

"'Aḥmad,' we asked, 'what's going on? We haven't seen you in days.'

"'Someone stole my clothes.'

"'I have some dinars with me,' I said. 'Take it as a loan or a gift, whichever you prefer.'

"He refused to take the money, so I asked him if he would copy reports for a fee. He said he would, so I offered him a dinar, but he wouldn't take it.

"'Buy me a robe,' he said, 'and cut it in half,' gesturing to show that he meant to wear half of it as a breechclout and the other half as a shirt. 'And bring me the change,' he said.

"I did as he asked. Then I brought him some paper and he copied some texts for me, and here they are in his writing."

41.11 [Aḥmad ibn Muḥammad ibn Shāhīn:] I heard Aḥmad ibn Muḥammad ibn Ḥammād al-Muqri' say that 'Alī ibn al-Jahm once saw one of his neighbors carrying a document in Aḥmad's handwriting. He asked him where he had found Aḥmad ibn Ḥanbal's notebook.

"So you know his writing?" asked the man.

"I do."

"Well, this isn't Aḥmad's notebook," said the neighbor. "It's my notebook in his writing."

"How did that happen?"

"One year," said the man, "we were studying with Sufyān ibn 'Uyaynah. We were the only two from our neighborhood studying with him that year. Aḥmad disappeared for a few days and I went to go look for him. I followed people's directions until I ended up at a sort of cave in Jiyād with a lattice blocking the entrance.

"'Peace be upon you!' I called out.

"'And you,' came the reply.

"'May I come in?'

"'No,' he answered. A moment later he said, 'Now you may.'

"I went in and found him wrapped in a ragged piece of felt.

"'Why did you keep me waiting?' I asked.

"'So I could cover myself.'

"'What happened to you?'

"'Someone stole my clothes.'

"I rushed home and brought back a hundred dirhams wrapped in a piece of cloth. I offered it to him but he refused to take it. I told him he could pay me back, but he still refused. I tried offering him less, going all the way down to twenty, but it was no use. Finally I turned to go, saying, 'It's wrong for you to kill yourself when I'm here offering to help you!'

"'Come back,' he said.

"I turned back. He said, 'Didn't Ibn 'Uyaynah teach both of us a lot of Hadith reports?'

"'Of course.'

"'What if I copy them out for you?'

"'All right,' I said.

"'Buy some paper,' he said, 'and bring it here.'

"He wrote so many dirhams' worth (the man mentioned the amount). He spent twelve dirhams on two garments and kept the rest for expenses."

[Ismāʿīl ibn Abī l-Ḥārith:] We used to live near an elderly man 41.12
from Marv. One day Aḥmad ibn Ḥanbal went in to see him and then came out again and left.

"Why did Aḥmad come to see you?" I asked him.

"He's a friend," answered the old man. "We've known each other for a long time."

He kept on evading the question but we pestered him until he broke down.

"He had borrowed two or three hundred dirhams from me," he said, "and he came here to repay it. I told him I never intended for him to pay me back, but he said that he never intended not to."

[Ṣāliḥ:] In the days of al-Wāthiq, when we were living in condi- 41.13
tions best left to the imagination, I went into my father's room while he was away at afternoon prayers. He had a piece of felt that he used to sit on, so old that it was almost worn through. Under the felt I noticed a piece of paper with writing on it. It said:

> Aḥmad, we have learned that you are poor and in debt. We have sent So-and-So with four thousand dirhams to pay off your debt and take care of your family. This is neither charity nor alms-tax: it is an inheritance from my father.

I read the note and put it back. When my father came in I said, "Dad, what's this note?"

He blushed. "I was hoping you wouldn't see it." Then he said, "Deliver this reply." He wrote:

> We have received your letter in good health. The debt is owed to a man who will not press us, and the family enjoys the bounty of God, thanks be to Him.

I took this reply to the man who had delivered the original note. "What a shame!" he said. "Even if Aḥmad had accepted the gift and then thrown it into the Tigris, it would have been a good deed: this man never does anything for anybody."

Some time later, we received another letter saying the same thing. My father answered it as he had the first.

About a year later the subject came up, and my father said, "See? If we'd taken the money, it'd be gone by now."

41.14 [Ibn Abī Ḥātim:] I heard Aḥmad's son Ṣāliḥ report the very same story, except without the part where he says, "Even if Aḥmad had accepted the gift and then thrown it into the Tigris."

[The author:] Abū Bakr al-Khallāl also tells the story, adding that the would-be benefactor was al-Ḥasan ibn ʿĪsā ibn Māsarjis, the client of Ibn al-Mubārak.

41.15 [Al-Tirmidhī:] A friend arrived from Khurasan and told me that he had done some business with the intention of giving the profits to Aḥmad ibn Ḥanbal and made ten thousand dirhams on the deal. He asked me to take the money to Aḥmad.

"First let me go see how he feels about it," I said.

I went to him, greeted him, and mentioned the man's name. It turned out he knew of him.

"He's made a profit of ten thousand dirhams," I said, "and he wants to give it to you."

"May God reward him for his trouble!" said Aḥmad. "But we have all we need." He refused to take the money, God have mercy on him.

[The author:] The same story is told by Abū Bakr al-Khallāl, who cites al-Marrūdhī. The man is identified as Muḥammad ibn Sulaymān al-Sarakhsī. In this version, the narrator adds that the man tried again but Aḥmad replied: "Let me live with some self-respect."

[Al-Barbarī:] Al-Ḥasan ibn ʿAbd al-ʿAzīz al-Jarawī inherited a hundred thousand dinars, which was delivered to him from Egypt. To Aḥmad ibn Ḥanbal he sent three sacks, each containing a thousand dinars. 41.16

"It's from a legitimate inheritance," he said. "Take it and support your family."

"I don't need it," he replied. "I have enough."

He returned the money and refused to take anything from the man.

[Ṣāliḥ:] I was there when Ibn al-Jarawī, the brother of al-Ḥasan, came to see my father after the sunset prayer. 41.17

"Everybody knows who I am," said al-Jarawī. "I've come here today because I want to give you something. It's money I've inherited, and I'd like you to accept it."

He kept insisting until finally my father got up and went back inside.

Later al-Ḥasan told me that his brother told him, "I saw that the more I insisted the more distant he got, so I figured I would tell him how much it was. I said, 'Aḥmad, we're talking about three thousand dinars.' That's when he walked out."

Abū Nuʿaym added that Ṣāliḥ said, "One day my father said to me, 'When there's not a single coin in the house, I'm happy.'"

[Al-Jarawī:] I went to Aḥmad ibn Ḥanbal and said, "This is a thousand dinars. Take it and buy a property to support the children." But he refused to take it. 41.18

He always used to welcome me, but after that, he said, "If you need something, I'd prefer you didn't come here in person. If you want to ask me about something send a message." So I ended up depriving myself of his company.

41.19 [Ismāʿīl ibn Ḥarb:] Somebody made an estimate of how much money Aḥmad turned down after he was brought to Samarra. It turned out to be seventy thousand.

41.20 [Ṣāliḥ:] One day I was with my father and the women of the house called me in.

"Tell your father that we're out of flour"—or maybe "bread."

I told him, and he said, "I'll take care of it right away."

He didn't, and so they called me back in. I told him again, and he said, "Right away."

At that moment came a knock on the door. I went out and found a man from Khurasan dressed like a courier and carrying a staff with a sack tied onto it.

"What can I do for you?" I asked him.

"I need to see Aḥmad ibn Ḥanbal."

I went in and told my father.

"Go out and ask him what he wants. Is it a legal problem or a Hadith?"

The man said it was neither, and my father said, "Bring him in."

The man came in, put down the staff and the bag, and asked, "Are you Aḥmad ibn Muḥammad ibn Ḥanbal?"

"Yes."

"I'm from Khurasan. One of my neighbors got sick and I went to visit him. I asked him if there was anything I could do, and he said, 'See this five thousand dirhams? When I'm dead, take it and give it to Aḥmad ibn Ḥanbal.' So here I am with the money, all the way from Khurasan."

"Was this man any relation of mine?"

"No."

"Was he a member of the family?"

"No."

"Is he returning some favor we did for him?"[215]

"No."

"So take it back, and thank you."

The man resisted and my father spoke to him roughly. Finally he took the money and left.

Some time later he was sitting and looking at his books when he raised his head and remarked, "Ṣāliḥ, do you know how long it's been since that man from Khurasan was here?"

"No."

"Today makes sixty-one days. Have you been hungry once during that time, or needed anything and not had it?"

['Abd Allāh:] I heard Fūrān report, "'Aḥmad got sick"—this was before the year 200—"and a lot of people came to call on him. One of them was 'Alī ibn al-Ja'd, who left a little bag at his bedside. I told Aḥmad about it, and he said, 'Return it to him just the way you found it.' So I went and returned it." 41.21

[Ṣāliḥ:] Fūrān said to my father, "I've got some shoes I'll send you." 41.22

My father said nothing. Fūrān said it again, and my father replied, "Don't! The thought of them is distracting me."

Another time a man sent Chinese paper to a number of Hadith-men, including Yaḥyā. He sent a crate of it to my father, who refused it.

My father once told me, "Not since Ibn al-Mubārak has anyone like Ibn Ma'īn come out of Khurasan. Well, his son came to me and said that his father wanted to send me a jacket to remember him by. I told him to bring it. But when he arrived with a whole bundle of clothes, I told him, 'Thank you and good-bye.'"

By that he meant that he refused to take it.

[Muḥammad ibn Mūsā:] I heard Ibn Nayzak say, "I was following Aḥmad and Yaḥyā to Ibn Sa'duwayh's"—or someone else's place. "He"—I think it was Sa'duwayh—"had prepared a pot of food for them. When Aḥmad realized what was going on, he said, 'It's almost prayer time,' and went out. No one dared say anything. He went to a public conduit[216] where there was a pitcher. There he took out some crumbs of bread he had wrapped in a rag. He filled a jug from the pitcher and ate the crumbs out of his hand, washing them down 41.23

with water. Afterward he prayed the afternoon prayer. Then, after the others had eaten and said their prayers, he came back, asked permission to enter, sat down, and began writing."

41.24 [Ḥumayd ibn al-Rabīʿ al-Kūfī:] One day Aḥmad asked the Hadith-men whether any of them lived in al-Karkh.

"I do," said one young man.

"Stay after," he said. "I need you to do something."

Aḥmad gave the young man some dirhams and told him to buy paper and bring it next time.

The young man went and bought the paper. He also hid a number of dirhams between the pages.[217] Then he came back and gave it to Aḥmad. After that he stopped coming.

Some time later, Aḥmad opened up the paper and the coins went flying. After he had gathered them up, he asked the Hadith-men if they knew the young man who had bought the paper.

"I know where he lives," said one man.

"Stay after," he said. "I need you to do something."

Picking up the money, Aḥmad followed the man out. When they reached Qaṭīʿat al-Rabīʿ, they found the young man sitting there.

"That's the one you want," said the man.

"You can go now," said Aḥmad. Then he went over to the young man, greeted him, dumped the money in his lap, and left.

41.25 [Al-Tustarī:] There was a boy who used to come to Ibn Ḥanbal's circle. One day Aḥmad gave him two dirhams and said, "Buy me some paper."

The boy went out and bought the paper. Then he put five hundred dinars inside it, rolled it up and tied it, and sent it to Aḥmad's house.

Later Aḥmad asked if anything white had been delivered. "Yes," he was told, and the package was brought over to him. No sooner had he opened it than the coins went flying. After he had put them all back, he went looking for the boy. When he found him, he put the package down in front of him and walked away. The boy ran after him, saying, "The paper's yours— I bought it with the two dirhams you gave me!" But Aḥmad wouldn't take the paper either.

[Al-Marrūdhī:] I was told that when Aḥmad was sent back from the frontier, Abū Bakr al-Mustamlī went with him to look after him. He told the following story. 41.26

"When we stopped at one of the way stations, we found that one of his friends had sent him a hundred dinars, telling him to spend it on his travels. But he wouldn't take it. I said, 'Aḥmad, I'm a frontiersman with mouths to feed. Let me take it!'

"'That won't do,' he said. 'What they give you the first time isn't like the second.[218] Better to live with some dignity.'

"Then he sent it back."

['Abd Allāh:] One night we heard a tapping on the door. I opened it and saw a man putting down a large footed tray covered with a white cloth. "Take this," he said, then ran off before I could say anything. 41.27

It was a big tray. I brought it inside and put it in front of my father.

"What's this?" he asked. "Did it come from Abū Muḥammad's house?"—meaning Fūrān's.

"No," I said.

"Where, then? Who brought it here?"

"Whoever it was put it down and left."

Under the cloth was some wholesome-looking food, along with goblets of sweets that had clearly cost someone a lot of money.

My father sat for a while, thinking hard. Finally he said, "Send some of it to your uncle's house and give some to Ṣāliḥ's children," pointing to the girl and the boys. "Take some for yourself, too."

Later I found out where it had come from.

Several people used to send him gifts but he would never partake. 'Abdūs al-'Aṭṭār often sent things, but he would never taste them.

Chapter 42

His Generosity

42.1 [Al-Ṭarasūsī:] Aḥmad ibn Ḥanbal once dropped a pair of clippers[219] into the well. One of his tenants came along and fished it out. Aḥmad immediately handed him some money—half a dirham, more or less.

"The clippers aren't worth more than a *qīrāṭ*,"[220] said the man. "I won't take anything."

A few days later, Aḥmad asked him, "How much rent do you owe on your shop?"

"Three months' worth," said the man, "at three dirhams a month."[221]

"Consider it paid," said Aḥmad, drawing a line through his account.

42.2 [ʿAbd Allāh:] Abū Saʿīd ibn Abī Ḥanīfah al-Muʾaddib told me, "When I used to come see your father, he would often give me things and say, 'This is half of what we've got in the house.' One day I came and stayed for a long time. He brought out four loaves of bread and said, 'This is half of what we have.'

"'I'd rather have these four from you,' I told him, 'than four thousand from anyone else.'"

42.3 [Al-Warrāq:] I once went to Muḥammad ibn ʿAbd Allāh ibn Numayr to ask for help. He gave me four or five dirhams, saying, "This is half of what I have."

Another time I went to Aḥmad ibn Muḥammad ibn Ḥanbal. He took out four dirhams and said, "This is all I have."

[Al-Mustamlī:] I once told Aḥmad that we had nothing left. He gave me five dirhams and said, "This is all I've got."

42.4 [Al-Marrūdhī:] Aḥmad often used to give away food. One day, Abū Saʿīd al-Ḍarīr came to ask for help.

"All I've got," said Aḥmad, "is this tree trunk. Bring a porter and take it."[222]

I sold it for nine dirhams and two *dāniq*s.[223]

Aḥmad was of the kindest and most unassuming disposition, and it always made him happy to give things away.

[Al-Nasāʾī:] Once during a feast day, Aḥmad invited me in. I went in and saw a table table and a dish with some bones in it sitting on a footed tray, and a pot off to the side. 42.5

"Have something to eat," he said. Seeing that I was too shy to join him, he said, "Al-Ḥasan used to say, 'Let us eat, by God!' And Ibn Sīrīn used to say, 'Food is there to be eaten.' And Ibrāhīm ibn Adham used to sell pieces of his clothing and spend the money on his friends. For him, the things of this world were worth no more than that," pointing to a discarded length of palm trunk.

Hearing all that, I relaxed and ate.

[ʿAlī ibn Yaḥyā:] I prayed the Friday prayer next to Aḥmad ibn Ḥanbal. After the imam had dismissed the congregation, a beggar stood up and asked for alms. Aḥmad found a coin and gave it to him. A man then said to the beggar, "I'll give you a dirham for that coin." He kept upping the amount and finally reached fifty dirhams before the beggar said, "I'm not giving it up. I want it for the same reason you do!"[224] 42.6

[Al-Marrūdhī:] I was with Aḥmad on the way to Samarra when we stopped at a way station. I took out a loaf of flatbread and put a jug of water before him. Then a dog appeared. It stood beside him on its hind legs and started wagging its tail. He tossed it a bit of food. Soon he was tossing it a bit to eat for every bite he took himself. Afraid that at that rate Aḥmad would starve, I got up and shooed the dog away. Then I looked and saw that Aḥmad was red with embarrassment. "Let it be," he said. "According to Ibn ʿAbbās, they have malicious souls."[225] 42.7

Chapter 43
His Accepting Gifts and Giving Gifts in Return

43.1 [Ṣāliḥ:] A man whose wife had just had a baby gave my father a footed tray of honey nut pudding. In return my father gave him some sugar worth a good deal of money.

43.2 [Ṣāliḥ:] Someone sent my father some fruit as a gift. In return, my father sent him an entire garment.

43.3 [Al-Marrūdhī:] I remember that Aḥmad, when a man made him a gift of some water from Zamzam, reciprocated by sending him barley meal and sugar. Once he told me to spend five dirhams on a gift for someone, saying, "Go see his children, since he gave Sa'īd[226] a gift."

43.4 [Isḥāq ibn Ibrāhīm:] One of Aḥmad's neighbors, a man named Jūwīn,[227] gave him some walnuts, raisins, and figs in a bowl, the lot worth three dirhams or less. Aḥmad gave me a dinar and said, "Go buy ten dirhams' worth of sugar and seven dirhams' worth of dates, and drop it off at his place at night."

I did as he asked.

43.5 [Ibrāhīm ibn Hāni':] A man from Samarqand came with a letter of recommendation from 'Abd Allāh ibn 'Abd al-Raḥmān, so Aḥmad ibn Ḥanbal agreed to teach him. One day the man gave him a garment as a gift. Aḥmad gave it to my father and said, "Take it to the market and find out what it's worth."

My father said, "I took it to the market and they told me it was worth twenty-some dirhams, and I came back and told Aḥmad. He stopped letting the man in until he could buy two garments and two face veils—or a garment and a face veil—to give him in return. Once he had sent the gifts, he allowed the man in again to hear Hadith."

43.6 [Ḥanbal:] Aḥmad had a friend named Maḥfūẓ who had traveled with him to study with 'Abd al-Razzāq. The two had a real liking for each other. One day, a messenger of his appeared out of nowhere bringing some baskets of premium Barnī dates. I went in and told Aḥmad. He accepted the gift, but he sent Maḥfūẓ a garment in return. Maḥfūẓ came to see him and said, "Aḥmad, your gift distressed me."

"And yours distressed me too," he replied.

Chapter 44

His Renunciation[228]

44.1 [Ibn al-Ashʿath:] I don't think I ever heard Aḥmad ibn Ḥanbal mention the things of this world.

44.2 [ʿUmar ibn Sulaymān:] I performed the Ramadan nighttime prayers with Aḥmad ibn Ḥanbal, led by Ibn ʿUmayr. When he performed his additional night prayer, he clasped his hands to his chest. He and the others at the mosque prayed so softly that I couldn't hear anything they said. The mosque had no hanging lamps,[229] mats, or incense[230]—only a lamp placed on the step.

44.3 [Al-Samarqandī:] I once asked Abū Muḥammad ʿAbd Allāh ibn ʿAbd al-Raḥmān about Aḥmad ibn Ḥanbal.

"Is he an exemplar?"

"Indeed he was, by God: he suffered poverty for seventy years!"

44.4 [Ṣāliḥ:] I once said to my father, "I heard that Aḥmad al-Dawraqī got a thousand dinars."

He replied: «The provision of your Lord is better and more lasting.»[231]

I also mentioned Ibn Abī Shaybah, ʿAbd al-Aʿlā l-Narsī, and the other Hadith-men who had been taken to Samarra.

"It didn't take long," he said, "before all of them started climbing over each other to go there, but none of them got much out of it."

On another occasion, when someone was described as successful, my father said, "Son, success means being successful in the end without owing anything to anybody."

44.5 [Ibn Abī l-Qudūr:] When prices were high, Aḥmad would come to me with woven cloth which he would hide on his person and have me sell for him. Sometimes I would get a dirham and a half for it and sometimes two dirhams. One day he didn't come to see me. The next day, I said, "Aḥmad, where were you yesterday?"

"Umm Ṣāliḥ was sick."

He gave me some woven cloth, which I sold for four dirhams. When I brought it to him, he didn't like it.

"You didn't add any of your own money, did you?" he asked.

"No," I replied. "It was finely woven."

44.6 [Ṣāliḥ:] My father said, "When prices were high, your mother would weave fine cloth. She'd sell four and a half *mithqāls*[232] for about two dirhams, and that's how we'd eat."

My father once came into my house after we had put in a new ceiling. He called me over and dictated the following report: "We heard Sulaymān ibn Ḥarb report that he heard Ḥammād ibn Salamah report, citing Yūnus, citing al-Ḥasan, that al-Aḥnaf ibn Qays returned from a journey to find that they had put a new roof on his house and painted some of the planks red and green.[233] They told him to look at it, and he said, 'I'm sorry I didn't notice. Anyway, I can't come in until you change it.'

"When I bought a slave woman, my wife complained to him about it. He said, 'I've always tried to keep them away from the things of this world. But I haven't heard the same about you.'

"My wife said, 'Is there anyone besides you who hates having money?'

"'Deal with her yourself, then,' he replied.[234]

"We often bought things and hid them so he wouldn't find out about them and rebuke us."

44.7 [Al-Marrūdhī:] When we were in Samarra, Aḥmad ibn ʿĪsā l-Miṣrī and a number of other Hadith-men came to see Aḥmad.

"Why do you look so upset?" asked al-Miṣrī. "Islam is the one true faith, without harshness or constraint, and there's room in it for everyone."

Aḥmad, who was lying down, simply stared at them. After they had left, he said, "Did you see them? I don't want any of them in here again."[235]

[Al-Naysābūrī:] Aḥmad once said to me, "Some morning, come by early and we'll compare our copies of *Renunciation*." 44.8

So I went to see him early one morning. I asked his son's mother[236] to bring me a mat and a pillow, and I put them out in the anteroom. Then Aḥmad came out with the book and his inkpot. When he saw the mat and the pillow, he said, "What's this?"

"For you to sit on," I said.

"Take it away," he said. "We can't study renunciation without renouncing."

So I took the things away and Aḥmad sat down on the ground.

[Al-Sarī ibn Muḥammad:] One day Aḥmad's grandson came over 44.9
to help him with his ablutions.[237] Seeing that his grandfather had taken a wet rag and put it on his head, he asked him if he had a fever.

"What would I get a fever from?" he replied.[238]

[Ibn Jabalah:] I was at Aḥmad ibn Ḥanbal's front door, which was 44.10
ajar, and I heard his son's mother[239] telling him, "Here I am suffering with you, but over at Ṣāliḥ's house they've got plenty to eat," and so on and so forth.

"Speak no ill," he kept telling her.

When he came out, his little boy came out with him and began crying.

"What do you want?" he asked him.

"Raisins!" cried the boy.

"Go tell the grocer," said Aḥmad, "to give you a *ḥabbah*'s worth."[240]

[Hāniʾ:] When he returned from Samarra, Aḥmad told me to go to 44.11
the bathhouse and ask the man who ran it to clear the place for him. So I went and asked, and the man agreed. I went back and told Aḥmad, who said, "It's been fifty years since I've entered a bathhouse.[241] I might as well not go now, either. Tell him to open it up again." So I did.

44.12 [Ṣāliḥ:] My father used to depilate himself at home. One winter day he said, "After sunset I want to go to the bathhouse, so go tell the owner."

But after sunset, he said, "Let him know I've changed my mind," and depilated himself at home.

44.13 ['Abd Allāh:] One day when I was sitting with my father he looked at my feet, which were smooth and had no cracks on the soles.

"Look at those feet!" he said. "Why don't you walk barefoot and toughen them up?"

44.14 [Al-Marrūdhī:] I heard Aḥmad say to Shujā' ibn Makhlad al-'Aṭṭār, "What difference does it make what I eat or what I wear? It will all be over soon enough."

44.15 [Al-Marrūdhī:] I heard Aḥmad say, "My happiest days are when I wake up with nothing in the house."

Chapter 45

His House and Furniture[242]

45.1 ['Alī ibn al-Madīnī:] When I saw Aḥmad ibn Ḥanbal's house, all I could think of was how much it resembled Suwayd ibn Ghafalah's, which was said to be very humble and sparsely furnished.

[The author:] Suwayd ibn Ghafalah was one of the great Successors. He set out on behalf of his tribe to see the Emissary of God, who died before his arrival. He became a companion of Abū Bakr, 'Umar, 'Uthmān, and 'Alī. He was a great renouncer of the world.

45.2 ['Imrān ibn Muslim:] Whenever Suwayd ibn Ghafalah heard it said that So-and-So had received a sum, or So-and-So had been appointed to an office, he remarked, "A crust and a bit of salt are enough for me."

45.3 [Al-Maymūnī:] Aḥmad's house was small and cramped. Even in the heat he would sleep downstairs. His uncle told me that he was always telling him to sleep upstairs but he wouldn't.[243] I saw where he slept, too. All he had was a quilt[244] and a dirty mattress.[245]

[Ḥasan ibn Sayyār:] When I was an apprentice, I went with my master to plaster a room for Aḥmad ibn Ḥanbal. Aḥmad told him to plaster it by hand, not with a trowel. We also tiled the floor. When we were finished, he looked pleased and said, "That's good and clean. A man can pray on that." 45.4

There were no mats or floor coverings in the room.

He gave me a handful of dates.

[Al-Ḥasan ibn Muḥammad ibn al-Ḥārith:] I once went into Aḥmad's house. In the open space inside, I saw a threadbare mat and a leather cushion, with his books and papers scattered all around it. There was also a clay water jug. 45.5

[Ibn ʿAbd al-Ḥamīd:] Aḥmad had an arched doorway inside his house. I noticed he had hung a hair-cloth across the entrance.[246] 45.6

[Abū Dāwūd:] I noticed that the door of Aḥmad's house had a matted, threadbare cloth hanging across it. Nearby I saw something like the stands that travelers use, with several jars on it. 45.7

[Muḥammad ibn Mūsā:] Aḥmad had a big doorway made of brick. When I saw it some time later, he had stretched a curtain of hair-cloth across it. 45.8

[Al-Zuhrī:] Aḥmad once said, as he led me into his house, "See this doorway of mine? I went into debt to build it."[247] 45.9

[Aḥmad ibn al-Ḥasan:] More than once I found Aḥmad sitting cross-legged on a small piece of felt cloth he owned, in front of a three-legged coal-pan[248] made of clay, with embers in it. 45.10

Chapter 46
His Diet

[Ṣāliḥ:] I remember seeing my father take dry crusts of bread, dust them off, put them in a dish, and pour some water over them to soften them. Then he'd eat them with salt. I never saw him buy pomegranates, quinces, or any other fruit except for melons, which he'd eat with bread, and grapes or dates, but that's all. Sometimes people would prepare dishes for him in the oven. He'd put lentils, 46.1

suet, and Shihrīz dates into a clay pot, and set aside a dish for the children. He would call them and put the dish in front of them, but they would laugh and refuse to eat any of it. He'd often dip his bread in vinegar. They could buy him a dirham's worth of suet and it would last him a month. After he got away from al-Mutawakkil he started fasting and stopped eating fat. I had the feeling that he had vowed that if he survived he would give up eating fat.

46.2 [Al-Marrūdhī:] Al-Naysābūrī, who worked for Isḥāq ibn Ibrāhīm, told me that the emir said, "When Aḥmad's family brings him a meal, let me see it."

What they brought him turned out to be two loaves of flatbread and a cucumber. When I showed the food to the emir, he said, "If he can live on that, we'll never win him over."[249]

46.3 [Al-Marrūdhī:] Once during the festival I heard Aḥmad say, "Yesterday they bought beans for us, and they were quite good."[250]

46.4 [Abū l-Sarī:] Aḥmad and I were once at Abū Bakr al-Aḥwal's house for his son's circumcision. I was sitting by Aḥmad at the table. He was eating, but then when they brought out a honey nut pudding, he stopped. When Abū Bakr urged him to have some, saying that it was a first-rate dish, he took just one bite.

46.5 [Al-Ḥasan ibn Khalaf:] During Aḥmad's illness, al-Marrūdhī came to me for help, so I found the doctor and we went to Aḥmad's house. The doctor asked him how he was feeling.

"I had myself cupped yesterday," he said.

"What did you eat afterward?"

"Bread and fermented grain paste."[251]

"What?" exclaimed the doctor. "You have yourself cupped and then eat only bread and grain paste?"

"What else am I supposed to eat?" asked Aḥmad.

46.6 [Ḥanbal:] When Aḥmad fell ill, ʿAbd al-Raḥmān prescribed almond oil,[252] but he refused to drink it, saying he wanted sesame oil instead. His condition grew worse and so they prepared it for him, but when he realized what it was he pushed it away.

[Al-Marrūdhī:] I heard Aḥmad say, "My hands and feet are cold. It must be the vinegar and salt I put on my bread." 46.7

Isḥāq ibn Ibrāhīm ibn Hāni' reported: "Aḥmad never ate anything cooked with pepper or garlic. Once I had dinner with him and some of his relatives. As we talked, I noticed that after every bite, he would wipe his hand on a napkin and say 'God be thanked!' Later he said to me, 'Eating with thanks is better than eating in silence.'" 46.8

Chapter 47
His Indulgences

[Ṣāliḥ:] When my father got sick, he let them take care of him. To keep him warm in winter, they would buy thorn-bush roots and burn them in a narrow coal-pan. 47.1

[Al-Muṭawwiʿī:] My father reported that Aḥmad ibn Ḥanbal didn't eat pudding with a spoon. Instead, he would eat it out of his hand. He also said that he ate thin flatbread. 47.2

"How do you know?" I asked.

"Once I happened to be outside his door just after his son Ṣāliḥ had done some baking for him. A beggar came to the door begging, and they sent out a crust of flatbread. I realized that Aḥmad must eat the same thing, since the Prophet, God bless and keep him, said, 'Don't give away anything you don't eat.'"

Chapter 48
His Clothing[253]

[Al-Maymūnī:] Aḥmad ibn Ḥanbal wore garments of a medium length.[254] His outermost garment[255] was worth fifteen dirhams, while his tunic[256] was of the sort that could be bought for about a dinar. The tunic was neither too fine nor too coarse. His outermost garment was fringed. 48.1

48.2 [Ḥamdan ibn ʿAlī:] Aḥmad's clothing was nothing special, beyond being of clean cotton. Toward the end of his life, after his sons no longer depended on his income and he could spend it on himself, he wore clothing of better quality.

48.3 [Al-Fadl ibn Ziyād:] I remember seeing Aḥmad dressed for winter in two long tunics, with a colored gown between them. He often wore a tunic and a heavy fur: when it got very cold, I would see him wearing the fur over his gown. I also saw him wearing a heavy wrap, with a turban wound around his cap.[257]

One day I heard Abū ʿImrān al-Wirkānī say to him, "That's quite a lot you've got on!" He laughed and said, "I don't like the cold."

He often wore a cap without winding a turban around it.

48.4 [Jaʿfar ibn Muḥammad:] I saw Aḥmad wearing a tightly threaded striped gown[258] and a cap with a turban. In the winter he sometimes wore a fur, sometimes a gown, and sometimes both.

48.5 [Muḥammad ibn Mughīrah:] I saw Aḥmad wearing a tunic, trousers, and a mantle[259] in the summer. He sometimes wore a tunic with a mantle thrown over it, often wearing the mantle directly over the tunic.

48.6 [Ḥanbal:] I saw Aḥmad wearing a pair of trousers pulled up above the waist, with a tunic on top.

48.7 [Al-Maymūnī:] I saw Aḥmad preside over a gathering of Hadith transmitters and other people while wearing one breechclout around his waist and another draped over his shoulder. I never saw him wear a cowl or shawl,[260] or a proper mantle, only a small breechclout that looked six cubits long. I asked his uncle about it and he confirmed that it was six cubits.[261]

48.8 [Ibn ʿAbd al-Ḥamīd:] I saw Aḥmad one summer day wearing a tunic and a breechclout tied around his waist. I never saw him with his sleeves unrolled (when he was out walking, that is).

48.9 [Ibn al-Ashʿath:] I used to see Aḥmad wearing his breechclout loosely draped.

48.10 [Ṣāliḥ:] My father had a cap he had sewed himself. It was lined with cotton. When he got up at night he would put it on.

[Aḥmad ibn al-Ḥusayn:] I saw one of Aḥmad's caps. It had one patch of striped cloth and another of Marawī[262] white. 48.11

[Ibn Zanjuwayh:] I saw Aḥmad wearing a green gown patched with a piece of white wool. 48.12

[Ḥamdān ibn ʿAlī:] I saw Aḥmad wearing a gown patched in a different color. 48.13

[Al-Marrūdhī:] Aḥmad needed to patch his shirt but didn't have a patch, so he decided to cut a patch from his breechclout. We cut it for him and sewed on the patch. More than once, when he needed a scrap of cloth, he cut it from his breechclout. 48.14

Once he asked me to repair some leather shoes he had worn for seventeen years. From the stitching on the outside I could see that they had already been repaired five or six times already.

[Ibn Maʿbad:] I saw Abū ʿAbd Allāh wearing yellow sandals. 48.15

[Al-Marrūdhī:] I once brought Aḥmad a new pair of leather shoes that had been made for him. He kept them overnight, but in the morning he said: "I've been thinking about those shoes"—he may even have said "most of the night"—"and couldn't sleep, so I've decided not to wear them. How much time do I have left, anyway? More than half my life is over." 48.16

Taking a battered old pair of shoes he had, he said, "Here, slap some patches onto these." He added, "Do you know how long I've had these? More than sixteen years, and they were used when I got them. These here"—meaning the new ones—"were weighing on my mind."

[Al-Muzanī:] I once noticed that Aḥmad wore trousers that ended above the ankle. 48.17

[Al-Marrūdhī:] I saw Aḥmad wearing a *murabbaʿ*[263] outer garment. He often put the end of it under his feet when he prayed. 48.18

Chapter 49

His Scrupulosity

49.1 [Al-Dūrī:] When Aḥmad ibn Ḥanbal wrote me a letter of introduction to some Hadith transmitters in Basra, he called me simply "someone seeking Hadith."

49.2 [Muḥammad ibn Ibrāhīm:] I heard that when Aḥmad ibn Ḥanbal was visited by a group of his fellow Hadith-men, he bought them something to eat using only the money he had on hand.[264] I also heard that when al-Mutawakkil brought him to Samarra he refused to touch anything prepared at the palace, and made a *kaylajah*—a fourth of barley meal[265]—last for fifteen days while he waited for money to reach him from Baghdad.

49.3 [Isḥāq ibn Mūsā l-Anṣārī:] Al-Ma'mūn gave me some money and ordered me to distribute it to the Hadith-men, "since some of them are poor."

Every one of them accepted some money—except for Aḥmad ibn Ḥanbal, who refused to touch it.

49.4 [Fūrān:] We were at Aḥmad ibn Ḥanbal's two nights before he died. With us was a young black slave whom his uncle Abū Yūsuf had bought with the money given him by al-Mutawakkil. The slave wanted to fan Aḥmad but he told him not to.

49.5 ['Abd Allāh:] When I was ill, my father came to check on me.

"Dad," I said, "we still have some of the money al-Mutawakkil gave us. What if I used it to make the pilgrimage?"

"You should," he said.

"But if you don't mind spending it," I asked, "why don't *you* take it?"

"I don't consider it forbidden, son," he answered. "But I'd rather abstain."

49.6 [Muḥammad ibn 'Ubayd Allāh:] Aḥmad ibn Ḥanbal told me, "Every year I survey the house I live in and pay the alms-tax on it, following what 'Umar ibn al-Khaṭṭāb said about the Black Land in Iraq."[266]

[Muḥammad ibn Yūnus:] Sulaymān ibn Dāwūd al-Shādhakūnī once told me, "Have you seen ʿAlī ibn al-Madīnī trying to emulate Aḥmad ibn Ḥanbal? That'll be the day! They're like chalk and cheese.[267] Once in Mecca I saw firsthand how scrupulous Aḥmad is. He had pawned a copper pail to a fruit-and-nut vendor so he could buy something to eat. When he had enough money to redeem the pail, he went to the vendor, who held out two of them and said, 'Take whichever one is yours.' 49.7

"'I can't tell,' said Aḥmad. 'Keep it, and keep the money.'

"So he left his pail.

"'One was his, I swear,' said the vendor. 'I was just testing him!'"

[Al-Ṭūsī:] Whenever he saw a Christian, Aḥmad ibn Ḥanbal would close his eyes. Asked why, he said, "I can't look at anyone who lies about God." 49.8

[ʿAbd Allāh:] Even with all the Hadith my father knew, there were fewer than a hundred reports I ever saw him recite without using a book. 49.9

[Al-Madīnī:] Aḥmad ibn Ḥanbal has a better memory than any of us, but I've heard that he only recites Hadith out of books—an example all of us should follow. 49.10

[Ibrāhīm ibn Jābir al-Marwazī:] We used to sit with Aḥmad ibn Ḥanbal and go over Hadith reports until we knew them well and could recite them correctly. Whenever we wanted to write something down, he would say, "The book remembers it better than we do." Then he would jump up to get the book. 49.11

[Al-Marrūdhī:] I once heard Aḥmad ibn Ḥanbal say, "I had to borrow sixty-five dirhams to spend on this entranceway, but all I get on the building is a quarter of the rent." 49.12

"Why didn't you let ʿAbd Allāh pay for it?" I said.

"I don't want him to taint my money."[268]

[Al-Tustari:] I heard that Aḥmad ibn Ḥanbal once went three days without eating and sent a message to a friend asking to borrow some flour. Realizing that he was starving, his family quickly baked 49.13

something for him. When they put the dish in front of him, he asked how they had managed to bake so fast.

"The oven in Ṣāliḥ's house was already warm," they told him.

"Take this away!" he said, and refused to touch it. Then he ordered them to seal up the door that joined his house to Ṣāliḥ's.[269]

49.14 [Al-Marrūdhī:] During Aḥmad's final illness, I heard him say to his wife, "Who told you to bake anything there?"—meaning at his son Ṣāliḥ's house. She had baked something there once before and he had refused to touch it, saying, "Who's going to eat that?"

49.15 [Al-Marrūdhī:] I was once with Aḥmad somewhere and he recited, «You lived in the dwellings of those who wronged themselves,»[270] adding, "We certainly have," or "That's where we are."

49.16 [Isḥāq ibn Ibrāhīm:] Aḥmad once sent me with three or four coins to buy spices for the cooking pot. Then gave me another coin and said, "Buy spices with this one too, but don't mix them with the others."

But the spices did get mixed up. When I brought them back and told him, he said, "Return what you bought and get the money back." I did, and he tossed it in with the money he paid the servant girl, since he couldn't sort out which coins were tainted.

49.17 [Ibn Hāni':] Aḥmad once gave me a coin and said, "Take this and buy me some beans in water."

Ḥusn, his son's mother, gave me another coin and said, "Take this and buy some beans for me too."

Aḥmad added, "And buy some beans in oil for the boys."

I ended up with one or two *ḥabbah*s in change from the coin I had spent on the beans in oil, so I told the bean vendor to give me some more oil. I took the oil and poured it over the beans I had bought for Aḥmad. When I brought the food back and put it in front of him, he noticed the trace of oil and asked, "What's this?"

I said, "There was a *ḥabbah* left over from the boys' coin so I spent it on oil for you."

"Take it away, you idiot," he said. "Who told you to do that? When are you going to learn?"

He didn't eat any of it.

[Al-Simsār:] I heard Aḥmad say to Isḥāq ibn Ibrāhīm al-Naysābūrī, "Go to Umm ʿAlī"—meaning his daughter—"and take whatever she gives you." 49.18

Isḥāq went in and came back out carrying a chicken. Then he and I left together.

"What did Umm ʿAlī say?" I asked him.

"She said her father needs a cupping but has no money, and asked her to give me the chicken and have me sell it."

When we got the chicken to market, Isḥāq was offered a dirham and two *dāniq*s for it, but changed his mind about the sale and took it back.

At the bridge, we ran across Aḥmad's son ʿAbd Allāh, who was sitting at Ibn Bukhtān's shop. He called Isḥāq over and asked, "Why are carrying a chicken? And whose is it?"

I told him that Umm ʿAlī had given it to us to sell.

"How much did you get for it?"

"We were offered a dirham and two *dāniq*s."

"Give it to me for one and a half."

Isḥāq took the money and gave him the chicken. When we got back, Umm ʿAlī asked him how much he'd gotten.

"One and a half dirhams."

"That's all?"

"The offer I got at the market was only a dirham and two *dāniq*s."

Then Aḥmad ibn Ḥanbal asked, "Who bought it?"

"Your son ʿAbd Allāh."

When he heard that, Aḥmad grabbed the money back from Umm ʿAlī. "Go," he shouted at me, "and return it!"

Isḥāq went running back to ʿAbd Allāh.

"Take your money back!" he said. "Your father shouted at me over it."

"Why did you tell him it was me?" asked ʿAbd Allāh, but took the money back.

Isḥāq continued the story:

[Isḥāq:] Aḥmad ibn Ḥanbal told me to go back to the market and keep his son out of it. So I sold the chicken to someone I didn't know for a dirham and a third, and then went back to Aḥmad.

"You'd better not have sold it to ʿAbd Allāh," he said.

"No," I replied. "I sold it to a stranger."

49.19 [Al-Simsār:] ʿAbd Allāh's mother had a house next to ours in the lane. The house had been part of Aḥmad's inheritance, and so he collected a dirham in rent on it. At one point she needed money and ʿAbd Allāh gave it to her. After that, Aḥmad stopped taking the dirham from her, saying that it was now tainted.[271]

49.20 [Muḥammad ibn ʿAlī:] Ṣāliḥ reported that when his father got sick, ʿAbd al-Raḥmān the healer advised him to roast a gourd and drink the juice.

"He told me not to cook it in my house or in ʿAbd Allāh's," said Ṣāliḥ.

I heard Abū Bakr al-Marrūdhī say that he took it and cooked it and brought it back to him.

49.21 [Ibn ʿAyyāsh:] Aḥmad sent me to buy him a single coin's worth of clarified butter. I brought it to him wrapped in a green leaf.[272] He took the butter, gave me back the leaf, and said, "Return it."

49.22 [Al-Ṣaḥnāʾī:] Aḥmad ibn Ḥanbal gave me a single coin to buy some beans on bread in broth. I came back with a lot of beans and he asked why.

"There were two bean vendors trying to undersell each other."

"Take it back," he said. "Give the vendor the food back and let him keep the money."

I did as he asked.

49.23 [Al-Mukharrimī:] Rawḥ ibn ʿUbādah came to stay with us and Aḥmad ibn Ḥanbal came to see him. Aḥmad slept right here. He kept some bread for himself in his sleeve and drank water from the watercourse, and he waited outside for Rawḥ to appear. Then Yaḥyā ibn Aktham showed up with an entourage. He sat in front of Aḥmad and started asking him questions. Aḥmad just kept looking down. When Yaḥyā realized he wasn't going to respond, he got up and left.[273]

[Jaʿfar ibn Muḥammad:] Someone from Aḥmad ibn Ḥanbal's house came to tell him that his son was ill and wanted butter. Aḥmad gave a coin to one of the men present and told him to buy some butter. The man brought back some butter wrapped in leaves of chard. As soon as he saw them, Aḥmad asked, "Where did those leaves come from?" 49.24

"From the grocer."

"Did you ask his permission to take them?"

"No."

"Take it all back!"

[Ṣāliḥ:] When I had a baby, one of my friends gave me a gift. Months later, the same friend decided to go to Basra. He asked me whether my father would write a letter of introduction to the elders there. When I asked my father he said, "I would write for him except that he gave you a gift." 49.25

[ʿAbd Allāh:] There was once an old man here who told us, "I noticed that Aḥmad was suffering from scabies, so I brought him some medicine and told him to put it on the rash. He took it but then gave it back. I asked him why, and he said, 'You study Hadith with me.'"[274] 49.26

[Al-Harawī:] We were at Hushaym's door when someone showed up with a letter of introduction. When they opened the door to let him in, we went in too, except for Aḥmad, who stayed back. He was a young man at the time—not even twenty. 49.27

"Aḥmad, come on in!" we said.

"No one gave me permission," he replied.

[Al-Marrūdhī:] Aḥmad had some repairs done on the roof of the house he rented out to the weavers. The repairs were done in such a way that the drainpipe emptied into the street. The next morning he said, "Call the carpenter and tell him to turn the pipe so it drains to the house." 49.28

I called the carpenter and he moved the pipe.[275]

[Al-Ḥarbī:] I attended Aḥmad Ibn Ḥanbal's Hadith sessions for two years. Whenever he came out to recite Hadith, he would bring 49.29

out a reed pen and an inkpot covered in red leather. If he found an error or an omission in his transcript, he would correct it using his own pen and ink; he was too scrupulous to take any of ours. We would ask if he knew certain reports by heart, and he'd say, "No, I need the transcript."

49.30 [Al-Ḥarbī:] Whenever Aḥmad ibn Ḥanbal—God have mercy on him—came out to teach us, he always had a reed pen and a leather-covered inkpot. He was too scrupulous to take any of our ink to correct an *S* or any such thing.[276]

49.31 [Ibn Shabīb:] I once asked Aḥmad ibn Ḥanbal about Muḥammad ibn Muʿāwiyah al-Naysābūrī, and he said to me, "Yaḥyā ibn Yaḥyā is a fine man."

[The author:] I say: Here Aḥmad indirectly condemned Muḥammad ibn Muʿawiyah, a known liar, by praising someone else. In another report he condemns him, but here and elsewhere he avoids doing so.

49.32 [ʿAbd Allāh:] I heard my father say to Yaḥyā ibn Maʿīn, "People tell me you say, 'I heard Ismāʿīl, son of ʿUlayyah, report.'"

"Yes, I do say that."

"Well, don't. Say 'Ismāʿīl, son of Ibrāhīm,' instead. I've heard that he doesn't like being called after his mother."

Yaḥyā accepted this instruction with good grace.

[The author:] A number of people are commonly known by their mothers' names. These include Bilāl son of Ḥamāmah, Muʿādh son of ʿAfrāʾ, Bashīr son of al-Khaṣāṣiyah, Ibn Buḥaynah, Yaʿlā son of Munyah, and many others, all mentioned in my book *Pollen for the Mind*. In any event, being scrupulous dictates that one avoid referring to people in a way they dislike.

49.33 [Al-Ruhāwī:] I once met Aḥmad ibn Ḥanbal in Baghdad and he asked me, "Whatever happened to that man al-Jawharī you have there in Ḥarrān? He was learned."

I replied that I knew of no one by that name teaching Hadith in Ḥarrān.

"You know who I mean: he was an associate of Abū Maʿbad Ḥafṣ ibn Ghaylān."

"I don't know him."

"Come on!" said Aḥmad. "He has a number of sons."

"Do you mean 'the Owl'?"

"Yes!" he said. "Learn from him: he's reliable."

[The author:] The man's name was Sulaymān ibn Abī Dāwūd and he was called "the Owl." Out of scrupulosity, our exemplar Aḥmad avoided using his nickname.

[Al-Sijistānī:] I once asked Aḥmad ibn Ḥanbal about the validity of a declaration of divorce pronounced by a drunken man. He said, "Ask someone else."[277] 49.34

[Al-Ḥarbī:] On his deathbed Aḥmad asked that we make expiation for him for one vow he had made, saying "I think I broke it."[278] 49.35

[Al-Marrūdhī:] More times than I can count, I asked Aḥmad ibn Ḥanbal about something and he said, "I don't know." 49.36

[Al-Yamāmī:] I heard Aḥmad ibn Ḥanbal say, "Many times I've waited three years before knowing what to think about a problem of law." 49.37

[Al-Athram:] I often heard Aḥmad ibn Ḥanbal, when someone asked him a question, say that he didn't know. He would say this even when he was aware of what had been said about it. When asked to give the answer he preferred, he would note that there was a difference of opinion. What he meant when he said "I don't know" was that he didn't know which view to choose. I often heard him say, "I don't know," and then start citing opinions. 49.38

[Al-Marrūdhī:] When I was with Aḥmad in Ītākh's palace in Samarra, I pointed out something that had been put up on the wall.[279] He told me not to look at it. 49.39

"But I already did," I said.

"Well, don't."

Chapter 50

His Shunning Appointment to Positions of Authority[280]

50.1 [Al-Muzanī:] Al-Shafiʿī said that he went to see Hārūn al-Rashīd and, after greeting him, said that he had just come from Yemen, which badly needed a strong hand. Al-Rashīd said, "Choose one of your students and we'll appoint him judge there."

Returning to his study session, and seeing that Aḥmad ibn Ḥanbal was among the best of those present, al-Shāfiʿī approached him and said, "I was talking with the Commander of Believers about appointing a judge in Yemen and he asked me to choose someone who studies with me. I've chosen you, so get ready: I'll take you in to meet him and he'll appoint you judge."

Ibn Ḥanbal turned on him and said, "The only reason I came to you was to learn something, and you want me to join them as a judge?"

Al-Shāfiʿī was shamed by this rebuke.[281]

[The author:] It is also reported that this incident took place during the reign of al-Amīn.

50.2 [Al-Athram:] I was told that al-Shāfiʿī said to Aḥmad, "The Commander of the Faithful"—meaning al-Amīn—"asked me to look for someone to serve him as judge in Yemen. I know you want to go see ʿAbd al-Razzāq, and now you can. Rule fairly, and get all the learning you want from him."

"If you ever mention this again," said Aḥmad, "that's the last you'll see of me." At the time, I think Aḥmad was thirty—or maybe twenty-seven—years old.[282]

50.3 [Al-Balkhī:] Al-Shāfiʿī, God have mercy on him, had a lot of pull with Muḥammad ibn Zubaydah.[283] One day Muḥammad mentioned that he was very concerned about not finding a good, trustworthy man who was an exemplar of the *sunnah* to serve as a judge. Al-Shāfiʿī told him that he had found just such a man: an exemplar of the *sunnah* who was gifted with religious understanding and well learned in Hadith.

"Who's that?" asked Muḥammad.

He told him it was Aḥmad ibn Ḥanbal.

Some time later, al-Shāfiʿī ran into Aḥmad and told him what he had said.

"Put that right out of your mind, and leave me out of it," he replied. "Otherwise I'll leave this place and go."

[Ṣāliḥ:] Isḥāq ibn Rāhawayh wrote to me saying: 50.4

> Emir ʿAbd Allāh ibn Ṭāhir sent for me and, when I went in, I was carrying a letter from your father in my hand. When the emir saw it, he asked what it was, and I told him. He took it and read it and said, "I have a lot of regard for him and for Ḥamzah ibn al-Hayḍam al-Būshanjī because neither of them ever got mixed up with people in power."

When he learned that Isḥāq ibn Rāhawayh had brought his letter to the attention of ʿAbd Allāh ibn Ṭāhir, my father stopped corresponding with him.

[Al-Ribāṭī:] I went to see Aḥmad ibn Ḥanbal, but he wouldn't look at me. I told him that I dictated Hadith in Khurasan and that if people there knew how he was treating me they would toss away the reports I had taught them. 50.5

"On the Day of Resurrection," he replied, "when they call forth ʿAbd Allāh ibn Ṭāhir and his entourage, do you think you'll have anywhere to run? Make sure you won't be standing there with him when that happens."[284]

Chapter 51

His Love of Poverty and His Affection for the Poor

[Al-Marrūdhī:] Aḥmad loved the poor. I never saw poor men treated as well as they were when sitting in his company. 51.1

[Al-Marrūdhī:] Aḥmad once mentioned someone who was poor and ill, and told me, "Go and ask him what he wants us to do for him." 51.2

Then he handed me some scent and said, "Put this on him."

51.3 [Al-Marrūdhī:] Aḥmad ibn Ḥanbal once said, "Nothing does as much good as poverty—nothing! When there's no money here I rejoice."

I once mentioned someone who bore poverty steadfastly despite living in rags. After that he would ask me about him, saying, "Go and see how he's doing! God be praised: there's nothing like bearing poverty—nothing like it at all. Do you understand what it means?"

Once he said, "Some people have the things of this world given to them in order to test them. It's much better when the world leaves you alone!"

I once mentioned how al-Fuḍayl and Fatḥ al-Mawṣilī had lived in destitution but bore up without complaint. "God have mercy on them," he said, as his eyes filled with tears. "They used to say that when the righteous are recalled, God's grace descends."

One day he said, "When there's no money here, I'm glad."

No sooner had he said it than his little son came to ask him for something. "Your father doesn't have a single coin," he replied, "or anything else."

Chapter 52
His Humility

52.1 [Muḥammad ibn Ṭāriq:] I was sitting next to Aḥmad ibn Ḥanbal and I asked him if I could use his inkpot.

He looked at me. "Neither one of us is as scrupulous as all that," he said with a smile.

52.2 [Yaḥyā ibn Maʿīn:] I never met anyone like Aḥmad ibn Ḥanbal. We sat with him for fifty years, and never once did he hold his piety and goodness over us.

52.3 [Ṣāliḥ:] I often saw my father pick up an adze and go over to the tenants' rooms to take care of jobs with his own two hands. He would go to the grocers and buy a bundle of kindling or whatever, and carry it back himself.

['Abd Allāh:] I remember that whenever any tribesman of Quraysh, young or old, or anyone of the Prophet's family came to see him, he'd refuse to walk through the doorway of the mosque until after they had gone through ahead of him. 52.4

['Ārim ibn al-Faḍl:] Aḥmad ibn Ḥanbal was here with us in Basra. He had come to me with a knapsack—or maybe a knotted bundle—with some dirhams in it, and every so often he would come and take a little out. One day I said, "Aḥmad, I hear you're an Arab. What tribe are you from?" 52.5

"A poor one," he would say.

Every time he came over, I would ask him the same question and he would give me the same answer. It wasn't until he left Basra that I found out the truth.[285]

[Al-Thaqafī:] The first time I saw Aḥmad, I asked if I could kiss his head. He said, "I've done nothing to deserve your respect." 52.6

[Al-Marrūdhī:] I asked Aḥmad whether you can tell a man to his face that he's revived the *sunnah*. 52.7

"You'll just give him a swelled head," he replied.

[Ibn Abī Mūsā:] A man from Khurasan once said to Aḥmad, "I thank God that I've met you!" 52.8

"Come off it," he replied. "What's all this? I'm nobody."

[Al-Ḥusayn ibn Ḥassān:] We went in to see Aḥmad ibn Ḥanbal, and an elderly man from Khurasan said, "For God's sake, think of us! We need you. There's no one left who knows anything. If you can't teach Hadith, then answer legal questions. People need your help!" 52.9

"Mine?" he replied. He sighed and his face fell. To me he looked miserable.

Once someone said to him, "May God reward you for all you've done for Islam!"

"No," he replied, "may He reward Islam for what it's done for me!" Then he added, "Who am I? No one!"

He was once handed a note from a man asking him to pray for him. "If I do that," he said, "who will pray for me?"

52.10 [Muḥammad ibn Aḥmad:] More than once I heard Aḥmad say, "Who am I that you should come to me? Who am I that you should come to me? Go seek Hadith!"

52.11 [Al-Ṭayālisī:] I once laid my hand on Aḥmad ibn Ḥanbal and then ran it down my body for a blessing. He saw me do it and grew furious. Flapping his hands as if to shake something off them, he said, "Who taught you to do that?"

It was clear that he didn't approve at all.

52.12 [Khaṭṭāb ibn Bishr:] Abū ʿUthmān al-Shāfiʿī once began lavishing praise on Aḥmad ibn Ḥanbal, saying things like, "Everyone will be all right as long as God keeps you here with us."

"Don't say those things, Abū ʿUthmān," said Aḥmad. "I'm no one at all."

Another time I asked him a question about being scrupulous. I saw his face fall and assume such a mournful expression of self-reproach that I felt sorry for him. I said to someone who was with me, "Some days he seems so despondent, and all I did was make him feel worse."

52.13 [Al-Marrūdhī:] Once, after mentioning men famous for being scrupulous, Aḥmad ibn Ḥanbal said, "I hope God doesn't despise me. How can I compare with men like that?"

Once I said to him, "So many people are praying for you!"

"I'm afraid it may be a ruse to make me feel complacent," he said. "I pray to God to make me better than they think I am and forgive the sins they don't know I've committed."

Another time I told him that a Hadith-man had said, "Aḥmad has given up more than money: he's given up other people, too."

"Who am I to renounce anyone?" he said. "They should be renouncing me!"

52.14 [ʿAbd Allāh:] I remember that whenever any tribesman of Quraysh, young or old, or anyone of the Prophet's family came to see him, he'd refuse to walk through the doorway of the mosque until after they had gone through ahead of him.

[Al-Abbār:] I once heard a man tell Aḥmad ibn Ḥanbal, "I've sworn an oath but I don't know what kind of oath it is." 52.15

"If you ever figure it out," replied Aḥmad, "maybe I will too."

Chapter 53

His Accepting Invitations and His Withdrawal upon Seeing Things He Disapproved Of

[Al-Ḥarbī:] Aḥmad ibn Ḥanbal would accept invitations to marriages, weddings, and circumcisions, and eat what was served. 53.1

[Al-Daʿʿāʾ:] A man once invited Aḥmad ibn Ḥanbal to an event and Aḥmad accepted. Later, he tried to back out of it, but the man wouldn't take no for an answer. At the event the man went and seated Aḥmad next to someone he did not want to sit with. "Ibn Sīrīn, God bless him, had it right," said Aḥmad. "He said, 'Never try to honor your brother by doing something that will cause him hardship.' That's what this brother of mine has done to me." 53.2

[Ṣāliḥ:] There was man called Aḥmad ibn al-Ḥakam al-ʿAṭṭār who used to frequent the circle of ʿAffān. When it came time for him to circumcise one of his sons, he invited Yaḥyā, Abū Khaythamah, and a number of other Hadith-men, including my father. The others went ahead and my father and I came along after them. When we arrived, we were given a seat in a room with several other Hadith-men. At some point one of them said, "Aḥmad, there's something made of silver here." My father turned and saw a chair.[286] So he got up and left, and everyone who was in the room with him followed him out. 53.3

Hearing of this, the host, al-ʿAṭṭār, rushed out and caught up with him, swearing that he hadn't brought the item in and didn't know it was there, and asking my father to come back. My father refused. When ʿAffān came along, al-ʿAṭṭār asked him to speak with my father and persuade him to return. ʿAffān spoke with him but it did no good, and al-ʿAṭṭār was devastated.

53.4 [Al-Sawwāq:] We were at the banquet at the Pitch-Worker's Gate[287] when Aḥmad ibn Ḥanbal arrived. As soon as he set foot in the house, he saw a chair with silver ornamentation, and went out again. The host came out after him, but Aḥmad waved him away and left, saying, "Magian finery! Magian finery!"

Chapter 54

His Preference for Solitude

54.1 ['Abd Allāh:] My father could bear solitude better than anyone. Bishr,[288] great as he was, couldn't stand to be alone: he would go out visiting an hour here, an hour there.

54.2 ['Abd Allāh:] The only places anyone saw my father were in the mosque, at a funeral, or at the home of someone taken ill. He hated walking through the markets.

54.3 ['Abd Allāh:] My father could bear solitude better than anyone. The only places anyone saw him were in the mosque, at a funeral, or at the home of someone taken ill. He hated walking through the markets.

54.4 [Fatḥ ibn Nūḥ:] I heard Aḥmad ibn Ḥanbal say, "I wish for something I'll never have: a place with no one in it at all."

54.5 [Al-Marrūdhī:] Aḥmad said to me, "I don't care if I never saw anyone and no one saw me—though I would miss 'Abd al-Wahhāb."[289]

54.6 [Al-Maymūnī:] Ibn Ḥanbal said, "I've found that being alone is easier for me."

54.7 [Al-Iṣfahānī:] I was once at Aḥmad's door waiting to be given permission to go in. At one point his son 'Abd Allāh appeared. A man who was there said to him, "Tell your father that So-and-So died and we're carrying him to the cemetery this afternoon."

'Abd Allāh went in, came out again, and said to the man, "I told him. He asked for God's mercy on the deceased and prayed for him. But he doesn't like to go out when people know he's coming because he'll draw a crowd."

[Al-Musayyabī:] I once said to Aḥmad, "I'd like to visit you and pay my respects, but I'm afraid you wouldn't want me to."[290] 54.8

"I don't like that sort of thing," he said.

[Al-Marrūdhī:] I once suggested to Aḥmad that he meet up with 'Abd al-Wahhāb. 54.9

"Didn't some of the pious avoid meetings?" he said. Then he added, "He would make an effort to be pleasant with me and I with him. No, solitude is a better teacher. The one with true understanding fears God."[291]

I once heard Aḥmad say, "I want to go down to Mecca and throw myself into one of those ravines where no one will ever find me."

Chapter 55

His Wish to Live in Obscurity and His Efforts to Remain Unnoticed

['Ubayd al-Qāri':] Aḥmad ibn Ḥanbal's uncle once went to see him and found him with his chin cupped in his hand. "Nephew," he asked, "what's troubling you? Why so glum?" 55.1

"Uncle," Aḥmad replied, "happiness is when God makes sure that no one's ever heard of you."

[Abū Ḥātim:] My father said, "All you had to do was look at Aḥmad ibn Ḥanbal to see that he wasn't trying to show off how ascetic he was. I saw him wearing sandals that didn't look like the sandals that the Qur'an-readers[292] wear. The toe-end was big and curled back and the strap hung loose. They looked like something bought for him from the market. I also saw him wearing a breechclout and a striped gown of a sky-blue color."[293] 55.2

By dressing this way Aḥmad was trying to avoid—or so I think, though God alone knows the truth—looking like a Qur'an-reader, in the hope of losing his reputation for piety.

[Al-Marrūdhī:] Aḥmad once said to me, "Tell 'Abd al-Wahhāb to hide his light under a bushel. Fame has brought me nothing but suffering." 55.3

[Al-Khallāl:] I heard him say, "I swear that if I knew a way to leave this city, I'd leave it. Then no one would mention me to them, and they'd forget about me."[294]

55.4 [Isḥāq:] I once saw Aḥmad ibn Ḥanbal going back inside his house after praying the dawn prayer. He was telling people, "Stop following me around!"

55.5 [Ibn Hārūn:] I remember that Aḥmad didn't like it when people followed him down the street.

55.6 [ʿAbd Allāh:] When my father went out on Fridays he wouldn't let anyone follow him. He would often stop and wait until they gave up and went away.

55.7 [Isḥāq:] I saw Aḥmad ibn Ḥanbal walking all by himself as if he were a man of no importance.

Chapter 56

His Fear of God

56.1 [Ṣāliḥ:] Whenever someone said a prayer for my father, he would say, "Call no man blessed until his work is done."

I often heard him say, "God save us! God save us!"

I heard him report that he heard Yūnus ibn Muḥammad report that he heard Ḥammād ibn Zayd report that Yaḥyā ibn Saʿīd claimed that Saʿīd ibn al-Musayyab used to say, "God save us! God save us!" I also heard him report that he heard Zayd ibn al-Ḥubāb report that he heard ʿAyyāsh ibn ʿUqbah report that ʿUmar ibn ʿAbd al-ʿAzīz often used to say, "God save us! God save us!"

56.2 [ʿAbd Allāh:] All I want is to come out of this even, without winning or losing.[295]

56.3 [Al-Marrūdhī:] I brought Ibrāhīm al-Ḥuṣarī, who was a righteous man, to meet Aḥmad. Ibrāhīm told him that his mother had dreamed of him and said something about the Garden. "Brother," said Aḥmad, "People used to say the same kind of thing about Sahl ibn Salāmah, but he went on to shed blood."[296] He added, "A believer should find joy in dreams but never trust them."

[Muḥammad ibn Ḥāzim:] Once when I was at Aḥmad's an elderly man came to see him. "Aḥmad," he said, "I overheard some people talking about you and saying you were among the best." Aḥmad ignored him. 56.4

[Al-Marrūdhī:] I once heard Aḥmad say, "I'm too fearful of God to eat or drink, and now I don't want to eat at all." 56.5

During his final illness, Aḥmad needed to urinate, and called for a basin. I brought one, and saw that his urine was bright red. When I showed ʿAbd al-Raḥmān the healer, he said, "That's a man with innards torn apart by worry"—or "by sorrow."

[Al-Marrūdhī:] One morning I went in to see Aḥmad and asked him how he was. 56.6

"How can a man be," he answered, "with his Lord imposing obligations, his Prophet demanding that he follow the *sunnah*, his two angels waiting for good deeds, his soul clamoring for what it wants, the Devil goading him to lust, the Angel of Death seeking his life, and his family asking for money?"

Chapter 57

His Preoccupation and Absentmindedness

[Al-Marrūdhī:] I once went out with Aḥmad leaning on my arm. We were approached by a woman carrying a long-necked lute[297] out in the open. I took it from her, broke it, and started stamping on it. The whole time, Aḥmad stood there staring at the ground and saying nothing. Soon everyone knew about the incident—everyone except for Aḥmad, who said, "I have no recollection of you ever breaking a lute in my presence." 57.1

Chapter 58
His Devotions

58.1 [Ṣāliḥ:] My father would never let anyone else draw the water for his ablutions. Whenever the bucket came up full, he would say, "Praise God!"

I asked him what the reason was.

"Son," he replied, "haven't you heard what God says? «Say, 'Have you considered if your water were to sink into the ground, who could then bring you flowing water?'»"[298]

58.2 ['Abd Allāh:] My father used to pray three hundred cycles every twenty-four hours. After he was flogged he could no longer manage so many, so he started doing only 150. At that time he was nearly eighty. Every day he'd read a seventh of the Qur'an, finishing it all in a week, and so every seven nights he'd have completed a full reading of the Qur'an in addition to the ritual prayers he'd performed during the daytime. When he'd finish the evening prayer he'd take a nap then pray until morning.

58.3 [Ibn al-Shāfiʿī:] Aḥmad ibn Ḥanbal once told me, "Your father is one of the six people I pray for just before dawn."[299]

58.4 [Yūsuf ibn al-Ḥusayn:] Aḥmad ibn Ḥanbal once asked me about the elders of Rey. "How is Abū Zurʿah, may God protect him?"

"He's well," I said.

He said: "There are five people I pray for at the end of every prayer." He told me who they were: his parents, al-Shāfiʿī, Abū Zurʿah, and one more whose name I've forgotten.

58.5 [Hilāl ibn al-ʿAlāʾ:] Al-Shāfiʿī, Yaḥyā ibn Maʿīn, and Aḥmad ibn Ḥanbal went to Mecca. As soon as they reached the place where they were staying, al-Shāfiʿī lay down to rest and so did Yaḥyā ibn Maʿīn. Aḥmad, on the other hand, stayed up to pray.

The next morning al-Shāfiʿī said, "I've worked out a hundred legal problems for us Muslims."

"What did you do?" they asked Yaḥyā.

"I've refuted a hundred lies told of the Prophet."

"What about you?" they asked Aḥmad ibn Ḥanbal.

"I prayed two cycles and recited the entire Qur'an."[300]

[Ibn Abī Hāshim:] I heard Aḥmad ibn Ḥanbal say, "I've read through the whole Qur'an in a day and counted how many times the word 'fortitude' comes up. It's over ninety."[301] 58.6

[Ṣāliḥ:] My father had a cap he had sewed himself, lined with cotton. When he stayed up at night to pray he would wear it. I often used to hear him reciting the Chapter of the Cave.[302] 58.7

[Abū Bakr Muḥammad ibn Abī ʿAbd Allāh:] When Aḥmad was on the run from the authorities, he hid in the house of Ibrāhīm ibn Hāniʾ. I heard Ibrāhīm report that he never saw anyone deny himself so much, pray as earnestly, or push himself as hard as Aḥmad ibn Ḥanbal. 58.8

"He would fast all day," he recalled, "and then have a quick meal. After evening prayer he would do more cycles then take a nap. Then he would perform his ablutions and pray straight through until dawn. At dawn he'd pray a single *witr* cycle. That was his routine the whole time he stayed with me. He never let up for a single night. I couldn't keep up with him. I never saw him break his fast, except one day when he had himself cupped and then ate something."

[Ibrāhīm ibn Shammās:] I knew Aḥmad ibn Ḥanbal when he was a boy. Even then he'd stay up at night praying. 58.9

[ʿAbd Allāh:] After my father grew old, he pushed himself to read the Qur'an more and more often and to pray more frequently between the noon and late afternoon prayers. Whenever I went into his room he would stop praying. Sometimes he would talk to me and sometimes he would sit quietly. If he was quiet, I'd leave him and he'd go back to his prayers. When he was in hiding, I remember seeing him spend most of the time reading the Qur'an. 58.10

[Al-ʿIjlī:] The last time I saw Aḥmad, he came out and sat with me in an anteroom. 58.11

I said, "I remember there were some law questions you were thinking about. Have you reached any answers?"

"This is the time to make haste," he said, "to *live* by the law." He continued in that vein until we rose to go.

58.12 [Al-Mu'addib:] I saw Bishr ibn al-Ḥārith pray four cycles after the Friday prayer without breaking them up by doing the salutation after the first two. But I saw Aḥmad ibn Ḥanbal pray six cycles after the Friday prayer and do the salutation after every two.[303]

58.13 [Abū Bakr ibn ʿAnbar:] One Friday I followed Ibn Ḥanbal to the mosque of al-Manṣūr. He stood by the Poets' Cupola and started praying supererogatory prayers two cycles at a time. A beggar came and stood in front of him, and Aḥmad gestured at him angrily to go away. Then the beggar tried to pass in front of him, and we rushed over and pulled him aside.[304]

58.14 [ʿAbd Allāh:] When Abū Zurʿah came to Baghdad, he stayed with my father. He kept him so busy comparing reports and their transmissions[305] that my father said at one point, "Today all I've prayed is the ritual prayers. I've let all this comparing with Abū Zurʿah take the place of the rest."[306]

58.15 [Ibn Hāni':] I went with Aḥmad to the Friday mosque and overheard him reading the Chapter of the Cave.[307]

Chapter 59

His Performances of the Pilgrimage

59.1 [ʿAbd Allāh:] My father made five pilgrimages: three on foot and two riding. On some of them he spent only twenty dirhams.

59.2 [Ṣāliḥ:] I heard my father say, "I made five pilgrimages, three of them on foot. On one of them I spent only thirty dirhams."

59.3 [Al-Marrūdhī:] Aḥmad once said to me, "Some people can make it from Mecca back to Baghdad on only fourteen dirhams."

"Like who?" I asked.

"Me."

59.4 [ʿAbd Allāh:] In the anteroom of our house was a bench. When my father had a visitor he wanted to sit with privately, he would offer him a seat on the bench. With other callers, he would stand in the doorway with his hands on the doorposts and talk from there. One day a man came to the house and said, "Tell your father it's Abū Ibrāhīm the Wanderer."

The two of them sat down on the bench.

"Say hello to a great Muslim," my father told me (or "one of the best of the Muslims"). So I said hello. Then my father said, "Talk to us, Abū Ibrāhīm."

"I was passing through Such-and-Such a place," he said, "near the monastery there, when I got too sick to walk. I remember thinking that if I were closer to the monastery one of the monks might treat me. Suddenly a great lion appeared, walked up to me, and carried me along gently on its back until we reached the monastery, where it let me down. When the monks saw me arrive on the back of a lion, all four hundred of them embraced Islam.

"Now *you* talk to me, Abū 'Abd Allāh!"

"Four or five nights before the pilgrimage," said my father, "I dreamed of the Prophet, God bless and keep him. He said, 'Aḥmad, make the pilgrimage.' Then I woke up. Whenever I prepare to travel, I put some crumbled bread in a bag. So I did that. The next morning, I started for Kufa, and got there later the same day. In the Friday mosque, I met a handsome young man with a pleasant scent. I greeted him and then said 'God is great' to begin my prayer. When I finished I asked him whether anyone was still leaving for the pilgrimage. He told me to wait until one of his brethren came along. When he came, he turned out to be a man in the same situation as I was. As we walked along, he asked the young man if we would be carried.[308]

"'If Aḥmad ibn Ḥanbal is with us,' said the young man, 'then we will.'

"At that moment I realized that he was al-Khaḍir. Then I asked the man with me if he wanted something to eat.

"'Go ahead and eat your sort of food,' he said, 'and I'll eat mine.'

"Whenever we ate, the young man would disappear then return when we were done. Three days later we were in Mecca."[309]

Chapter 60

His Extemporaneous Prayers and Supplications

60.1 [ʿAbd Allāh:] At the end of his ritual prayers, my father often used to say, "God, you have safeguarded me from prostrating myself before any but You. Safeguard me likewise from seeking anything from any but You."

Finally I said, "I hear you saying that a lot. Are you following a precedent?"

"Yes," he answered. "Wakīʿ ibn al-Jarrāh used to say it often, so I asked him about it, just as you asked me now. He said that he heard Sufyān al-Thawrī say it and that Sufyān, when he asked him about it, said that he heard it from Manṣūr ibn al-Muʿtamir."

60.2 [Al-Razzāz:] Once when we were praying with Aḥmad ibn Ḥanbal, I heard him say, "God, if anyone has followed a caprice or an independent judgment, believing that he is right when he is mistaken, return him to the truth so that no member of this community goes astray.

"God, let us not trouble ourselves over the sustenance that You have undertaken to provide, nor make us dependent on others for that sustenance that comes from You.

"Let us achieve the best of those things that You have promised without being deterred by the worst.

"May You never see us doing what You have forbidden, nor find us shirking from what You have commanded.

"Ennoble us and do not abase us: ennoble us through obedience to You, and do not abase us through disobedience of You."

One time a man came to him and asked him something I couldn't make out. Aḥmad answered, "Hold out as long as you can; in strength is victory." Then he added, "The Prophet, God bless and keep him, said, 'In strength is victory, and after suffering comes relief. «Surely with every hardship there is ease; surely with every hardship there is ease.»'"[310]

[Al-Ṣaffār:] We were at Aḥmad ibn Ḥanbal's, and I asked him to pray for us. He said, "God, You know that we know that You desire for us most of what we seek for ourselves; make us rather seek for ourselves only what You desire for us." 60.3

He fell silent. Then someone said, "Give us more."

"God," he said, "we ask You, by that power You spoke of when You said to the heavens and the earth, «Come willingly or unwillingly, and they both said, 'We come willingly,'»[311] to guide us to what pleases You. We seek Your protection against all need except the need for You, and all subjection except to You. Give us not so much that we wax arrogant, nor so little that we become heedless. Grant us, in Your mercy, a sustenance that will suffice us, and a bounty that leaves us dependent on none but You."

[Al-Khawātīmī:] After Aḥmad Ibn Ḥanbal had been flogged and then sent out of the caliph's palace, I went to visit him. I found him lying face down in the house, praying. I overheard him say, "O You who reward us for what You do,[312] do to me whatever makes me deserving of Your reward." 60.4

I heard that al-Marrūdhī said that a group had gathered at Aḥmad's and asked him to pray. "God," he said, "do not demand from us a gratitude equal to Your blessings."

I heard Muḥammad ibn Yaʿqūb al-Ṣaffār say, "At the the end of every prayer, Aḥmad would say, 'God, I ask You to treat us as mercifully as Your mercy demands, and to forgive as as You have resolved to do. I ask You to let us reap the reward of our good deeds and to safeguard us from iniquity. I ask You to let us enter the Garden in triumph and to escape the Fire. If we sin, pardon us; if we worry, dispel our care. Let us want for nothing, but provide.'"

[Al-Warrāq:] When we were in Tarsus we met someone who was leaving the city and asked Aḥmad to supply him with a prayer. He told him to say, "O guide to the errant! Lead me to the path where the truthful walk, and make of me a righteous servant." 60.5

The man left. On the road, he ran into some trouble and was separated from his companions. He uttered the prayer Aḥmad had taught him and shortly afterward caught up with the party. Later he came to Aḥmad and told him what had happened.

"Keep it a secret," said Aḥmad.

60.6 [Saʿd ibn Masʿadah:] I heard Ṭalḥah ibn ʿUbayd Allāh al-Baghdādī, who lived in Egypt, report that he and Aḥmad happened to travel by ship together. Aḥmad did not speak except to say, "God, let me die a Muslim and a follower of the *sunnah*."

Chapter 61

His Manifestations of Grace and the Effectiveness of His Prayers

61.1 [ʿAbd Allāh:] Once I saw my father threaten some ants and ask them to leave his house. They left in a great dark mass and never returned.

61.2 [Muḥammad ibn ʿAlī l-Simsār:] One night Aḥmad went over to Ṣaliḥ's house because Ṣaliḥ's son was bleeding from the nose. The doctors[313] had come and were treating him with acacia and so on,[314] but the blood was coming too fast.

"What's wrong, son?" said Aḥmad.

"Grandpa, I'm going to die!" said the boy. "Call to God for me."

"You'll be all right," said Aḥmad. He moved a hand as if praying for him and the blood stopped. This was after everyone had given the boy up for dead, since he had been bleeding continuously.

61.3 [Abū Ṭālib:] Once I was taking dictation from Aḥmad and my pen snapped. He gave me one of his own. Later I showed it to Abū ʿAlī l-Jaʿfarī, telling him that it was a pen that Aḥmad had given me. "Take it," he told his serving boy, "and lay it on the palm tree: let's see if that will fertilize it."

The boy did as he was asked and the tree grew fruit.

61.4 [Al-ʿAbbās ibn Muḥammad:] One of my neighbors, a man named ʿAlī ibn Abī Ḥarārah, told me this story.

"My mother had been unable to walk for almost twenty years. One day she said, 'Go ask Aḥmad ibn Ḥanbal to pray to God for me.'

"I went to his house and knocked on the door. He was in the anteroom but he didn't open up.

"'Who is it?' he called out.

"I told him I lived in the neighborhood and my mother was an invalid who couldn't walk and wanted him to pray for her. Through the door came an angry reply: 'She's the one who should be praying for me!'

"I turned away. As I was leaving an old woman came out of the house and said, 'Are you the one who was talking to Abū 'Abd Allāh?'

"'Yes.'

"'I just heard him praying for her.'

"I rushed home. When I knocked on the door, my mother came out walking on her own two feet to open it, saying, 'God cured me!'"

[Ibrāhīm ibn Hāni']: So-and-So the weaver, who rented from 61.5
Abū 'Abd Allāh, told me: "Once when I was sick I kept moaning all night. In the middle of the night Aḥmad came out and said, 'Who's that in pain over there?'

"They told him, and he prayed for me. 'God, cure him!' he said, and went back inside. The pain suddenly stopped, as if someone had poured water on a fire."

[Fāṭimah:] My brother Ṣāliḥ had a fire in his house. He'd married 61.6
into a wealthy family who sent over a dowry that looked like it was worth four thousand dirhams, but all of it went up in smoke. Ṣāliḥ said, "All I care about is losing the robe that my father used to wear when he prayed. I liked to put it on for a blessing and pray in it."

When the fire was put out, they went back in. On the bed they found the robe. Everything around it had burned up but the robe was unharmed.

[The author:] I heard a similar story from the chief judge, 'Alī 61.7
ibn al-Ḥusayn al-Zaynabī. He had a fire and everything in the house burned up except a book that had some of Aḥmad's writing in it.

As for myself, when Baghdad was flooded in 554 [1159–60] and my books were ruined, one thing that was spared was a volume containing two sheets in Aḥmad's handwriting.

61.8 [Al-Lakkāf:] ʿAbd Allāh ibn Mūsā, who was a good Sunni, told me: "One dark night, my father and I went out to visit Aḥmad, but it got too dark to see. My father said, 'Let's call on God, invoking His righteous servant Aḥmad, and ask Him to light our way. For thirty years, everything I've asked for in his name has been granted.' My father prayed and I said 'Amen.' The sky lit up as if it were a moonlit night and stayed that way until we arrived."

61.9 [Al-Rāzī:] A group of us accompanied Aḥmad ibn Ḥanbal as far as al-Mutawakkil's gate. He was admitted at the Intimates' Gate, but before going in, he said, "All of you can go back now. May God keep you in health!"

Since that day, not one of us has fallen ill.

Chapter 62
The Number of Wives He Had

62.1 [Al-Marrūdhī:] I heard Aḥmad say, "I didn't marry until I was forty."

[The author:] His first wife was ʿAbbāsah bint al-Faḍl, who was Ṣāliḥ's mother.

62.2 [Al-Khallāl:] Aḥmad ibn Ḥanbal's grandson Zuhayr dictated the following to us. "My grandfather, God have mercy on him, married my father's mother, ʿAbbāsah bint al-Faḍl, an Arab from just outside Medina. She had only one child—my father—and then she died."

62.3 [Al-Marrūdhī:] I heard Aḥmad say, "Ṣāliḥ's mother and I lived together for thirty years and never had an argument."[315]

His Second Wife, Rayḥānah, ʿAbd Allāh's Mother[316]

62.4 [Zuhayr:] After Ṣāliḥ's mother, ʿAbbāsah, died, my father married an Arab woman named Rayḥānah. She bore him only one child: my uncle ʿAbd Allāh.

62.5 [Muḥammad ibn Baḥr:] I heard my uncle report: "When we all gathered to marry Aḥmad and Muḥammad ibn Rayḥān's sister, her father said to him, 'Abū 'Abd Allāh, she's—' and laid a finger on his eye, meaning 'She's one-eyed.'

"Aḥmad said, 'I knew that.'"

[Aḥmad ibn 'Anbar:] When Ṣālih's mother died, Aḥmad said to one of the women of the house, "Go to my cousin So-and-So and ask her if she'll agree to marry me." 62.6

The cousin reported: "So I went and asked, and she agreed. But when I came back, he asked, 'Was her sister listening?'

"I told him that the sister"—who was one-eyed—"had been listening. He said, 'Go back and ask for the one with one eye.' So I did, and she accepted."

This was 'Abd Allāh's mother. After seven years of marriage, she asked him, "Cousin, how do things seem to you? Is there anything you don't like?"

"Nothing," he answered, "except that those sandals of yours squeak."

Al-Khallāl also said: "I remember Khaṭṭāb ibn Bishr saying that one of Aḥmad's wives said to him a few days after she came into the household: 'Is there anything I'm doing wrong?' 62.7

"'No,' he answered, 'except that those sandals you're wearing didn't exist at the time of the Prophet, God bless and keep him.'"

So she sold them and bought a *maqṭūʿ*,[317] which she would wear.

Al-Khallāl added that the woman he was talking about is this one: that is, 'Abd Allāh's mother.

He also heard al-Marrūdhī say that he heard Aḥmad mention a wife and ask God to have mercy on her. Then he said, "We lived together for twenty years and never had an argument."

That's this woman: 'Abd Allāh's mother.

[The author:] I've already quoted Aḥmad as saying that Ṣāliḥ's mother lived with him for thirty years, and this last report says that he and a wife lived together for twenty. Although both reports are attributed to al-Marrūdhī, one of them must be wrong. Aḥmad did not marry at all until he was forty and did not marry again until after Ṣāliḥ's mother had died. If he spent thirty years with her and 62.8

another twenty with the second wife, he would have to have lived for ninety years. Yet he only lived to be seventy-seven. Moreover, he would need to have married ʿAbd Allāh's mother when he was over seventy, but we know that by the time he died, ʿAbd Allāh was already transmitting his reports and traveling with him. Aḥmad used to say that ʿAbd Allāh—who had already begun seeking Hadith and had heard many teachers while his father was still alive—had a good head for memorizing Hadith. Therefore, I think that the person Aḥmad lived with for twenty years was Ṣāliḥ's mother—though God knows best.

These, in any case, are the two wives he is known to have had. We have not heard of a third.

Chapter 63
His Concubines

63.1 Aḥmad, God have mercy on him, bought a concubine named Ḥusn.

63.2 [Abū Yūsuf ibn Bukhtān:] When Aḥmad asked us to buy the girl for him, Fūrān and I went. As we were leaving, Aḥmad came after me and said, "Make sure she's got some meat on her."

63.3 [Zuhayr:] When ʿAbd Allāh's mother died, Aḥmad bought Ḥusn. She bore him Umm ʿAlī, whose name was Zaynab. Later she bore al-Ḥasan and al-Ḥusayn, who were twins, but they died soon after they were born. Then she bore Muḥammad and al-Ḥasan, who lived till about forty. After them she bore Saʿīd.

63.4 [Ḥusn:] I asked my master whether I should sell one of my anklets. He asked if I really meant it, and I said I did.

"Praise God," he said, "who led you to make this choice."

So I gave the anklet to Ṣāliḥ's son Abū l-Ḥasan, who sold it for eight-and-a-half dinars. When I got pregnant, my master distributed the money. When I had Ḥasan, he gave a dirham to Karrāmah—an old woman who served us—and told her to go to Ibn Shujāʿ—a neighbor of ours who was a butcher—and tell him to take it and buy a head.[318] He bought the head, she brought it home, and we ate it.

"Ḥusn," he said to me, "all I have left is this dirham, and this is the only day you'll get anything from me."[319]

Whenever there was no money in the house my master was happy all day.

One day he came in and said he needed a cupping but had no money. So I went to my jar, took out half a *mann*[320] of weaving I kept there, and sent it out to one of the weavers, who sold it for four dirhams. I spent half a dirham on meat, and he spent a dirham on the cupping. I also bought some perfume for another dirham.

When my master went out to Samarra, I wove a length of soft cloth and used it to make a beautiful robe. When he came back I brought out the robe—this was after I'd been paid fifteen dirhams for it out of the rental income[321]—but when he saw it he said, "I don't want it."

"Master," I said, "I have other things I made from different cotton."

So I gave the robe to Fūrān, who sold it for forty-two dirhams. With that I bought some cotton and wove it into a large gown. When I told Aḥmad, he said, "Don't cut—leave it be!" He ended up using it as his shroud and they wrapped him up in it. I took out the coarse material and he cut it.[322]

Once when he was sick at the end I baked something for him.

"Where did you bake this?" he asked.

"At ʿAbd Allāh's," I said.

"Take it away," he said, and refused to eat it.

[The author:] As far as we know, Aḥmad married only two 63.5
women—Ṣāliḥ's mother and ʿAbd Allāh's—and had only the one concubine whose reports we have cited. Her name is Ḥusn. Yet, in his *Virtues of Aḥmad*,[323] Abū l-Ḥusayn Aḥmad ibn Jaʿfar ibn al-Munādī reports that Aḥmad asked his wife for permission to buy a concubine in order to emulate the practice of the Prophet. She gave her permission and he bought an inexpensive girl he named Rayḥānah, following the *sunnah* of the Prophet. If this is right, he must have bought two slaves, one during his wife's lifetime. But God alone knows best![324]

Chapter 64

The Number of His Children

64.1 We have already mentioned that Ṣāliḥ was born to one mother and ʿAbd Allāh to another, and that Ḥusn the slave bore him al-Ḥasan and al-Ḥusayn, then a third child also named al-Ḥasan, then Muḥammad, Saʿīd, and Zaynab, who was called Umm ʿAlī.

64.2 [Ṣāliḥ:] My father once started apologizing to me for Ḥasan and Saʿīd, saying, "Every soul that acknowledged God as his Lord has to be born sooner or later."[325]

64.3 [ʿAbd Allāh:] When one of the babies was born, ʿAbd al-Aʿlā gave me a note of congratulations to deliver to my father. But my father flung it away, saying, "No man of learning would write a note like that, or any Hadith-man either. It's what you'd expect from a scribe!"

64.4 [Fūrān:] I was a close associate of Aḥmad ibn Ḥanbal. He felt comfortable with me and he would even borrow money from me.

Whenever he had a baby born at night when I wasn't there to hear about it, he would come in the very early morning and sit by my door. But he wouldn't knock, so I never knew he was there until I came out to pray. Then he would get up and join me. I'd ask him what he was doing there so early and he'd say, "We had a baby."

Then he'd leave and I'd pray the morning prayer. Afterward I'd go to the bridge[326] or the Straw Gate[327] to buy what the women needed and have it delivered to his house.

Chapter 65

The Lives of His Children and Descendants

Ṣāliḥ ibn Aḥmad ibn Ḥanbal, His Children, and His Descendants

65.1 Ṣālih, who was called Abū l-Faḍl, was the oldest of Aḥmad's children. He was born in 203 [818–19]. His father loved him and treated him generously. Burdened with children when he was still young, Ṣāliḥ was unable to transmit as many of his father's reports as he might have, though he still transmitted quite a few, along with reports he learned from Abū l-Walīd al-Ṭayālisī, Ibrāhīm ibn al-Faḍl al-Dhāriʿ (the taker of measures),[328] and ʿAlī ibn al-Madīnī. Transmitting in turn from him were his son Zuhayr, al-Baghawī, and Muḥammad ibn Makhlad, among others. He moved to Isfahan after being appointed judge there, and there he died.

[Al-Khallāl:] Ṣāliḥ was always eager to spend money. Al-Ḥasan ibn ʿAlī l-Faqīh told me in Miṣṣīṣah that Ṣāliḥ once had his blood let and afterward invited his friends to celebrate his recovery. He must have spent twenty dinars on scent and that sort of thing. 65.2

I think it was also al-Ḥasan who told me the following.

At one point Aḥmad knocked on the door. One of the guests, Ibn Abī Maryam, said to Ṣāliḥ, "Let down that curtain so we don't get in trouble with your father! And don't let him smell the scent!"

Aḥmad came in, sat down, and asked Ṣāliḥ how he was feeling. Then he said, "Here, take these two dirhams and spend them on yourself today." With that, he got up and left.

"You so-and-so!" said Ibn Abī Maryam to Ṣāliḥ. "How could you think of taking those dirhams?"

[Muḥammad ibn ʿAlī:] I was with Ṣāliḥ when he arrived in Isfahan. The first place he went was the Friday mosque, where he prayed two cycles. Then, when the notables and elders had gathered, he sat down to hear the letter of appointment that the caliph had given him. As the letter was being read he began to weep uncontrollably. Soon the elders sitting near him were weeping as well. When the reading was finished, they prayed aloud for him. "Everyone in our town treasures the memory of Abū ʿAbd Allāh," they told him, "and wishes you the best." 65.3

"Do you know," he asked them, "why I'm crying? I imagined my father seeing me like this"—dressed, that is, in the black robes of his office. "Whenever a shabby ascetic would come to visit him, my father would send for me so I could meet him. He wanted me to be like that—or look like that. As God is my witness, I had no choice but to take this position: I have a debt to pay and all my father's children to feed."[329]

More than once, as he left the judicial session and removed his black robe, Ṣāliḥ said to me, "Just think: I might die in these clothes!"

Ṣāliḥ died in Ramaḍān 265 [April–May 879] in Isfahan.

65.4 His son Zuhayr transmitted reports from him, and Zuhayr's reports, in turn, were transmitted by his nephew Muḥammad ibn Aḥmad ibn Ṣālih and by Aḥmad ibn Sulaymān al-Najjād. Al-Dāraquṭnī describes Zuhayr as reliable. According to Judge Aḥmad ibn Kāmil, he died in Rabīʿ I 303 [September–October 915].

Muḥammad ibn Aḥmad ibn Ṣāliḥ ibn Aḥmad ibn Ḥanbal

65.5 Called Abū Jaʿfar, he transmitted reports he learned from his father, his uncle Zuhayr, and Ibrāhīm ibn Khālid al-Hisinjānī, among others. Transmitting in turn from him was al-Dāraquṭnī. He died in 330 [941–42].

ʿAbd Allāh ibn Aḥmad ibn Ḥanbal

65.6 Called Abū ʿAbd al-Raḥmān, he transmitted more of his father's reports than anyone else, having heard most of his compilations and his Hadith. He also heard reports from ʿAbd al-Aʿlā ibn Ḥammād, Kāmil ibn Ṭalḥah, Yaḥyā ibn Maʿīn, Abū Shaybah's sons Abū Bakr and ʿUthman, Shaybān ibn Farrūkh, and many others.

He had a very retentive memory. His father used to say, "My son ʿAbd Allāh has a gift for learning"—or "memorizing"—"Hadith."

In his last illness, he was asked where he wanted to be buried. He replied, "I'm certain that there's a prophet buried somewhere in the Qaṭīʿah, and I'd rather be near a prophet than near my father."

He died on Sunday, the twenty-first of Jumādā II 290 [May 22, 903], and in the late afternoon was buried in the Straw Gate cemetery. His nephew Zuhayr prayed over him with a great crowd in attendance.

Sa'īd ibn Aḥmad ibn Ḥanbal

According to Ḥanbal ibn Isḥāq, Sa'īd was born about fifty days before Aḥmad died. According to others, Sa'īd was appointed judge in Kufa and died in 303 [915–16]. 65.7

[The author:] This is incorrect. I cite Abū Manṣūr al-Qazzāz, who reports hearing Aḥmad ibn 'Alī ibn Thabit say that Sa'īd ibn Aḥmad ibn Ḥanbal repeated reports he had heard from Abū Mujālid Aḥmad ibn al-Ḥusayn al-Ḍarīr, and Judge Abū 'Imrān Mūsā ibn al-Qāsim al-Ashyab transmitted reports from *him*. Sa'īd died quite a long time before his brother 'Abd Allāh.

I have also mentioned, in the chapter on those learned men who praised Aḥmad, that Ibrāhīm al-Ḥarbī visited 'Abd Allāh to express his condolences on the death of his brother Sa'īd.

Regarding al-Ḥasan and Muḥammad we have no information at all. As for Zaynab, we have reported, in the chapter on Aḥmad's scrupulosity, the story where she tells Isḥāq ibn Ibrāhīm, "Take this chicken and sell it! My father needs a cupping but he has no money." Said Isḥāq, "I saw Aḥmad beat his daughter and scold her for speaking bad Arabic."[330] 65.8

[Al-Marrūdhī:] I went in to see Aḥmad and found a woman there combing the hair of one of his daughters. 65.9

"Have you put ties[331] in her hair yet?" I asked the woman.

"She won't let me," came the reply. "She said, 'My daddy said I can't.'"

"He'd get mad," said the girl.

It is reported that Aḥmad had a daughter named Fāṭimah, who is apparently someone other than Zaynab. On the other hand, Zuhayr's report, cited earlier, on the number of Aḥmad's children does not mention her. Fāṭimah may be the same person as Zaynab, since women sometimes have two names, or she may be someone else. In the chapter on Aḥmad's manifestations of grace, we cited Fāṭimah in this report:

[Fāṭimah:] My brother Ṣāliḥ had a fire in his house. Afterward they went in and found that a robe that had belonged to my father was untouched even though everything around it had burned. 65.10

Chapter 66

How and Why the Inquisition Began

66.1 Before the rise of the Secessionists, there was general agreement on the ancestral principle that the Qur'an is the speech of God and not created.[332] Even when the Secessionists adopted the belief that the Qur'an is created, they kept it a secret. Thus the principle remained inviolate down through the reign of al-Rashīd.[333]

66.2 [Muḥammad ibn Nūḥ:][334] I heard Hārūn al-Rashīd, the Commander of the Faithful, say, "I hear that Bishr al-Marīsī claims the Qur'an is created. If God puts him in my hands, I swear I'll kill him more painfully than I've ever killed anyone."

66.3 [Al-Dawraqī:] I heard Muḥammad ibn Nūḥ report, citing al-Masʿūdī, judge in Baghdad: "I hear that Bishr al-Marīsī claims the Qur'an is created. If God puts him in my hands, I swear I'll kill him more painfully than I've ever killed anyone."

Bishr thus remained in hiding for twenty years. When Hārūn died, he reappeared and began advocating his misguided belief. That's how the Inquisition started.

66.4 [The author:] Even after al-Rashīd died and al-Amīn became caliph, the official position remained the same. But when al-Ma'mūn came to power, a number of Secessionists insinuated themselves into his company and persuaded him to adopt the view that the Qur'an is created. Fearful of those elders who were still alive, al-Ma'mūn hesitated to call for assent to the new creed. Eventually, though, he resolved to impose it on the community.[335]

66.5 [Ibn Aktham:][336] Al-Ma'mūn once remarked that if not for Yazīd ibn Hārūn, he would proclaim that the Qur'an is created. One of those present asked whether Yazīd was really someone to worry about.

"Fool!" said the caliph. "What if I make a statement and he condemns it? People will have to choose sides. And if there's one thing I hate, it's conflict."

"Let me go and see for myself," said the man.

"You go ahead," said al-Ma'mūn.

So the man traveled to Wāsiṭ, where he found Yazīd in his mosque and sat down with him.

"Yazīd," said the man, "the caliph sends his regards and wants you to know that he intends to declare that the Qur'an is created."

"You're lying," said Yazīd. "The caliph would never force people to take a position they don't understand or accept. If you want to see for yourself, come back when the study circle gathers. When everyone's here, you can tell them what you told me."

The next day the man waited for the people to gather and then said, "God be pleased with you, Yazīd! The caliph sends his regards and wants you to know that he intends to declare that the Qur'an is created. What do you have to say about that?"

"You're lying," said Yazīd. "The caliph would never force people to take a position they don't understand or accept, and that no one has ever believed in before."

So the man came back and said to the caliph, "You were right! Here's what happened," and told the story.

"Now do you see?" said al-Ma'mūn. "He played you perfectly."

Chapter 67

His Experience with al-Ma'mūn[337]

67.1 According to his biographers, al-Ma'mūn sent a letter from al-Raqqah[338] to the chief of the Baghdad police, Isḥāq ibn Ibrāhīm, telling him to put the community to the test, which he did.

67.2 [Ṣāliḥ:] I heard my father say, "When they took us in to be questioned by Isḥāq ibn Ibrāhīm, the first thing they did was to read aloud the letter written by the one in Tarsus"—that is, al-Ma'mūn.[339] "They recited some verses to us, including «Nothing is like Him»[340] and «He is the creator of everything.»[341] When I heard 'Nothing is like Him,' I recited «He is the One who hears and sees.»[342]

"Then those present were put to the test. Those who withheld their assent were taken away and locked up. Of them all, only four resisted. Their names are Muḥammad ibn Nuḥ; ʿUbayd Allāh ibn ʿUmar al-Qawārīrī; al-Ḥasan ibn Ḥammād, called Sajjādah; and my father. Later ʿUbayd Allāh ibn ʿUmar and al-Ḥasan ibn Ḥammād gave in too, leaving only Muḥammad ibn Nūḥ and my father in confinement. There they stayed until, several days later, a letter arrived from Tarsus ordering the two of them to be transported there. They were duly sent, shackled one to the other."

67.3 [Abū Maʿmar al-Qaṭīʿī:] I was there when Aḥmad ibn Ḥanbal was brought to the palace during the Inquisition. He had always been a meek man, but when he saw the members of the community giving their assent, his veins swelled, his eyes went red, and all the meekness was gone. Seeing him, I remember thinking to myself, "He's standing up for God."

"Abū ʿAbd Allāh," I told him, "this is good news! Haven't we heard Muḥammad ibn Fuḍayl ibn Ghazwān report, citing al-Walīd ibn ʿAbd Allāh ibn Jumayʿ, citing Abū Salamah ibn ʿAbd al-Raḥmān ibn ʿAwf, who said, 'Among the Prophet's Companions were some who, if challenged on any matter of religion, would glower and roll their eyes like madmen'?"

67.4 [Ibn Abī Usāmah:] I remember hearing that during the Inquisition, someone said to Aḥmad ibn Ḥanbal, "See? Right loses and wrong wins!"

"Never!" he retorted. "Wrong wins only if people's hearts wander off and lose their way, but ours haven't done that yet."

67.5 [Ṣāliḥ:] My father and Muḥammad ibn Nūḥ were carried off in chains and we went with them as far as al-Anbār. There Abū Bakr al-Aḥwal asked my father, "Abū ʿAbd Allāh, if they threaten you with a sword, will you give in?"

"No," he answered. Then he and Muḥammad ibn Nūḥ were taken away.

Later my father told me:

"When we got to al-Raḥbah[343] it was the middle of the night. As we were leaving, a man came up to us and said, 'Which of you is Aḥmad ibn Ḥanbal?'

"Someone pointed me out. 'Slow down,' said the man to the camel-driver. Then to me: 'Listen, you! What does it matter if they kill you right here and now? You'll enter the Garden, here and now.' Then he said, 'I leave you in the care of God,' and left.

"I asked who he was and they told me: 'He's an Arab of Rabīʿah named Jābir ibn ʿĀmir who composes poetry in the wilderness. People speak highly of him.'"

[Ibrāhīm ibn ʿAbd Allāh:] Aḥmad ibn Ḥanbal said, "The most powerful thing anyone said to me during my ordeal was what a desert Arab said to me at Raḥbat Ṭawq: 'Aḥmad, if you die for the truth you die a martyr, and if you live you live a hero.'" 67.7

With that he strengthened my resolve.

[Aḥmad:] "Nothing has ever made more of an impression on me than the words of a desert Arab from Raḥbat Ṭawq: 'Aḥmad, if you die for the truth you die a martyr, and if you live you live a hero.'" 67.8

Ibn Abī Ḥātim quoted his father as saying, "In the end he was right. By the time the Inquisition was over, God had made Aḥmad ibn Ḥanbal a name to be reckoned with."

[The author:] We have also heard that al-Shāfiʿī, may God be pleased with him, had a dream where the Prophet asked him to warn Aḥmad that he would be tried regarding the creation of the Qurʾan. This report will be given along with its chain of transmitters in the chapter on dreams. 67.9

[Al-Anbārī:] When I found out that Aḥmad ibn Ḥanbal was being taken to see al-Maʾmūn, I crossed the Euphrates and found Aḥmad sitting in a caravanserai. When I greeted him he said, "Abū Jaʿfar, you shouldn't have troubled yourself!" 67.10

"It was no trouble," I told him. Then I said, "Listen here! As of today, you have people prepared to follow your example. If you say the Qurʾan is created, many of them will say the same. If you resist, many of them will too. Think about it: even if that man doesn't kill you, you're going to die sooner or later anyway. So fear God and don't give in!"

"God's will be done!" said Aḥmad, weeping. "God's will be done!" Then he said, "Abū Ja'far, repeat what you said for me."

So I repeated it, and again he said "God's will be done! God's will be done!"

67.11 [Ṣāliḥ:] My father told me: "We were just leaving Adana when the city gate opened behind us and someone called out: 'Good news! That man is dead!'[344]

"I had been praying I would never meet him."

67.12 [Al-Būshanjī:] I heard Aḥmad ibn Ḥanbal say, "Three times I've asked God for something and twice seen my request granted. I asked Him to keep me away from al-Ma'mūn, and I told Him I didn't want to see al-Mutawakkil. Well, I never saw al-Ma'mūn."[345]

Al-Ma'mūn died at the Badhandūn—a river in Byzantine territory—while Aḥmad was locked up in al-Raqqah. Al-Mu'taṣim received the oath of allegiance in Anatolia and returned to Iraq. Aḥmad was brought back to Baghdad in 218 [833], and it was al-Mu'taṣim who tried him. As for al-Mutawakkil, when he brought Aḥmad to the palace to instruct his children in Hadith, he observed him from a secret compartment, meaning that he saw Aḥmad but Aḥmad never saw him.

67.13 [Ṣāliḥ:] My father and Muḥammad ibn Nūḥ were sent back from Tarsus still in irons. When they reached al-Raqqah, they were put onto a boat. At 'Ānāt,[346] Muḥammad ibn Nūḥ died and his chains were removed. My father prayed over his body.

67.14 [Ḥanbal:] I heard Aḥmad ibn Ḥanbal say: "I never saw anyone so young or so unlearned stand up for God more bravely than Muḥammad ibn Nūḥ. I hope God saved him when he died!

"One day, when the two of us were alone, he said to me, 'Aḥmad, fear God! Fear God! We're nothing alike, you and I. You're a man people follow and everyone is watching and waiting to see what you'll do. Fear God, and stand firm!'—or words to that effect. Imagine him trying to keep me strong and warn me to do the right thing! And look what happened to him: he fell sick and ended up dying by the side of a road somewhere. I prayed over him and buried him."

He may have added: "That was in 'Ānah."

Aḥmad ibn 'Alī ibn Thābit reported that Muḥammad ibn Nūḥ died in 218 [833].

Chapter 68

What Happened after the Death of al-Ma'mūn

As soon as al-Ma'mūn's death was announced, Aḥmad ibn Ḥanbal and Muḥammad ibn Nūḥ were sent back to Iraq in irons, as we have seen. Muḥammad ibn Nūḥ died on the way and Aḥmad, still in chains, completed the journey. 68.1

[Al-Būshanjī:] During the reign of al-Ma'mūn, Aḥmad was taken away to the Byzantine frontier. He had traveled as far as al-Raqqah when al-Ma'mūn died at al-Badhandūn, so the two never met.[347] That was in 218 [833]. 68.2

Abū l-'Abbās al-Raqqī, a Hadith scholar, told me that he and some others went to visit Aḥmad during his imprisonment in al-Raqqah. There they confronted him with the reports that allow a Muslim to conceal his beliefs when his life is in danger.

"But what do you do," responded Aḥmad, "with Khabbāb's report that says: 'Before your time there were believers who could be sawed in half without renouncing their faith'?"

When they heard that they gave up hope.

"I don't care if they keep me locked up," he went on. "My house is already a prison. I don't care if they kill me by the sword, either. The only thing I'm afraid of is being flogged. What if I can't take it?"

One of the prisoners had overheard him. "Don't worry, Aḥmad," he said. "After two lashes you don't feel the rest."

Aḥmad looked relieved.

After that he was brought back from al-Raqqah and jailed in Baghdad.

[Ṣāliḥ:] When the news came that al-Ma'mūn had died, Muḥammad ibn Nūḥ and my father, still in chains, were sent back 68.3

to al-Raqqah. From there they continued their journey on a prison ship. When they reached ʿĀnāt, Muḥammad ibn Nūḥ died and they buried him there. Finally my father, still in chains, reached Baghdad.

First he stayed for a few days in Yāsirīyah.[348] Then they held him in a house rented for that purpose near the Palace of ʿUmārah.[349] After that he was transferred to the Commoners' Prison[350] in Mawṣilī Street—or, according to another report, a street called al-Mawṣiliyyah.[351]

68.4 [Ṣāliḥ:] My father said, "I used to lead the prisoners in prayer with the chains still on me."[352]

68.5 [Abū Bakr al-Aʿyan:] I told Ādam al-ʿAsqalānī I was traveling to Baghdad and asked him if he wanted anything.

"Yes," he said. "When you get there, go to Aḥmad ibn Ḥanbal, greet him for me, and tell him this. 'You there! Fear God, and seek closeness to Him, by staying the course. Let no one dismay you: you stand—God willing—at the very gate of the Garden.' And tell him: 'We heard al-Layth ibn Saʿd report, citing Muḥammad ibn ʿAjlān, citing Abū l-Zinād, citing al-Aʿraj, citing Abū Hurayrah, that the Prophet, God bless and keep him, said: "If any ask you to disobey God, heed him not."'"

So I went to see Aḥmad ibn Ḥanbal in jail. When I found him, I greeted him, conveyed al-ʿAsqalānī's greeting, and repeated his words, along with the Hadith. Aḥmad lowered his gaze for a time, then raised his head and said, "God have mercy on him in life and death alike! His is good counsel indeed."

68.6 [Al-Aʿyān:] I went to Ādam ibn Abī Iyās [al-ʿAsqalānī] and told him that ʿAbd Allāh ibn Ṣāliḥ had sent him his regards.

"Convey no greetings to me from him," he said, "or to him from me!"

"Why not?" I asked.

"Because he said that the Qur'an is created."

"He's just explained that he didn't mean it," I said, "and he's announced to everyone that he takes back what he said."

"In that case, convey my greetings."

As I was leaving, I told al-ʿAsqalānī I was going to Baghdad and asked him if he wanted anything.

"Yes," he said. "Go to Ibn Ḥanbal and give him my regards. Tell him this: 'You there! Fear God, and seek closeness to Him, by staying the course. Let no one dismay you: you stand—God willing—at the very gate of the Garden.' And tell him: 'We heard al-Layth ibn Saʿd report, citing Muḥammad ibn ʿAjlān, citing Abū l-Zinād, citing al-Aʿraj, citing Abū Hurayrah, that the Prophet, God bless and keep him, said: "If any ask you to disobey God, heed him not."'"

So I went to see Aḥmad ibn Ḥanbal in jail. When I found him, I conveyed al-ʿAsqalānī's greeting and his advice, along with the Hadith. Aḥmad lowered his gaze for a moment, then said, "God have mercy on him in life and death alike! His is good counsel indeed."

Chapter 69

His Experience with al-Muʿtaṣim

When al-Maʾmūn died, Aḥmad was brought back to Baghdad and 69.1
imprisoned there. Then he was tried by al-Muʿtaṣim. The chief
judge at the time was Aḥmad ibn Abī Duʾād, who had persuaded 69.2
the caliph to test people's belief that the Qurʾan is created.[353]

Al-Marrūdhī said:

When Aḥmad ibn Ḥanbal was put in prison, the jailer came and asked him whether the Hadith about tyrants and those who serve them was authentic.[354] Aḥmad told him it was.

"Am I one of those who serve them?" asked the jailer.

"Those who serve are the ones who cut your hair, wash your clothes, prepare your food, and do business with you. What *you* are is one of the tyrants."

[Aḥmad:] In Ramadan of '19 [September or October 834] I was 69.3
moved to Isḥāq ibn Ibrāhīm's house. Every day they sent over two men—Aḥmad ibn Rabāḥ, one was called, and the other was Abū Shuʿayb al-Ḥajjām—to debate with me. When they were ready

to leave they would call for a fetter and add it to the fetters that I already had on me. I ended up with four fetters on my legs.[355]

On the third day one of the two came and started debating with me. At one point I asked, "What do you say about God's knowledge?"[356]

"God's knowledge is created," he replied.

"You're an unbeliever!"

Present also was a man sent by Isḥāq ibn Ibrāhīm. When he heard me, he said, "You're talking to the emissary of the Commander of the Faithful!"

"Whoever he is," I replied, "he's still an unbeliever."

69.4 On the fourth night, he—that is, al-Muʿtaṣim—sent Bughā, called the Elder, to fetch me from Isḥāq's. On the way out, I was taken to see Isḥāq, who said, "By God, Aḥmad, it's your life we're talking about here. He won't behead you and be done with it: he's sworn that if you don't do as he asks he'll flog you senseless and then throw you where you'll never see the sun. Now look here: doesn't God say «We have made it an Arabic Qur'an?»[357] How could He make it without creating it?"

I answered with a different verse: «He made them like stubble cropped by cattle.»[358] Then I asked him whether "made them" meant "created them." He didn't know how to answer me so he said nothing. Finally he said, "Take him away!"

69.5 When we got to the place called the Orchard Gate, they took me out.[359] Then they brought a riding animal and put me on it, fetters and all. There was no one with me to hold me up, and more than once I nearly fell over with the weight of the fetters. They took me inside—inside al-Muʿtaṣim's palace, that is—put me in a room, and locked the door. I wanted to clean myself off for prayer, but it was the middle of the night and there was no lamp in the room. But when I stuck out my hand I found a pitcher of water and a basin nearby. So I did my ablutions and prayed.

69.6 The next morning, I pulled the drawstring out of my trousers and used it to tie the fetters together so I could lift them, leaving my trousers hanging down on one side. Then al-Muʿtaṣim's messenger came, took me by the arm, and told me to come along. So I appeared before al-Muʿtaṣim holding up my fetters with the cord. He was sitting there with Ibn Abī Du'ād and a crowd of his associates.

[Ibrāhīm ibn Muḥammad:] Aḥmad ibn Ḥanbal was brought before the caliph. Aḥmad ibn Abī Du'ād and Abū ʿAbd al-Raḥmān, the disciple of al-Shāfiʿī, were there too. Aḥmad was given a seat in front of the caliph. They had said things to frighten him, and they had just finished beheading two men. Upon seeing Abū ʿAbd al-Raḥmān, Ibn Ḥanbal asked, "Do you know any reports from al-Shāfiʿī on passing hands over one's shoes?"[360] 69.7

"Look at that!" exclaimed Ibn Abī Du'ād. "We bring him here to behead him, and he wants to discuss jurisprudence!"

[Al-Būshanjī:] Al-Muʿtaṣim returned to Baghdad from the Byzantine front in Ramadan of '18. It was then that he tried Aḥmad and had him flogged in open court.[361] 69.8

[Aḥmad:] When I came before al-Muʿtaṣim, he kept telling me to come closer. When I got up close to him he told me to sit, and I did, weighed down by the fetters. After a time I asked if I might speak.[362] 69.9

"Go ahead," he said.

"What did the Prophet call on us to do?" I asked.

After a moment of silence, he replied: "To testify that there is no god but God."

"Well, I testify that there is no god but God." Then I went on: "Your grandfather Ibn ʿAbbās reports that when the delegation from the tribe of Qays came to see the Prophet, they asked him about faith. He answered, 'Do you know what faith is?'

"'God and His Emissary know best,' they said.

"'It means testifying that there is no god but God, and Muḥammad is His Emissary. It means holding the ritual prayer, paying the alms tax, and giving up one-fifth of your spoils.'"[363]

"If my predecessor hadn't left you for me to deal with," said al-Muʿtaṣim, "I wouldn't be doing this to you." Then, turning to

ʿAbd al-Raḥmān ibn Isḥāq, he said, "Didn't I ask you to stop the Inquisition?"

69.10 "Thank God!" I thought to myself. "The Muslims' suffering is over!"

But then he said to them, "Debate with him. Talk to him!" and then again to ʿAbd al-Raḥmān: "Talk to him!"

"What do you say about the Qur'an?" asked ʿAbd al-Raḥmān.

"What do you say about God's knowledge?" I asked. He fell silent.

One of the others broke in. "But didn't God say, «God is the creator of all things»?[364] And isn't the Qur'an a thing?"

"God also mentioned a wind," I said, "that would «destroy everything at the behest of its Lord,»[365] but it destroyed only what He wanted it to."[366]

Then another one spoke up: "God says, «Whenever any new admonition comes to them from their Lord.»[367] How can something be new without having been created?"

I replied: "God also said, «*Ṣād*. By the Qur'an, containing the admonition.»[368] This admonition is the Qur'an. In the other verse there's no 'the.'"

One of them cited the Hadith of ʿImrān ibn Ḥuṣayn that God created the remembrance. "That's wrong," I said. "I have it on more than one source that he said, 'God wrote the remembrance.'"

Next they tried arguing with me using the Hadith of Ibn Masʿūd: "God has created nothing—not the Garden or the Fire or the heavens or the earth—greater than the Throne Verse."

I said: "The word 'created' applies to the Garden, the Fire, the heavens, and the earth, but not to the Qur'an."

One of them cited the Hadith of Khabbāb: "You there! Try as you may to come nearer to God, you will find nothing dearer to Him by which to approach Him than His word."[369]

"Yes," I said, "that's what it says."

Ibn Abī Du'ād glared at me.

69.11 And so it went. One of them would say something, and I would rebut him. Then another would speak and I would rebut him too.

Whenever one of his men was stymied, Ibn Abī Du'ād would interrupt: "Commander of the Faithful! By God, he's misguided, and misleading, and a heretical innovator!"

But al-Mu'taṣim kept saying, "Talk to him! Debate him!"

So again one of them would say something, and I would rebut him. Then another would speak and I would rebut him too. When none of them had anything left to say, he—meaning al-Mu'taṣim—said, "Come on, Aḥmad! Speak up!"

"Commander of the Faithful," I replied, "give me something I can agree to—something from the Book of God or the *sunnah* of His Emissary."

At that, Ibn Abī Du'ād exclaimed, "What! You only repeat what's in the Qur'an or the *sunnah* of His Emissary?"

"You have an interpretation," I said, "and that's your affair, but it's nothing to lock people up for, or put them in chains."

[Al-Būshanjī:] One of my associates reported that Ibn Abī Du'ād 69.12
confronted Aḥmad and tried to engage him in debate but Aḥmad ignored him. Eventually al-Mu'taṣim asked Aḥmad why he wouldn't address Ibn Abī Du'ād.

"I speak only with men of learning," said Aḥmad.

[Aḥmad:] "Commander of the Faithful," said Ibn Abī Du'ād, 69.13
"seeing him capitulate to you would mean more to me than a hundred thousand dinars, and another hundred thousand dinars,"[370] and so on, throwing out one number after another.

"If he tells me what I want to hear," said al-Mu'taṣim, "I swear I'll unchain him with my own hands. Then I'll lead my troops to him and march along behind him." Then he said, "Aḥmad, I want what's best for you, the same as if you were my son Hārūn. Come on, now: What can you tell me?"[371]

"Give me something from the Book of God," I said, "or the *sunnah* of His Emissary."

As the session dragged on, al-Mu'taṣim grew bored and restless. 69.14
"Go!" he said to the scholars. Then he ordered 'Abd al-Raḥmān ibn Isḥāq and me to stay behind so he could talk to me.

"Come on!" he said. "Why don't you give up?" Then he said, "I don't recognize you. Have you never come here before?"

"I know him, Commander of the Faithful," said ʿAbd al-Raḥmān ibn Isḥāq. "For thirty years, he's been saying that Muslims owe obedience to you and should follow you in the holy war and join you on the pilgrimage."

"By God," said al-Muʿtaṣim, "he's a man of learning—a man of understanding! I wouldn't mind having someone like him with me to argue against people from other religions." Then, turning to me, "Did you know Ṣāliḥ al-Rashīdī?"

"I've heard of him," I said.

"He was my tutor, and he was sitting right there," he said, pointing to a corner of the room. "I asked him about the Qur'an and he contradicted me, so I had him trampled and dragged out. So Aḥmad: find something—anything—you can agree to, and I'll unchain you with my own hands."

"Give me something from the Book of God," I said, "or the *sunnah* of His Emissary."

69.15 The session dragged on. Finally al-Muʿtaṣim rose and went back inside, and I was sent back to the place where they had been keeping me.

After sunset prayers, two of Ibn Abī Du'ād's associates were sent in to spend the night there and continue debating with me. They stayed until it was time to break the fast.[372] When the meal arrived they pressed me to eat but I wouldn't. Then, at some point during the night, al-Muʿtaṣim sent over Ibn Abī Du'ād.

"The Commander of the Faithful wants to know if you have anything to say."

I gave him my usual answer.

"You know," he said, "your name was one of the seven—Yaḥyā ibn Maʿīn and the rest—but I rubbed it out."[373]

The seven were Yāḥyā ibn Maʿīn, Abū Khaythamah, Aḥmad al-Dawraqī, al-Qawārīrī, Saʿduwayh, and—in some accounts—Khalaf al-Makhzūmī.[374]

Ibn Abī Du'ād continued: "I was sorry to see them arrest you." Then he said, "The Commander of the Faithful has sworn to give you a good long beating and then throw you somewhere where you'll never see the sun. But he also says that if you capitulate he'll come and unchain you himself."

Then he left.

The next morning—on my second day there—al-Muʿtaṣim's 69.16
envoy came, took me by the arm, and brought me before him. Again al-Muʿtaṣim ordered them to debate me. "Talk to him!" he said.

So the debate began again. One of them would speak from over here and I would answer him, and another from over there and I'd answer him too. Whenever they mentioned anything not in the Book of God or the *sunnah* of His Emissary, or in a report about the early Muslims, I would say, "I don't know what you mean."

"Commander of the Faithful," they would protest, "when he has an argument against us he stands his ground, but whenever we make a point he says he doesn't know what we're talking about."

"Keep debating him!" said al-Muʿtaṣim.

"All I see you doing," said one of them, "is citing Hadith and 69.17
claiming to know what it means."

"What do you say," I asked him, "about the verse «Concerning your children, God enjoins you that a male shall receive a share equivalent to that of two females»?"[375]

"It applies only to believers," he said.

I asked him: "What about murderers, slaves, or Jews?"

He fell silent. I had resorted to that tactic for one reason: they had been arguing on the basis of the plain text of the Qur'an while accusing me of citing Hadith for no good reason.[376]

They kept at it until nearly noon. When al-Muʿtaṣim had had enough, he sent everyone away except for ʿAbd al-Raḥmān ibn Isḥāq, who continued to argue with me. Finally al-Muʿtaṣim rose and went back inside, and I was sent back to the place where they had been holding me.

69.18 [ʿAbd Allāh:] Al-Fatḥ ibn Shakhraf wrote to me in his own hand saying that he heard from Ibn Ḥuṭayṭ—a man of learning from Khurasan, whose name he gave in full—that before Aḥmad ibn Ḥanbal was flogged, he and some of his fellow victims of the Inquisition were kept in confinement in a house somewhere.

"Night fell," said Aḥmad, "and the others went to sleep, but I couldn't stop thinking about what would happen to me. Then I saw a tall man picking his way around the sleepers toward me.

"'Are you Aḥmad ibn Ḥanbal?' he asked.

"I said nothing and he asked again. When I didn't answer, he asked a third time: 'Are you Aḥmad ibn Ḥanbal?'

"'Yes.'

"'Only endure,' he said, 'and the Garden is yours.'

"Later, when I felt the burning of the whips, I remembered what he'd told me."

69.19 [Aḥmad:] I remember thinking to myself on the third night that something was bound to happen the next day. I asked one of the men who were assigned to me to find me a cord. He found one and I used it to pull up my chains. Then I put the drawstring back on my trousers to hold them up so I wouldn't be exposed if something happened to me.

69.20 On the morning of the third day,[377] al-Muʿtaṣim sent for me again. I entered the hall to find it packed with people. As I came slowly forward, I saw people with swords, people with whips, and so on—many more than on the first two days. When I reached him, he told me to sit down. "Debate him," he told the others. "Talk to him!"

They began to argue with me. One would talk and I would answer him, and then another would talk and I'd answer him too. Soon I was winning.[378] One of the men standing near al-Muʿtaṣim began pointing at me. After the session had gone on for a while, al-Muʿtaṣim had me led away to one side so he could confer with them alone. Then he sent them to the side and had me brought over.

"Come on, Aḥmad!" he said. "Tell me what I want to hear, and I'll unchain you with my own hands."

When I gave him my usual answer, he cursed me, then said, "Drag him away and strip him!"

I was dragged away and stripped.[379]

Some time before, I had acquired some of the Prophet's hair. Noticing that I had something knotted up in the sleeve of my shirt, Isḥāq ibn Ibrāhīm sent someone over to ask what it was. I told him it was some of the Prophet's hair. When they started tearing my shirt off, al-Muʿtaṣim told them to stop and they pulled it off me without ripping it. I think he held back because of the hair that was knotted up inside. 69.21

Sitting down on a chair, al-Muʿtaṣim called for the posts and the whips. They brought out the posts and made me stretch out my arms. From behind me someone said, "Hold on to the tusks and pull," but I didn't understand, so I ended up spraining both my wrists.[380] 69.22

[Al-Būshanjī:] They say that when Aḥmad was suspended from the posts, al-Muʿtaṣim, seeing him undaunted, so admired his bravery that he was prepared to be lenient with him; but then Aḥmad ibn Abī Duʾād provoked him, saying, "If you let him go, people will say that you've renounced al-Maʾmūn's creed and are refusing to enforce it." It was this that pushed al-Muʿtaṣim to go ahead and flog him. 69.23

[Aḥmad:] When they brought the whips, al-Muʿtaṣim looked at them and said, "Bring different ones," which was done.[381] Then he said to the lictors,[382] "Proceed!" 69.24

One at a time, they came at me, and struck two lashes apiece, with al-Muʿtaṣim calling out, "Harder, damn you!" As each one stepped aside another would come up and hit me twice more, with him shouting all the while, "Harder, damn you all!"[383]

After I had been struck nineteen lashes, he—meaning al-Muʿtaṣim—rose from his seat and walked up to me. 69.25

"Aḥmad," he said, "why are you killing yourself? I swear to God, I want what's best for you."

Then ʿUjayf began jabbing at me with the hilt of his sword. "Do you think you can win against this whole lot?"

"For shame!" someone called out. "The caliph is standing there waiting for you."

"Commander of the Faithful!" cried another. "Kill him, and let his blood be on my hands!"

Then more of them chimed in. "Commander of the Faithful, you've been fasting, and now you're standing in the sun!"[384]

"Come on, Aḥmad," he said. "Say something!"

"Give me something I can believe," I said, "from the Book of God or the *sunnah* of His Emissary."

He went back to his chair and sat down.

"Proceed," he said to the lictor. "Let him feel it, damn you!"

69.26 Soon he rose a second time, saying, "Come on, Aḥmad! Tell me what I want to hear."

The others joined in, saying, "Shame on you, Aḥmad: your imam is standing here waiting for you."

"Which of your associates," asked ʿAbd al-Raḥmān, "is doing what you're doing?"

"Tell me whatever you can manage," al-Muʿtaṣim said to me, "and I'll unchain you with my own hands."

"Give me something I can believe," I said, "from the Book of God or the *sunnah* of His Emissary."

Again he went back to his chair and sat down. "Proceed," he said to the lictors. Again they came up one by one and struck me two lashes apiece, with al-Muʿtaṣim calling out, "Harder, damn you!" As each stepped aside another would come up and hit me twice more, with him shouting all the while, "Harder, damn you all!"

That's when I passed out.[385]

Some time later I came to my senses to find that my chains had been removed.

"We threw you face down," said one of the men who had been there. "Then we rolled you over on the ground and trampled you."

I had no memory of that.

They brought me some barley water and told me to drink it and vomit.

"I can't break the fast," I told them.

They took me back to Isḥāq ibn Ibrahīm's place, where I attended the noon prayer.[386] Ibn Samā'ah stepped forward to lead the prayer. When he finished he asked me, "How could you pray when you're bleeding inside your clothes?" 69.27

"'Umar prayed with blood spurting from his wounds," I answered.

Ṣāliḥ said: 69.28

My father was released and went home. From the time he was first arrested to the time he was flogged and let go was twenty-eight months.

One of the two men who were with my father—in jail, that is—heard and saw everything. Later he came to see me and said, "Cousin, may God have mercy on Abū 'Abd Allāh! I never saw anyone like him. When they sent food in, I would remind him that he was fasting, and tell him he was allowed to save himself.[387] I also remember that he was thirsty. He asked the attendant for something to drink. The man gave him a cup of water with ice in it. He took it and looked at it for a moment, but then he gave it back without drinking it. I was amazed that he could go without food or water even in that terrifying place."

Ṣāliḥ said: 69.29

At the time, I was doing everything I could to smuggle some food or a loaf or two of flatbread in to him, but none of my pleading did any good.

A man who was there told me that he kept his eye on him for the entire three days, and not once during all the argument and debate did he mispronounce a single word. "I didn't think it was possible for anyone to be as tough as he was."

[Al-Būshanjī:] Al-Mu'taṣim returned to Baghdad from the Byzantine front in Ramadan of '18. It was then that he tried Aḥmad and had him flogged before him. 69.30

A trustworthy associate of mine reported to me what he was told by Ibrāhīm ibn Muṣ'ab, who at that time was standing in for Isḥāq ibn Ibrāhīm as al-Mu'taṣim's chief of police: "I've never seen anyone brought face to face with kings and princes show as little fear as Aḥmad did that day. To him we were nothing but a cloud of flies."

69.31 [Al-Zuhrī:] I read from my own notes what al-Marrūdhī said at the trial of Aḥmad ibn Ḥanbal, as Aḥmad was hanging between the posts.[388]

"Master," said al-Marrūdhī, "God says, «Do not kill yourselves.»"[389]

"Marrūdhī," said Aḥmad, "go and look outside and tell me what you see."

Al-Marrūdhī reported: "I went out and there, in the courtyard of the caliph's palace, was a vast crowd of people—God only knows how many—with their sheets of paper, their pens, and their pots of ink. I asked them what they were doing, and they said, 'We're waiting to hear what Aḥmad says so we can write it down.'"

He told them to stay where they were, then went back inside, where Aḥmad was still hanging between the posts. He told him that he had seen a crowd of people holding pen and paper and waiting to write down whatever he would say.

"Can I mislead all those people?" asked Aḥmad. "I'd rather kill myself."[390]

69.32 [The author:] Here then is a man who, like Bilāl, was willing to give up his life for the sake of his God.[391] Of Saʿīd ibn al-Musayyab, similarly, it is reported that his life meant as little to him as the life of a fly. Such indifference to self is possible only when one has glimpsed the life that lies beyond this one and trained one's gaze on the future rather than the present. Aḥmad's great suffering is evidence of his strong faith, for, as the Prophet is known to have said, "A man suffers in proportion to his faith." Praise the One who helped Aḥmad, granted him the gift of perception, strengthened his resolve, and came to his aid.

69.33 [Ibn al-Aṣbagh:] I was in Baghdad and heard a clamor. I asked what it was about and people told me that Aḥmad ibn Ḥanbal was being tried. So I went home, collected a substantial sum of money, and bribed my way into the session. Inside the palace, I saw soldiers with their swords drawn, their spears fixed, their shields planted, and their whips at the ready. I was fitted out with a black cloak, a sash, and a sword, and given a seat close enough that I could hear what was being said.

The caliph appeared and seated himself in a chair. Then Ibn Ḥanbal was brought in.

"I swear by my ancestor the Prophet," said the caliph, "that if you don't say as I say, I'll have you flogged!"

Turning to the lictor, he said, "Take him away!"

At the first blow, Aḥmad said, "In the name of God!"

At the second, he said, "There is no might or power except by God!"

At the third, he said, "The Qur'an is the speech of God, and uncreated!"

At the fourth he said, "«Say: we will suffer only what God has decreed for us!»"[392]

The lictor had struck him twenty-nine lashes when Aḥmad's trouser cord—which was made of nothing more than a strip of garment lining—broke. His trousers slipped down as far as his groin.

"He'll be left with nothing on," I thought to myself. But then he looked up to the heavens and moved his lips. Instantly the trousers stopped slipping and remained in place.

Seven days later, I went to see him. "Aḥmad," I asked, "I was there the day they beat you and your trousers came apart. I saw you look up and move your lips. What were you saying?"

He said, "I said, 'God, I call You by Your name, which has filled the Throne! If You know me to be in the right, do not expose my nakedness.'"

[Aḥmad ibn al-Faraj:] I was there when Aḥmad was whipped. 69.34
Abū l-Dann came up and struck him more than ten lashes. Blood started pouring from his shoulders. He was wearing a pair of trousers, and the cord broke. I noticed that as the trousers began to come down, he said something inaudible and they went back up.

Later I asked him about it, and he told me what he had said: "'My God and Lord, You've put me here, and now You're going to expose my nakedness to the world?' That's when my trousers came back up."[393]

69.35 [Al-Qurashī:] When they brought Aḥmad ibn Ḥanbal forward to be flogged, they stripped him of everything but his trousers. As he was being flogged, the trousers came loose. His lips moved, and then I saw two hands appear from under him as he was being whipped and pull the trousers back up. When the flogging was over, we asked him what he had said when the trousers came loose. He told us, "I said, 'I call on You who alone knows where Your Throne is. If I'm in the right, do not expose my nakedness.' That's what I said."

69.36 [Al-Rāzī:] Isḥāq ibn Ibrāhīm used to say, "By God, I was there the day Aḥmad was flogged and his trousers came down and went up again, and reknotted themselves after coming loose. The people there with him were too preoccupied to notice. But I never saw a more terrible day for al-Muʿtaṣim. If he hadn't stopped the flogging, he would never have made it out alive."[394]

69.37 [Al-Anṣārī:] I heard one of the lictors say, "Aḥmad ibn Ḥanbal turned out to be as tough as a bandit.[395] If a camel knelt down and I hit it as hard as I hit him, I would have split open its belly."

69.38 [Shābāṣ:] I struck Aḥmad ibn Ḥanbal eighty lashes. If I'd hit an elephant that hard I would've knocked it down.[396]

69.39 [Al-Rāshidī:] One of my associates reported: "When the whips began to tear into Abū ʿAbd Allāh, he said, 'To You, Sovereign of the heavens and the earth, I cry for help!'"

69.40 [ʿAbd Allāh:] I often heard my father say, "God have mercy on Abū l-Haytham! God pardon Abū l-Haytham! God forgive Abū l-Haytham!"

"Dad," I finally asked, "who is Abū l-Haytham?"

"Don't you know?"

"No."

"It's Abū l-Haytham al-Ḥaddād. The day they took me and stretched my arms out for the flogging, I felt someone pulling at my clothes from behind.

"'Do you recognize me?' he asked.

"'No.'

"'I'm Abū l-Haytham, and I'm a bandit, a cutpurse, and a thief. At one time or another, I've been struck eighteen thousand lashes—all on record with the Commander of the Faithful—for the sake of Satan and the things of this world. So bear up and take your beating for God and Islam.'

"They struck me eighteen lashes instead of his eighteen thousand. Then the attendant came out and said, 'The Commander of the Faithful has pardoned him!'"

[The author:] In his *History*, Ibrāhīm ibn Muḥammad ibn ʿArafah reports that Aḥmad was struck thirty-six lashes.[397]

[Yaḥyā ibn Nuʿaym:] As Aḥmad ibn Ḥanbal was being taken out 69.41
to al-Muʿtaṣim to be flogged, the officer escorting him said, "Go ahead and curse whoever did this to you!"

"Cursing your oppressor," said Aḥmad, "shows a lack of fortitude."

[Al-Baghawī:] I saw Aḥmad ibn Ḥanbal going into the mosque 69.42
of al-Manṣūr wearing a green over-garment, his sandals in his hand, bare-headed. To me he looked to be a tall, dark-skinned, white-bearded old man. Sitting in the gallery of the minaret were members of the caliph's entourage. When they saw him, they came down to pay their respects. Kissing his head and hands, they said, "Curse the one who mistreated you."

"Cursing your oppressor," said Aḥmad, "shows a lack of fortitude."[398]

[Aḥmad:] When they took me to the palace I went without food 69.43
for two days. After they flogged me they brought me some barley water, but I didn't have any so as not to break my fast.

[Al-Makhzūmī:] I was in Mecca walking around the Kaʿbah with 69.44
Saʿīd ibn Manṣūr when I heard a voice behind me say: "Today is the flogging of Aḥmad ibn Ḥanbal."

Later I found out that he had been flogged that day.

In another telling:

Saʿīd ibn Manṣūr asked me, "Did you hear what I heard?"

I told him I had.

"Remember what day this is," he said.

Later we found out that he had been flogged that day.

69.45 [Al-Ṭaḥḥān:] On the day Aḥmad ibn Ḥanbal was flogged, I was with Abū ʿUbayd al-Qāsim ibn Sallām, Ibrahīm ibn Abī l-Layth, and several others at the home of ʿĀṣim ibn ʿAlī.

"Will anyone come with me and talk to that man?" asked ʿĀṣim.[399] He repeated the question several times but no one answered, until finally Ibrāhīm said, "I'll come."

ʿĀṣim shouted to the servant boy to bring his boots. But then Ibrāhīm said, "Let me go and see my daughters first. I haven't seen them in a while and I have some things to tell them."

He left, and we suspected that he had gone to perfume himself and put on his shroud.

When he returned, ʿĀṣim again called for his boots.

"I went to see my daughters," said Ibrāhīm, "and they wept."

Then a letter came from ʿĀṣim's two daughters in Wāsiṭ. It read, "Father, we've heard that that man has taken Aḥmad ibn Ḥanbal and flogged him to make him say that the Qur'an is created. If he asks you to do the same thing, be fearful of God and refuse. By God, we'd rather hear that you'd died than that you gave in."

69.46 [Al-Ḥarrānī:] While Aḥmad was being flogged, Abū ʿUbayd al-Qāsim ibn Sallām and I were waiting at al-Muʿtaṣim's gate. Abū ʿUbayd started saying, "Are we going to let them do this to the best of us? It's unbearable!"

I said:

They had no right to flog him so
  But let them strike, for firm he stood,
And even as they stretched him flat
  As highland earth, he said, inspired:
"I may die, but you, not I, will burn
  With the liars in the pits of Hell!"

[Abū Ḥātim:] The day they flogged Aḥmad, I decided to go and see for myself what had happened to him. I arrived early and found an old man standing there saying, "God, give him strength! God, help him!" He continued, speaking as if caught in some terrible dilemma, "I need to know if he's given in and I have to go take his place." 69.47

Then someone came out, saying, "He didn't give in."

"Thank God!" said the old man.

I asked someone who the old man was.

"Bishr ibn al-Ḥārith," I was told.[400]

[The author:] We are aware of other accounts of the flogging, but we doubt their accuracy and have therefore omitted them.[401] 69.48

More on What He Achieved by Remaining Steadfast throughout His Ordeal

The Prophet, God bless and keep him, said: "There will come a time when anyone who suffers bravely for his faith will be rewarded fifty times more than you." 69.49

"More than us?" asked his Companions.

"Yes," he said, repeating it three times.

[Al-Shāfiʿī:] "The hardest three things are these: being generous when you have little, being scrupulous when you're alone, and speaking truth to power." 69.50

[Abū Zurʿah:] I always used to hear people speaking highly of Ibn Ḥanbal and giving him precedence over Yaḥyā ibn Maʿīn and Abū Khaythamah, though never as much as after he was tried. After he was tried, his reputation knew no bounds. 69.51

[Ibn Abī ʿAbd al-Raḥmān:] I heard Aḥmad ibn Yūnus recite the Hadith: "In the Garden are palaces open only to prophets, truth-tellers, or those given power over their own souls." 69.52

Someone asked, "Who are 'those given power over their own souls'?"

"Aḥmad ibn Ḥanbal, for example," he replied.

[The author:] This Hadith is traced back to Kaʿb al-Aḥbār, as follows:

We cite Muḥammad ibn ʿAbd al-Bāqī ibn Aḥmad ibn Sulaymān, who cites Ḥamd ibn Aḥmad, who cites Aḥmad ibn ʿAbd Allāh al-Iṣfahānī, who heard ʿAbd Allāh ibn Muḥammad report that he heard ʿAbd al-Raḥmān ibn Muḥammad ibn Salm report that he heard Hannād ibn al-Sarī report that he heard Muḥammad ibn ʿUbayd, citing Salamah ibn Nubayṭ, citing ʿAbd Allāh ibn Abī l-Jaʿd, citing Kaʿb al-Aḥbār, report:

[Kaʿb al-Aḥbār:] Belonging to God are dwellings of pearl upon pearl, or nacre upon nacre, in which are seventy thousand palaces. In each palace are seventy thousand courts, and in each court seventy thousand rooms, where none may live but prophets, truth-tellers, martyrs, just rulers, and those given power over their own souls.

[The author:] According to Hadith scholars, one of the words in this report may be pronounced two different ways. *Muḥakkam*, "given power," means—according to Abū ʿUbayd al-Harawī—someone who is asked to choose between death and unbelief and chooses death. If pronounced *muḥakkim*, it means, according to Wakīʿ, someone capable of judging himself.

69.53 [ʿAbd Allāh:] My father once said to me, speaking of the Inquisition: "Son, I gave all I could."

He[402] also said that some Catacombers[403] wrote to Aḥmad ibn Ḥanbal saying, "If you change your mind about your creed, we'll change our minds about being Muslims."

69.54 [Abū Ghālib:] Aḥmad was flogged for the sake of God and stood where the truth-tellers stand during the last ten days of Ramadan 220 [mid- to late September 835].

69.55 [Jaʿfar ibn Abī Hāshim:] Ibn Ḥanbal was in jail through '17, '18, and '19, and was let out in Ramadan.

More on How He Left the Palace of al-Muʿtaṣim

69.56 [Ibn al-Ḥārith:] Abū Muḥammad al-Ṭufāwī asked Aḥmad ibn Ḥanbal to tell him what they had done to him.

"After they had flogged me," said Aḥmad, "that one with the long beard"—meaning ʿUjayf—"came up and jabbed me with the hilt of his sword. I remember thinking it was finally over. Let him cut my throat so I can rest!

"Ibn Samāʿah said to the caliph, 'Commander of the Faithful! Behead him and let his blood be on my hands.'

"But then Ibn Abī Dū'ād said, 'Commander of the Faithful: better not to! If you kill him here or let him die inside the palace, they'll say he held out till the end. They'll make a hero of him and they'll think they've been proven right. No: let him go right away. If he dies outside they won't know what happened. Some will say he resisted[404] but no one will know for sure.'"[405]

[Abū Zurʿah:] Al-Muʿtaṣim summoned Aḥmad ibn Ḥanbal's uncle and asked the people, "Do you know who this is?" 69.57

"Yes," they said. "It's Aḥmad ibn Ḥanbal."

"Look at him. Do you see that he's unharmed?"

"Yes."

If he hadn't done that, I suspect that an unstoppable outburst of violence would have ensued.[406] When he said, "I give him to you unharmed," the people were mollified.

[Ibn al-Aṣbagh:] Only after a crowd had gathered at the gate and begun to raise an outcry was Ibn Ḥanbal released. The authorities were frightened and let Aḥmad out. 69.58

Chapter 70

His Reception by the Elders after His Release, and Their Prayers for Him

[Muhanna' ibn Yaḥyā:] I saw Yaʿqūb ibn Ibrāhīm ibn Saʿd al-Zuhrī kissing Aḥmad on the forehead and the face after he was released from jail. I also saw Sulaymān ibn Dāwūd al-Hāshimī kissing his head and forehead. 70.1

[Al-Jarawī:] I said to al-Ḥārith ibn Miskīn: "That man"—meaning Aḥmad ibn Ḥanbal—"is being flogged. Come on: let's go to him." 70.2

We arrived just as he was being flogged. Later he told us, "After they beat me I fell down and I heard that one"—meaning Ibn Abī

Du'ād—"saying, 'Commander of the Faithful, he's gone astray, and will lead others astray.'"

Al-Ḥārith remarked: "Yūsuf ibn 'Umar ibn Yazīd told me, citing Mālik ibn Anas, that al-Zuhrī was maliciously denounced to the authorities and then flogged. When he was told that al-Zuhrī had been subjected to a public inquisition with his books hanging around his neck, Mālik said, 'Sa'īd ibn al-Musayyab was flogged, and had his hair and beard shaved off. Abū l-Zinād and Muḥammad ibn al-Munkadir were also flogged. 'Umar ibn 'Abd al-'Azīz once said, "Do not envy anyone who hasn't suffered for Islam."' And Mālik didn't even mention himself."

Aḥmad was impressed with what al-Ḥārith told him.

70.3 [The author:] People have always suffered through ordeals for the sake of God. Many prophets were killed; and among the ancient nations, many good people were killed or immolated, with some of them being sawed in half without renouncing their faith. If not for my aversion to prolixity and my preference for brevity, I would list the reports I have in mind, along with their chains of transmission.

70.4 The Prophet, God bless and keep him, was poisoned, as was Abū Bakr. 'Umar, 'Uthmān, and 'Alī were assassinated. Al-Ḥasan was poisoned, and al-Ḥusayn, Ibn al-Zubayr, al-Ḍaḥḥāk ibn Qays, and al-Nu'mān ibn Bashīr were assassinated. Khubayb ibn 'Adī was crucified. Al-Ḥajjāj executed 'Abd al-Raḥmān ibn Abī Laylā, 'Abd Allāh ibn Ghālib al-Ḥuddānī, Sa'īd ibn Jubayr, Abū l-Bakhtarī l-Ṭā'ī, Kumayl ibn Ziyād, and Ḥuṭayṭ al-Zayyāt. He also crucified Māhān al-Ḥanafī, and before him Ibn al-Zubayr. And al-Wāthiq killed and crucified Aḥmad ibn Naṣr al-Khuzā'ī.

70.5 Among the great scholars who were flogged is 'Abd al-Raḥmān ibn Abī Laylā, who was struck four hundred lashes and then executed by Ibn al-Ḥajjāj.

Another is Sa'īd ibn al-Musayyab, who was struck one hundred lashes by 'Abd al-Malik ibn Marwān for refusing to swear allegiance to al-Walīd in Medina. At 'Abd al-Malik's orders, he was flogged, drenched with water on a cold day, and dressed in a woolen cloak.[407]

Another is Khubayb ibn ʿAbd Allāh ibn al-Zubayr, who was struck a hundred lashes by ʿUmar ibn ʿAbd al-ʿAzīz at the command of al-Walīd, all for reciting a Hadith where the Prophet—God bless and keep him—says, "When the descendants of Abū l-ʿĀṣ reach thirty in number, they will make God's servants their own, and take turns plundering His treasury."

Whenever ʿUmar was told, "Rejoice!" he would reply, "How can I rejoice with Khubayb blocking my way?"[408]

Others include Abū l-Zinād, who was flogged by the Umayyads; 70.6
Abū ʿAmr ibn al-ʿAlāʾ, struck five hundred lashes by the Umayyads; Rabiʿat al-Raʾy, flogged by the Umayyads; ʿAṭiyyah al-ʿAwfī, struck four hundred lashes by al-Ḥajjāj; Yazīd al-Ḍabbī, struck four hundred lashes by al-Ḥajjāj; Thābit al-Bunānī, flogged by Ibn al-Jārūd, the deputy of Ibn Ziyād; ʿAbd Allāh ibn ʿAwn, struck seventy lashes by Bilāl ibn Abī Burdah; Mālik ibn Anas, struck seventy lashes by al-Manṣūr for saying that a person who swears an oath under compulsion is not bound by it; and Abū l-Sawwār al-ʿAdawī and ʿUqbah ibn ʿAbd al-Ghāfir, who were both flogged.

Aḥmad ibn Ḥanbal thus had a formidable list of exemplars.[409]

More on His Exempting al-Muʿtaṣim and the Others Present from Liability for Flogging Him

[Ṣāliḥ:] I heard my father say, "I exempt that dead man[410] from lia- 70.7
bility for flogging me." Then he said, "I just came across the verse «Whoever pardons and amends will find his reward with God»[411] and looked into what it means. I cite Hāshim ibn Qāsim, who cites al-Mubārak ibn Faḍālah, who cites someone who heard al-Ḥasan say, 'On the Day of Resurrection, all the nations will come crawling before God, mighty and glorious. Then only those to whom God owes a reward will be called upon to rise.'

"He said: 'The only ones to rise will be those who forgave others.'

"So I decided to exempt the deceased from liability for flogging me."

Then he added, "I'd rather not have God torment anyone for my sake."

70.8 [Aḥmad ibn Sinān:] I heard that Aḥmad ibn Ḥanbal forgave al-Muʿtaṣim the day he defeated Bābak, or the day he captured Amorium. He said, "I exempt him from any liability for flogging me."

70.9 [Aḥmad:] Al-Wāthiq sent me a message asking me to forgive al-Muʿtaṣim for flogging me. I responded, "I forgave him the moment I left the palace because of what the Prophet said: 'None will rise on Resurrection Day except those who forgive.'"

70.10 [Aḥmad:] Isḥāq ibn Ibrāhīm asked if I would exempt Abū Isḥāq [al-Muʿtaṣim] from liability. I told him that I already had. I had been thinking about the Hadith that says: "On the Day of Resurrection a cry will sound: 'Let none rise but those who have forgiven!'" I also remembered what al-Shaʿbī said, "Forgive once and be rewarded twice."

70.11 [Al-Khiraqī:] I once spent the night at Aḥmad ibn Ḥanbal's. Every time he lay down, he would weep, straight through until morning. I asked him why he had been weeping so much. He said, "I was thinking about how al-Muʿtaṣim had me flogged. Then during the lesson we came across the verse «Let harm be requited by an equal harm. But whoever pardons and amends will find his reward with God.»[412] So I prostrated myself and decided to forgive him."

70.12 [Al-Ḥarbī:] Aḥmad ibn Ḥanbal forgave everyone, including al-Muʿtaṣim, who attended his flogging or helped carry it out under instructions from others. He said, "If Ibn Abī Duʾād weren't summoning others to unbelief, I would forgive him, too."

70.13 [Fūrān:] One night Aḥmad ibn Ḥanbal sent for me. When I arrived he asked, "You once reported something Faḍl al-Anmāṭī said. What was it?"

I told him, "Faḍl said to me: 'I will never forgive the one who ordered me flogged so I would say the Qurʾan is created, or the ones who carried out the flogging, or any of the followers of Jahm—present or absent—who rejoiced in it.'"

Aḥmad said: "But I've forgiven al-Muʿtaṣim, the ones who flogged me, and anyone who was there, or who wasn't. I thought it was better not to have anyone tormented in the Fire on my account.

I also remembered two Hadiths reported of the Prophet, God bless and keep him: ‘God, mighty and glorious, will raise palaces, and people will lift their eyes to them and say, “Whose are these? How beautiful they are!”

"‘The answer will come: “They belong to those who have paid for them.”

"‘“What price did they pay?”

"‘“Forgiving a fellow Muslim.”’

“The other report is: ‘God, mighty and glorious, will order a banner to be raised and a crier to cry, “Let all who have a claim on God follow this banner into the Garden.”

"‘The people will ask, “Tell us who has a claim!”

"‘The answer will come, “Whoever forgave his fellow Muslim.”’”

[ʿAbd Allāh:] I once read to my father a report narrated by Rawḥ citing Ashʿath citing al-Ḥasan: “The Garden has a door that God has placed there only for those who have forgiven an injustice done them.” 70.14

“Son,” my father said, “the moment I left al-Muʿtaṣim’s palace, I forgave him and everyone with him, with two exceptions: Ibn Abī Du’ād and ʿAbd al-Raḥmān ibn Isḥāq, who were calling for my blood. But I’m too insignificant in the eyes of God for Him to torment anyone on my account, so I declare them forgiven as well.”

More on the Effects of the Flogging

[Ṣāliḥ:] A man who treated flogging victims came to look after my father.[413] “I’ve seen people who’d been struck a thousand lashes,” he told us, “but nothing as bad as this. They struck him from the front as well as behind.” 70.15

Then he took an instrument and probed some of the wounds. “They didn’t puncture anything,” he said.

He began to come regularly to treat my father. Some of the blows had struck him in the face, and he had been left lying face down for some time. At one point the man said, “There’s something I want to remove.” He took out a piece of metal and used it to fold back the flesh while cutting some of it away with a knife. My father bore it all, praising God the whole time, and eventually recovered. He continued to feel pain in certain places, and the scars were visible on his back until the day he died.

I heard him say, "By God, I have given all I could. I was afraid, and all I wished for was to come out of it even, not winning or losing."

70.16 [Abū Ḥātim:] I went to see Aḥmad ibn Ḥanbal three or so years after he was flogged.

"Do you still feel any pain?" I asked him.

He put his right hand on his left elbow and said, "Here," as if to say that it had been dislocated and still hurt.

70.17 [Ibn Munādī's grandfather:] After the ordeal was over, I saw Aḥmad sitting with a censer in front of him. He would take a rag he had wrapped around his hand and warm it over the fire then hold it to his side, where they had hit him. "Abū Jaʿfar," he said, turning to me, "no one showed more compassion for me that day than al-Muʿtaṣim."

Chapter 71

His Teaching of Hadith after the Death of al-Muʿtaṣim

71.1 [Al-Būshanjī:] In '27 [842], Aḥmad ibn Ḥanbal taught Hadith openly in Baghdad. That was right after al-Muʿtaṣim died. We were in Kufa when we heard the news. I headed back to Baghdad and caught up with him in Rajab of that year, while he was still teaching. Then, with three days left in Shaʿbān, he stopped of his own accord. The authorities hadn't told him to stop, but al-Ḥasan ibn ʿAlī ibn al-Jaʿd, who was then judge in Baghdad, had written to Ibn Abī Duʾād to tell him that Aḥmad was openly teaching Hadith. When Aḥmad learned of this, he stopped without having to be asked. As far as we know, he had not taught during al-Muʿtaṣim's reign, which lasted for eight years and eight days. After that he did not teach again at all until he died.

Chapter 72

His Experience with al-Wāthiq

In Rabīʿ I 227 [January 842], Abū Jaʿfar Hārūn al-Wāthiq, son of al-Muʿtaṣim, succeeded to the caliphate. Although Ibn Abī Du'ād persuaded him to continue putting people to the test over the createdness of the Qur'an, he avoided another confrontation with Aḥmad, either because he was aware of his ability to withstand coercion or because he was afraid of what would happen if Aḥmad were punished. He did, however, write to him saying, "Take care that we never find each other in the same place." Aḥmad accordingly went into hiding for the remainder of al-Wāthiq's reign. After several months spent moving from one place to another, Aḥmad disappeared into his house, where he remained until al-Wāthiq died. 72.1

[Aḥmad ibn ʿAlī:] When he was a fugitive, Aḥmad ibn Ḥanbal stayed with Isḥāq ibn Ibrāhīm ibn Hāniʾ al-Naysābūrī. 72.2

[The author:] Isḥaq's father, Ibrāhīm ibn Hāni', is sometimes named instead, but the house is one and the same.

[Al-Baghawī:] At the beginning of '28 [late in 842], I heard Aḥmad ibn Ḥanbal recite the Hadith reported by Muʿawiyah where the Prophet, God bless and keep him, says, "Nothing remains in this present world but adversity and tribulation, so prepare yourselves to be steadfast." 72.3

Afterward he said, "God, I accept Your charge," over and over.

[Ibrāhīm ibn Hāni':] Aḥmad ibn Ḥanbal hid at my place for three days. Then he said, "Find me somewhere else to go." 72.4

I told him it wasn't safe, but he insisted, and promised to tell me something useful if I did as he asked. So I found a place for him to go. As he was leaving, he said, "The Emissary of God hid in a cave for three days and then moved elsewhere, and it's wrong to follow his example in good times but not in bad."[414]

[Ibrāhīm ibn Hāni':] Aḥmad ibn Ḥanbal hid at my place for three nights. Then he said, "Find me somewhere else to go." 72.5

I told him it wasn't safe. He replied, "The Prophet, God bless and keep him, hid in a cave for three days and then moved elsewhere, and it's wrong to follow his example in good times but not in bad."

Fatḥ added: I recited this report for Ṣāliḥ and ʿAbd Allāh, who said it was the first they had heard of it. I also recited it for Ibrāhīm's son Isḥāq, who said that his father had never said any such thing to him.

72.6 [Abū Zurʿah:] I asked Aḥmad ibn Ḥanbal how he had escaped al-Muʿtaṣim's sword and al-Wāthiq's lash. He said, "Apply truthfulness to any wound, and it heals."[415]

Addendum

72.7 It is reported that al-Wāthiq put an end to the Inquisition after watching a debate that persuaded him of the better course.[416]

72.8 [Al-Muhtadī:] Whenever my father al-Wāthiq was going to execute anyone, we would attend the session. One day an elderly man with a dyed beard was brought in, weighed down with fetters. My father summoned Ibn Abī Du'ād and his associates, then had the man brought forward.

"Peace be upon you," said the elder.

"May God not grant you peace!" retorted my father.

"Commander of the Faithful," said the elder, "you've been poorly raised. God says «When you are greeted by anyone, respond with a better greeting or at least return it.»[417] But you neither returned my greeting nor offered a better one."

"It seems we have a debater on our hands," said Ibn Abī Du'ād.

"Debate him, then," said my father.

72.9 "Old man! What do you say regarding the Qur'an?"

"That won't do. Let me ask first."

"Go ahead."

"What do you say regarding the Qur'an?"

"It's a created thing."

"Is that something that the Prophet, Abū Bakr, ʿUmar, ʿUthmān, ʿAlī, and the Righteous Caliphs were aware of, or not?"

“They weren’t aware of it.”

“God preserve us!” cried the elder. “The Prophet didn’t know about it, and neither did Abū Bakr, or ʿUmar, or ʿUthmān, or ʿAlī, or the Righteous Caliphs, but you do!”

Ibn Abī Duʾād was stymied and abashed. “Give me a moment,” he said.

“Same question again?”

“Yes.”

“What do you say regarding the Qurʾan?”

“It’s a created thing.”

“Is that something that the Prophet, Abū Bakr, ʿUmar, ʿUthmān, ʿAlī, and the Righteous Caliphs were aware of, or not?”

“They were aware of it,” said Ibn Abī Duʾād, “but they didn’t call on anyone to proclaim it.”

“So why can’t you do the same?” asked the elder.

My father rose, went into his private chamber, lay down, and 72.10
crossed his legs, repeating to himself: “The Prophet didn’t know about it, or Abū Bakr, or ʿUmar, or ʿUthmān, or ʿAlī, or the Righteous Caliphs, but you do! God preserve us! The Prophet, Abū Bakr, ʿUmar, ʿUthmān, ʿAlī, and the Righteous Caliphs did know about it, but they didn’t call on anyone to proclaim it; why can’t you do the same?”

Then he summoned ʿAmmār the chamberlain and told him to remove the old man’s fetters, give him four hundred dinars, and let him go. He lost all regard for Ibn Abī Duʾād and stopped the Inquisition then and there.

[The author:] I have heard a different telling of the story. 72.11

[Ṣāliḥ ibn ʿAlī:] I once saw the Caliph al-Muhtadī billāh presiding over the Grievance Court at Commoners’ Gate. I watched the cases being read aloud to him from beginning to end, and saw him make a ruling on each one. I watched as the orders were issued, the wording settled, and the documents sealed and handed over to the petitioners under his supervision. It was a fine and impressive sight to see. At one point, al-Wāthiq caught me staring at him and I averted my eyes. The same thing happened twice more: when he looked at me I would look away, but then when he turned back to his work I would begin staring again. Finally he said, "Ṣāliḥ!"

I rose. "At your service, Commander of the Faithful!"

"You have something you want"—or "you would like"—"to tell me."[418]

"Yes, sire!"

"Resume your place."

So I went back and waited until he closed the session and said to the chamberlain, "Have Ṣāliḥ stay."

After everyone had left, I was admitted to his presence. I greeted him with a prayer for his well-being.

"Sit," he said.

I sat.

"Do you want to tell me what you were thinking, or do you want me to tell you what I think you were thinking?"

"Whichever you decide, Commander of the Faithful!"

"I'll tell you what I think, then. You approved of what you saw me doing and you thought, 'What a great caliph we have—if only he didn't believe that the Qur'an is created!'"

His words struck terror into my heart. But then I reminded myself that I wasn't going to die any earlier than God had already decreed, that I was only going to die once no matter what, and that lying is wrong, no matter how grave or how trivial the subject. So I said, "Commander of the Faithful, those were my thoughts exactly."

He bowed his head for a moment, then said, "Hmph! Well then, listen: I'll be honest with you."

With a great sense of relief, I said, "Who better, sire, to speak the truth than the deputy of the Lord of the Worlds and the nephew of the Chief of Prophets?"

Al-Muhtadī then told me the following story.

72.12 [Al-Muhtadī:] Beginning in the reign of al-Wāthiq, I always believed that the Qur'an was created. But then Aḥmad ibn Abī Du'ād brought in an elderly man—a Syrian, from Adana—weighed down with fetters, to face al-Wāthiq. He was a handsome fellow, well built, with a fine head of gray hair. I could see that al-Wāthiq had taken a liking to him and was uncomfortable with the thought of arguing with him. He beckoned him closer and closer. When he had come right up next to him, the elder greeted him most properly and intoned an eloquent prayer for his well-being. Al-Wāthiq invited him to sit down, then said, "Sir, I want you to debate whatever point Ibn Abī Du'ād raises with you."

The elder replied, "Commander of the Faithful, Ibn Abī Du'ād is an apostate[419] and too weak-witted to debate with me."

When al-Wāthiq heard this, his kindness toward the man disappeared, to be replaced by anger. "Ibn Abī Du'ād is an apostate and too weak-witted to debate with *you*?"

"Forget I mentioned it, Commander of the Faithful," he replied. "I'll debate with him."

"That's why I brought you here," said al-Wāthiq.

"Then would you mind keeping score, Commander of the Faithful?"

"Agreed."

"Tell me, Aḥmad," said the elder to Ibn Abī Du'ād,[420] "is this 72.13
creed of yours an obligatory part of our religion, such that one's religion is incomplete unless one holds the same view as you do?"

"Yes."

"Tell me, then: When God sent His Emissary to humankind, did the Emissary keep back anything that God had commanded him to tell us regarding our religion?"

"No."

"And did he summon the community to espouse this creed of yours?"

Ibn Abī Du'ād was left speechless.

"That's one for me, Commander of the Faithful," said the elder.

"All right then, one for you."

"Now then, Aḥmad," said the elder, "recall that when God revealed the Qur'an to His Emissary, he said: «Today I have perfected your religion for you and completed my blessing upon you; I am satisfied with Islam as a religion for you.»[421] Which of you is right: God, when He speaks of perfecting His religion; or you, when you say that something is missing and can only be completed by adding this doctrine of yours?"

Again Ibn Abī Du'ād was stymied.

"Say something," said the elder. But Ibn Abī Du'ād had nothing to say.

"That's two for me, then, Commander of the Faithful."

"Two it is."

"Now then, Aḥmad," said the elder, "tell me: Was the Emissary of God aware of this doctrine of yours, or not?"

"He was aware of it."

"And did he summon people to espouse it?"

Again, silence.

"That's three, Commander of the Faithful."

"Three it is," said al-Wāthiq.

"Now then, Aḥmad," said the elder, "you're claiming that the Emissary of God was content to know it but not press it upon the community?"

"Yes."

"And the same goes for Abū Bakr al-Ṣiddiq, 'Umar ibn al-Khaṭṭāb, 'Uthmān ibn 'Affān, and 'Alī ibn Abī Ṭālib, God be pleased with them all?"

"Right."

72.14 Thereupon the elder turned away and addressed al-Wāthiq. "As you may recall, Commander of the Faithful, I said that Ibn Abī Du'ād is an apostate and too weak-minded to debate with me. If he's right, and we can't keep this doctrine back, even though the Emissary of God, 'Umar, 'Uthmān, and 'Alī all managed to, then I say: may God give no good to anyone who's too good to do what was good enough for them!"

"Why yes," said al-Wāthiq. "If we're too good to keep quiet about a doctrine that the Emissary of God, 'Umar, 'Uthmān, and 'Alī all kept quiet about, then may God be no good to us! Remove the man's fetters."

As the fetters were being removed, the elder reached for them but the blacksmith pulled them away.

"Let the man have them," said al-Wāthiq. The elder took them and put them into his sleeve.

"Why did you try to wrestle them away from the smith?" asked al-Wāthiq.

"Before I die," the elder said, "I intend to give them to my executor and tell him to put them inside my shroud so that when the Day of Resurrection comes, I can use them as proof before God against my abuser. 'Lord,' I'll say, 'ask this creature of yours why he chained me up and terrified my wife, my children, and my friends for no good reason at all?'"

He burst into tears, and so did al-Wāthiq, and so did we all. Then al-Wāthiq asked him to exempt him from any liability for what he had suffered at his hands.

"By God," said the elder, "I forgave you from the beginning, out of respect for the Emissary of God, since you're a descendant of his."

"Will you do something for me?"

"If I can."

"Stay here so that we and our children can learn from you."

"Commander of the Faithful," said the elder, "you're better off sending me back to where this abuser found me, and I'll tell you why: so I can stop my wife and children from cursing you, which is what they were doing when I left them."

"In that case," said al-Wāthiq, "let us give you something to make sure you're well taken care of."

"I can't accept it," he replied, "as I don't need it, and I'm able-bodied."

"Ask me for any other favor, then."

"And you'll grant it?"

"Yes."

"Let me go back to the frontier this minute."

"Granted."

The elder bid him farewell and went out. That's when I renounced the doctrine, and I think al-Wāthiq did too.

72.15 [Abū Bakr ʿAbd Allāh:] Abū Bakr Aḥmad ibn ʿAbd al-Raḥmān al-Shīrāzī l-Ḥāfiẓ reported the story of the elder from Adana and what happened at the debate. He added that the elder was Abū ʿAbd al-Raḥmān ʿAbd Allāh ibn Muḥammad ibn Isḥāq al-Adhramī.

[The author:] It is reported that before he died, al-Wāthiq disavowed the doctrine of the createdness of the Qurʾan.

72.16 [Al-Muhtadī:] By the time he died, al-Wāthiq had renounced the doctrine of the createdness of the Qurʾan.[422]

Chapter 73

His Experience with al-Mutawakkil

73.1 On Wednesday, with six nights left in Dhu l-Hijjah 232 [August 11, 847], al-Mutawakkil ʿalā llāh, who was then twenty-six years of age, succeeded al-Wāthiq as caliph. Through him God brought about the triumph of the *sunnah* and put an end to the suffering caused by the Inquisition, much to the gratification of the people.

73.2 [Al-Taymī:] There were three great caliphs: Abū Bakr, who fought the apostates until they surrendered; ʿUmar ibn ʿAbd al-ʿAzīz, who made good the abuses of the Umayyads; and al-Mutawakkil, who abolished heretical innovations and publicly proclaimed the *sunnah*.

73.3 [ʿAlī ibn al-Jahm:] The Caliph al-Mutawakkil sent for me and said, "ʿAlī, I dreamed I saw the Prophet. I rose to greet him, and he said, 'You're rising for me even though you're a caliph?'"

"It's a good dream, Commander of the Faithful," I said. "Your rising for him symbolizes your standing up for the *sunnah*. And he called you a caliph!"

Al-Mutawakkil was pleased.

73.4 [ʿAlī ibn Ismāʿīl:] In Tarsus I dreamed that I saw al-Mutawakkil sitting in a place full of light.

"Al-Mutawakkil?" I asked.

"Yes," he said.

"What has God done with you?"

"He forgave me."

"Why?"

"Because of the little bit of *sunnah* I was able to restore."

[The author:] Al-Mutawakkil extinguished the fires of heretical innovation and lit the lamps of *sunnah*.

[Ibrāhīm ibn Muḥammad:] In 234 [848–49], al-Mutawakkil chose a number of jurists and Hadith-men, including Muṣʿab al-Zubayrī, Isḥāq ibn Abī Isrāʾīl, Ibrāhīm ibn ʿAbd Allāh al-Harawī, and ʿAbd Allāh and ʿUthmān, the sons of Ibn Abī Shaybah, to receive awards and regular stipends, and ordered them to hold public Hadith sessions to teach the reports that refute the Secessionists and the followers of Jahm, as well as the reports that describe seeing God. ʿUthmān ibn Abī Shaybah had a pulpit set up for him to lead a session inside the City of al-Manṣūr. Some thirty thousand people gathered to hear him. Abū Bakr ibn Abī Shaybah held his session in the mosque of al-Ruṣāfah, where another thirty thousand gathered to hear.[423] 73.5

[Ghulām Khalīl:] In ʿAbbādān, after the end of the Inquistion, Abū Jaʿfar al-Khawwāṣ recited for me: 73.6

The heretics' rope has frayed and snapped
Their turn in power come and gone;
And gone with them is the Devil's horde
That gathered round to cheer them on.
Tell me, friends: In all that lot
Was there an exemplar? Even one?
One like Sufyān of Thawr, who taught us all
What to accept and what to shun?
Or Sulaymān of Taym, who never slept,
For fear of God's all-seeing gaze?
Or like Mālik, that sea, that pasture-ground
Where the jurists come to graze?

Or Ibn Ḥanbal, Islam's brave young man,
As stout a heart as God e'er made;
Who, though ringed about with whip and sword,
Faced their clamor unafraid.[424]

Addendum

73.7 Five months into his reign, al-Mutawakkil sent for Aḥmad ibn Ḥanbal.

[Ṣāliḥ:] Al-Mutawakkil ordered Isḥāq ibn Ibrāhīm to send my father to him. So Isḥāq summoned my father and said: "The Commander of the Faithful requires your presence. Prepare yourself for a journey!"

73.8 My father said:

Isḥāq also asked me to forgive him for being present when I was flogged. I told him that I had already forgiven everyone who was there. Then he said he wanted to ask me about the Qur'an—not to test me, but because he genuinely wanted to know.

"Just between us, then: What do you say about the Qur'an?"

"It's the speech of God," I told him, "uncreated."

"Why uncreated?"

"God has said, «His is the creation, His the command,»[425] which shows that what He creates is not the same as what He commands."

"But His command is created," said Isḥāq.

"God help us!" I said. "Can one created thing create another?"

"But what authority tells you it isn't created?"

"Ja'far ibn Muḥammad says, 'It is neither a creator nor a created thing.'"

He fell silent.

The next night, he sent for me and asked, "How do you feel about going?"

"That's up to you."

73.9 [Ṣāliḥ continued:]

When al-Mutawakkil sent for my father, a number of Helpers and Hāshimī dignitaries came to see him and asked whether he would really speak to him.

"I had made up my mind to speak to him," said my father, "about his family, about the Helpers and Emigrants, and about the best interests of the Muslims."

It was in 237 [851–52] that my father was sent to al-Mutawakkil. He was taken out of Baghdad and made it as far as a place called Buṣrā, where we spent the night in a mosque. In the middle of the night, al-Naysābūrī arrived and said, "He says, 'Go back!'"

"I hope this is for the best," I said.

"I've been praying all this time," he said.

An Account of What Happened When Aḥmad's Enemies Denounced Him to the Authorities, Claiming That He Was Harboring a Partisan of ʿAlī

After Aḥmad was taken to see al-Mutawakkil and then sent back again, Isḥāq ibn Ibrāhīm died and was succeeded by his son, ʿAbd Allāh ibn Isḥāq. Then Aḥmad's enemies denounced him to al-Mutawakkil, claiming that he was harboring a partisan of ʿAlī.[426] 73.10

[Ṣāliḥ:] The Caliph al-Mutawakkil sent a message to ʿAbd Allāh ibn Isḥāq, the new governor in Baghdad, telling him to warn Aḥmad ibn Ḥanbal against hiding anything from the caliph. The caliph then dispatched his chamberlain, Muẓaffar, as well as the chief of the courier service, a man named Ibn al-Kalbī, to whom he had sent the same message. Late at night, after most people had gone to bed, al-Muẓaffar and Ibn al-Kalbī confronted Aḥmad and passed on the message that ʿAbd Allāh ibn Isḥāq had conveyed to them: that is, that he should be wary of hiding anything from the caliph. 73.11

[Ṣāliḥ:] There was a knock, and my father, who was dressed only in his breechclout, answered the door. The callers read aloud a message from the caliph suggesting that he was harboring a partisan of ʿAlī. He said, "I don't know what he means. I believe that obedience is due him in good times and bad, willingly or not, even if he should favor others over me. I regret not being able to pray with my fellow Muslims, attend Friday prayers, or address the community."[427] 73.12

Before he died, Isḥāq had told my father to remain at home and not to come out for Fridays or other group prayers, warning him that if he did, he would suffer what he had suffered under al-Muʿtaṣim.

Ibn al-Kalbī then said: "The Commander of the Faithful has ordered me to ask you to swear that you are not concealing anyone."

"If you want me to swear," he said, "I will."

They made him swear by God, and to swear that he would divorce his wife if he was not telling the truth.

Then Ibn al-Kalbī said, "I want to search your house and your son's"—meaning mine—"as well."

Muẓaffar and Ibn al-Kalbī searched the house while two women who had come with them searched the women. Then they did the same with my house. They even lowered a candle into the well and looked down it. They also sent women into the women's quarters. Finally they left.

Two days later came a letter from ʿAlī ibn al-Jahm saying: "The Commander of the Faithful is reassured of your innocence of the slanderous accusations made against you and praises God, who did not allow your enemies to succeed in their plan. He herewith asks you to come to see him, and calls upon you in the name of God not to plead for exemption or to return the money he sends you."[428]

73.13 [Al-ʿUkbarī:] In 236 [850–51], I went to look for Aḥmad ibn Ḥanbal to ask him about a problem. I asked where to find him and was told that he had gone out to pray, so I sat down and waited. Upon his return, I greeted him and he returned my greeting. Then he headed down an alley and I walked along beside him. At the end of the alley was a door. As he pushed it open and went through, he said, "Leave now, with God's blessing!"

I asked my question again, but again he asked me to go. Then another man came out. I asked him why Ibn Ḥanbal was dodging me. He said, "Someone went to the authorities and accused him of harboring a partisan of ʿAlī. So Muḥammad ibn Naṣr came and searched the whole neighborhood without finding anyone. Now Aḥmad won't talk to people who aren't scholars."

73.14 [Al-Marrūdhī:] I heard Aḥmad ibn Ḥanbal say: "I had a visit from Abū ʿAlī ibn Yaḥyā[429] ibn Khāqān, who told me that he had received a letter from the Commander of the Faithful sending me his regards and then saying: 'If anyone should remain safe from harm, it is you. I must nevertheless inform you that a man held here as our prisoner claims that he is an associate of yours and that you sent him to receive a partisan of ʿAlī who recently arrived from Khurasan. If you wish, I can flog this associate of yours, lock him up, or send him to you.'"

Aḥmad said, "I told Abū ʿAlī, 'I don't know what this supposed associate of mine is talking about, so my reply to the letter is: let the man go unharmed!'"

I said, "But why should you care if something happens to him? He's threatened your life!"

"What he's after," said Aḥmad, "is to rip us out, root and branch. But he must have someone—a mother, or brothers, or daughters—who would care if something happens to him. That's why I asked them to let him go."

73.15 [Ibrāhīm ibn Isḥāq:] Al-Mutawakkil took the partisan of ʿAlī who denounced Aḥmad to the authorities and sent him to Aḥmad to repeat the accusation. But Aḥmad forgave him, saying, "He might have boys who would mourn if he were killed."

His Journey to Samarra after the Accusation Had Been Cleared Up

73.16 [Ṣāliḥ:] My father received a letter from ʿAlī ibn al-Jahm saying: "The Commander of the Faithful herewith sends you Yaʿqūb, called Qawṣarrah, with a gift for you, and orders you to come to him. He calls upon you in the name of God not to plead for exemption or to return the money he has sent you, for doing so will strengthen the hand of those working against you."

The next day, Yaʿqūb returned and went in to see him. "Abū ʿAbd Allāh," he said, "the Commander of the Faithful conveys his greetings to you and says: 'I am now convinced of your innocence.

Desiring, as I do, the comfort of your presence and the blessing of your prayers, I herewith send to you ten thousand dirhams to cover the expenses of your journey.'"

Yaʿqūb then brought out a bag with a knotted pouch containing about two hundred dinars and the rest filled with untrimmed dirhams. My father didn't even look at it. Yaʿqūb tied it back up, saying, "I'll be back tomorrow to find out what you've decided to do." He added, "Praise God, who prevented the innovators from rejoicing in your downfall."

Then he left.

I brought in a green washtub,[430] turned it over, and dropped it on top of the bag. When it was time for the evening prayer, my father said, "Ṣāliḥ, take this and put it in your house."

So I put it on the roof next to where I slept. Early the next morning I heard him calling me so I got up and went over. He told me he hadn't slept. When I asked him why not, he began weeping and said, "Here I thought I'd escaped them, but now they've come to torment me at the end of my life!" He went on, "I've decided to give that thing away as soon as it's morning."

"That's up to you," I said.

In the morning al-Ḥasan al-Bazzāz and the elders came to see him. "Ṣāliḥ," he told me, "bring me a scale." Then he added, "Send for the descendants of the Emigrants and Helpers. And send for So-and-So, and So-and-So, and tell them to distribute the money in their neighborhoods."

So it went, until he had given all the money away and emptied the bag. This was at a time when we were living in a state of deprivation best known to God. At one point one of my little boys came over, looked at me, and said, "Daddy, give me a dirham!" So I got out a coin and gave it to him.

The chief courier reported that my father had given the money away that very day. He even gave away the bag.

73.17 ʿAlī ibn al-Jahm said:

I told the caliph that Aḥmad had given the money away. People did see him accept the gift, but they also knew that he had no use for it: "He lives on a loaf of flatbread!"

The caliph said, "You're right, ʿAlī."

Sāliḥ said: 73.18

After my father gave away the money, they escorted us outside. It was nighttime, and there were guardsmen with us carrying torches. When it grew light out, my father asked me if I had any dirhams. I told him I did, and he said, "Give them something." So I gave each guardsman a dirham.[431]

When we reached the grain merchants' district, Yaʿqūb said, "Stop here." Then he sent word to al-Mutawakkil that we had arrived. My father kept his eyes on the ground as we entered Samarra.

At that moment Waṣīf came past, heading for the palace. Seeing the mass of people gathered there, he asked, "What's all this?"

"Aḥmad ibn Ḥanbal's here," he was told.

After my father had been checked through by Yaḥyā ibn Harthamah,[432] Waṣīf sent him a message saying, "The Commander of the Faithful conveys his salutations and expresses his gratitude to God for preventing the heretics from rejoicing in your downfall. You are aware of where Ibn Abī Duʾād stood, and must therefore understand how important it is for you to state a position satisfactory to God."[433]

We were given lodgings in Ītākh's palace. My father's first visitor was ʿAlī ibn al-Jahm, who told me that the Commander of the Faithful had sent ten thousand dirhams to replace the money my father had given away. The caliph had also forbidden anyone to tell my father about the gift, which would only upset him. 73.19

The next visitor was Aḥmad ibn Muʿāwiyah, who told my father, "The Commander of the Faithful is always talking about you and wishing you were here close to him. He wants you to live here and teach Hadith."

"I'm not well enough," my father said. He laid his finger on his teeth. "I haven't told my sons," he said, "but some of my teeth are loose."

Later he was sent a question: "Say two beasts fight. If one is gored by the other, falls to the ground, and is slaughtered, may it be eaten?"

He replied: "If it can blink and move its tail, and if it is bleeding, then yes."

73.20 The next visitor was Yaḥyā ibn Khāqān, who said, "The Commander of the Faithful has ordered me to escort you to see his son al-Muʿtazz. I need to have a suit, a cowl, and a cap made for you in black, so you'll have to tell me what kind of cap you wear." I said I had never seen him wear a cap. "The Commander of the Faithful is going to grant you one of the higher ranks and place al-Muʿtazz in your care." Then he turned to me. "He's also ordered a stipend of four thousand dirhams for you and the other members of the family."

The next day Yaḥyā came to see us again. He asked my father, "Will you ride with us?"

"That's up to you," he answered.

"Put it in God's hands, then, and come along."

My father put on his breechclout and his shoes. The shoes were about fifteen years old and had been repaired many times over. Yaḥyā signaled that he should put on a cap.

"He doesn't have one," I said. "I've never seen him wear one."

"He can't go in bareheaded!"

We asked for a mount. Yaḥyā said, "Make it a *muṣallī*."[434]

My father sat down on the ground, reciting, «From the earth We have created you and We will return you thereto.»[435] Then he mounted a mule belonging to a merchant. We joined him as he rode to the heir apparent's palace, where he was given a seat in a room adjoining the entryway. Yaḥyā came to take his arm and escort him inside. There was a partition there, but it was removed so we could see him. My father sat down and Yaḥyā said, "The Commander of the Faithful has brought you here to derive blessing from your presence and to place his son in your care."

One of the staff later told us that al-Mutawakkil had been sitting behind a screen. When my father came in, the caliph had said to his mother, "Look, Mother! He lights up the whole room."[436]

Then a servant appeared carrying a bundle. Yaḥyā took it and pulled out a lined outer garment with a shirt inside it. He put my father's arm into one sleeve, then took him by the arm and lifted him up to get the neck-hole of the garment over his head. After that he reached into the garment and pulled my father's right hand, then his left, out through the sleeves, with my father doing nothing to help him. Finally Yaḥyā took a cap and put it on my father's head and draped a cowl over his shoulders. The one thing they didn't bring was a pair of shoes, so he was left wearing his old ones.

As soon as my father was dismissed and we returned to the place where we were staying, he tore the clothes off, then burst into tears. "I kept myself well away from these people for sixty years, but now at the end of my life they've come to torment me! I don't think I can get out of attending that boy, not to mention all the people I'll have to advise from the moment I lay eyes on them to the moment I leave." Then he said: "Ṣāliḥ, send these clothes to Baghdad, have them sold, and give the money away in alms. I don't want any of you buying anything with it."

I sent the clothes back to be sold, and he gave the money away.

[Zuhayr:] I was the first to meet Aḥmad when he got out of the 73.21
boat. He disembarked wearing the wrap they had put on him. It slipped off and fell, but instead of putting it back on and adjusting it, he dragged it along after him.

[Ṣāliḥ:] After we sent the clothes away, we told my father that the 73.22
house where we were staying belonged to Ītākh.

"Write a note to Muḥammad ibn al-Jarrāḥ," he said, "and ask him to let us stay somewhere else."

After we wrote the note, al-Mutawakkil gave us permission to leave. But the new place he assigned us was available only because he had evicted the people living there, so my father wouldn't go there either. Next the caliph rented a property for two hundred dirhams for us to stay in, with delivery of food and ice. Punkahs[437] were installed and carpets from Ṭabaristān spread out on the floor. When my father saw the punkahs and the carpets, he left the place and threw himself down on a quilt he had with him.

At one point my father had something wrong with his eye, but then it cleared up. "Isn't that something?" he said. "My eye was bothering me for a while, but look how quickly it got better."

73.23 [Al-Marrūdhī:] When we were in Samarra, Aḥmad told me at one point that he had gone eight nights without eating or drinking anything except some barley water—less than a quarter-measure. He would go three nights without eating. On the fourth, I would put an eighth-measure of barley water in front of him. Sometimes he would finish it and sometimes he'd leave some. If there was anything bothering him, he wouldn't eat at all, and break his fast with only a drink of water.

73.24 [Ṣāliḥ:] In Samarra my father started fasting for three days at a time and breaking his fast with Shihrīz dates. He did this for fifteeen days, eating every third day. Then he started eating every other night, but only a loaf of flatbread. Whenever a table was brought in, they set it down in the anteroom where he wouldn't see it and the rest of us would eat.

73.25 Whenever the heat got too much for him, he would lay a wet rag on his chest. Every day al-Mutawakkil would send Ibn Māsawayh over to examine him. "Abū ʿAbd Allāh," he would say, "I like you and I like the people you have with you. There's nothing wrong with you except inanition and infrequent bowel movements. You know, we often tell our monks to eat sesame oil to relax the bowels." He started bringing him things to drink but he would pour them out.

73.26 Among his other visitors were Yaʿqūb and ʿAttāb, who would come to ask him on behalf of the caliph what he thought should be done with Ibn Abī Duʾād and his estate, but he would never answer. They started coming every day to tell him how the case was coming along. Finally it was testified that Ibn Abī Duʾād's estates could be sold off, and he himself was sent down to Baghdad.

Yaḥyā would sometimes come to see him, and wait in the anteroom until he was finished praying. When ʿAlī ibn al-Jahm came to see my father, he would remove his sword and cap before coming in. 73.27

At one point al-Mutawakkil ordered a house to be bought for us. My father called me over and said, "Ṣāliḥ, if you let them buy a house I'll never speak to you again. All they want is to find a way to keep me here for good."

He remained so obstinate that the idea was finally dropped.

At one point the caterer came to me and said, "Would you rather I stopped sending food over and give you the three thousand dirhams a month instead?"

I told him no.

Al-Mutawakkil's messengers continued coming over to ask after my father and then going back to the caliph and saying that he didn't look well. Meanwhile they would tell my father that the caliph needed to see him. My father would say nothing. After they left, he would say, "Isn't that strange? How would they know whether he needs to see me or not?" 73.28

Then Yaʿqūb came over and said, "The Commander of the Faithful is eager to see you. Think about when you can come see him, and let me know."

"That's up to you," my father replied.

"He has Wednesday free," said Yaʿqūb, and went out.

The next day Yaʿqūb came back and said, "Good news! The Commander of the Faithful sends his regards and informs you that he has excused you from wearing the black, attending the heirs apparent, and coming to the palace. If you prefer to wear cotton or wool, you may do so."

My father praised God for this turn of events.

Then Yaʿqūb said, "I have a son who's dear to my heart. I wonder if you would recite some Hadith for him."

My father said nothing. After Yaʿqūb left, he said to me, "Doesn't he see what I'm going through?"

73.29 [Al-Marrūdhī:] I heard Yaʿqūb, the caliph's messenger, ask Abū ʿAbd Allāh, "If my son comes here between sunset and evening prayers, would you teach him one or two Hadith?"

"No," said Abū ʿAbd Allāh. "Tell him not to come."

After Yaʿqūb had left, I heard Aḥmad say, "Even if his nose touched the sky I wouldn't teach him. Does he want me to put my own head through a noose?"[438]

73.30 [Ṣāliḥ:] My father would start reading the Qurʾan every Friday and finish it by the following Friday. Whenever he finished a reading, he would make a supplication and we would say, "Amen!" Then he would say, "God, guide me," over and over. Finally I asked him what he was concerned about and he said, "Whether to make a vow to God, knowing that I'll be held accountable for it. «Believers, fulfill your obligations.»[439] I'm considering a vow never to recite a full Hadith report again for the rest of my life—not to anyone, not even all of you."

Then ʿAlī ibn al-Jahm arrived. When we told my father, he said, «We belong to God and to Him we shall return»[440] and ʿAlī reported this back to al-Mutawakkil.

My father told us, "They want me to recite Hadith so they can keep me here. The scholars who ended up staying here were the ones who accepted what they were offered for teaching Hadith, or obeyed when they were ordered to teach."

73.31 Meanwhile my father continued to receive visits from Yaḥyā, Yaʿqūb, ʿAttāb, and others. They would talk and he would sit with his eyes closed as if ill. He gradually became very feeble. When his condition was reported to al-Mutawakkil, the stricken caliph sent message after message asking about his health. All the while, he continued to send us money, telling the messengers, "Give it to the family without telling the father. What does he expect of them? He might not care about the things of this world, but why should he stop his family from enjoying them?"

"He won't eat any of the food you give him," the caliph was told. "He won't sit on your carpets, and he declares what you drink to be forbidden."

"Even if al-Muʿtaṣim himself came back to life and spoke against Aḥmad," said the caliph, "I wouldn't listen."

[Al-Marrūdhī:] I once heard Aḥmad say, "For some time I've been asking God to guide me on whether I should vow not to teach Hadith any more." 73.32

He added, "I've stopped teaching, but they still won't leave me alone."

[Ṣāliḥ:] Some time later I went back down to Baghdad and left ʿAbd Allāh there with our father. Not long afterward ʿAbd Allāh appeared, bringing with him the clothes I had left in Samarra. I asked him what was going on. 73.33

ʿAbd Allāḥ replied: "He said, 'Go back, and tell Ṣāliḥ not to come back here. All of you are the cause of my troubles. If I could do it all over again, I would have left you in Baghdad and come here by myself. If you hadn't been here, they wouldn't have brought us food or laid down carpets or started sending us you-know-what every month.'"[441]

So I wrote to my father telling him what ʿAbd Allāh had said. He wrote back in his own hand:

> *In the name of God, full of compassion, ever-compassionate*
> May God give you a just reward and protect you from all misfortune.
>
> I am writing to tell you the same thing I told ʿAbd Allāh: all of you need to stay away. If you do they may forget that I'm here, but as long as you're with me I'll be the center of attention. We even had people coming to see you so they could report back about what we're doing. That's why I'm asking, not because I'm angry at you. Please understand, son, that if you and your brother stay in Baghdad and stop coming here you'll be doing what I want. So don't worry and don't be upset with me.
>
> Peace be upon you, and the mercy of God, and His blessings.

73.34 Then I received another letter in his handwriting addressed to me. It said:

> *In the name of God, full of compassion, ever-compassionate*
> May God give you a just reward and in His mercy protect you from all harm.
>
> I write to you enjoying successive blessings from God, whom I ask to complete them and to aid me in expressing my gratitude for them. I've been released from some of my obligations.[442] Only those who were offered rewards and accepted them remained in confinement here. They were given stipends and ended up where you see them now. They've taught Hadith and consorted with those people. I ask God to protect us from them and to free us from this predicament. If you could see the wretched state I'm in, you would gladly give up your property and your families to free me. But don't let what I'm telling you trouble you. Just stay home; perhaps God will find a way to set me free.
>
> Peace and the blessings of God.

Later I got another letter similar to the one above.

After we left, the food stopped being delivered and the carpets, cushions, and other items put there for us were removed.

73.35 Then my father made a will:

> *In the name of God, full of compassion, ever-compassionate*
> This is the testament of Aḥmad ibn Muḥammad ibn Ḥanbal.
>
> He declares that there is no god but God, alone, without partner; and that Muḥammad is His servant and Emissary, bringing right guidance and a true religion that he carried to victory over all other cults and creeds despite the resistance of the polytheists.
>
> All those members of his family willing to heed him he enjoins to partake with the like-minded in worshipping and praising God and in giving good counsel to the Muslim community.

He testifies that he accepts God, mighty and glorious, as his lord; Islam as his religion; and Muḥammad, God bless him and grant him peace, as his prophet.

I declare that I owe ʿAbd Allāh ibn Muḥammad, known as Fūrān, approximately fifty dinars; he is to be believed when he says so.[443] Let him be repaid out of the income from the house, God willing. Once the debt is paid, let ten dirhams be given to each of Ṣāliḥ's children,[444] male and female, after the money due Abū Muḥammad is paid back.

Witnessed by Abū Yūsuf as well as Ṣāliḥ and ʿAbd Allāh, sons of Aḥmad ibn Muḥammad ibn Ḥanbal.

[Al-Marrūdhī:] One night after he had been fasting continuously, Aḥmad woke me up. He was sitting up and saying, "I'm so hungry that my head's spinning. Find me something to eat!" 73.36

I found part of a loaf of flatbread for him and he ate it.

"If I weren't afraid of helping them break my resistance," he said, "I wouldn't eat at all."

He would often get out of bed and try to leave the house but then find himself so weakened by hunger that he would have to sit down and rest. Sometimes I would have to moisten a rag and give it to him to lay on his face in order to revive him. At one point he was so weak—from starvation, not illness—that he made a will and had it witnessed. Here's what I heard him say when making his will in Samarra:

In the name of God, full of compassion, ever-compassionate
This is the testament of Aḥmad ibn Muḥammad.

He declares that there is no god but God, alone, without partner; and that Muḥammad is His servant and Emissary, bringing right guidance and a true religion that he carried to victory over all other cults and creeds despite the resistance of the polytheists.

All those members of his family willing to heed him he enjoins to partake with the like-minded in worshipping God and giving good counsel to the Muslim community.

He testifies that he accepts God, mighty and glorious, as his lord; Islam as his religion; and Muḥammad as his prophet.

He also testified that he owed fifty dinars, to be repaid out of the income of the rental property.

73.37 [ʿAbd Allāh:] My father spent sixteen days at the caliph's palace in Samarra without eating anything but a quarter-measure of barley meal. Every night he would have a drink of water, and every third night eat a handful of meal. Even after he came home it took him six months to recover. The inner corners of his eyes seemed to have receded toward the pupil.[445]

73.38 [Al-Marrūdhī:] When we were in Samarra, Aḥmad used to ask me if I could find him some bean broth. Many times I would moisten some bread in water and he would eat it with salt. From the time we entered Samarra to the time we left, he tasted no cooked food or any fat.

73.39 [Al-Marrūdhī:] Aḥmad ibn Ḥanbal once said to me, "All day long I hope for death. I'm afraid of being tempted by the things of this world. Yesterday I was thinking that it's been two trials. Before, they tested my religion, and this time they're trying me with the things of this world."

Once in Samarra he said, "Isn't it surprising? Before this, I lived on bread, and stopped craving food altogether. When I was in jail, I ate. To me, that meant that my faith had increased. But now it seems to have decreased."

On another occasion he said, "Today makes eight days I've gone without eating or drinking anything except some barley meal—less than a quarter-measure."

He would go three days without eating—and I was with him all the time. On the fourth night I would serve him an eighth-measure of barley meal. Sometimes he would drink it and sometimes he wouldn't. For fourteen or fifteen days, he survived on less than two quarter-measures of barley meal. Whenever he was upset about something he wouldn't eat at all and would drink only water. People tried to make him stop doing what he was doing to himself, suggesting that if he asked for a cooked meal he would feel much better.

"You can enjoy a cooked meal," he replied, "only if you're sure of being saved. Abū Dharr lived for thirty days on nothing but water from the well of Zamzam, Ibrāhīm al-Taymī went for days without eating. Ibn al-Zubayr could go for seven."

[Ṣāliḥ:] Al-Mutawakkil had rented a house for them, but my father asked to move out of it and rented another place himself. When al-Mutawakkil asked how my father was faring, he was told that he was ill. "I had hoped to keep him close, but I grant him leave to go. ʿUbayd Allāh! Give him a thousand dinars to distribute, and tell Saʿīd to prepare a boat to take him back to Baghdad." 73.40

Late that night, ʿAlī ibn al-Jahm arrived, followed by ʿUbayd Allāh with the thousand dinars.

"The Commander of the Faithful has exempted me from doing anything I don't want to do," said Aḥmad. "So take the money back." Then he said, "I don't like the cold. It would be more comfortable for me to travel by land."

A document of safe passage was written up for him as well as a letter to Muḥammad ibn ʿAbd Allāh instructing him to take care of him. He arrived back home that afternoon.

[Ibn al-Ashʿath:] Al-Mutawakkil wrote to his deputy ordering Aḥmad to be sent to him. When Aḥmad arrived, al-Mutawakkil had a palace vacated and furnished for his use, with food of various kinds delivered every day. He wanted Aḥmad to teach his son Hadith, but Aḥmad refused. He also refused to sit on the carpets or look at the food provided him even though he was fasting. When it came time to break the fast, he told his companion to buy him some bean broth. He went on this way for some days. Then, ʿAlī ibn al-Jahm, who was a Sunni and favorable to Aḥmad, said to the caliph, 73.41

"A renunciant like him is no good to you. Would you consider giving him permission to leave?"

So the caliph gave his permission, and Aḥmad came home.

73.42 [Al-Marrūdhī:] While we were in Samarra, I heard Isḥāq ibn Ḥanbal pleading with Aḥmad to go see the caliph so he could command him to do right and forbid him to do wrong.[446]

"He would listen to you," said Isḥāq. "Look at Ibn Rāhawayh: Doesn't he preach to Ibn Ṭāhir?"

"Ibn Rāhawayh is no example because I think what he's doing is wrong. As far as I'm concerned he does no good, and he thinks the same of me. If there's anyone who needs to hear me preach, it's him. Consorting with the high and mighty is a trial. We've tried to steer clear of them, but still they've managed to cause trouble for us. Think how much worse it'll be if we start associating with them."

73.43 Al-Marrūdhī also said:

I heard Ibn al-Mubārak's nephew Ismāʿīl arguing with Aḥmad and trying to persuade him to go see the caliph.

"Your uncle," said Abū ʿAbd Allāh, "said, 'Keep away from them, and if you can't, speak the truth.' I'm afraid of not speaking the truth."

I also heard Aḥmad say, "If I were to see the caliph, the only subject I'd raise is the Emigrants and the Helpers."[447]

According to another account, Aḥmad's uncle said, "Why don't you go see the caliph? He thinks highly of you."

"That's what worries me," said Aḥmad.

73.44 [Ibn al-Munādī:] Eight years or so before he died, Aḥmad stopped teaching Hadith. As far as I know, the reason was that al-Mutawakkil sent him a message conveying his greetings and asking him to take his son al-Muʿtazz as a pupil and teach him Hadith. Aḥmad replied: "Convey my greetings to the Commander of the Faithful and tell him that I have sworn a solemn oath never to recite a complete Hadith again as long as I live. The Commander of the Faithful has exempted me from doing anything I detest, and this is something I detest."

Hearing this, the messenger departed.

More on What Happened between Him and al-Mutawakkil after His Return from Samarra

[Ṣāliḥ:] My father used to receive visits from messengers conveying al-Mutawakkil's greetings and asking after his health. We were happy to receive the visitors, but my father would shudder so violently that we had to bundle him up in heavy clothes. He would bunch his fingers together and say, "If I had my soul in my hand, I would let it go," then open his hand. 73.45

Some time later, al-Mutawakkil and his entourage were passing through al-Shammāsiyyah on their way to al-Madā'in. My father told me that he didn't want me to go to them or send them word of any kind. I said I wouldn't.

The next day I was sitting outside and there right in front of me—even though it was a rainy day—appeared Yaḥyā ibn Khāqān, who had come, rain and all, with a vast entourage.

"Is this any way to act?" he said, dismounting just outside our alley. "You didn't come and convey your father's greetings to the Commander of the Faithful, so he sent *me* to *you*."

I tried to persuade him to come through the alley on horseback, but he refused and began sloshing his way through the mud instead. When he reached the door, he removed the galoshes he was wearing over his boots and went into the house.

My father was sitting in the corner wearing a patched wrap and a turban. The only curtain across the door was a strip of burlap. Yaḥyā greeted him, kissed him on the forehead, and asked after his health.

"The Commander of the Faithful conveys his greetings and asks, 'How are your spirits and how is your health?' He says that he took comfort in having you close by and asks you to pray for him."

"Not a day passes," says my father, "that I don't pray for him."

"He's sent along a thousand dinars for you to distribute to those in need."

"Abū Zakariyyā," he replied, "I don't leave the house and I don't see anyone. And he's exempted me from doing what I detest, and this is something I detest."

"Abū 'Abd Allāh! Caliphs will only tolerate so much."

"Do what you can to handle it discreetly, Abū Zakariyyā."

Yaḥyā wished him well and rose. On the way out he turned around and came back.

"Would you say the same thing if it was one of your associates who was giving you the money?"

"Yes."

When we reached the anteroom, he said, "The Commander of the Faithful has ordered me to give you the money to distribute to your families."

"Keep it with you for now," I said. After that a messenger came from al-Mutawakkil nearly every day.

73.46 ['Abd Allāh:] I heard my father say, "All I wish for is death. Living this way is worse than dying. What happened before was a test of faith. Flogging and prison I could stand, since I was the only one who suffered. But now we're being tested by the things of this world," or words to that effect.

73.47 ['Abd Allāh:] I heard my father say, "This time it's worse. Flogging and prison I could stand, since I was the only one involved. But now we're being tested by the things of this world."

73.48 Al-Marrūdhī:] Aḥmad told me, "Yaḥyā ibn Khāqān came bearing that pittance of his," and went on about how meager a sum it was.

"But I heard he brought a thousand dinars," I said.

"That's right," he said. He went on: "I wouldn't take it from him. He got as far as the door and then turned around and asked, 'If one of your associates brought you something, would you take it?' I told him I wouldn't. He said he had asked so he would know what to tell the caliph."

"But would it have been so wrong," I asked, "if you had accepted the money and then given it away?"

He glowered at me. "If I did that, what do you think it would mean? Am I supposed to be his housekeeper?"

73.49 [Ṣāliḥ:] 'Ubayd Allāh ibn Yaḥyā wrote to my father saying, "The Commander of the Faithful has ordered me to write and ask you about the Qur'an—not to test you, but instead to learn from you and benefit from your insight."

In response, Aḥmad dictated the following letter to me, for delivery to 'Ubayd Allāh ibn Yaḥyā:[448]

In the name of God, full of compassion, ever-compassionate

May God reward you, Abū l-Ḥasan, as you deserve, in all matters; and in His mercy stave off all that is hateful in this world and the next. I am writing to you—may God be pleased with you!—to convey such thoughts as occur to me in response to the question posed by the Commander of the Faithful. I ask God to perpetuate the guidance with which He has favored him, inasmuch as the people had waded deep into the treacherous waters of falsehood and disagreement and were floundering there until the Commander of the Faithful succeeded to the caliphate and God, acting through him, banished every heretical innovation. The wretchedness, suffering, and constraint endured by the community vanished all at once, swept away by a Commander of the Faithful doing God's will; and great was the rejoicing of the Muslims, who pray for his well-being. I pray God answer every righteous prayer for the caliph, strengthen his good intentions, and aid him in his quest.

Of Ibn 'Abbas it is related that he said, "Do not strike one 73.50
verse of God's Book against another for doing so will cast doubt into your hearts."

Citing 'Abd Allāh ibn 'Amr it is related that a group of people were sitting at the door of the Prophet's house. One said, "Did God not say such-and-such?" Another said, "But did He not also say such-and-such?" Overhearing them, the Prophet came out, looking as if a pomegranate had been split open and spattered his face with bitter juice.

"Is this what you've been told to do?" he asked. "To strike the verses of God's Book one against another? That's how the nations before you went astray. What you're doing has no place

> here. Look to what you are enjoined to do, and do it; look to what is forbidden you, and forbid yourself to do it!"

73.51 Aḥmad cited additional Hadith reports, then said:

> God—exalted be He—has said «so that he may hear the word of God»[449] and «His is the creation, His the command»[450] thereby conveying that command and creation are two different things.

After citing additional verses, he wrote:

> I am no man for Disputation. I do not approve of speculation regarding any of these matters except what is in the Book of God or in reports of what was believed by the Prophet—may God bless and keep him—his Companions, or their Successors.

Chapter 74
His Refusing Ibn Ṭāhir's Request to Visit Him

74.1 [Ṣāliḥ:] When Muḥammad ibn ʿAbd Allāh ibn Ṭāhir came to Baghdad, he sent a message to my father saying, "I'd like you to come and see me. Tell me the day you prefer and I'll make sure there's no one else here."

My father replied, "I am a man who has never consorted with rulers. Furthermore, the Commander of the Faithful has exempted me from doing anything I detest. This I detest."

Muḥammad strove to change his mind but to no avail.

I then received a letter from Isḥāq ibn Rāhawayh saying:

> I went to see Ṭāhir ibn ʿAbd Allāh and he told me that Muḥammad had invited Aḥmad to call on him but Aḥmad had refused.

I said, "May God correct the emir! Aḥmad has vowed never to teach Hadith again. Perhaps he was afraid that if he went, he would ask him to teach."

He asked, "Are you serious?"

I said, "I am."

I told my father about this but he said nothing.

[The author:] I think Aḥmad refused to visit Ibn Ṭāhir because he was a ruler. He did visit people so long as they were men of piety and learning.

['Abd Allāh:] After my father was released by the Inquisition, he was worried that Isḥāq ibn Rāhawayh would come to see him so he decided to go see him first. No sooner had he reached Rey and gone into a mosque when the clouds opened like waterskins. He sheltered there until night fell and he was told to leave the mosque because they wanted to close it. 74.2

"This is a house of God," he said, "and I'm a worshipper of God."

"Either leave," they said, "or we'll drag you out by the feet. Your choice."

My father continued the story:

"Good-bye,"[451] I said, and went out into the thunderstorm with no idea where to go. Then a man came out of his house and said, "You there! Where are you going at a time like this?"

"I have nowhere to go," I said.

"Come in," he said.

He brought me in, had me undress, and gave me dry clothes to change into. I performed my ablutions and then went into a room where there was a heater full of coals, a blanket of felt on the floor, and a laden table. The members of the family invited me to join them. After we ate, the man said, "Where are you from?"

I told them I was from Baghdad.

"Do you know a man named Aḥmad ibn Ḥanbal?"

"I'm Aḥmad ibn Ḥanbal."

"Well," said the man, "I'm Isḥāq ibn Rāhawayh."[452]

Chapter 75
What Happened When His Two Sons and His Uncle Accepted Gifts from the Authorities

75.1 [Ṣāliḥ:] A short while after my father came back from Samarra, he summoned me and said, "Ṣālīh, I want you to give up that stipend. Stop accepting it and don't transfer it to anyone else, either. It's only because of me that you get it at all. When I'm gone you can do as you think best."

I said nothing.

"What's wrong?"

I said: "I don't like to tell you one thing to your face and then do something else behind your back, so I'm not going to lie to you or tell you what you want to hear. No one here has more dependents than I do and no one has a better excuse to take that money. When I would come complaining to you, you'd say, 'Your fate is bound up with mine. I wish God would remove that burden from me!' Now it seems He's granted your wish."

"So you're not going to turn down the money?"

"No."

"Get out, damn you!" he said.

After that he had someone block up the door between our houses.

75.2 When I ran into my brother ʿAbd Allāh, he asked me what was going on and I told him.

"What should I say to him?" he asked me.

"That's up to you."

My father made the same request of him as he had made of me. ʿAbd Allāh also said he wouldn't turn down the stipend, and our father got angry at him too.

Later we saw his uncle, who asked why we had said anything about it at all. "If you took something, how would he know?"

His uncle then went to see him. "Abū ʿAbd Allāh," he said, "I'm not taking any of that money."

"Thank God!" said my father.

With that he stopped talking to us, shut up all the doors between our houses, and said that nothing should come from our homes into his. Before we began accepting stipends from the ruler, he used to eat with us. Often we would send him something and he would eat part of it.

Two months later we received our designated payment, delivered to our door, and the first to arrive and claim a share was his uncle. 75.3

When he learned what was going on, my father came to the door that had been blocked up and spoke through a hole that the boys had made.

"Call Ṣāliḥ for me!" he said.

Someone brought me the message.

"I'm not coming," I said.

My father sent another message to ask why not.

"There are plenty of people who depend on this stipend," I said. "I'm not the only one, but I am the most entitled. If you've chosen me of all people for a scolding, I'm not coming."

A bit later his uncle called everyone to prayer. My father came out of the house and was told that his uncle had gone out to the mosque. I went there too, but stopped and waited in a spot where I could hear what they were saying. As soon as the prayer was over, my father turned to his uncle and said, "You enemy of God! You lied to my face even though other people need the money more than you. You said you wouldn't take any of it and then you did—even though you've got a property that pays you two hundred dirhams and you were hoping to make more by taking over a public road! When the Day of Resurrection comes, I'm afraid we'll find you with seven tracts of land tied around your neck!"[453] 75.4

With that he stopped speaking to him. He also stopped praying in our mosque and started going out to pray in someone else's mosque.

75.5 [Al-ʿUkbarī:] In 236 [850–51] I went looking for Aḥmad ibn Ḥanbal so I could ask him about something. I asked for him and they told me he had gone out to pray, so I sat down to wait by the alley gate. When he appeared, I rose and greeted him and he returned the greeting. He went down the alley and I walked beside him all the way to the end, where there was an open door. He pushed it open and went in, saying, "Go away now, and may God spare you!"

As I turned, I saw that the gate opened onto a mosque where an elder with a dyed beard was standing and leading the congregation in prayer. I sat and waited until he spoke the parting salutation. When someone came out, I asked him who the elder was.

"That's Isḥāq, Aḥmad ibn Ḥanbal's uncle," he said.

"Why won't Aḥmad pray behind him?"

"He won't talk to him, or to his own sons, because they accept a stipend from the authorities."

75.6 [Ṣāliḥ:] At some point when my father wasn't speaking to us, he found out that we'd been sent another sum.[454] My father came to the opening in the door and said, "Ṣāliḥ! Find out which parts are for Ḥasan and Umm ʿAlī[455] and take them to Fūrān. Tell him to go to wherever the money came from and give it away as alms."

"How would Fūrān know where it came from?"

"Just do as I say."

So I sent the two portions to Fūrān.

Meanwhile, my father, after he heard that we had accepted the money, went to bed without eating. I didn't see him for a month. Then the boys opened the door and went in. But he still wouldn't let them bring in anything from my house. Finally I sent him a message saying: "This has gone on long enough, and I miss you." Then I went in. He wouldn't speak to me. I bent down and embraced him.

"Dad," I asked, "why are you doing this to yourself?"

"It's something I can't help, son."

75.7 After that we didn't accept anything for a while. Then we were granted something more and we took it. When my father found out he stopped talking to us for months. Finally Fūrān had a word with him and I went in.

"It's Ṣāliḥ," said Fūrān. "Remember how much you care for him."

"Ṣāliḥ was the dearest person in the world to me," said my father. "All I wanted was for him to have what I wanted for myself. What's wrong with that?"

"Dad," I said, "have you ever met anyone who could survive what you put yourself through?"

"So now you're arguing with me?"

Then he wrote to Yaḥyā ibn Khāqān demanding that he stop paying the stipend and never mention it again. No sooner had the message reached Yaḥyā than the chief of intelligence took it and sent a copy to al-Mutawakkil.

"How many months are due to Aḥmad's sons?" the caliph asked.

"Ten."

"Have forty thousand dirhams—whole coins from the treasury—sent to them immediately without telling Aḥmad."

"I'll write to Ṣāliḥ and let him know," said Yaḥyā to the official.

When I received Yaḥyā's letter, I sent word to my father.

The one who delivered the message reported: "Aḥmad sat silently for a while staring at the ground. Then he raised his head and said, 'If I want one thing but God decrees another, there's nothing more I can do.'"

[Al-Būshanjī:] Someone quoted al-Mutawakkil as saying, 75.8
"Aḥmad won't let us take care of his family." This was because he had sent vast sums to Aḥmad's children, grandchildren, and uncle, who had taken it without telling him. When Aḥmad realized what had happened, he reproached them and told them to return the money. "How could you take it when the frontier is undefended and no one is distributing the spoils to the Muslims who deserve a share?"[456]

Everyone pleaded that they had already paid the money to their creditors.

Then al-Mutawakkil sent another sum, ordering that it be given 75.9
to his sons without his knowing about it. Again, they accepted it.

When Aḥmad found out, he summoned them and said, "With the first amount, you claimed that you had spent it already or used it to pay your debts. This one, though, you can still send back."

I myself saw him block off the door that joined his house to his son Ṣāliḥ's. I also saw him stay away from the mosque that adjoined his house, where the prayer caller was his uncle and the prayer leader was Ibn ʿUmayr. It was because of the money that he stopped talking to them. I saw him walk all the way through the alley, into the lane, onto the main thoroughfare, and then down another lane where there was a mosque called the Sidrah Mosque, big enough for Friday prayers.

75.10 When Aḥmad was sent to Samarra during the reign of al-Mutawakkil, they took him to the palace to recite Hadith for caliph's children al-Muʿtazz, al-Muntaṣir, and al-Mu'ayyad, his heirs apparent. Aḥmad responded by feigning illness and, if asked about a report, saying, "I don't remember, and I don't have my books here." In the end al-Mutawakkil relented and let him go, signing an order that read as follows: "We herewith excuse Aḥmad from doing anything he detests."

On one occasion Aḥmad received a gift of dates bearing al-Mutawakkil's seal but refused to taste them. To explain himself, he reportedly said, "The Commander of the Faithful has excused me from doing anything I detest." He said the same thing whenever anything was sent to his house, and that became his custom.

75.11 [ʿAbd Allāh:] When I was ill, my father came to check on me.

"Dad," I said, "we still have some of the money al-Mutawakkil gave us. What if I used it to make the pilgrimage?"

"You should," he said.

"But if you don't mind spending it," I asked, "why didn't *you* take it?"

"I don't consider it forbidden, son," he answered. "But I'd rather abstain."

Chapter 76

Some Major Figures Who Capitulated to the Inquisition

Among the prominent men of learning who capitulated were ʿAlī ibn al-Jaʿd; Ismāʿīl ibn Ibrāhīm ibn ʿUlayyah;[457] Saʿīd ibn Sulaymān al-Wāsiṭī, known as Saʿduwayh; Isḥāq ibn Abī Isrāʾīl; Abū Ḥassān al-Ziyādī; Bishr ibn al-Walīd; ʿUbayd Allāh ibn ʿUmar al-Qawārīrī; ʿAlī ibn Abī Muqātil; al-Faḍl ibn Ghānim; al-Ḥasan ibn Ḥammād Sajjadah; Ismāʿīl ibn Abī Masʿūd; Muḥammad ibn Saʿd, scribe to al-Wāqidī; Aḥmad ibn Ibrāhīm al-Dawraqī; Ismāʿīl ibn Dāwūd al-Jawzī; Yaḥyā ibn Maʿīn; ʿAlī ibn al-Madīnī; Abū Khaythamah Zuhayr ibn Ḥarb; Abū Naṣr al-Tammār; and Abū Kurayb. 76.1

The capitulations that were hardest for Aḥmad ibn Ḥanbal to bear were those of Abū Naṣr al-Tammār, Yaḥyā ibn Maʿīn, and Abū Khaythamah. He had a high opinion of them all and did not expect any of them to give in as quickly as they did. Abū Naṣr al-Tammār was a Worshipper who heard Hadith from Mālik, the two Ḥammāds, and many others, but was unable to withstand the Inquisition and caved in. Aḥmad consequently held that one should not write down the reports he transmitted, and refused to pray over him when he died. 76.2

[Abū Ḥafṣ:] The day Abū Naṣr al-Tammār was taken in for questioning by Isḥāq ibn Ibrāhīm, Bishr asked me to find out what happened. When I told him that al-Tammār had capitulated, he recited «We are of God, and to Him we return!»[458] several times, then said, "How beautiful that beard of his would have been if he had dyed it"—meaning with blood—"and resisted until death." 76.3

[ʿUbayd Allāh:] Abū Maʿmar al-Qaṭīʿī was such a fervent adherent of the *sunnah* that he used to say, "If my mule could talk, she'd say she was a Sunni." 76.4

But then when he was put to the test, he gave in. After he was released he said, "We denied our faith and they let us go."

76.5 [Ibn ʿAskar:] After Saʿduwayh was called in, I saw him come out of the emir's residence and say, "Boy, bring the donkey. Your master has denied his faith!"

[The author:] I say: Saʿduwayh is Saʿīd ibn Sulaymān Abū ʿUthmān al-Wāsiṭī, known as Saʿduwayh. He recited Hadith citing Ibn Saʿd and others and performed the pilgrimage sixty times.

[Al-ʿIjlī:] After his interrogation, Saʿduwayh was asked what he had done.

76.6 "We denied our faith and they let us go," he said.

Chapter 77

His Comments on Those Who Capitulated

77.1 [Abū Zurʿah:] Aḥmad held that one should not write down reports transmitted by Abū Naṣr al-Tammār, Yaḥyā ibn Maʿīn, or anyone else who capitulated to the Inquisition.

77.2 [Al-Maymūnī:] I have it on good authority that he—meaning Aḥmad ibn Ḥanbal—did not attend the funeral of Abū Naṣr al-Tammār. I believe the reason was al-Tammār's capitulation to the Inquisition.

77.3 [Ḥajjāj ibn al-Shāʿir:] I heard Aḥmad ibn Ḥanbal say, "If I were to transmit Hadith from anyone who gave in, I'd transmit from Abū Maʿmar and Abū Kurayb."

[The author:] Abū Maʿmar's full name is Ismāʿīl ibn Ibrāhīm al-Hudhalī and he capitulated under duress. He later regretted doing so, reproaching himself and expressing envious admiration of those who resisted. As for Abū Kurayb, his real name is Muḥammad ibn Abū l-ʿAlāʾ. After his capitulation he was given a stipend of two dinars. When he discovered that they were rewarding him for giving in, he renounced the stipend even though he needed it.

77.4 [Ṣāliḥ:] Al-Ḥizāmī came to see us after having been to see Ibn Abī Duʾād. As soon as my father went out and saw him there, he shut the door in his face and went back inside.

[The author:] He did the same with Abū Khaythamah, who came and knocked on the door. When Aḥmad came out and saw him there he shut the door and went back inside muttering angrily to himself. Abū Khaythamah, who could hear whatever it was that Aḥmad was saying, never came back.

When Aḥmad fell ill, Yaḥyā ibn Maʿīn came to see him; but Aḥmad turned his back on him and refused to say a word. Finally Yaḥyā got up and left, grumbling, "After all that time together he won't even speak to me!"

[Al-Marrūdhī:] When Aḥmad ibn Ḥanbal fell ill, Yaḥyā ibn Maʿīn 77.5
came to visit him. But Aḥmad, who had vowed never to speak to anyone who had capitulated, did not return his greeting. Yaḥyā began offering excuses, including the Hadith of ʿAmmār, and the verse «with the exception of one who is forced to do it, while his heart rests securely in faith.»[459] Aḥmad's only response was to turn his head away. Finally Yaḥyā said, "I give up!" and got to his feet, muttering "It's no use explaining anything to him."

I followed him out and found him sitting by the door.

"Did Aḥmad say anything after I left?" he asked.

"He said, 'I can't believe he's citing the Hadith of ʿAmmār! (The Ḥadīth of ʿAmmār runs as follows: "As I passed them, I heard them cursing you; and when I told them not to, they beat me.")[460] All they did was *threaten* to beat you.'"

Finally I heard Yaḥyā say, "Go on, then, Aḥmad, and may God forgive you! Never on God's green earth have I met anyone who knew His Law better than you."

Addendum

Someone might well ask why, if it can be shown that certain indi- 77.6
viduals capitulated under duress, which the Law allows, did Aḥmad end his relationship with them? There are three possible responses:

1. The persons in question were threatened but not beaten before they capitulated. Threats do not count as coercion, as is evident from the aforementioned report about Yaḥyā ibn Maʿīn.

2. Aḥmad may have ended his relationship with them in order to make a point: to show the common people what a heinous doctrine it was that the offenders had assented to and thus help the mass of believers stay on the right path.

3. Upon giving their assent, most of the offenders accepted payments and began associating with members of the regime. In doing so they went beyond what the Law allows and thus deserved ostracism and condemnation.

77.7 [Al-Marrūdhī:] From the time we entered Samarra to the time we left, Aḥmad tasted no cooked food or any fat. At one point he said, "That lot"—meaning Ibn Abī Shaybah, Ibn al-Madīnī, and ʿAbd al-Aʿlā—"have certainly been enjoying themselves. I had no idea they were so attached to this world. How can they bring themselves to hang about palace doors like that?"

[The author:] One of the most damning things reported about Ibn al-Madīnī was that he recited a report transmitted by al-Walīd ibn Muslim, including a verbal error that al-Walīd had made, to Ibn Abī Du'ād in order to help his side argue for its point of view. This was one of the things that Aḥmad held against him.

77.8 [Al-Marrūdhī:] I told Aḥmad that ʿAlī l-Madīnī was reciting a report transmitted by al-Walīd ibn Muslim, citing al-Awzāʿī, citing al-Zuhrī, citing Anas citing ʿUmar, saying: "Leave it to its Creator."[461]

"He's a liar!" said Aḥmad. "Al-Walīd ibn Muslim's report says 'Leave it to its Maker.'" He added: "Al-Madīnī knows that al-Walīd made an error when he transmitted it. So why would he recite it for those people? Why give them a wrong report?"

He thus declared al-Madīnī to be a liar.

77.9 [Qahm:] Ibn Abī Du'ād told al-Muʿtaṣim that Aḥmad ibn Ḥanbal claimed that God will be visible in the afterlife even though the eye can perceive only finite objects. When al-Muʿtaṣim asked Aḥmad to explain himself, he replied that he was citing the Emissary of God.

"And what did the Emissary say?"

"I heard Muḥammad ibn Jaʿfar Ghundar report," said Aḥmad, "that he heard Shuʿbah report, citing Ismāʿīl ibn Abī Khālid, citing

Qays ibn Abī Ḥāzim, citing Jarīr ibn ʿAbd Allāh al-Bajalī: 'We were once with the Prophet on the fourteenth night of the month when he looked at the full moon and said, "You will most certainly see your Lord as clearly as you see the moon; you will not be cheated of seeing him."'" Then he turned to Ibn Abī Du'ād. "What do you say to that?"

"I'll have to look into the chain of transmitters," he replied.

This exchange took place on the first day of Aḥmad's trial. After the session ended, Ibn Abī Du'ād sent for ʿAlī ibn al-Madīnī, who was then living in Baghdad without a dirham to his name. No sooner had al-Madīnī arrived than Ibn Abī Du'ād, without further ado, gave him ten thousand dirhams. Then he said, "That's a gift from the Commander of the Faithful." By his command, al-Madīnī also received the two years' worth of stipends that were owed him. Then Ibn Abī Du'ād asked him about the Hadith of Jarīr ibn ʿAbd Allāh regarding the visibility of God.

"It's authentic," said al-Madīnī.

"Do you have any criticism of it at all?"

"I ask His Honor the Judge for permission not to discuss this."

"ʿAlī," he said, "this is the most serious question you'll ever be asked."

After regaling him with new clothes, bottles of scent, and a riding animal complete with saddle, bridle, and reins, Ibn Abī Du'ād continued to press his question until al-Madīnī finally said, "One of the transmitters is unreliable. It's Qays ibn Abī Ḥāzim, who was no more than a desert Arab who used to piss on his own heels."

Ibn Abī Du'ād rose and embraced him.

The next day, when the trial had resumed, Ibn Abī Du'ād said, "Commander of the Faithful, Aḥmad cited the Hadith of Jarīr and named Qays ibn Abī Ḥāzim as a transmitter, but Qays was no more than a desert Arab who used to piss on his own heels."

Aḥmad later said that he realized immediately that this was the work of ʿAlī l-Madīnī.

[The author:] If this story is true, Ibn al-Madīnī is guilty of a terrible crime: volunteering an assessment he knew to be false. Qays 77.10

ibn Abī Ḥāzim was one of the leading Successors and the only one to have met all ten of the foremost Companions and transmitted reports on their authority. This is the view of most men of learning, though Abū Dāwūd Sulaymān ibn al-Ashʿath says that he transmitted from only nine of the ten, the missing one being ʿAbd al-Raḥmān ibn ʿAwf. In any event, Qays did transmit from a great many Companions and was never criticized for any reason. Anyone who does what al-Madīnī reportedly did therefore deserves to be ostracized.

77.11 [Muḥammad ibn ʿAbd Allāh al-Shāfiʿī:] Ibrāhīm al-Ḥarbī was asked why he didn't transmit reports transmitted by ʿAlī ibn al-Madīnī. He replied, "One day I saw him walking along with his sandals in his hand and the hem of his garment between his teeth.[462]

"'Where are you off to?' I asked.

"'I need to get to Abū ʿAbd Allāh's in time to pray behind him.'

"I thought he meant Aḥmad ibn Ḥanbal, but when I asked him he said he meant Ibn Abī Duʾād.

"'By God,' I said, 'I'm never citing another word I heard from you.'"

77.12 [Ibrāhīm al-Ḥarbī:] Whenever ʿAlī ibn al-Madīnī came across a Hadith transmitted by Aḥmad in a document, he would say, "Cross it out," to please Ibn Abī Duʾād.

77.13 [Yaḥyā ibn ʿUthmān:] I heard Bishr ibn al-Ḥārith say: "I would rather have seen their hair dyed with blood than see them give in."

Chapter 78

Those Who Defied the Inquisition

78.1 [Al-Marwazī:] Only four men, all of them from Marv, remained steadfast throughout the Inquisition: Aḥmad ibn Ḥanbal, Aḥmad ibn Naṣr, Muḥammad ibn Nūḥ, and Nuʿaym ibn Ḥammād.

Abū l-Ḥusayn ibn al-Munādī mentions the following men as having remained steadfast as well: Abū Nuʿaym al-Faḍl ibn Dukayn, ʿAffān, al-Buwayṭī, Ismāʿīl ibn Abī Uways al-Madanī, Abū Muṣʿab al-Madanī, and Yaḥyā l-Ḥimmānī.

Reports Concerning the Prominent Dissenters

ʿAffān ibn Muslim

[Ḥanbal ibn Isḥāq:] The first to be called for interrogation was ʿAffān. The next day, after his return, I was there, as were all of us, including Aḥmad ibn Ḥanbal. Yaḥyā ibn Maʿīn asked ʿAffān to tell us what Isḥāq had said to him and how he had answered. 78.2

"I did nothing to dishonor you or your associates," he said, meaning that he had not said what Isḥāq wanted him to say.

"So what was it like?"

"Isḥāq ibn Ibrāhīm called me in. When I got there, he read out the letter that al-Maʾmūn had sent to al-Raqqah from northern Iraq. In the letter it said, 'Test ʿAffān, and call on him to say that the Qurʾan is such-and-such. If he does so, confirm him in his position. If he refuses, cut off his stipend.'"

Al-Maʾmūn had been paying ʿAffān five hundred dirhams a month.

"When the letter had been read out, Isḥāq asked me to state my position. By way of reply, I recited «Say, He is God, the One, the *ṣamad*»[463] through to the end, then asked, 'Is that created?'

"Isḥāq said, 'Listen, elder, the Commander of the Faithful says he'll cut off your stipend, and if he does I will too.'

"I told him that God says «In heaven is your sustenance, and also that which you are promised.»[464] He had no reply to that and let me go."

Aḥmad and those of our associates who were there were heartened by this report.

[Ibrāhīm ibn al-Ḥusayn:] I was working for ʿAffān, holding the reins of his mule, when he was called in for trial. When he went in, he was asked to agree to what they said but he wouldn't. They told him they would keep back his stipend, which came to a thousand dinars a month, but he said, «In heaven is your sustenance, and also that which you are promised.»[465] 78.3

When we got back, the women of the house, and everyone else there, started berating him. There were about forty people living in that house. Then we heard a knock on the door. In came a man who looked to me like a seller of ghee or oil carrying a thousand dirhams in a bag. "You've supported the faith," he said to ʿAffān, "and may God support you! You'll be getting a bag like this every month."

Abū Nuʿaym al-Faḍl ibn Dukayn

78.4 [Aḥmad ibn ʿUmar:] Of all the elders' gatherings I've seen, the greatest was the one I saw in Kufa during the Inquisition. After the letter with the doctrine in it was read aloud, Abū Nuʿaym spoke up and said, "I've heard reports from 870-some teachers, from al-Aʿmash on down, but I never met anyone who held that view"—that the Qur'an is a created thing—"nor saw anyone espouse it without being accused of heresy."

Hearing this, Aḥmad ibn Yūnus rose and kissed Abū Nuʿaym's head, saying, "May God reward you on behalf of Islam!"

78.5 [Muḥammad ibn Yūnus:] When Abū Nuʿaym was taken in to the governor, he said, "I've seen all the elders in Kufa—that's more than seven hundred, from al-Aʿmash on down—say that the Qur'an is the speech of God, and my neck means as little to me as this button."

At that, Aḥmad ibn Yūnus rose and kissed him on the head even though there had been bad blood between them and said, "May God reward you for the great elder you are!"

78.6 [Ibn Abī Shaybah:] When the Inquisition came to Kufa, Aḥmad ibn Yūnus told me to go find Abū Nuʿaym and let him know. When I found him and told him, he said, "It's just a flogging." Then he tore a button off his garment. "My head means less to me than this button."

78.7 [Ḥanbal ibn Isḥāq:] I heard Abū ʿAbd Allāh—meaning Aḥmad ibn Ḥanbal—say, "Two elders stood up for God better than anyone else"—or "nearly everyone else"—"ever has: ʿAffān and Abū Nuʿaym."

He was referring to their refusal to capitulate.

Nuʿaym ibn Ḥammād

[Muḥammad ibn Saʿd:] Nuʿaym ibn Ḥammād was from Marv. He pursued Hadith extensively in Iraq and western Arabia before settling in Egypt, where he stayed until he was summoned to Iraq during the caliphate of al-Muʿtaṣim. He was questioned regarding the Qurʾan but refused assent to what was demanded of him. He was then jailed in Samarra, where he died, still in prison, in 228 [842–43]. 78.8

[Ibrāhīm ibn Muḥammad ibn ʿArafah:] Among those who died in 228 [842–43] was Nuʿaym ibn Ḥammād, who perished in chains in a dungeon because he refused to say that the Qurʾan was a created thing. He was dragged by his chains and thrown into a pit, and died without being wrapped in a shroud or having anyone pray over his body. This was the doing of Ibn Abī Duʾād's man.[466] 78.9

Abū Yaʿqūb Yūsuf ibn Yaḥyā l-Buwayṭī

He was taken away during the Inquisition and pressured to espouse the claim that the Qurʾan is a created thing. When he refused, he was jailed in Baghdad and died in prison. He was a renunciant and a man who understood the Law. 78.10

[Al-Rabīʿ ibn Sulaymān:] I saw al-Buwayṭī mounted on a mule with a manacle around his neck and a fetter on his legs. The manacle and the fetter were joined by an iron chain. Suspended from the chain was a brick weighing thirty-five pounds.[467] He was saying, "God created the world by saying 'Be.' If 'be' is created, then one created thing brought another created thing into being." He went on: "By God, I'll die with this very chain still on me, so that when I'm gone, people will know that men died in irons for this cause. If they put me before him"—meaning al-Wāthiq—"I'll speak my mind."

[ʿAbd al-Raḥmān ibn Aḥmad:] Al-Buwayṭī lived a life of pious self-denial. During the Inquisition, he was taken from Egypt to Iraq, where he refused to capitulate and was clapped into irons and thrown in jail. He died, in prison and in fetters, in 232 [846–47]. 78.11

Aḥmad ibn Naṣr ibn Mālik ibn al-Haytham al-Khuzāʿī, called Abū ʿAbd Allāh

78.12 The Little Market of Naṣr in Baghdad is named after his father. His grandfather, Mālik ibn al-Haytham, was one of the leaders of the Abbasid revolutionary movement. Ibn Naṣr himself was a man of piety and rectitude who called upon others to do right. He heard Hadith from Mālik ibn Anas, Ḥammād ibn Zayd, and Hushaym, among others. Yaḥyā ibn Maʿīn and others transmitted on his authority.

78.13 Ibn Naṣr was accused of seeking the caliphate, but when he was arrested and brought before al-Wāthiq, the latter said, "Never mind what you were arrested for. What do you have to say about the Qur'an?"

"It's the word of God," said Ibn Naṣr.

"But is it a created thing?"

"It's the word of God."

"Well then: Can you see God on the Day of Resurrection?"

"That's what the reports say."

"Hah!" said al-Wāthiq. "You mean He'll be visible as if he were a finite object with a body?"

Al-Wāthiq then called for the sword and the leather mat. At his command, Ibn Naṣr, still in chains, was sat upon. Next a rope was put around his neck and he was stretched out. Finally al-Wāthiq marched up to him and hacked off his head. At his command, the severed head was sent to Baghdad and displayed for several days on the East Side and then on the West.

78.14 [Al-Marrūdhī:] At the mention of Aḥmad ibn Naṣr, I heard Aḥmad ibn Ḥanbal say, "God have mercy on him! How generous he was: he gave up his life!"

78.15 [Ismāʿīl ibn Khalaf:] Aḥmad ibn Naṣr was my friend. After the Inquisition killed him and displayed his head, I heard that the head was reciting the Qur'an. So I went and spent the night in a spot overlooking the head, which was guarded by men on horse and men on foot. As soon as everyone had dozed off, I heard the head reciting

«Do people think that once they say, "We believe," they will be left alone and not be put to the test?»[468] When I heard it, I shuddered.

Later I dreamed of seeing him draped in fine silk and heavy brocade[469] with a crown on his head. "Brother," I asked him, "how have you fared?"

"God has forgiven me," he answered, "and admitted me to the Garden. But I did spend three unhappy days first."

"Why?"

"The Emissary of God came to visit me, but when he passed the stake where my head was he averted his eyes. Finally I asked him whether I had died for the truth or for a falsehood.

"'For truth,' he said. 'But it was a member of my family who killed you, so whenever I pass you I feel ashamed.'"

[Ibrāhīm ibn al-Ḥasan:] The night after Aḥmad ibn Naṣr was killed, one of my associates saw him in a dream. He asked him how God had judged him. 78.16

"It felt as if I had dozed off for a moment," he replied, "and then I saw God smiling at me."

Al-Khaṭīb reports: Ibn Naṣr's head remained on display in Baghdad, and his body crucified in Samarra, for six years before his remains were finally taken down. The head and body were brought back together in Shawwāl of '37 [851–52] and buried in al-Mālikiyyah, a cemetery on the East Side. 78.17

Those arrested during the Inquisition include al-Ḥārith ibn Miskīn, Abū ʿAmr al-Miṣrī. 78.18

He heard reports from Sufyān ibn ʿUyaynah and others, and followed Mālik in his judgments of the Law. He was a reliable transmitter of Ḥadith. During the Inquisition, he was taken to Baghdad by order of al-Maʾmūn, who jailed him when he refused to espouse the creed of the created Qurʾan. He remained in jail until the accession of al-Mutawakkil, who released all the detainees.

Another victim of the Inquisition was ʿAbd al-Aʿlā ibn Mushir, Abū Mushir, al-Dimashqī l-Ghassānī, who was sent to al-Maʾmūn in al-Raqqah. 78.19

[Muḥammad ibn Saʿd:] Abū Mushir al-Ghassānī was sent from Damascus to al-Raqqah to meet with ʿAbd Allāh [al-Maʾmūn] ibn Hārūn, who asked him about the Qurʾan.

"It's the speech of God," he said, refusing to say it was created.

Al-Maʾmūn called for the sword and the mat. Seeing that he was going to be beheaded, Abū Mushir said, "It's created!"

Al-Maʾmūn spared his life but said, "If you had said that before I called for the sword, I would have sent you back home to your family. But if I let you go now you'll say you were coerced. Take him to Baghdad and lock him up until he dies!"

Abū Mushir was accordingly sent from al-Raqqah to Baghdad in Rabīʿ II 218 [April–May 833], and remained in jail only a short time before he died on the first day of Rajab '18 [July 23, 833]. A great many people in Baghdad witnessed the removal of his body for burial.

78.20 [The author:] Of those who refused to capitulate, some were overlooked or ignored while others were imprisoned and forgotten. None received as much attention as Aḥmad ibn Ḥanbal, a man of standing whose story was especially memorable.

Chapter 79
His Final Illness

79.1 [ʿAbd Allāh:] My father told me: "I've lived seventy-seven years and started my seventy-eighth."

That same night he took fever. He died on the tenth, in '41 [855].

79.2 [Al-Jawharī:] I went to visit Ibn Ḥanbal in jail and found Abū Saʿīd al-Ḥaddād there with him. Abū Saʿīd asked him how he was feeling.

"Well," he answered. "In good health, praise God!"

"Did you have any fever last night?"

"If I say I'm in good health," said Aḥmad, "don't ask any more questions. I don't want to talk about anything detestable."

79.3 [Ṣāliḥ:] On the first day of Rabīʿ I 241, on a Tuesday night,[470] my father took fever. The next day I went to see him. He was feverish and he was breathing only with great effort. I knew how his illnesses went and I was the one who nursed him whenever he was unwell.

"What did you eat last night, Dad?" I asked him.

"Bean broth," he said.

Then he tried to get up.

"Take my hand," he said.

I took it. When he reached the privy his legs gave way and he had to lean on me.

He was attended by several healers, all of them Muslims. One of them, a man called ʿAbd al-Raḥmān, advised him to roast a gourd and drink the juice. That was on the Tuesday before the Friday when he died.

"Ṣāliḥ," he said.

"Yes."

"Don't roast it in your house or ʿAbd Allāh's either."

Al-Fatḥ ibn Sahl came to check on him but I didn't let him in. 79.4
Then ʿAlī ibn al-Jaʿd[471] came but I didn't let him in either. But as people kept arriving, I finally told my father he had visitors.

"What do you think we should do?" he asked me.

"Let them in to pray for you."

He agreed, and in they came, pouring into the house until it was full, asking him how he was feeling and calling on God to cure him. As soon as one group went out, another would come crowding in. As more and more arrived, the street filled up and we had to close the alley gate.

Among the callers was a neighbor of ours who had just dyed his beard. As soon as my father saw him, he said, "Now there's a man who's keeping some *sunnah* alive. That makes me happy." The man went in and began praying for my father, who kept adding, "And for him, and for all Muslims."

Another man came and said, "Find some way to get me in to see him. I was there the day they flogged him at the palace and I want him to forgive me."

79.5 When I told my father, he said nothing. But I kept at him until he relented. When I let the man in, he stood there weeping. "Abū ʿAbd Allāh," he said, "I was there the day they flogged you at the palace. Now here I am before you. If you want revenge, take it. If you can forgive me, forgive me."

"On one condition," said my father. "Don't do anything like it again."

"I won't," said the man.

"I forgive you."

The man went out in tears and all those present wept as well.

79.6 My father kept some scraps of coin in a bit of rag. Whenever he needed anything, we would give some of the money to whoever was doing the shopping for him. On that Tuesday, he asked me if there was anything in the rag. I looked and found a dirham.

"Find one of the tenants to run an errand," he said. So I sent word and one of the women was given some money.[472]

"Send out and get me some dates so I can expiate a broken oath," he said. I sent out for the dates, bought them, and expiated his oath.[473] After that there were about three dirhams left. When I told him, he said, "Praise God!" Then he said, "Read out my will."

I read it out to him and he affirmed that it was his.

[The author:] We have already cited his will in our account of the Inquisition and will therefore refrain from citing it again.

79.7 [Al-Marrūdhī:] Aḥmad fell ill on Tuesday night, two nights into Rabīʿ I 241, and remained unwell for nine days. As word spread that he was growing worse, crowds of visitors appeared at the gate and remained there through the night. When the authorities learned that a crowd had gathered, they posted watchers and horse-troopers at the door of the house and the gateway into the alley. Up to that point Aḥmad had been allowing people in to see him. They would crowd into the house calling out greetings, and he would respond by lifting his hand. That ended with the arrival of the mounted troops, who stopped people from going in and shut the alley gate. But so many people had crowded into the streets and mosques that some of the vendors could no longer do business. The only way to see Ibn Ḥanbal was to find a way in through the adjoining houses or the weavers' tenements, or to climb over a wall. After sending men to take up positions near the gate and report back to him, Ibrāhīm ibn ʿAṭāʾ came twice a day—once in the morning and once in the evening—to ask after Ibn Ḥanbal but as often as not went away without seeing him. Meanwhile, watchers acting on behalf of Ibn Ṭāhir were making inquiries as well.

Aḥmad told me, "Ibn Ṭāhir's chamberlain came to see me and reported, 'The caliph sends his salutations; he wishes to see you.' I told him that was something I would detest doing, and the Commander of the Faithful had exempted me from doing what I detest."

Ibn Ṭāhir's chamberlain came back at night and asked questions of the doctors who were attending my father. Meanwhile, the watchers were sending reports back to Samarra, and the courier horses came and went every day. The members of the clan of Hāshim came to see him and wept. A number of judges and other officials arrived but were not admitted. A boy belonging to his uncle Yūsuf was sent to fan him, but my father waved him away because he had been purchased with funds he disapproved of.

"Stay with me," he said. "It won't be long now."

"I'm right here," I told him.

Whenever he needed to buy anything for his health, he would 79.8
take out a bit of rag containing some scraps of coin and give them to me and I would buy what he needed.

He had us witness his will, which he had written in Samarra. I heard that he said, "Read it out," and it was read aloud for him. Then he asked us to buy some dates to expiate an oath. Afterward he was left with a *dāniq* and a half, more or less. When I came in he asked how it had gone, and I told him that we had taken the dates and sent them. He turned his face to the heavens and began praising God.

He also had a visit from ʿAbd al-Wahhāb. "It means a lot to me," said Aḥmad when he was admitted, "that he came here in this heat."

ʿAbd al-Wahhāb bent over him and took his hand. The two sat hand in hand until it was time for ʿAbd al-Wahhāb to leave.

At one point a group of people came in, one of them an elder with a dyed beard. Aḥmad said, "It makes me happy to see that he's dyed his beard," or words to that effect.

One of his visitors said, "May God give you what you asked Him to give all of us." "May God grant your prayer!" replied Aḥmad. As his visitors began naming him in their prayers, he kept saying, "For all Muslims too!"

Several of his visitors were people he disapproved of for one reason or another. Whenever such a person entered, Aḥmad would close his eyes as if to dismiss him. Often he would refuse to return his greeting.

One elder came to see him and said to him, "Be mindful of the moment when you'll stand before God!" At that, Aḥmad gave a sob and the tears streamed down his cheeks.

79.9 A day or two before he died, he slurred out the words, "Call the boys," meaning the little ones. As the children gathered around him one by one, he held them close to inhale their scent and, tears in his eyes, ran his hand over their heads. Someone said, "Don't worry, Abū ʿAbd Allāh: they'll be fine." But Aḥmad made a gesture as if to say, "That's not what I was thinking."

When he could only sit, he would pray from that position; and when he couldn't rise he would pray lying down, tirelessly, by lifting his hands as if performing a cycle of prostrations.

When I put a basin under him I saw that his urine was nothing but bright red blood with no other fluid in it at all. I mentioned this to the doctor, who said that anyone who spent that much time in suffering and sorrow might well shred his own innards.

On Thursday he grew worse. I washed him so he could pray. "Get the water between my fingers," he said.

On Thursday night he stopped moving. Thinking he was dead, we were trying to stretch him out when he began to bend his knees with his face turned toward Mecca. We began saying "There is no god but God" for him to repeat but he had already started saying it. He on his side to face Mecca.

On Friday, throngs of people began to gather, filling the streets and alleys. At noon he was taken from us. A great cry arose and people began to weep so loudly that it felt as if the earth were shaking. When everyone sat down, we realized that we might miss Friday prayers, so I found a place where I could look out over the crowd and announced that we would bring him out after the prayer.

[Ḥanbal:] While Ibn Ḥanbal was in jail, one of al-Faḍl ibn al-Rabīʿ's sons gave him three hairs, saying that they belonged to the Prophet.[474] As he lay dying, Aḥmad asked that one hair be put over each of his eyes and the third on his tongue. This we did for him when he died. 79.10

[Ṣāliḥ:] During his illness my father prayed by having me hold him upright so he could bow and prostrate himself, which he did by having me lift him. 79.11

At one point Mujāhid ibn Mūsā came in, saying, "No need to be afraid, Abū ʿAbd Allāh! With all these people to testify on your behalf, there's nothing to fear when you meet God!" He began kissing my father's hand and weeping. When he asked for his counsel, my father pointed to his tongue.

Another visitor was Judge Sawwār, who reassured him that God would not hold him to the strictest accounting, citing the report transmitted by Muʿtamir to the effect that his father had said to him as he lay dying, "Tell me about God's lenience."[475]

He began to suffer from retention of urine and other pains but his mind remained clear. All the while he would ask what day of the month it was and I would tell him. At night I slept beside him. If he wanted anything he would shake me and I would hand it to him. Once he asked me to bring him the notes where he'd written that Ibn Idrīs cites Layth ibn Ṭāwūs as saying he hated to moan. I read the report for him and he never moaned after that except on the night he died. 79.12

79.13 ['Abd Allāh:] During his final illness, my father asked me to find where he had written the reports transmitted by 'Abd Allāh ibn Idrīs. When I found the book for him, he asked me to find the report related by Layth and read it to him. The report ran: "I told Ṭalḥah that Ṭāwūs disapproved of moaning when ill, and did not moan until he died." After I read this to my father, I didn't hear him moan until he died, God have mercy on him.

More on His Final Moments

79.14 ['Abd Allāh:] As my father lay dying, I sat beside him holding the rag I would use to tie his mouth closed. He was slipping in and out of consciousness and gesturing with his hand three times, like this, as if to say, "Not yet!" After the third time, I asked him, "Dad, what are you trying to say? You pass out and we think you're gone, and then you come back and say 'Not yet.'"

"Don't you understand, son?"

"No."

"The Devil, damn him, is standing in front of me biting his fingers in frustration and saying 'Aḥmad, you've escaped me,' and I keep telling him 'Not yet I haven't—not till I'm dead.'"[476]

79.15 [Aḥmad ibn Muḥammad ibn 'Umar:] 'Abd Allāh ibn Aḥmad was asked whether his father was conscious when he saw the Angel of Death.

"He was. We were washing him so he could pray and he started gesturing. Ṣāliḥ asked me what he was trying to say, and I told him that he wanted us to spread his fingers and wash between them. When we did that, he stopped gesturing. A little later he died."

79.16 [Ṣāliḥ:] My father's tongue kept moving until he died.

Chapter 80

His Date of Death and His Age When He Died

[Ḥanbal:] Aḥmad died on a Friday in Rabīʿ I 241 [July or August 855], at the age of seventy-seven. 80.1

[Ḥanbal:] Aḥmad ibn Ḥanbal died in 241, on a Friday in Rabīʿ I, at the age of seventy-seven. 80.2

[Al-Ḥaḍramī:] Aḥmad ibn Ḥanbal died twelve nights into Rabīʿ I 241. 80.3

[ʿAbd Allāh:] My father died before noon on Friday, and we buried him after praying the afternoon prayer, twelve nights into Rabīʿ I 241.[477] 80.4

[Ṣāliḥ:] It was on Friday, twelve nights into Rabīʿ I, about two hours after dawn, that my father died—God have mercy on him! 80.5

[Al-Marrūdhī:] Aḥmad died on Friday, twelve nights into Rabīʿ I 241, and his funeral procession took place after Friday prayers had ended. 80.6

[Al-Aḥmasī:] Aḥmad ibn Ḥanbal died in 241, at sunrise on a Friday. We lifted the body in the afternoon and buried him at sunset. 80.7

[Al-Būshanjī:] Aḥmad ibn Ḥanbal died in 241. 80.8

[Ṣāliḥ:] My father died at the age of seventy-seven. 80.9

Addendum. The Virtue Manifested in His Dying on a Friday

[The Prophet:] "If a Muslim dies on a Friday, God mighty and glorious spares him the ordeal of the tomb." 80.10

A great number of preeminent Muslims died on a Friday. It was on a Friday, for example, that ʿUthmān ibn ʿAffān was assassinated and ʿAlī ibn Abī Ṭālib struck down, though he expired on the Sunday; and on a Friday that al-Ḥusayn was killed. Al-ʿAbbās ibn ʿAbd al-Muṭṭalib, al-Ḥasan al-Baṣrī, Ibn Sīrīn, and others too numerous to mention also died on a Friday.

Chapter 81

How His Body Was Washed and Shrouded

81.1 [Ṣāliḥ:] When my father died the streets filled with mourners. I sent word that I would bring his body out when the afternoon prayer was over.

Ibn Ṭāhir sent us his chamberlain Muẓaffar with bundles of cloth, perfumes, and a message: "The emir conveys his greetings and says, 'I am doing what the Commander of the Faithful would do if he were here.'"

I said, "Return the greeting and tell him that while Aḥmad was alive, he was exempt from doing anything he detested. I'm not going to inflict anything detestable on him now that he's dead."

"Wrap him in this cloth," he replied, "and put something else over it."

I repeated what I had said.

My father's slave woman had spun a ten-cubit length of cloth worth twenty-eight dirhams to be used to make two shirts. From it we cut two strips to wrap him in. Taking another strip from Fūrān, we had three layers of cloth to wrap the body.[478] We bought the aromatics ourselves. An associate of ours who was a perfumer asked if he could send us some of his but I wouldn't let him.

Meanwhile, someone had taken a jar of ours and poured water into it. I told them to tell Fūrān to buy a waterskin and fill the jar my father used to drink from, since he would never take anything from our houses.

When the body had been washed we wrapped it in the shrouds with some hundred members of the clan of Hāshim looking on. As soon as we got the body onto the bier they began kissing him on the forehead.

81.2 [Al-Marrūdhī:] As I was preparing to wash him, enough tribesmen of Hāshim arrived to fill the house. So we took him into his set of rooms, let down the door curtain, and covered him with a cloth while we worked. No outsiders were present for the washing of the corpse. When that was done, we prepared to shroud him, but the Hāshimīs pushed us aside, weeping, pushing their children forward over the body, and kissing it. Finally we got him onto the bier and bound him to it using strips of turban cloth. Ibn Ṭāhir had sent some shrouds but I sent them back. His uncle told the messenger, "He wouldn't even let my slave fan him." Someone else said, "He asked to be shrouded in his own clothes."

In the end we shrouded him in a piece of Marawī fabric that he had been planning to make some clothes from. We added another piece to it and so wrapped him in three layers of cloth.

Chapter 82

On Who Sought to Pray over Him

['Abd Allāh:] My father died before noon on a Friday. Muḥammad 82.1
ibn 'Abd Allāh ibn Ṭāhir pushed us aside and performed the funeral prayer for him, though we and the tribesmen of Hāshim prayed over the body while it was still in the house. We buried him after the afternoon prayer.

[Ṣāliḥ:] When my father died, Ibn Ṭāhir sent a message asking 82.2
who was going to pray for him. I told him I was.

When we reached the desert, we found Ibn Ṭāhir standing there waiting for us. He approached us and offered his condolences. The bier was lowered to the ground. I waited a bit, then stepped forward and began lining everyone up. Then Ibn Ṭālūt and Muḥammad ibn Naṣr came forward and, each seizing one of my arms, said, "Make way for the emir!" I tried to stop them but they took me aside and Ibn Ṭāhir ended up performing the prayer. The mourners didn't realize what had happened. The next day, when they found out, they began praying at the gravesite. That went on for a good while: people coming and praying at the grave.

82.3 [ʿUbayd Allāh:] I heard al-Mutawakkil say to Ibn Ṭāhir: "What a blessing for you: praying over Aḥmad ibn Ḥanbal!"

Chapter 83

The Number of People Who Prayed over Him

83.1 [Al-Haytham ibn Khalaf:] We buried Aḥmad ibn Ḥanbal in 241, after the afternoon prayer. I never saw so many people in one place.

83.2 [Al-Qanṭarī:] I've seen forty pilgrimages but never so many people as I did then.

83.3 [Al-Warrāq:] We've never heard of more people gathering in one place, whether in the Age of Ignorance or in the Age of Islam. We've even heard that the place was surveyed and a proper estimate made of the number of people there. It came to about a million, plus the sixty thousand or so women I counted looking on from the walls. People had opened the gates of the houses all along the streets and alleys to anyone who wanted to come in and do their ablutions. People also bought great quantities of drinking water.

83.4 [Al-Baghawī:] Bunān ibn Aḥmad al-Qaṣabānī told us that he was present for the funeral of Aḥmad ibn Ḥanbal.

"There were people lined up from the square as far as the bridge at Bāb al-Qaṭīʿah. The estimates I heard were of eight hundred thousand men and sixty thousand women."

83.5 [Mūsā ibn Hārūn:] The flat tracts of land where people stood after Aḥmad ibn Ḥanbal died were surveyed and the number of people present was calculated to have been more than six hundred thousand, not counting the ones off to the side, around the edges, on the roofs, and scattered around, who if counted would have brought the total to more than a million.

83.6 [Al-Warrāq:] Not counting a certain funeral that took place among the Children of Israel, we have never heard of there being more Muslims gathered in one place than there were for Ibn Ḥanbal's funeral procession.

[Al-Fatḥ ibn al-Ḥajjāj?:] The Commander of the Faithful sent twenty men to estimate how many people prayed over Aḥmad ibn Ḥanbal. They counted 1,300,000, plus the people who were on boats. 83.7

[Abū Zurʿah:] I heard that al-Mutawakkil ordered a survey of the area where people were standing while the funeral prayer was said for Aḥmad. It turned out there was room for 2,500,000 people. 83.8

[Al-Ḥasan al-Maqāniʿī:] I was in Baghdad, alone in an orchard belonging to a friend, when I saw two men—one old, one young—dressed in ragged hair shirts. I greeted them and said, "You look like strangers here." 83.9

"We are," they said. "We're from the Lukkām Mountains[479] and we're here for Aḥmad ibn Ḥanbal's funeral. Every one of God's friends has come to see it."

[Al-Sulamī:] Abū l-Ḥasan al-Dāraquṭnī and I attended the funeral of Abū l-Fatḥ al-Qawwās the renunciant. Seeing the crowd, al-Dāraquṭnī said, "I've heard Abū Sahl ibn Ziyād al-Qaṭṭān say that he heard ʿAbd Allāh, son of Aḥmad ibn Ḥanbal, say that he heard his father say: 'Tell the innovators that if we compare funerals, we win.'" 83.10

Chapter 84

The Praising of the *Sunnah* and the Decrying of Innovation That Took Place during His Funeral Procession

[Al-Būshanjī:] During the funeral prayers for Aḥmad ibn Ḥanbal, some of the mourners cursed al-Karābīsī openly. The cursing was reported to al-Mutawakkil, who asked who he was. Told that al-Karābīsī had invented a doctrine previously unknown, he ordered him confined to his house until he died. 84.1

[Al-Nasawī:] I attended Aḥmad ibn Ḥanbal's funeral. It was very crowded. Al-Karābīsī was cursed loud and long, as was al-Marīsī. 84.2

[Al-Warrāq:] At Aḥmad ibn Ḥanbal's funeral, the mourners made an open display of adherence to the *sunnah* and cursed the 84.3

purveyors of reprehensible innovation. By showing them the ascendancy and might of Islam as well as the suppression of errant guides, dissenters, and reprehensible innovators, God consoled the Muslims for the calamity they had suffered. Some mourners camped out at the gravesite, and women began to visit as well. The authorities accordingly sent patrolmen to clear the area and restore order.

84.4 [ʿAlī ibn Mahruwayh's aunt:] On the day Ibn Ḥanbal died, the only place in Baghdad where the afternoon prayer was performed was Ḥārith's mosque.

Chapter 85

The Crowds That Gathered around His Grave

85.1 [Al-Ḥasan ibn al-Bannā:] Abū Ḥasan al-Tamīmī cites his father as saying that his grandfather attended the funeral of Aḥmad ibn Ḥanbal and reported, "I stayed for an entire week hoping to reach the grave but there were too many people there. It took a week for me to get through."

Chapter 86

His Estate

86.1 [Isḥāq:] When Aḥmad ibn Ḥanbal died, he left six or seven coins in a rag, worth two *dāniq*s, that he used to use to wipe his face.

Chapter 87

Reactions to His Death

87.1 The day Aḥmad ibn Ḥanbal died, there was an outpouring of grief from four communities: the Muslims, the Jews, the Christians, and the Magians; and of the latter three, twenty thousand—or, as reported by Abū Nuʿaym, ten thousand—embraced Islam.[480]

[Ibn Ḥurayth:] The day Aḥmad died, the news spread swiftly to every household except where sinners dwelt.[481] 87.2

Chapter 88

Reaction to His Death on the Part of the Jinns

[Al-Marrūdhī:] I heard this from a man in Tarsus. 88.1

"I'm from Yemen, and I have a daughter who was possessed. I brought in some exorcists who drove out her jinni and made it promise not to return. But then a year later it came back.

"'Didn't you promise not to come back?' I asked.

"'I did,' said the jinni. 'But a man named Aḥmad ibn Ḥanbal has died in Iraq and all the jinns—except for the demons, like me—have gone to pray over him. But I won't be back again.'

"He never returned."

This story has also come down to us in another telling.

[Abū Muḥammad al-Yamānī:] When I was in Yemen, a man told me that his daughter had been possessed by a demon. So I took him to one of our Yemeni exorcists, who drove out her jinni and made it promise not to return. But then about six months later her father came to me and said the demon had returned. 88.2

"Go back to the exorcist," I said.

So he went back. The exorcist drew out the jinni and got it talking.

"Shame on you!" said the exorcist. "Didn't you promise to leave her alone?"

"I did," said the jinni. "But we've heard that Aḥmad ibn Ḥanbal is dead. All the righteous jinns have gone to mourn him, and the demons like me are tagging along behind."

[Al-Khallāl:] Aḥmad ibn Muḥammad ibn Maḥmūd told me the following: 88.3

I was on my way back from Sind on board ship. At one point I woke up in the night and heard a voice calling from the sea, "Aḥmad ibn Ḥanbal, the faithful servant of God, is dead!"

"What was that?" I asked one of the others on board.

"That was a righteous jinni."

We later learned that Aḥmad had died that night.

[Al-Khallāl:] I also heard that Abū Zurʿah said that where he was from in Khurasan, the jinns announced Aḥmad's death forty days before it happened.

I also heard Aḥmad's son Ṣāliḥ say, "Forty days after my father died, after everyone had gone to bed, my family said they heard a sobbing, unlike any sound a human would make, coming from my father's house."

Chapter 89

On the Condolences Offered to His Family

89.1 Aḥmad's children reported that many people, including certain righteous men who had kept their identities a secret, came to offer their condolences. Without spending too much time on the subject, I will present a few of the more famous accounts.

89.2 [Ibn Abī Ḥātim:] We heard Aḥmad's son Ṣāliḥ report:

A few days after my father died, Muḥammad ibn ʿAbd Allāh ibn Ṭāhir received a letter from al-Mutawakkil ordering him to pay us a visit of condolence and to carry off the books. But I gathered up the books first and told him, "All of the reports we've ever heard are in here. If you want them, stay here and copy them."[482]

"I'll tell the caliph," he said.

[Ibn Abī Ḥātim:] Ṣāliḥ kept putting him off and the books stayed in our hands, thank God!

89.3 [Ṣāliḥ:] One of my friends wrote me this letter of condolence:

> *In the name of God, full of compassion, ever-compassionate*
> God, mighty and glorious, has decreed that death deal impartially with humankind, dooming His creatures to a finite span until fate comes to claim them all. Bowing now to God's decree

is Abū ʿAbd Allāh—may God have mercy on him!—whom He has summoned to Himself. Accepting God's welcome with a willing heart, he came faultless as always, unsullied, and immaculate, firm in tradition, inerrant, and guiding aright, unswerving from the path of good guidance, unswayed by caprice, and dauntless in adversity, until God drew him close to Himself. Let all aspire to the grace that he has gained; and though losing him brings a wrenching grief that bites deep into the heart, and I console you and any other Muslim who reads this letter by reminding you of God's promised blessings, mercies, and signs vouchsafed to those who ponder well, suffer long, and submit with good grace to the fate God has decreed for all things He has made. I remind you that he left us in the best possible way: present in mind, confident of God's guidance, and unshaken in his courage and resolve. The world pursued him but he spurned it, and he brooked no rebuke when he stood up for God; his passing leaves a ragged scar on the heart of Islam.

I pray to God, who gives freely of His bounty, to bless Muḥammad, His servant and Emissary; and to grant Aḥmad no lesser reward than that He grants to any of the allies He has created to serve Him. May He raise him in rank, exalt him in standing, and seat him among the prophets, the truth-tellers, the martyrs, and the saints—goodly companions all! I ask God to give you strength, and the reward promised to the strong; and grant you that certainty that confers the reward promised to those who live out their faith. I ask Him, for He is the fount of all blessing, the dispenser of all good things, and the One for whom nothing is impossible.

[Al-Ṣūfī:] The night we buried Abū ʿAbd Allāh, one of our scholars— 89.4
a kindly, learned man named Abū Jaʿfar—asked me, "Do you know who was buried today?"

"Who?"

"The sixth of five."

"What do you mean?"

"The first is Abū Bakr al-Ṣiddīq," he said. "The second was ʿUmar ibn al-Khaṭṭāb. ʿUthmān ibn ʿAffān was the third, ʿAlī ibn Abī Ṭālib the fourth, ʿUmar ibn ʿAbd al-ʿAzīz the fifth, and now we have a sixth: Aḥmad ibn Ḥanbal."

I appreciated his saying that. What he meant was that each man was the greatest in his own time.

Chapter 90

A Selection of the Verses Spoken in Praise of Him in Life and in Commemoration of Him in Death[483]

90.3 [Al-Hayḍam's father:]

When now you told of learning and of Aḥmad gone
  You might have said the foaming sea was dry.
Of a gen'rous heart, of piety and lordly sway,
  Of one so firm in faith are we bereft.
At his approach, you felt the breath of spring;
  As befits his name, all spoke of him to praise.[484]
Most like Sufyān in piety was he
  Nor did Misʿar or Miʿḍad leave him far behind.
Like them, he little sought, and guided right,
  Denied himself, and showed us how to live.
In all these things was his alone the prize,
  In all these things did we him call unmatched.
Come back! Your hands an edifice of faith
  Did build, not a palace to inhabit in this world.
You craved no eagle-footed steed,
  Nor shapely slave, bewitching as the jinn,
In finery bedecked, and golden weave,
  Swaying like a cane-brake when she walks.

But to each must come that fateful hour when death
Arrives, the tenants of the world to lead away;
And from this world can they but one thing take:
The deeds they stored away while yet they could.[485]

Al-Hayḍam recited a poem by his father, including these lines: 90.5

To the tears that world-renouncers weep, add tears;
And let the ones who fear their Lord behold
And fear the more. They mourn for you, their eyes
Bereft of sleep, their only comfort tears.
Embraced by earth good Aḥmad lies, as far
From us as anyone can be. May clouds refresh
His grave with rain as days turn into years![486]

[The author:] I have copied many of the praise poems and elegies composed for him but confined myself here to a few selections. May God guide me aright!

Chapter 91

His Dreams

[ʿAbd Allāh:] I heard my father say, "The Lord of Glory appeared to me in a dream and I asked Him how best to draw nearer to Him. 91.1

"'Through my Speech, Aḥmad,' He said.

"'Do we have to understand it?' I asked.

"He said, 'It works whether you understand it or not.'"

[Ṣadaqah ibn al-Faḍl:] I was traveling from Kufa to Baghdad without any money to spend. By the time I reached the Ṣarṣar Canal I was starving. I went into a mosque there and fell asleep. I woke up to find a man joggling me with his foot. It was Aḥmad ibn Ḥanbal. With him was a porter carrying bread. 91.2

"Last night I had a dream," he said. "A voice said, 'Your friend Ṣadaqah ibn al-Faḍl has arrived from Kufa in a bad way so go help him.'"

Chapter 92

Dreams in Which He Appeared to Others[487]

92.1 [Muḥammad ibn Mihrān al-Jammāl:] Aḥmad Ibn Ḥanbal appeared to me in a dream wearing a striped mantle, or one with lozenges. He seemed to be in Rey, trying to get to Friday prayer. I asked a dream interpreter what it meant. He said Aḥmad would become renowned for some great deed. It wasn't long after that we heard about what he had done during the Inquisition.

92.2 ʿAbd al-Raḥmān added: I heard my father say, "Aḥmad ibn Ḥanbal appeared to me in a dream. He looked larger than life and had very beautiful features. I began asking him about Hadith and comparing reports."

92.3 [Ibn Khurrazādh:] A neighbor of ours had a dream where an angel came down from the heavens carrying seven crowns. The first person on earth to receive one was Aḥmad ibn Ḥanbal.

92.4 [Zakariyyā ibn Yaḥyā l-Simsār:] Aḥmad ibn Ḥanbal—God have mercy on him—appeared to me in a dream with a jeweled crown on his head and sandals on his feet, strutting around. I asked him how God had judged him.

"He forgave me," he said, "brought me near Him, and placed this crown on my head with His own hands, saying that He was rewarding me for saying that the Qur'an was His uncreated speech."

I remarked that I had never seen him strut on earth.

"This is how servants walk in Paradise," he said.

92.7 [Al-Marrūdhi:] I dreamed I saw Aḥmad ibn Ḥanbal in a garden. He was dressed in green with a crown of light on his head and walking in a way I had never seen him walking before.

"Aḥmad," I said, "what's this new stride of yours?"

"This is how servants walk in Paradise," he said.

"What's the crown I see on your head?"

"My Lord, mighty and glorious, stood me before Him, judged me lightly, dressed me in these clothes, honored me, drew me near, let me gaze upon Him, and crowned me with this crown, saying, 'Aḥmad, this is the crown of glory that you earned by saying that the Qur'an is My uncreated speech.'"

92.9 [Ibn Khuzaymah:] When Aḥmad ibn Ḥanbal died I was grief-stricken. That night he appeared to me in a dream. He was swaggering as he walked. I asked him why he was walking that way and he said, "This is how servants walk in Paradise."

"And how did you fare?"

"God forgave me, crowned me, and gave me sandals of gold, saying, 'Aḥmad, this is your reward for saying that the Qur'an is My speech.'

"Then He said, 'Aḥmad, call upon Me with those prayers you learned from Sufyān al-Thawrī and[488] used to recite on earth.'

"So I said, 'Lord of all things! By your power over all things, hold me accountable for nothing, and forgive me for everything.'

"'Aḥmad, this is the Garden. Rise, and enter.'

"I went into the Garden, and there was Sufyān al-Thawrī. He had wings and he was flying from one palm tree to another, saying, «Praise be to God who has fulfilled His promise to us and made us the inheritors of this land, letting us settle in the Garden wherever we want. How excellent is the reward of those who labor!»"[489]

I[490] asked him how 'Abd al-Wahhāb al-Warrāq had fared.

"I left him swimming in a sea of light, in pure water made of light, visiting his Lord."

"What about Bishr?"

"Fortunate Bishr!" said Sufyān. "Who could match him? I left him in the presence of the Glorious One, sitting at a laden table, with the Glorious One addressing him directly, saying 'Eat, you who never ate; drink, you who never drank; revel, you who never did,' or words to that effect."

92.10 [Ibn Khuzaymah:] When Aḥmad ibn Ḥanbal died I was grief-stricken. That night he appeared to me in a dream. He was swaggering as he walked. I asked him why he was walking that way and he said, "This is how servants walk in Paradise."

"And how did you fare?"

"God forgave me, crowned me, and gave me sandals of gold, saying, 'Aḥmad, this is your reward for saying that the Qur'an is My speech.' Then He asked, 'Aḥmad, why did you write down reports via Jarīr ibn 'Uthmān?' I said he was trustworthy. 'True,' said God, 'but he hated 'Alī, God curse him!'[491]

"Then He said, 'Aḥmad, pray to me using those prayers you learned from Sufyān al-Thawrī and used to recite on earth.'

"So I said, 'Lord of all things!'

"'Go on.'

"'By Your power over all things.'

"'Go on.'

"'Hold me accountable for nothing, and forgive me for everything.'

"'Aḥmad, this is the Garden. Rise, and enter.'

"I went into the Garden, and there was Sufyān al-Thawrī. He had wings and he was flying from one palm tree to another, saying, «Praise be to God who has fulfilled His promise to us and made us the inheritors of this land, letting us settle in the Garden wherever we want. How excellent is the reward of those who labor!»"[492]

I asked him how 'Abd al-Wahhāb al-Warrāq had fared.

"I left him swimming in a sea of light, in pure water made of light, visiting his merciful King and Lord."

"What about Bishr?" I asked, meaning Bishr the Barefoot.

"Fortunate Bishr!' he replied. "Who could match him? I left him in the presence of the Glorious One, sitting at a laden table, with the Glorious One addressing him directly, saying 'Eat, you who never ate; drink, you who never drank; revel, you who never did.'"

Then I woke up and gave away ten thousand dirhams—or some such amount—in charity.

92.13 [Al-Anṣārī:] A man from Bākharz, which is in the region of Nishapur, told me, "I dreamed that it was Resurrection Day. I saw a man on a splendid horse and heard a crier calling out: ‘Let no one precede him this day!’

“I asked who the rider was and they told me it was Aḥmad ibn Ḥanbal.”

[ʿAbd Allāh:] I dreamed I saw my father. I asked him how God had judged him. 92.14

“He stood me before Him and said, ‘Aḥmad, for My sake were you tried and flogged. Here: behold My countenance, which I grant you leave to see.’”

[ʿAlī ibn al-Muwaffaq:] I dreamed I entered the Garden and there saw three men. The first was sitting at a table where God had assigned one angel to serve him food and another to pour him drink. The second was standing at the gate of the Garden with some other people, looking into their faces and letting them inside. And the third was standing in the middle of the Garden gazing at the Throne and looking at the Lord. 92.17

I went to Riḍwān and asked, “Who are those three?”

“The first one,” he said, “is Bishr the Barefoot, who came here parched and starving. The one standing in the middle of the Garden is Maʿrūf al-Karkhī, who worshipped God because he desired to see Him, and now he can. And the one standing at the gate is Aḥmad ibn Ḥanbal. God has commanded him to look into the faces of the Sunnis, take them by the hand, and bring them inside.”

[Al-Ramlī:] I traveled to Iraq and copied what the Iraqis and the Hijazis had written, but found their views so different that I couldn’t choose which school to follow. Late one night, I got up, performed my ablutions, prayed two cycles, and asked God to guide me as He wished. Then I went to bed and dreamed of the Prophet. I saw him march through the Gate of the Banū Shaybah and sit down with his back resting on the Kaʿbah. He was smiling at al-Shāfiʿī and Aḥmad ibn Ḥanbal, who were on his right. Off to the other side was al-Marīsī. 92.18

I said, “Emissary of God! They’re so divergent I don’t know which to follow.”

Pointing to al-Shāfiʿī and Aḥmad, he recited «Those are the ones to whom We gave the Scripture, wisdom, and prophethood.»[493] Then, gesturing at al-Marīsī, he recited «If these people reject it, We shall entrust it to a people who will never refuse to acknowledge it. Those were the people whom God guided, so follow their guidance.»[494]

92.19 [Yaḥyā l-Jallā' or ʿAlī ibn al-Muwaffaq:] At one point during the Inquisition, I debated a group of Stoppers, who trounced me. I went home heartsick. My wife put out some dinner, but I told her I wasn't eating, and she took it away. Then I went to bed and dreamed I saw the Prophet coming into the mosque. There were two circles there: in one, Aḥmad ibn Ḥanbal and his associates had gathered, and in the other Ibn Abī Du'ād and his cronies. Standing between the two, the Prophet gestured toward Ibn Abī Duʿād and his circle and recited «If these people reject it . . .» and then, pointing to the circle of Aḥmad ibn Ḥanbal, recited «. . . We shall entrust it to a people who will never refuse to acknowledge it.»[495]

92.21 [Isḥāq ibn Ḥakīm:] Aḥmad ibn Ḥanbal appeared to me in a dream. Written on his back, in light instead of ink, were the words «God will surely suffice to defend you against them, for He is All Hearing, All Knowing.»[496]

92.22 [Al-Anṭākī:] We had a visit from an Iraqi who was reputed to be one of the most learned in that region. One day he asked me to direct him to a good interpreter who could explain a dream he had had.

"I saw the Prophet," he explained, "standing on a plain with some other people. I asked one of them who he was and he said, 'That's Muḥammad.'

"'What's he doing here?'

"'Waiting for his community to arrive.'

"In the dream I thought to myself, 'I'll stay here and see what happens.'

"After the people had gathered around, I noticed that one of them was carrying a spear, as if intending to dispatch an expedition. The Prophet looked out and saw a spear taller than any of the others and asked whose it was.[497]

"'It belongs to Aḥmad ibn Ḥanbal.'

"'Bring him to me!'

"Aḥmad came forward, spear in hand. The Prophet took the spear, brandished it, and gave it back, saying, 'Go forth and lead these people!' Then he called out to the people, 'This is your leader. Follow him, heed him, and obey him!'"

"Your dream," I said to the man, "needs no explanation."

[Al-Sijistānī:] I dreamed it was Resurrection Day. The people 92.23
were lined up at a bridge that no one could cross unless he had a stamp. Off to one side was a man making stamps with his seal-ring and handing them out. Whoever got one could cross the bridge. I asked who was making the stamps and they told me it was Aḥmad ibn Ḥanbal.

[Ibn Yūnus:] After Aḥmad ibn Ḥanbal died, I dreamed I was in 92.24
the Garden. A voice said, "You're in the Garden of Eden." Then I saw three horsemen in front of me, with a fourth horsemen riding ahead with a banner. I asked who they were.

"The one on the right is Gabriel and the one on the left is Michael. The one in the middle is Aḥmad ibn Ḥanbal. The one with the banner is Isrāfīl. God has given him that banner and ordered him to admit to Eden only those who love Ibn Ḥanbal."[498]

[Al-Maqdisī:] In a dream I saw the Prophet lying asleep under a 92.25
garment with Aḥmad and Yaḥyā[499] whisking the flies away from him.

[Sahl ibn Abī Ḥalīmah:] We were camped out at Ismāʿīl ibn 92.26
ʿUlayyah's gate when Aḥmad ibn Ḥanbal appeared to me in a dream, dragging his robe. I took the robe to mean knowledge.

[Al-Shaybānī:] In Ascalon I dreamed I was in Tarsus. I went into the 92.27
Friday mosque. I looked to the right of the niche and saw the Prophet sitting there with Abū Bakr on his right, ʿUmar on his left, and Bilāl in front, all in green, with beautiful cloths covering their heads.

"Peace be upon you, Emissary of God!" I said.

"And upon you be peace, my son."

"Emissary of God, in the Hadith of Abū l-Zubayr citing ʿAbd Allāh ibn ʿAmr, you said 'My community will be pelted and disfigured.'"[500]

"Yes. That refers to the proponents of free will."

"Emissary of God, to whom can we entrust this religion?"

"To this man here," he replied.

I looked to the right of Abū Bakr and saw a man lying on his back covered in a white garment. I lifted it away from his face and saw a well-built man with a wide beard and rosy cheeks. Not recognizing him, I asked, "Emissary of God, who is he?"

"Don't you recognize him?"

"No."

"That's Aḥmad ibn Ḥanbal."

92.28 [Muḥammad ibn Isḥāq:] I dreamed that Resurrection Day had come. I saw the Lord of Glory and I could hear Him speak and see His light. He asked me, "What do you believe about the Qur'an?"

"It is Your speech, o Lord of the Universe."

"Who told you so?"

"Aḥmad ibn Ḥanbal."

God praised Himself and summoned Aḥmad.

"What do you believe about the Qur'an?"

"It is Your speech, o Lord of the Universe."

"How do you know?"

Aḥmad turned over two sheets of paper. On one it said "Shuʿbah citing al-Mughīrah," and on the other "ʿAṭāʾ citing Ibn ʿAbbās."

God then summoned Shuʿbah and asked, "What do you believe about the Qur'an?"

"It is Your speech, o Lord of the Universe."

"How do you know?"

"We cite ʿAṭāʾ citing Ibn ʿAbbās."

ʿAṭāʾ was not summoned but Ibn ʿAbbās was.

"What do you believe about the Qur'an?"

"It is Your speech, o Lord of the Universe."

"How do you know?"

"We cite Muḥammad, the Emissary of God."

So the Prophet was summoned.

"What do you believe about the Qur'an?"

"It is Your speech, o Lord of the Universe."

"Who told you?"

"Gabriel, on Your authority."

"You have spoken the truth," said God, "and so have all of them."

[Abū ʿAbd Allāh al-Zubayrī:] A man from Basra named Abū Muḥammad al-Qurashī, who was a man of learning, untarnished reputation, and rectitude, came to me and said, "I had a dream you'll enjoy hearing about; let me tell you. I saw the Prophet. With him were Abū Bakr, ʿUmar, ʿUthmān, and ʿAlī. Then four more people came up to him and he invited them to come closer. I was surprised, and so I asked someone who was there who they were. 92.29

"'Mālik, Aḥmad, Isḥāq,[501] and al-Shāfiʿī.'

"Then I saw the Prophet take Mālik's hand and seat him next to Abū Bakr, take Aḥmad's hand and seat him next to ʿUmar, take Isḥāq's hand and seat him next to ʿUthmān, and take al-Shāfiʿī's hand and seat him next to ʿAlī."

I asked a dream interpreter about this and he told me: "Mālik has the same standing among men of learning that Abū Bakr does among the Companions: no one disputes his rank.

"Aḥmad has the same standing as ʿUmar: he's famous for being tough and unflinching and brooking no opposition when doing God's work. That's because Aḥmad never wavered from the truth about the Qur'an and never succumbed to the Inquisition despite the brutality he had to endure.

"Isḥāq is like ʿUthmān: the Postponers caused him so much suffering that he had to leave his home town.

"And al-Shāfiʿī is like ʿAlī. Of them all, ʿAlī was the best judge; and al-Shāfiʿī was the most learned in the derivation of law and the judging of legal matters."

[Ṣadaqah:] I had always resented Aḥmad ibn Ḥanbal. Then I had a dream where I saw the Prophet walking down a road holding his hand in perfect amity. I tried to catch up to them but couldn't. When I woke up the resentment was gone. Then I dreamed I was among crowds of people at pilgrimage time. Prayer was announced 92.30

and everyone lined up. "Let Aḥmad lead the prayer!" said a voice. Then Aḥmad appeared and led the prayer. After that, whenever I was asked about anything, I would say, "Ask my exemplar Aḥmad ibn Ḥanbal."

92.31 [Muḥammad ibn ʿUbayd:] Ṣadaqah said, "I dreamed we were at ʿArafah. Everyone was waiting for the ritual prayer to start. I asked what they were waiting for and someone said, 'They're waiting for the prayer leader.' Then Aḥmad ibn Ḥanbal arrived and led the prayer."

This Ṣadaqah was inclined to the opinion of the Kufans,[502] but after the dream, whenever he was asked a question, he would say, "Ask the exemplar."

92.32 [Al-Daʿʿāʾ:] Ibn Ḥanbal died on a Friday. That night, I asked God to show him to me in a dream. Then I slept and dreamed of seeing him perched on a steed of light that hung between the heavens and the earth. He was holding it by a halter that was also made of light. I reached for the halter but he pulled it away, saying, "Hearing is one thing but seeing is another." He said it twice. Then I woke up.

92.33 [ʿAbd Allāh:] I was on my way to Samarra and stayed at the inn where my father had stayed on his way to Samarra. I spent some time looking for traces of his presence. That night, he came to me in a dream. I told him that I was going to Samarra to accomplish something and asked if I would succeed. When he said nothing, I asked again, and he said "No." I ended up spending two months in Samarra but came home empty-handed.

A year later, I went again, and stayed at the same inn. Again I saw my father in a dream, and I asked him the same question. After a moment he said, "Yes," or made a gesture that meant yes. This time I got what I wanted.

92.34 [Al-Ṭabarī:] I dreamed of seeing Aḥmad ibn Ḥanbal and telling him, "Have you seen how no one agrees with anyone any more?"

"So long as God is on your side," he said, "nothing can harm you."

92.35 [Al-ʿUkbarī:] Aḥmad ibn Ḥanbal appeared to me in a dream with people around him as if it were a study circle.

"I just had a cupping," I told him. "What should I eat?"

"Pomegranates," he said.

[Al-Ḥarbī:] Aḥmad appeared to me in a dream standing there wearing a lined outer garment but nothing on his head. 92.36

"I hear you've edited a work on the virtues of the Prophet," he said.

"I have."

"Well done!" he said.

"How could I do otherwise? If not for him we'd be Magians. After all, we were born among non-Arabs, not Arabs."

"Magians!" he cried. "Magians! Magians!" Then he fell against the wall in a faint.

[The author:] I have encountered this story in another source, though it may actually be a different story, meaning that there were two different dreams.

[Al-Ḥarbī:] I saw Aḥmad in a dream and he asked me what I was writing. 92.37

"*Proofs of Prophethood*," I told him.

"If not for that Prophet," he said, "we'd be Magians."

[Lūlū:] Aḥmad appeared to me in a dream and I asked him, "Aren't you dead?" 92.38

"I am."

"How did God deal with you?"

"He's forgiven me and everyone who prayed over me."

"But some of them were innovators!"

"They were left till the end."

[Bundār:] Aḥmad appeared to me in a dream looking angry. I asked him why. 92.39

"How could I not be angry," he replied, "when Munkar and Nakīr came and asked me to name my Lord. 'Do you know who you're talking to?' I asked them.

"'We know,' they said. 'But it's our duty to ask, so forgive us!'"

[Al-Ṭalmakhūrī:] Aḥmad ibn Ḥanbal appeared to me in a dream. 92.41

"May I tell you something useful?" he asked.

"Yes!"

He said: "From the niche to the grave."[503]

92.42 [Al-Zāghūnī:] I dreamed of going to Aḥmad's tomb and seeing him sitting there on top of it. He looked like a very old man.

"Our friends are dead," he said, "and our allies few." Then he said, "Whenever you need help, say, 'Great One! Great One, greater than all who think themselves great!' Do that, and your prayers will be answered."

92.43 [Abū Bakr:] One year, a few days before Ramadan, we had heavy rains. Later, during Ramadan, I went to sleep one night and dreamed I had gone as usual to visit Aḥmad ibn Ḥanbal's tomb. But it had sunk so deep into the ground that only a *sāq*[504] or two was left above ground.

"It must be the rain that did this," I thought.

"No," said Aḥmad from inside the tomb. "It was the terrifying presence of the One True God, mighty and glorious, who came to visit me. I asked Him why He came every year, and He said, 'Because you stood up for My speech, which is read aloud from every niche.'"

I bent toward his grave-shaft to kiss it, then asked him, "Why is yours the only grave that one can kiss?"

"Son," he said, "it's not out of respect for me, but for the Emissary of God. I have some of his hairs with me. Why don't those who care for me come visit me in Ramadan?"

He asked the question twice.

Chapter 93

Dreams in Which He Was Mentioned[505]

93.1 [Al-Rabīʿ:] Al-Shāfiʿī told me to take a letter he had written, deliver it to Aḥmad ibn Ḥanbal, and bring back his reply. When I reached Baghdad, I found Ibn Ḥanbal praying the dawn prayer and I joined him. As soon as he finished I handed him the letter, saying, "This is from your brother al-Shāfiʿī in Egypt."

"Have you read it?"

"No."

He broke the seal and read the letter, tears welling up in his eyes.

"What is it?"

"He says the Prophet came to him in a dream and told him to write to me and convey his greetings. I'm going to be tested and asked to call the Qur'an created, but if I don't give in, God will raise a banner in my honor that will fly until the Day of Resurrection."

"That's good news, then," I said. "What's my reward?"

Aḥmad removed the shirt he was wearing next to his skin and handed it to me. I took it, and his reply, and returned to Egypt. When I handed the letter to al-Shāfiʿī he asked what Aḥmad had given me.

"The shirt off his back," I said.

"I won't take it away from you," he said, "but soak it and give me the water so I can share in the blessing."

[Al-Rabīʿ:] Al-Shāfiʿī asked me to deliver a letter he had written 93.2
to Aḥmad ibn Ḥanbal, saying, "Sulaymān, take this letter down to Iraq and don't read it."

I took the letter and left Egypt for Iraq. When I reached Ibn Ḥanbal's mosque, I found him praying the dawn prayer and I joined him. I hadn't prayed the usual number of cycles, so I continued praying after he had finished. It took him a moment to recognize me but he did. When I finished praying, I greeted him and handed him the letter. He spent a long time asking about al-Shāfiʿī before he even looked at the letter. Finally he broke the seal and began reading. At one point he burst into tears, saying, "I pray to God to do what al-Shāfiʿī says!"

"What did he say?" I asked.

"He says the Prophet came to him in a dream and said, 'Tell that young man Aḥmad ibn Ḥanbal that he'll be tried on account of God's religion and asked to say that the Qur'an is created. He should refuse. He'll be flogged, but God will unfurl a banner for him that will fly until the Day of Resurrection.'"

"That's good news, then," I said. "What's my reward?"

He was wearing two garments, one on top of the other. He took the under-garment off and handed it to me, then handed me a reply to the letter. I went back and told al-Shāfiʿī what had happened.

"Where's the garment?" he said.

"Right here."

"I won't try to buy it from you," he said, "or ask for it as a gift. But wash it and give me the water."

So I washed it and brought him the water. He put it in a bottle, and every day I'd see him take a little bit and dab it onto his face so he could share in Ibn Ḥanbal's blessing.

93.3 [Ibn al-Faraj:] Ibn Ḥanbal's imprisonment and beating had a devastating effect on me. But then I dreamed I heard a voice say, "Aren't you glad that he'll have the same standing with God as Abū l-Sawwār al-ʿAdawī?"[506]

I found Aḥmad and told him about this. He protested: «We are of God, and to Him we return!»[507]

93.5 A dissolute member of the Muslim community summoned Abū l-Sawwār al-ʿAdawī and asked him a question about a religious matter.[508] Abū l-Sawwār gave the answer he thought was right, but the other man didn't like it, and said: "If you insist on that opinion, I declare you quit of Islam!"

"Which religion should I go to, then?"

"Well then, consider your wife divorced!"

"So where I am I supposed to go at night?"

At that the man struck him forty lashes.

Abū Jaʿfar added: I visited Aḥmad and told him this story, and he was happy to hear it.

[The author:] Abū l-Sawwār al-ʿAdawī's name was Ḥassān ibn Ḥurayth. He transmitted Hadith via ʿAlī ibn Abī Ṭālib and ʿImrān ibn Ḥuṣayn. He was a scholarly renunciant, and he matched Aḥmad in the endurance he displayed while being flogged.

93.6 [Hishām:] Whenever someone would insult Abū l-Sawwār al-ʿAdawī, he would say, "If I'm what you say I am, I suppose I'm a bad man."

93.7 [Isḥāq al-Madāʾinī:] I dreamed that the Black Stone cracked open and from it a banner emerged.

"What's going on?" I asked.

"Aḥmad ibn Ḥanbal has sworn allegiance to God."[509]

This was on the day he was flogged.

[Salamah ibn Shabīb:] We were once sitting with Aḥmad when a man appeared and asked, "Which of you is Aḥmad ibn Ḥanbal?" 93.8

None of us spoke up, but Aḥmad said, "I'm Aḥmad. What do you need?"

"I've crossed four hundred leagues of land and sea to find you. I had a visit from al-Khaḍir on a Friday night.[510] He said, 'Why don't you go visit Aḥmad ibn Ḥanbal?' I said I didn't know you but he said, 'Go to Baghdad and ask. Tell him that the Lord of Heaven on His throne is pleased with you, and all the angels too, because of your endurance for the sake of God.'"

[Salamah ibn Shabīb:] I was once with Aḥmad in his mosque in 93.9
Baghdad. There were several others there too. We had just finished the morning prayer when a man came in and asked, "Which of you is Aḥmad ibn Ḥanbal?"

Out of deference to Aḥmad, no one said anything. Then he himself said, "I'm Aḥmad. What do you need?"

"I've crossed four hundred leagues of land and sea to find you. I had a visitor on a Friday who said he was al-Khaḍir. He told me to go to Baghdad and ask for you, and tell you that the Lord of Heaven on His throne is pleased with you, and all the angels too, because of your endurance."

"Count no one meritorious before his work is done," said Aḥmad.

When the man rose to go, Aḥmad asked him if there was anything else he could do for him. The man said no and went out.

[Al-Marrūdhī:] One day I was sitting on the Straw-Sellers' Bridge 93.13
when I saw two men clearing the way for a Bedouin on camelback. They stopped in front of me and told the Bedouin, "That's him: the one sitting there."

"Are you Aḥmad ibn Ḥanbal?" the Bedouin asked.

"No," I said. "But I know him. What do you want him for?"

"I have to see him."

"Shall I take you?"

"Aye."

I led the way to Aḥmad's place and knocked on the door.

"Who is it?"

"Al-Marrūdhī."

"Come in."

"I have someone with me."

"Bring them too."

The Bedouin knelt his camel and tethered her, and we went inside. When he saw Aḥmad, he said, "Aye, by God," three times, and greeted him.

"What do you need?"

"I'm an emissary sent by God's Emissary."

"What on earth do you mean?"

"I'm a Bedouin, with quarters forty miles outside Medina. My family needed some wheat and some dates, so I went to Medina and bought what they wanted. Then it got dark. I prayed the last evening prayer of the day in the Prophet's mosque and lay down to sleep. Then I felt someone shaking me, and a voice said, 'Will you run an errand for the Emissary of God?'

"I said I would. He put his right hand on my left arm, walked me over to the wall of the Prophet's tomb, and placed me by his head.

"'Emissary of God!' he called out.

"From behind the wall a voice said, 'Will you do an errand for me?'

"'Aye, by God,' I said, three times.

"'Go to Baghdad'—or 'Crooked Town'[511]—al-Marrūdhī couldn't remember which he said, 'and ask for the house of Aḥmad ibn Ḥanbal. When you find him, tell him: "The Prophet sends his greetings, and a warning that God is preparing to subject you to a grievous ordeal; but I have asked Him to give you the strength to bear it, so fear not."'"

After that, whenever anyone marveled at his endurance during the flogging, he would say, "I knew it was coming."

Twenty-five days after the Bedouin departed, the Inquisition began.

[Abū Bakr al-Nāqid:] Sarī l-Saqaṭī said, "I dreamed I had been admitted to the Garden of Paradise. As I was wandering through it, I found myself looking down into a room and seeing a slave. I asked her whose she was and she said, 'Aḥmad ibn Ḥanbal's.'" 93.14

Abū Bakr added: I myself saw Sarī in a dream after he died. I asked him what had become of Aḥmad and Bishr.

"They've just entered the Garden of Eden," he said, "and they're eating."

[Ḥubaysh:] The Prophet appeared to me in a dream. I asked him what had become of Aḥmad ibn Ḥanbal. 93.15

"Moses will be along," he said. "Ask him."

When Moses appeared, I asked him and he said, "Aḥmad ibn Ḥanbal was put to the test in good times and bad. He proved himself sincere and has joined the truth-tellers."

[Abū Naṣr:] I dreamed I was praying along with the Prophet. When he finished I said, "May my father redeem you, Emissary of God![512] There's a member of your community I want to ask you about." 93.16

"Who?"

"Aḥmad ibn Ḥanbal."

"Ask my brother Moses."

I woke up. Then I dozed off again, and there was Moses.

"O Addressee of God![513] The Prophet came to me in a dream and I asked him about a member of his community but he said to ask you."

"Is it Aḥmad ibn Ḥanbal you want to know about?"

"Yes."

"He was put to the test in good times and bad but endured it all, and now he's in 'Illiyyīn."[514]

[Bundār:] Sufyān al-Thawrī came to me in a dream and I asked him how he had fared. 93.17

"Better than I expected," he said.

"What's that in your sleeve?"

"Pearls, rubies, and gems," he said. "When Aḥmad ibn Ḥanbal's spirit joined us, God greeted him with a shower of precious stones. This is my share."

93.18 [Bundār:] I asked ʿAbd al-Raḥmān ibn Mahdī to describe al-Thawrī for me, and he did. Then I asked God to show him to me in a dream. No sooner had ʿAbd al-Raḥmān[515] died than I dreamed of Sufyān, who matched the description ʿAbd al-Raḥmān had given me. I asked what God had done with him.

"He's forgiven me," he said.

I noticed that he was carrying something in his sleeve and I asked him what it was.

"Aḥmad ibn Ḥanbal's spirit has been brought here, and God commanded Gabriel to shower it with pearls, gems, and chrysolite. This is my share."

Al-Khaṭīb added: Bundār would seem to have had this dream upon the death of Aḥmad ibn Ḥanbal, but God alone knows the truth.

93.20 [Al-Bukhārī:] Al-Muḥāribī said that he dreamed of seeing ʿAbd Allāh ibn al-Ṣabbāḥ sitting by the niche in the mosque. He greeted him and asked how he had fared.

"Well," he said. "Follow Ibn Ḥanbal! Follow him! Follow him!"[516]

He also dreamed of seeing al-Faḍl ibn Ziyād. He described the dwelling where he saw al-Faḍl, and then said that he asked him what he had done to earn it.

"'Follow the *sunnah,*' said al-Faḍl.

"'What about Aḥmad ibn Ḥanbal?'

"'He's on the other side of something we can't see through.'"

93.22 [Aswad ibn Sālim:] Once in my sleep I sensed a presence that spoke to me and said, "Aswad! God sends His greetings and says, 'Aḥmad ibn Ḥanbal is bringing this community back to the right path, so be sure to follow him. If you don't, you'll perish.'"

93.23 [Al-Ḥasan al-Ṣawwāf:] The Lord of Glory appeared to me in a dream and said, "Ḥasan, anyone who disagrees with Ibn Ḥanbal will be tormented."

93.24 [Ibn Mijmaʿ:] We had a neighbor who was killed in Qazwīn. The morning after Aḥmad ibn Ḥanbal died, the neighbor's brother came over and said, "I had the strangest dream last night! I saw my brother, looking better than he ever did, riding on a horse. I said, 'Brother, weren't you killed? What are you doing here?'

"He said, 'God commanded all the martyrs and the blessed in Heaven to attend Aḥmad ibn Ḥanbal's funeral, so here I am.'"

Later we checked the date and it was the same day Aḥmad died.

[Yaʿqūb ibn ʿAbd Allāh:] Sarī l-Saqaṭī came to me in a dream and I asked him how he had fared. He said that God had permitted him to gaze upon His countenance. 93.26

"What about Aḥmad ibn Ḥanbal and Aḥmad ibn Naṣr?"

"They're busy eating fruit in the Garden."

[Al-Sijistānī:] The Emissary of God came to me in a dream. I asked him who he'd left in our time for members of his community to emulate in their religion. 93.27

"Aḥmad ibn Ḥanbal."

[Hibat Allāh ibn al-Sarī:] I saw the Emissary of God in a dream and said, "Emissary of God! Our thinkers all disagree and we don't know whose view to follow." 93.29

"Follow Aḥmad ibn Ḥanbal's," he replied.

[Al-Sijistānī:] I had a dream in 228 [842–43] where I was in the Friday mosque and a man who looked like a eunuch came out of the enclosure toward me saying, "The Emissary of God has said, 'After I'm gone, follow Aḥmad ibn Ḥanbal and . . .'" someone else whose name I can't remember. 93.30

I thought, "What a strange report!" When I asked someone to interpret the dream, he said, "The one who looked like a eunuch was an angel."

[Al-Marwazī:] I dreamed I was by Aḥmad's tomb. A cloud of dust appeared, and out of it an elder came riding. 93.31

"The prince is here!" came the cry.

The man dismounted by the tomb. I asked who he was and they told me, "'Abd Allāh ibn 'Umar ibn al-Khaṭṭāb."[517]

[Ḥajjāj:] An uncle of mine who had written down reports heard from Hushaym appeared to me in a dream. I asked him about Aḥmad ibn Ḥanbal and he said, "He's an associate of 'Umar ibn al-Khaṭṭāb." 93.32

93.33 [Ibn Abī Qurrah:] I dreamed that I had gone into the Garden. There I saw a palace made of silver. The door opened and out came Aḥmad ibn Ḥanbal wearing one garment of light as a breechclout and another as a sash. I raced up to him and he said, "Are you here already?"

"Yes," I said.

He kept asking the question until I woke up.

I also dreamed of walking through a gate whose doors were made of gold. On the other side were mountains of musk and people saying, "The warrior is here!"

Then Aḥmad ibn Ḥanbal came in wearing a sword and carrying a spear.

"This is the Garden," he said.

My sister Fāṭimah bint Abī Qurrah told me that one Friday she dreamed of seeing birds made of light coming down from Heaven and people using them to fly up.

"I asked what the light was and they said, 'It's Aḥmad ibn Ḥanbal's spirit, and it takes you up to God.'"

93.34 [Ibn al-ʿAbbās:] I dreamed we were waiting for Aḥmad's funeral procession to come out. When it appeared, I looked and saw that it was rising into the sky. It kept on rising until it disappeared.

93.35 [Al-Warrāq:] The Prophet came to me in a dream and asked me, "Why do you look so sad?"

"How could I not look sad," I answered, "when your community has fallen on such hard times?"

"Tell everyone to cleave to the path of Aḥmad ibn Ḥanbal," he said, twice.

93.36 [Abū Zurʿah:] I saw the Prophet in a dream and complained to him about the trouble we were having with the followers of Jahm.

"Have no fear," he said. "Aḥmad ibn Ḥanbal stands in their way."

93.37 [Ibn al-Mubārak al-Zamin:] I saw Zubaydah in a dream and asked her how God had judged her.

"The moment we broke ground for the Mecca road, He forgave me."

"But why do you look jaundiced?"

"A man called Bishr al-Marīsī was buried among us. Hell wanted him so badly it gave a groan that made my skin crawl and turned my face yellow."

"What happened to Aḥmad ibn Ḥanbal?"

"He just passed me in a boat of white pearl that sails on a fathomless red sea, on his way to visit the Merciful One."

"What did he do to deserve his reward?"

"Saying that the Qur'an is the speech of God and not created."

[Ḥanbal:] Someone I trust told me that he dreamed of a woman whose hair had turned white at the temples. When he asked her about it, she said, "When Aḥmad was flogged, Hell breathed such a sigh that all of us went grey." 93.38

[Al-Qawārīrī:] A certain man of spiritual standing was said to have had a dream vision and I wanted to hear about it from him. He came and we sat alone for a while. Later my little girl said, "He had light coming from his face." 93.39

He told me that he had seen the Prophet sitting with Aḥmad ibn Naṣr.

"The Prophet said, 'God's curse on So-and-So,' three times, 'and So-and-So and So-and-So! They're plotting against Aḥmad ibn Ḥanbal and al-Qawārīrī, but they won't get anywhere, God willing!' Then he said to me, 'Greet Aḥmad and al-Qawārīrī and tell them that I pray to God to reward them on my behalf and on behalf of my community.'"[518]

[Al-Maḥāmilī:] Abū Sa'īd al-Nahratīrī was a man of Qur'an, Hadith-learning, and religious understanding. After he died, he came to me in a dream, as if he were meeting me at the gate of Cotton House.[519] 93.40

"What happened to you?" I asked him. Using gestures, he conveyed that he had suffered an ordeal but gained salvation in the end.

"What about us here?"

"Only two things matter," he said. "The Qur'an and Hadith-knowledge."

"What about our study circle?"

"The way you've taken"—meaning the legal school of al-Shāfiʿī—"is right."

"What about Aḥmad ibn Ḥanbal?"

He conveyed with a gesture that Aḥmad had attained a lofty rank.

93.41 [Abū Bakr:] A man from Tarsus told me this story.

"I used to pray to God to show me dead people in their graves so I could ask them what had happened to Aḥmad ibn Ḥanbal. Ten years after his death, I dreamed that the dead were standing on their graves and calling out to me.

"'You there! How much longer will you ask God to show us to you? Ever since he left you, the one you've been asking about has been under the Ṭūbā tree,[520] with angels piling him with finery.'"

93.42 [Al-Ḥimmānī:] I dreamed I was sitting under a portico at home when the Prophet appeared. He stood in the doorway with his hands on the jambs, called to prayer, and announced that prayer had begun. Then he said, "The saved are saved and the damned damned."

"Emissary of God," I said. "Who are the saved?"

"Aḥmad ibn Ḥanbal and his followers."

93.43 [Al-Warrāq:] In Ramla there lived a man named ʿAmmar who people claimed was one of the Substitutes. He fell ill and I went to see him. I had heard about a vision he'd had, and so I asked him about it.

"It's true," he said. "I saw the Prophet in a dream and I asked him to pray to God to forgive me, and so he did. Later I saw al-Khaḍir and asked him, 'What do you say about the Qur'an?'

"He said, 'It's God's speech, and not created.'

"'What do you say about Bishr ibn al-Ḥārith?'

"'The day he died, he left behind him no one more fearful of God.'

"'What about Aḥmad ibn Ḥanbal?'

"'He was a truth-teller.'

"'What about al-Ḥusayn al-Karābīsī?'

"In response he vilified him. Then I asked, 'What's going to happen to my mother?'

"He said, 'She'll fall ill and live for seven days before she dies,' and that's what happened."

[Al-Dahhān:] I saw al-Khaḍir in a dream and asked him if he was the one who was with Moses.[521] He said he was. Then I asked him what he thought of Aḥmad ibn Ḥanbal. 93.44

"He's a truth-teller."

[Abū Bakr:] I dreamed I was in the mosque of al-Khayf and there I saw the Prophet. I asked, "How is Bishr doing with you?" 93.45

"He was given a place in the middle of the Garden."

"What about Aḥmad ibn Ḥanbal?"

"Haven't you heard that when God admits the people of remembrance[522] to the Garden, he smiles at them?"

[Ibn al-Fatḥ:] Bishr ibn al-Ḥārith came to me in a dream, sitting and eating at a table laid for him in an orchard. I asked him how God had judged him. 93.46

"He took pity on me and forgave me, and opened the whole Garden to me."

"And where's your friend Aḥmad ibn Ḥanbal?"

"Standing at the gate to intercede for Sunnis who declare the Qur'an to be the uncreated speech of God."

['Alī ibn al-Muwaffaq:] I had some personal devotions to do at night, so I stayed up from Thursday night until Friday morning then went to bed. I dreamed that I had entered the Garden. There I saw three men. The first was sitting at a table with one angel serving him food and another pouring him drink. The second was standing in the middle of the Garden gazing at God, Mighty and Glorious, without blinking. The third would leave the Garden, take hold of people, and bring them inside. 93.47

I asked Riḍwān, "Who are those three who've been so well rewarded?"

"Your brothers who died sinless."

"Tell me more."

"The first one," he said, "is Bishr the Barefoot, who from the time he reached the age of reason never once ate his fill or drank as much water as he wanted, all for fear of God, who has assigned him two angels: one to feed him and one to pour for him. The second man—the one gazing at the throne—is Maʿrūf al-Karkhī, who worshipped God because he longed for Him, not for fear of the Fire or in hope of the Garden; and now God has allowed him to gaze at Him all he wants. And the third one is Aḥmad ibn Ḥanbal, who was truthful in his speech and scrupulous in his religion. God has commanded him to look into the faces of the Sunnis and bring them into the Garden."

93.48 [Ibn al-Muthannā:] I saw Bishr ibn al-Ḥārith in a dream and asked him how God had judged him.

"He's forgiven me."

"What about Aḥmad ibn Ḥanbal and ʿAbd al-Wahhāb al-Warrāq?"

"They're in Paradise"—or "in the Garden"—"eating and drinking."

93.49 [Al-Anṭākī:] I dreamed it was the Day of Resurrection. From inside the Throne a herald called out, "Bring Abū ʿAbd Allāh, Abū ʿAbd Allāh, Abū ʿAbd Allāh, and Abū ʿAbd Allāh into the Garden!"

I asked an angel next to me, "Who are they?"

"Mālik, al-Thawrī, Muḥammad ibn Idrīs, and Aḥmad ibn Ḥanbal."

In another telling he added: "Those four are the exemplars of Muḥammad's community, and they were brought to the Garden ahead of everyone else."

93.50 [Al-Maḥāmilī:] Al-Qāshānī came to me in a dream and I asked what he knew about Aḥmad ibn Ḥanbal.

"God forgave him," he said.

93.51 [Thābit al-Marwazī:] I used to think that Ibn Shabbuwayh, who fought in the jihad, ransomed prisoners, and lived on the frontier, had more merit than Aḥmad. I asked my brother ʿAbd Allāh ibn Aḥmad which of the two he preferred.

"Aḥmad ibn Ḥanbal."

I wasn't convinced, and couldn't bring myself to admire anyone but Ibn Shabbuwayh.

A year later, I had a dream where an elder was speaking to a group of people gathered around him. When he rose to go I followed him and said, "Tell me who has more merit and a higher rank: Aḥmad ibn Ḥanbal or Aḥmad ibn Shabbuwayh?"

"What a question!" he replied. "Aḥmad ibn Ḥanbal was put to the test and stood firm while Aḥmad ibn Shabbuwayh was spared. How can you compare someone who survived an ordeal to one who never went through it? I can't! There's a world of difference between them."

[Al-Jallā':] A friend told me that he saw the Prophet in a dream and asked him about some of the issues that jurists disagree on. The Prophet told him, "All jurists are right about some things and wrong about others. Aḥmad ibn Ḥanbal has God's help, and makes fewer errors, so cleave to his example and cite him when you make an argument. You live in an age that will see no other like him." 93.52

[Muḥammad ibn al-ʿAbbās:] Bishr's associate al-Khayyāṭ told me that a man who was an intimate of Bishr ibn al-Ḥārith once came to Bishr and said, "On one of the festival days I dreamed that it was the end of the world. Everyone was so terrified that I saw people weeping tears of blood. A herald came forward and called out, 'Where is Bishr and where is Aḥmad ibn Ḥanbal?' 93.53

"They took the two of you and brought you into God's presence.

"'If those two are found wanting,' said the people waiting to be judged, 'then we're all doomed.'

"Then an angel appeared. 'What happened to Bishr and Aḥmad?' we asked.

"'They're being judged on how well they showed their gratitude to God for blessing them with untarnished reputations.'"

Hearing this story, Bishr said, "One of the two can never do enough. As for the other, experience shows how grateful he is."

[Muḥammad ibn ʿAbd Allāh:] I saw Abū l-Ḥasan ibn ʿAbdūs in a dream. He was dressed in white. I said, "Have you seen al-Shāfiʿī?" 93.54

"He's a sea that never runs dry," he said, "and the community should gather around him."

"What about Mālik ibn Anas?"

"Head and shoulders above the others."

"What about Aḥmad ibn Ḥanbal?"

"His is the closest approach to God."

93.57 [Bilāl al-Khawwāṣ:] Al-Khaḍir came to me in a dream and I asked him about Bishr ibn al-Ḥārith.

"He was the last of his kind," he said.

Then I asked about Aḥmad ibn Ḥanbal.

"A truth-teller," he said.

"How is it that I'm able to see you?"

"It's because of your kindness to your mother."

[The author:] It has also been reported that Bilāl saw al-Khaḍir while awake. The story appears in our chapter on al-Khaḍir's praise of Aḥmad.

93.58 [Haydhām:] A man dreamed he heard someone saying, "God has chosen certain persons among you to protect you from disaster—or words to that effect—and Aḥmad ibn Ḥanbal is one of them."

93.59 One night I fell to thinking about Aḥmad ibn Ḥanbal and how he survived being flogged despite how frail he was. I was moved to tears. That night I dreamed of a voice that said, "If only you could have seen how proud the angels in Heaven were as they saw him being beaten!"

"What?" I asked. "The angels knew about Aḥmad's flogging?"

"There wasn't a single one who wasn't looking down."

93.60 [Yaʿqūb ibn Yūsuf:] One night during the Inquisition, I was sleeping when a man wearing a sleeveless woolen cloak came into the room.

"Who are you?" I asked.

"Moses, son of ʿImrān."

"You're the Moses who had God speak to him directly, without an interpreter?"

"That's right."

It was at that moment that a second man, this one curly-haired and dressed in two robes, fell from the ceiling.

"Who's that?" I asked.

"Jesus, the son of Mary."

Then Moses spoke again. "I, the Moses who had God speak to him directly, without an interpreter, and Jesus the son of Mary, and your Prophet, and Aḥmad ibn Ḥanbal, and the Carriers of the Throne, and all the angels bear witness that the Qur'an is the speech of God and not created."

['Abd Allāh ibn al-Ḥasan:] In a dream I saw a Hadith-man who had just died. I asked him how God had judged him and he said, "He's forgiven me." 93.61

"Really?"

"I swear to God He's forgiven me!"

"Why?"

"Because I loved Aḥmad ibn Ḥanbal."

"And are you comfortable?"

He smiled. "Comfortable and happy."

[Al-Fasawī:] When Ḥamdūn al-Bardha'ī came to Abū Zur'ah to study Hadith, he saw that the house was full of utensils, carpets, and the like—which, as it happened, belonged to Abū Zur'ah's brother. Ḥamdūn was on the verge of leaving without copying any Hadith. That night, however, he dreamed that he was standing on the shore of a lake. He saw a man's shadow reflected in the water and heard a voice say, "Are you the one who thinks Abū Zur'ah needs to be more of a renunciant?" The voice continued: "You should know that Aḥmad ibn Ḥanbal was one of the Substitutes, and when he died, God sent Abū Zur'ah to take his place." 93.62

Chapter 94
The Benefit of Visiting His Grave

[Al-Hindibā'ī:] I used to visit Aḥmad ibn Ḥanbal's grave but then stopped. After some time had passed, I had a dream where a voice said, "You've stopped visiting the exemplar of the *sunnah*." 94.1

[Aḥmad ibn al-Ḥasan:] My father cited Abū Ṭāhir al-Maymūn as saying, "Son, I met a man in the Ruṣāfah mosque—this was in Rabī' 94.2

II 466 [December 1073]—who told me when I asked him that he had traveled six hundred leagues to be there.

"'Why?'

"'One Friday night back home,' he said, 'I dreamed I was in the desert, or in a great wilderness. All the people in creation were standing there, the gates of Heaven were open, and angels were coming down. The angels were dressing certain people in green and flying back up with them. I asked who the special ones were.'

"'The ones who visited Aḥmad ibn Ḥanbal.'

"As soon as I woke up, I put my affairs in order and came here. I've visited him several times and now I'm going home, God willing."

94.3 [Abū Bakr ibn Abruwayh:] The Emissary of God and Aḥmad ibn Ḥanbal appeared to me in a dream.

"Emissary of God," I asked, "who's that?"

"This is Aḥmad ibn Ḥanbal, God's ally and the ally of His Emissary. Listen, Abū Bakr! Every day God looks over at Aḥmad's grave seventy thousand times and forgives anyone he sees there."

I woke up, washed, and prayed two cycles in gratitude to God. Then I took off my clothes, gave them away to the poor, and set off on the pilgrimage. After that I visited Aḥmad's tomb and spent a week there.

94.4 [Abū Bakr al-Najjād:] I had heard that anyone in need who visits Aḥmad's grave on a Wednesday and prays there will receive generous sustenance from God. So once when I was in need, I visited the grave on a Wednesday. I was on my way back in a dismal frame of mind when an old woman called out to me from one of the cemeteries.

"Abū Bakr!" she said.

"What is it?"

"Your mother left a bag with me and told me that if I saw you looking needy I should give it to you. Do you need it?"

"Yes," I said, and took it. In it was—

The amount is missing, may God care for the worthy elder who transmitted the story!

[Abū l-Ḥasan al-ʿUkbarī:] When I was a boy I traveled from ʿUkbarā down to Baghdad without any money to spend. I stayed in the mosque inside the Round City for several days ["without eating," he may have added]. On Wednesday I went to visit Aḥmad's tomb. There I found a man who greeted me—I was wearing fine clothes[523]—and asked me if I was hungry. When I said nothing, he gave me some bread and enough gold to live on for a while. For a while he continued to check on me. 94.5

Chapter 95

The Benefit of Being Buried Near Him

[Ibn Abī l-Dunyā:] I heard Abū Yūsuf ibn Bukhtān—who was a good Muslim—report that when Aḥmad ibn Ḥanbal died, someone had a dream where he saw a lamp on every grave. When he asked why, he was told, "Don't you see? As soon as that man was put in among them, the tombs of all the dead were illuminated. Some of the dead who were being tormented were forgiven." 95.1

[ʿUbayd ibn Sharīk:] A drag queen[524] who died was seen in a dream saying, "I've been forgiven: as soon as Aḥmad was placed among us, everyone dead and buried was forgiven." 95.2

[Al-Ḥasan ibn Aḥmad:] When al-Qaṭīʿī's mother died, he had her buried near Aḥmad ibn Ḥanbal. A few nights later she appeared to him in a dream. He asked her how she had fared and she said, "God bless you, my son! Every night"—or "Every Friday night"—"a wave of mercy descends on the grave of the man you buried me near, and it covers all of us buried here, including me." 95.3

[Al-Jammāl:] One night, in the cemetery where Aḥmad is buried, I recited the verse «Among those some shall be damned, and others shall be blessed.»[525] Then I nodded off and heard a voice say, "Because of Aḥmad's presence, no one here is damned, thank God!" 95.4

[The author:] One of the early Muslims is said to have told the following story. 95.5

Where I lived there was an old woman, a Worshipper, who had spent fifty years serving God. One day she woke up in terror.

"Last night a jinni came to me," she said. "He said he was my male counterpart.[526] He told me that the jinns had overheard the angels offering each other condolences on the imminent death of a righteous man named Aḥmad ibn Ḥanbal who would be buried in Such-and-Such a place. God will forgive anyone who takes up residence nearby, so if you can go there when you feel death coming on, do it. Please believe me: I'm telling you this for your own good. You'll die the night after he does."

And that's what happened, so we knew it was a truthful dream.

95.6 [Abū l-Barakāt:] I had a friend named Thābit: a righteous man who read the Qur'an, called on people to do good, and forbade them to do ill. When he died, I didn't pray over him because something happened to prevent me. Then he came to me in a dream. When I greeted him, he didn't answer, and turned aside.

"Thābit!" I said. "How can you ignore me when we've been such good friends?"

"So if we're friends, why didn't you pray over me?"

I apologized to him then asked him to tell me how things were in Aḥmad's burial ground, since he'd been buried there.

"No one here feels the Fire," he said.

"What about the burial ground of Quraysh?"

"I don't know about that," he said. "I've told you as much as I know."

"When someone new comes to join you, do you visit them and ask them questions?"

"We visit and ask about the living people they've left behind."

95.7 [The author:] I read something my teacher Abū l-Ḥasan ʿAlī ibn ʿUbayd Allāh ibn al-Zāghūnī wrote in his own hand, as follows: "When the Prophet's descendant Abū Jaʿfar ibn Abī Mūsā was buried next to him, Aḥmad ibn Ḥanbal's tomb was exposed. His corpse had not putrified and the shroud was still whole and undecayed."

Abū Jaʿfar died 129 years after Ibn Ḥanbal.

Chapter 96

The Punishments That Befall Anyone Who Attacks Him

[Muḥammad ibn Fuḍayl:] I made some remarks critical of Aḥmad ibn Ḥanbal after which my tongue started to hurt and wouldn't stop. One night I heard a voice in my sleep saying, "It's because of what you said about that good man," over and over. When I woke up, I expressed contrition to God until the pain went away. 96.1

[Muḥammad ibn Fuḍayl:] Once as I was criticizing Aḥmad ibn Ḥanbal my tongue started to hurt. Upset, I went to bed, and heard a voice saying, "Your tongue hurts because of what you said about that good man." 96.2

When I woke up, I said, "I seek God's forgiveness!" and "I won't do it again!" until the pain went away.

[Misʿar ibn Muḥammad ibn Wahb:] Before al-Mutawakkil became caliph, I was his tutor. When he became caliph, he gave me a room in the section reserved for his intimates. Whenever he had a question about religion he would send for me. During his intimate audiences, I would stand next to him. Whenever he needed me for any reason, he would summon me and I would take up my usual post. He kept me by his side day and night except when he wanted to be alone. 96.3

One day, after holding an intimate audience in the hall called The Serene, he moved into another room he had where the ceiling, walls, and floor were made of glass tiles. Water could be piped in and sent flowing in any direction across the top of the room, along the floor, and down the walls, and anyone sitting inside looked as if he were sitting underwater. The room was fitted out with Coptic textiles and pillows and cushions of Tyrian purple. Al-Mutawakkil was sitting with al-Fatḥ ibn Khāqān and ʿUbayd Allāh ibn Khāqān on his right and Bughā the Elder and Waṣīf on his left. I was standing in the corner of the room to his right and a servant stood in the doorway with his hand on the jamb. Suddenly al-Mutawakkil laughed out loud and everyone fell silent.

"Aren't you going to ask me why I laughed?" he said.

"Why did the Commander of the Faithful laugh?" they asked. "May God keep him smiling!"

96.4 "I remembered one day when I was attending al-Wāthiq. He had been holding an intimate audience in the hall where we were sitting before, and I was standing next to him. Suddenly he rose and went into the room where we are now, and sat where I'm sitting. I tried to follow him in but I was stopped, so I stood where the servant is standing now. Ibn Abī Du'ād was sitting where Fatḥ is now, Muḥammad ibn ʿAbd al-Malik ibn al-Zayyāt was sitting where ʿUbayd Allāh is, Isḥāq ibn Ibrāhīm was sitting where Bughā is, and Najāḥ was sitting where Waṣīf is now.

"Then al-Wāthiq said: 'I've been thinking about how I've demanded everyone's assent to the doctrine that the Qur'an is created. I've noticed how quickly some people adopted the belief and how stubbornly the others are resisting it. With the ones who resist, I've tried flogging, beheading, beating, and imprisonment, but none of it seems to have any effect. Not only that: the ones who've obeyed me did so because they wanted something from me, and so adopted my creed immediately hoping for a reward. The dissenters, on the other hand, have no motive except pious scruple, which sustains them even when they're killed or beaten or thrown in jail. All of this started me thinking, and I'm beginning to doubt whether what we're doing is right. Should we really be putting people on trial and torturing them over this? I've reached the point where I'm ready to stop the Inquisition and give up Disputation altogether, and I'm ready to send out some heralds to announce my decision and put a stop to all this fighting among ourselves.'

96.5 "The first to respond was Ibn Abī Du'ād. He said: 'Have a care, Commander of the Faithful! You've revived a precedent and restored an element of the faith, so think twice before you annul it and kill it off. Try as they did, your predecessors never achieved as much as you have. May God reward you as generously as he awards any of His allies on behalf of Islam and true religion!'

"The others sat silently, their heads bowed in thought, for a time. Then Ibn Abī Du'ād, who was afraid that al-Wāthiq would say something to contradict him and undo the work he had done to promote his creed, again took the initiative and said: 'The creed that we've adopted and that we're asking people to espouse is the one God chose for His prophets and emissaries and the one he sent Muḥammad to propagate. It's just that people have become too blind to accept it.'

"'Well then,' said al-Wāthiq, 'I want you to swear an oath of good faith.'

"Ibn Abī Du'ād promptly called on God to strike him down with paralysis in this world, not to mention the torments of the next, if the caliph was wrong about the Qur'an being created. Muḥammad ibn 'Abd al-Malik al-Zayyāt called on God to drive iron spikes through his hands in this world, not to mention the torments of the next, if the caliph was wrong about the Qur'an being created. Isḥāq ibn Ibrāhīm called on God to make him stink so badly in this world that his friends and relatives would flee from him, not to mention the torments of the next, if the caliph was wrong about the Qur'an being created. And Najāḥ called on God to kill him by confining him in the smallest of prison cells if the caliph was wrong about the Qur'an being created.

"While this was going on, Ītākh came in and they challenged him to come up with his own oath. He called on God to drown him in the sea if the caliph was wrong about the Qur'an being created. Finally, al-Wāthiq himself called on God to set him on fire if he was wrong about the Qur'an being created.

"And now I'm laughing because every one of the things they pro- 96.6
posed came true. Ibn Abī Du'ād was stricken with paralysis, as I saw with my own eyes. I myself put Ibn al-Zayyāt into a brazen bull and drove steel spikes through his hands. During his final illness, Isḥāq ibn Ibrāhīm gave off a stinking sweat that drove everyone away.

Twenty times a day they changed the gown he was wearing and threw the old one into the Tigris because it smelled like carrion and stank too much to be used again. For Najāḥ, I built a cell one cubit by two and kept him there until he died. Ītākh was executed by Isḥāq ibn Ibrāhīm at my command: when he returned from the pilgrimage he was weighed down with chains and dropped in the water.

96.7 "Now about al-Wāthiq. He had a great love for women and sex. One day he sent for Mikhāʾīl the physician, who was called in to see him and found him in a sunroom lying under a silken sheet.

"'Mikhāʾīl,' said al-Wāthiq, 'I need you to get me an aphrodisiac.'

"'Commander of the Faithful,' said the physician, 'I don't approve of putting stress on the body. Too much sex wears the body down, especially if a man has to force it. Respect the body God has given you and take care of it, since it's the only one you have!'

"'No,' said al-Wāthiq, 'I must have something.' He lifted up the sheet and clamped there between his legs was a concubine whom Mikhāʾīl later described as extraordinarily beautiful and shapely. 'Who could resist someone like this?'

"'Well then, if you must have it, then what you need is lion meat. Have them prepare four hundred grams and boil it seven times in aged wine vinegar. When you sit down to drink, have them weigh out three dirhams' worth. Take one dirham's worth with wine for three nights running and you'll get the results you want. But be careful not to take too much. Whatever you do, don't exceed the dosage I've prescribed.'

"For several days al-Wāthiq neglected to pursue the matter, but then one day as he was sitting and drinking he remembered the prescription.

"'Bring me lion meat right away!' he cried.

"A lion was brought up out of the pit and slaughtered on the spot, and the meat put on the grill. At his orders, it was then boiled in vinegar, cut into strips, and dried. He began taking some of it as an accompaniment to wine.

"After some time he began to suffer from a dropsy of the belly. The physicians were summoned and agreed that the only remedy was to light an open-topped oven, stoke it with olive branches until it was full of coals, then sweep out the coals, turn it over, fill it with green clover, and have al-Wāthiq sit inside it for three hours.[527] If he asked for water he was not to have it. After three full hours had passed, he was to be taken out and made to sit upright in the manner they prescribed. He was likely to feel severe pain if exposed to a breeze, but if he asked to be put back into the oven he must instead be kept as he was for two hours. At that point, the water in his belly should come out as urine. If he were to take water or go back into the oven before the two hours had passed, he would expire. 96.8

"The oven was accordingly lit, stoked, emptied, turned over, and filled with clover, and al-Wāthiq was stripped and put inside. He began shouting, 'I'm burning up! Bring me water!'

"But there were people there assigned to prevent anyone from giving him water, and to stop him from getting out of the place where he'd been put, or moving around. Even after his whole body broke out in blisters and parts of it swelled up as big as the largest melon, he was kept where he was until the three hours had passed. Then he was taken out. He was nearly burned to death—and those who saw him thought he had been. The doctors put him into a seated position. Whenever there was a breeze, it hurt him, and he would bellow like a bull.

"'Put me back in the oven!' he would say. 'If you don't I'll die!'

"Seeing him in agony, and hearing his cries, his intimates and the women of his family gathered and begged them to put him back in the oven in the hope that it would give him some relief. So they put him back inside. As soon as he felt the heat, he stopped shouting, and the swellings on his body burst and subsided. After the inside of the oven had cooled, he was taken out. This time he had been burnt black as coal. Within an hour he died.

"So," said al-Mutawakkil, "I'm laughing because God answered the prayers of every one of them by inflicting the punishment he had called down on himself."

96.9 [The author:] I've also heard a different telling of the story.

[Al-Marwazī:] No sooner had al-Mutawakkil become caliph than ʿAbd al-ʿAzīz ibn Yaḥyā l-Makkī appeared before him and said, "Commander of the Faithful, something extraordinary happened when al-Wāthiq executed Aḥmad ibn Naṣr: Aḥmad's head continued reciting the Qur'an until it was buried!"

Al-Mutawakkil found this news upsetting, especially because of what it implied for his brother. When Muḥammad ibn ʿAbd al-Malik ibn al-Zayyāt appeared, al-Mutawakkil told him he was upset about Aḥmad ibn Naṣr.

"May God burn me alive," said Muḥammad, "if Aḥmad ibn Naṣr didn't die an Ingrate."

Then Harthamah appeared and al-Mutawakkil said the same thing.

"May God chop me into pieces," said Harthamah, "if Aḥmad ibn Naṣr didn't die an Ingrate."

Then Ibn Abī Du'ād appeared and al-Mutawakkil said the same thing.

"May God strike me with paralysis," said Ibn Abī Du'ād, "if Aḥmad ibn Naṣr didn't die an Ingrate."

Later al-Mutawakkil was to say, "Al-Zayyāt ended up burned to death at my command. Harthamah fled and was captured by some Arabs who blamed him for killing their cousin and chopped him to pieces.[528] And Ibn Abī Du'ad was imprisoned in his own skin."

[The author:] Ibn Abī Du'ād served as chief judge under al-Muʿtaṣim and al-Wāthiq and urged both caliphs to try people regarding the createdness of the Qur'an. As a result, God struck him with paralysis.

96.10 [Al-Makkī:] I went to see Ibn Abī Du'ād after he had his stroke.

"I didn't come to check on you," I said, "but to thank God for imprisoning you in your own skin."

96.11 [Abū Yūsuf Yaʿqūb:] I dreamed that my uncle and I were walking along the ʿĪsā Canal and heard a woman say, "Don't you know what happened tonight? God has taken Ibn Abī Du'ād."

"How did he die?" I asked.

"He made God angry, and God sent his anger down from seven heavens high."

One of my associates told me that he was at Sufyān ibn Wakīʿ's place the morning after fires had been sighted in Baghdad and elsewhere.

Sufyān asked, "Do you know what I dreamed last night? I dreamed that Hell gave a sigh and a flame rose up," or words to that effect. "I asked what was happening and someone said, 'They're preparing to receive Ibn Abī Du'ād.'"

96.12 [Khālid ibn Khidāsh:] I dreamed I heard a voice say, "Ibn Abī Du'ād and Shuʿayb have been transformed into animals, Ibn Samāʿah has suffered a stroke, and So-and-So"—he didn't say who—"has choked on his own blood."

[The author:] The Shuʿayb mentioned here is Ibn Sahl, the judge; he was a follower of Jahm. Ibn Abī Du'ād suffered a stroke, had his property confiscated, and in the year 240 [854–55] perished in disgrace.

96.13 [The Prophet:] Anyone who challenges God's authorities on earth with the intention of demeaning them will suffer crushing humiliation in this world, apart from the shame and disgrace that await him in the next.

[The author:] "God's authorities on earth" means the Book and the *sunnah* of the Prophet.

96.14 [The Prophet:] "God's authorities on earth" means His Book and the *sunnah* of His Prophet.

96.15 [Al-Ṭūsī:] The day Aḥmad ibn Ḥanbal was flogged, Khālid ibn Khidāsh wrote to my father to let him know that when the news came of what had been done to Aḥmad, a certain man went into a mosque to offer a prayer of thanksgiving but the earth gave way under him and he sunk chest-deep into the ground. When he cried out for help some people came and pulled him out.

96.16 [Khālid ibn Khidāsh:] A certain man was rejoicing over the flogging of Aḥmad ibn Ḥanbal when the ground he was standing on suddenly gave way.

96.17 [Al-Najjād:] An elder who used to tutor us and study Hadith with us told me that he once went to visit the grave of Aḥmad ibn Ḥanbal.

"There were only a few other graves around it at the time," he said. "Some people had gathered nearby to shoot pellets. One of them asked which was Aḥmad's grave. When it was pointed out to him, he shot a pellet at it. I knew him, and I saw him some time later. His hand had shriveled up."

96.18 ['Imrān ibn Mūsā:] I went to visit Abū l-'Urūq, the lictor who had flogged Aḥmad, just to get a look at him. For forty-five days, he could only bark like a dog.

Chapter 97

What to Think about Anyone Who Speaks Ill of Him

97.1 [Al-Mukharrimī:] If you hear a man slander Aḥmad ibn Ḥanbal, you know he's an innovator.

97.2 [Nu'aym ibn Ḥammād:] If you hear an Iraqi criticize Aḥmad ibn Ḥanbal, doubt his religion, and do the same if you hear a Khurasani criticize Isḥāq ibn Rāhāwayh.

97.3 [Abū Zur'ah:] If you hear a Kufan attack Sufyān al-Thawrī or Zā'idah, you can be sure he's a Rejectionist. If you hear a Syrian attack Makḥūl or al-Awzā'ī, you can be sure he's an 'Alī-hater. If you hear a Basran attack Ayyūb al-Sakhtiyānī or Ibn 'Awn, you can be sure he's an advocate of free will. If you hear a Khurasani attack 'Abd Allāh ibn al-Mubārak, you can be sure he's a Postponer. And you should also know that all those sects have one thing in common: they hate Aḥmad ibn Ḥanbal because he's inflicted mortal wounds on them all.

97.4 [Al-Ṣāghānī:] The first time I realized that God no longer favored Isḥāq ibn Abī Isrā'īl was when I heard him refer to "some people who claim to be special because they've heard reports from Ibrāhīm ibn Saʿd," alluding to Aḥmad ibn Ḥanbal. The reason for his resentment was that God had left him in obscurity while making Ibn Ḥanbal famous.

97.5 [Al-Dawraqī:] If you hear anyone speak ill of Aḥmad ibn Ḥanbal, doubt his Islam.

97.6 [Sufyān ibn Wakīʿ:] We think of Aḥmad as the standard: anyone who finds fault with him is a sinner to us.

97.7 [Al-Hamadhānī:] Aḥmad is the test that separates Muslims from heretics.

97.8 [Al-Ṣāʾigh:] Whenever I meet a Hadith-man I don't know I make sure to bring up Aḥmad ibn Ḥanbal. If the man speaks of him with enthusiasm I know he's all right. If he says nothing I know he's no good.

97.9 [Abū Jaʿfar:] Ibn Aʿyan recited these verses about Aḥmad ibn Ḥanbal:

To know who holds religion firm
One test is the key:
A man who speaks of Aḥmad ill
Admits to heresy.[529]

97.10 [Al-Karābīsī:] People who go after Aḥmad ibn Ḥanbal might as well go up to Mount Abū Qubays and try to knock it down with their sandals.

Chapter 98

Why We Chose His Legal School over the Others

98.1 Recall—may God lead you aright!—that when faced with a difficult choice, the only way to discern the right course of action is to put personal feelings and partisanship aside and search systematically for the truth, without undue deference to the names and reputations of those involved. If you do this, the fog of perplexity will dissipate. If, on the other hand, you allow yourself to be led astray by your inclinations, it will be difficult to find your way back to the straight and narrow.

98.2 Note, then, that after examining the evidentiary basis of the Law and the foundations of jurisprudence, and delving into the biographies of those who exercised their faculties on behalf of the Law, I find our man to have been the most knowledgeable in those fields.

98.3 To begin with, he was active in the preservation and transmission of the Book of God.

98.4 [ʿAbd Allāh:] My father Aḥmad ibn Ḥanbal taught me the entire Qur'an by his own choice.[530]

Aḥmad himself read the text with Yaḥyā ibn Ādam, ʿUbayd ibn al-Ṣabbāḥ, Ismāʿīl ibn Jaʿfar, and others—omitting here the list of their authorities. When reading, he would not let the pronunciation of *a* approximate that of *i*, citing the Hadith: "The Qur'an was revealed with *a* pronounced closer to *u* than to *i*, so recite it that way." He would not assimilate adjacent letters except in the word *ittakhadhtum* ("you have taken")[531] and the like, as did Abū Bakr. And he would extend long vowels to a moderate extent.[532]

He also compiled works on the Qur'anic sciences, including exegesis, abrogation, transposition, and the like, as we have noted in the chapter on his writings.

98.5 Turning to Hadith, there is universal agreement that he was unique even among his fellow exemplars in the sheer amount he memorized as well as his ability to distinguish the authentic from the dubious. Among earlier men of learning, Mālik knew more Hadith than anyone who came before him. To see that Aḥmad in turn outdid Mālik, one need only compare Aḥmad's *Authenticated Reports* with Mālik's *Well-Trodden Path*.

If asked, furthermore, about the reputations of Hadith transmitters, Aḥmad could list their virtues and defects from memory whenever he was asked as easily as he might recite the opening chapter of the Qur'an. Anyone who looks at the *Defects* compiled by Abū Bakr al-Khallāl will see this immediately. None of his colleagues could match him in this respect, nor could any contest his mastery of the legal opinions, special virtues, points of agreement, and differences of opinion attributed to the Companions of the Prophet.

As for the study of the Arabic language, Aḥmad himself used to say, "I've written more Arabic than Abū ʿAmr al-Shaybānī." 98.6

As for ruling on legal questions on the basis of analogy, Aḥmad has more feats of deductive reasoning to his credit than we have room for, but several examples may be found in the chapter on his powers of intellect. 98.7

In addition to all of these scholarly attainments, he had the force of character to renounce the world and impose on himself a scrupulousness that none of his fellows could match. No other scholar is described as declining with such unremitting severity the gifts offered by his friends as well as the emoluments dangled by the authorities. Were I willing to risk the danger to their reputations, I could cite examples of gifts accepted by the other major figures and describe their willingness to relax their standards in such cases. Aḥmad, conversely, renounced even permitted things, as this book has shown in more than sufficient detail. 98.8

In addition to all of the above, Aḥmad proved himself capable of suffering great and terrible ordeals in the service of truth, a feat unmatched among his comrades.

[Al-Shāfiʿī:] Muḥammad ibn al-Ḥasan asked me who was better: his exemplar or mine?[533] I asked him if he wanted to give each man his due or merely have a boasting match. He replied that he wanted a fair comparison. 98.9

"In that case," I said, "tell me where your man excels."

"In the Book, consensus, *sunnah*, and analogy."

"Tell the truth now, with God as your witness! Who knows the Book of God better: our man or yours?"

"Well, if I'm under oath, then it's your man."

"What about the *sunnah* of the Prophet?"

"Your man again."

"And the opinions of the Companions?"

"Your man again."

"So what have you got left besides analogy?"

"Nothing."

"And even there, we have better claim to using analogy than you. The difference is that we draw analogies on the basis of revealed texts so that the reasoning is clear."

The comparison here is between Abū Ḥanīfah and Mālik ibn Anas.

98.10 By reporting this exchange, al-Shāfiʿī saves us the trouble of debating with the partisans of Abū Ḥanīfah. Aḥmad's superiority to Mālik is acknowledged, Aḥmad having learned everything Mālik knew and then added to it, as attested by any comparison of the *Well-Trodden Path* and the *Authenticated Reports*. Al-Shāfiʿī, for his part, was well versed in the various fields of learning but conceded Hadith transmission to Aḥmad; and Hadith is the pivot upon which legal reasoning turns.

98.11 [Aḥmad:] Al-Shāfiʿī told me, "You know Hadith better than I do. Whenever a Hadith turns out to be sound, let me know so I can adopt it."

98.12 [ʿAbd Allāh:] I heard my father say, "Al-Shāfiʿī once said to me, 'Aḥmad, whenever a report about the Emissary of God proves to be sound, let me know so I can use it.'"

98.13 [ʿAbd Allāh:] I heard my father say, "Muḥammad ibn Idrīs al-Shāfiʿī once said to me, 'Aḥmad, you know better than I which reports are sound. Whenever you find a sound one, whether from Kufa, Basra, or Syria, let me know so I can adopt it.'"

Whenever in his book al-Shāfiʿī says, "I cite a trustworthy source" or "I heard a trustworthy source report," he means my father.

This is why the book al-Shāfiʿī wrote in Baghdad is better argued than the one he wrote in Egypt.[534] When he was here, he would ask my father, who would correct him; but in Egypt there was no one to catch him when he used a weak report. I heard my father say, "Al-Shāfiʿī learned more from me than I did from him."

98.14 [Muḥammad ibn Isḥāq ibn Rāhawayh:] I heard my father say, "Al-Shāfiʿī never met anyone like Aḥmad ibn Ḥanbal."

[Aḥmad ibn Kāmil:] Several of Aḥmad's associates told me that he used to say, "Al-Shāfiʿī learned more from us than we did from him." 98.15

[Abū Ḥātim:] I'd give Aḥmad ibn Ḥanbal precedence over al-Shāfiʿī. Being a jurist and not a Hadith expert, al-Shāfiʿī learned about Hadith from Aḥmad. He would often ask him, "Is this report strong? Do people know it?" If Aḥmad said it was, he would take it and build on it. 98.16

[Al-Athram:] Once when we were in al-Buwayṭī's circle, he read to us, citing al-Shāfiʿī, that ablution with sand consists of two passes.[535] But when I recited the Hadith where ʿAmmār quotes the Prophet as saying, "Ablution with sand consists of one pass,"[536] he rubbed "two passes" out of his book and changed it to "one pass," as in the report of ʿAmmār. 98.17

He also said, "Whenever you find a reliable account of the Prophet, prefer it to whatever I might have said. Adopt the Hadith and use it as if it had come from me."

[Al-Būshanjī:] I think of Aḥmad as more learned and more insightful than Sufyān al-Thawrī. After all, Sufyān never had to suffer an ordeal as terrible as the one Aḥmad went through. Also, Sufyān and the other local scholars of his time cannot have known as much as Aḥmad did, since Aḥmad knew what all of them knew put together. He also had a clearer sense of which of them transmitted accurately and which ones made mistakes, not to mention which were honest and which ones lied. 98.18

[The author:] The foregoing should give a clear idea of the scholarly preeminence that has persuaded so many to join Aḥmad's interpretive tradition. Those of his associates who strive to know the Law do not merely imitate him. Rather, they act in accordance with the implication of his rulings. In doing so, they may favor one report of his view over another, and even choose a position that was never adopted by the original jurists of the school so long as it is consistent with the implication of his rulings. The position may thus be attributed to Aḥmad's school only in the sense that it conforms to the general spirit of his statements. 98.19

98.20 What if partisans of Abū Ḥanifah boast that their exemplar knew some of the Companions?

There are two rebuttals. The first is to cite al-Dāraquṭnī, who said, "Abū Ḥanīfah never met any of the Companions"; and Abū Bakr al-Khaṭīb, who said, "He saw Anas ibn Mālik." The second is to say that by that reasoning they should grant Saʿīd ibn al-Musayyab and others who did meet the Companions precedence over Abū Ḥanīfah.[537]

98.21 What if partisans of Mālik boast that their exemplar knew the Successors?

This claim is invalidated by reference to the Successors whom he met. Those Successors had known the Companions, and yet gave Mālik precedence over them.[538]

If they say, "Mālik is the repository of the knowledge of Medina," then concede the point, but then say that our exemplar Aḥmad acquired everything Mālik knew and added to it.

98.22 What if partisans of al-Shāfiʿī boast that his lineage strikes close to that of the Prophet, who said, "Put Quraysh first and do not step out ahead of them; learn from them and do not presume to teach them"?

To this we reply that kinship does not entail giving him precedence over others in learning. Among the Successors, almost all the learned men were non-Arab affiliates of the tribes. These include al-Ḥasan al-Baṣrī, Ibn Sīrīn, ʿAṭāʾ, Ṭāwūs, ʿIkrimah, Makḥūl, and others. By virtue of their great learning, they were perceived as having outdone those of their contemporaries whose nobility depended only on lineage. People accepted what Ibn Masʿūd and Zayd told them and rejected the same claim when it came from Ibn ʿAbbās.[539]

As for "Put Quraysh first," I refer you to Ibn al-Ḥarbī, who reports that Aḥmad was asked what it meant and said, "It means first in line for the caliphate. The phrase 'do not presume to teach them' is understood to refer to the Prophet."

Should they say that al-Shāfiʿī was faultless in his Arabic and therefore beyond reproach, concede the point, but then say that that does not give him precedence over others because precedence arises from how much one knows. Then again, he was caught making mistakes: saying, for example, "salty water" when the expression is "salt water"; or saying that *allā taʿūlū*[540] means "that you not have many dependents" whereas specialists in language say it means "that you not incline"; or saying "if you call a dog" when he meant "if you sic a dog," as the Arabs use the verb *ashlā* to mean only "call"; or saying "a robe that's *x*," even though the Arabs say "a robe that costs *x*." According to al-Marrūdhī, on the other hand, Aḥmad ibn Ḥanbal never made mistakes when he spoke. 98.23

Should anyone say, "It's been reported that Aḥmad recited Hadith on al-Shāfiʿī's authority," point out that al-Shāfiʿī was older. Not only that: al-Shāfiʿī himself would cite Mālik, who, according to al-Shāfiʿī's partisans, should have deferred to him. What's more, al-Shāfiʿī reported Hadith citing Aḥmad, as we have seen. 98.24

Al-Buwayṭī said that he heard al-Shāfiʿī say, "Everything is in my books," and a certain scholar explained that it came from Aḥmad ibn Ḥanbal.[541]

The foregoing will, I hope, suffice to make our case. Let God be merciful to all, and to each his own.

Chapter 99

On the Excellence of His Associates and Successors

[Al-Warrāq:] To criticize Aḥmad's associates is to attack Aḥmad himself. Anyone who does that must be harboring a grudge of some kind and is no Sunni. 99.1

[Al-Athram:] Aḥmad ibn Ḥanbal's associates sometimes decide to give up matters that have no consequence as far as God is concerned in order to avoid provoking any criticism of Aḥmad. 99.2

99.3 [Abū l-Faḍl:] I heard that after Aḥmad's death, someone mentioned to al-Mutawakkil that unpleasantness was liable to break out between his partisans and the innovators.

"Don't tell me anything more about them," al-Mutawakkil told the informant. "Instead, take their side. Aḥmad and his people are the lords of Muḥammad's community. God knows well enough the ordeal Aḥmad suffered, since He raised him to fame during his life and after his death; and his partisans are the best he could wish for. I daresay that God will give Aḥmad the reward He gives to the truth-tellers."

99.4 [Al-Marrūdhī:] Ibn Suḥt, who was Ibn Ḥubāb al-Jawharī's relation by marriage, said, "I dreamed I saw some people, and a man in white saying, 'God has forgiven Aḥmad ibn Ḥanbal and all who defend him.'"

99.5 [Abū l-Qāsim:] I heard a righteous man relate that one of his fellows appeared in a dream and was asked how God had judged him.

"He forgave me," was the reply.

"So who are the majority of people in the Garden?"

"Followers of al-Shāfiʿī."

"What about Aḥmad ibn Ḥanbal?"

"You asked me who the majority were, not who the highest ones were. Al-Shāfiʿī has the greater number, but Aḥmad's people have the higher rank."

99.6 [Al-Ḥimmānī:] I dreamed I was sitting under a portico at home when the Prophet appeared. He stood in the doorway with his hands resting on the jamb, issued the call to prayer, and announced that prayer had begun. Then he said, "The saved are saved and the damned damned."

"Emissary of God," I asked, "who are the saved?"

"Aḥmad ibn Ḥanbal and his followers."

99.7 [Al-Ḥarbī:] I dreamed I was in a group and we were being held against our will and I was unhappy about it. Then a voice asked, "What are you?"

I said, "Followers of Ibn Ḥanbal."

"Go, then; Ḥanbalīs aren't to be confined."

Then it felt as if a voice said, "No adherent of the Ḥanbalī school has ever been held accountable for his sins."

Ibn ʿAqīl—God have mercy on him!—used to say: 99.8

"The problem with our school is our own members. If a Ḥanafī or a Shāfiʿī excels in his studies, he's appointed to a judgeship or some other position and as a result of his appointment can devote himself to teaching and research. Aḥmad's people, on the other hand, can hardly study anything without deciding to devote themselves to pious exercises and renounce the world, given how godly the group tends to be. As a result, they stop being scholars."

Chapter 100

His Most Prominent Associates and Their Successors from His Time to Our Own

The number of Aḥmad's associates, and of those learned scholars 100.1
and good men who, during the years that have elapsed between his death and our own time, have followed his path is too large to count. Here I will mention only the most prominent, arranged in nine generations. May God ensure success![542]

Selected Members of the First Generation: Those Who Associated with Aḥmad and Transmitted Directly from Him

Aḥmad ibn Muḥammad ibn al-Ḥajjāj, Abū Bakr al-Marrūdhī. A 100.3
scrupulous and righteous man. He was devoted to serving Aḥmad, who would send him out on errands. Aḥmad used to tell him: "Anything you say counts as if I said it myself." He treated al-Marrūdhī with special consideration and would eat what he gave him.[543] After he returned from Samarra, he would often say, "God reward al-Marrūdhī!" It was al-Marrūdhī who closed Aḥmad's eyes and

washed him after he died. He also transmitted many of his reports and discussions of legal issues.

When Abū Bakr al-Marrūdhī left for the frontier, a crowd of people marched with him as far as Samarra. He kept telling them to turn back but they wouldn't. The size of the crowd was estimated at fifty thousand, not counting the ones who turned back before reaching Samarra.

"Be grateful to God," someone said to him, "that so many people admire you."

He burst into tears then said, "It's not me they admire, it's Aḥmad ibn Ḥanbal."

[Al-ʿAbbās ibn Naṣr:] I went to pray at al-Marrūdhī's grave and saw some old men there. One of them was telling another, "So-and-So slept here last night and woke up scared. I asked him what happened, and he said, 'I dreamed I saw Aḥmad ibn Ḥanbal riding along. I asked him where we were going, and he said, "To the Tree of Ṭūbā to catch up with Abū Bakr al-Marrūdhī."'"

Al-Marrūdhī died the sixth of Jumādā I 275 [September 16, 888] and was buried near Aḥmad's grave. His funeral prayer was led by Hārūn ibn al-ʿAbbās al-Hāshimī.

100.7 *Ibrāhīm ibn Isḥāq al-Ḥarbī.* Born in 198 [813–14], heard reports from Abū Nuʿaym al-Faḍl ibn Dukayn, ʿAffān ibn Muslim, ʿAbd Allāh ibn Ṣāliḥ al-ʿIjlī, Mūsā ibn Ismāʿīl al-Tabūdhakī, Musaddad, and many others. He was an exemplar in all fields of learning, a good compiler, and a worshipful renunciant who transmitted from Aḥmad some good discussions of legal problems.

Al-Dāraquṭnī said, "Ibrāhīm al-Ḥarbī was on a par with Aḥmad ibn Ḥanbal in renunciation, learning, and scrupulosity."

100.8 [Al-Ashyab:] A man once said to Ibrāhīm al-Ḥarbī, "How did you manage to collect all these books?"

"With blood and toil!" Ibrāhīm replied angrily. "Blood and toil!"

100.9 [ʿAbd Allāh:] My father used to tell me, "Go to Ibrāhīm al-Ḥarbī and have him dictate the *Book of Dividing Inheritances* for you."

['Abd Allāh ibn Aḥmad ibn Zayd:] Abū 'Alī l-Ḥusayn ibn Qahm once said to me, at the mention of Ibrāhim al-Ḥarbī, "By God, Abū Muḥammad, you'll never see another like him, at least not in this world. I've met people of learning and ability in every field, and studied with them, but never saw anyone as accomplished in all of them as he was." 100.10

[Ibn Durustuwayh:] Ibrāhīm al-Ḥarbī and Aḥmad ibn Yaḥyā Tha'lab once met, and Tha'lab said to Ibrāhīm, "When is it all right to do without meeting other scholars?" 100.11

"When one knows what they've said," answered Ibrāhīm, "and what positions they've supported."

Ibrāhīm al-Ḥarbī died in Baghdad in 285 [898–99]. Yūsuf ibn Ya'qūb al-Qāḍī prayed over him, and a great number of people attended the funeral. He was buried in his house, and his grave is known today and visited for blessings.

Muhanna' ibn Yaḥyā l-Shāmī. Related Hadith citing Yazīd ibn Hārūn and 'Abd al-Razzāq. A major figure among Aḥmad's associates. Aḥmad respected him and gave him the consideration due him as a student of long standing. He would tire him out with his incessant questions, but Aḥmad would bear it patiently. Al-Dāraquṭnī called him a trustworthy and upstanding authority. 100.18

Selected Members of the Second Generation

Aḥmad ibn Muḥammad ibn Hārūn Abū Bakr al-Khallāl. Dedicated himself to collecting the knowledge transmitted by Aḥmad ibn Ḥanbal. Traveling for that purpose, he documented Aḥmad's teachings both with few intermediaries and with many intermediaries,[544] and compiled a number of works, including his *Compendium* in some two hundred quires. None of Aḥmad's other associates accomplished anything on that scale. His study circle was in the mosque of al-Mahdī. He died before the Friday prayer on the third of Rabī' I 311 [June 20, 923]. 100.22

Al-Ḥasan ibn 'Alī ibn Khalaf, Abū Muḥammad al-Barbahārī. Combined learning and renunciation. Was an associate of al-Marrūdhī 100.23

and Sahl al-Tustarī. He renounced seventy thousand dirhams left him by his father on account of misgivings he had about its permissibility. He was severe in his denunciations of innovators, who eventually managed to turn the authorities against him. He moved from Muḥawwal Gate, where he had been staying, to the East Side, where Tūzūn's sister hid him in her house. After he had been there a month, he died of a hemorrhage.[545] The woman sent her servant to find someone to wash his corpse, then locked all the doors so no one would know the body was there. The corpse-washer arrived, washed the corpse, and stood praying alone over the body. Suddenly the woman looked up and saw that the house was full of men dressed in green and white. Summoning the servant, she asked, "Did you let them in?"

"My lady," he replied, "did you see what I saw?"

"I did!"

"Well, here are the keys; the door is still locked."

Hearing this, she told them to bury al-Barbahārī in the house. "When I die," she added, "bury me near him."

He was accordingly buried in the house, and when she died she was buried there as well. The place is in al-Mukharrim, near the royal palace.

I read a report in the handwriting of my teacher Abū l-Ḥasan al-Zāghūnī saying, "The grave of Abū Muḥammad al-Barbahārī was opened and his body found whole and undecayed. From the grave came a scent of perfume that filled the City of Salvation."[546]

Selected Members of the Third Generation

100.35 *ʿAbd al-ʿAzīz ibn Jaʿfar ibn Aḥmad, Abū Bakr, the Disciple of al-Khallāl.* Recited Hadith citing Muḥammad ibn ʿUthmān ibn Abī Shaybah, Mūsā ibn Hārūn, Qāsim al-Muṭarriz, and Abū l-Qāsim al-Baghawī, among many others. He is the author of several large and well-executed compilations. He died in Shawwāl 363 [June–July 974].

[Abū Yaʿlā:] I have heard that during his final illness, ʿAbd al-ʿAzīz ibn Jaʿfar said, "I'll be here with you until Friday."

Those around him wished him a speedy recovery, but he replied: "I heard Abū Bakr al-Khallāl say that he heard Abū Bakr al-Marrūdhī say, 'Aḥmad ibn Ḥanbal lived seventy-eight years, died on a Friday, and was buried after the ritual prayer.' Abū Bakr al-Marrūdhī himself lived seventy-eight years, died on a Friday, and was buried after the ritual prayer. And Abū Bakr al-Khallāl lived seventy-eight years, died on a Friday, and was buried after the ritual prayer. Now I'm seventy-eight, and I'll be here with you until Friday."

When Friday came he died. He was buried after the ritual prayer.

'Ubayd Allāh ibn Muḥammad ibn Muḥammad ibn Ḥamdān, Abū 'Abd Allāh ibn Baṭṭah al-'Ukbarī. Heard reports from al-Baghawī, Ibn Ṣā'id, and many others. He traveled extensively in search of Hadith. He was gifted with a generous share of learning and piety. 100.37

[Al-Lu'lu'ī:] After Abū 'Abd Allāh ibn Baṭṭah returned from his travels, he remained at home for forty years, during which he was never once seen at a market, nor ever seen to break his fast except on the Festival of Sacrifice and the Festival of Fast-Breaking. He constantly exhorted others to right action. Whenever he was told anything bad about anyone, he would change the story before repeating it.

[Al-'Atīqī:] Abū 'Abd Allāh ibn Baṭṭah died in Muḥarram 387 [January–February 997]. He was a righteous elder whose prayers were answered.

[Al-'Ukbarī:] We buried him on 'Āshūrā' [Muḥarram 10, 387/January 23, 997].

Muḥammad ibn Aḥmad Abū l-Ḥusayn ibn Sam'ūn. Unique in his day in his leading others to the remembrance of God. Generous in his gifts of learning, practice, and manifestations of grace. I have collected reports about him, and most of the others in this chapter, in my *Account of the Elite*. As I dislike repeating myself when I write, I will not provide complete biographies here, only short comments. 100.38

Al-Ḥasan ibn Ḥāmid Abū 'Abd Allāh. The leader of those who followed Aḥmad's way in this generation, and the author of many 100.40

large-scale compilations. He died on the Mecca road near Wāqiṣah after his return from the pilgrimage of 403 [ca. June 1013]. Shortly before his death, he was leaning against some rocks and a man approached him with some water. Though about to expire, al-Ḥasan asked, "Where did you get this?"[547]

"This is hardly the time to ask," said the man.

"On the contrary," said al-Ḥasan. "What better time than before I face God?"

Selected Members of the Fourth Generation

100.43 *Muḥammad ibn ʿAlī ibn al-Fatḥ, Abū Ṭālib al-ʿUshārī.* A prolific transmitter and a man of abundant religious feeling.

I heard my teacher ʿAbd al-Wahhāb al-Ḥāfiẓ say, "Abū Ṭālib al-ʿUshārī once went out on a day of unrest when no one was safe. He was accosted by a Turk who asked him, 'What have you got to give me?'

"'Nothing,' he said.

"The Turk walked off but Abū Ṭālib called him back. 'I have to tell you,' he said, 'that our stock in trade is being honest. I have two dirhams—take them!'

"The Turk not only left him unmolested but found out where he lived and extended protection to the whole neighborhood in appreciation of his honesty."

From the Fifth Generation

100.44 *The judge Abū Yaʿlā Muḥammad ibn al-Ḥusayn ibn Muḥammad ibn Khalaf ibn al-Farrāʾ.* Heard much Hadith, and studied legal reasoning with Abū ʿAbd Allāh ibn Ḥāmid. To him passed the knowledge of Aḥmad's way in his generation. He authored numerous compilations on the principles of jurisprudence and on particular applications of the law. He had many students. He was a man of propriety and integrity, and discerning in matters of law. He served as a judge and dictated Hadith in the mosque of al-Manṣūr from the chair formerly occupied by Ibn Ḥanbal's son ʿAbd Allāh. Vast crowds attended his sessions, and three men—Abū Muḥammad ibn Jābir, Abū Manṣūr ibn al-Anbāri, and Abū ʿAlī l-Baradānī—worked as his repeaters.[548] He died on Sunday night between the two night prayers and was buried on Monday, the nineteenth of Ramadan 458 [August 14, 1066]. So many people attended his funeral that a good number succumbed to the heat and had to break their fast.

Selected Members of the Sixth Generation

Abū Jaʿfar ʿAbd al-Khāliq ibn ʿĪsā l-Hāshimī. Heard much Hadith from Abū l-Qāsim ibn Bishrān, Abū Muḥammad al-Khallāl, Abū Isḥāq al-Barmakī, al-ʿUshārī, Ibn al-Mudhhib, and others, and studied jurisprudence with Judge Abū Yaʿlā. He was a jurisprudent and compiler, and a pious and self-restrained man. He was certified by Judge Abū Yaʿlā and served Abū ʿAbd Allāh al-Dāmaghānī as a notary-witness but stopped before he died. He taught at a mosque in the Ragdealer's Alley near the Basra Gate and at the mosque of al-Manṣūr, then moved to the East Side, where he taught at a mosque across from the caliphal palace. In '66, after the flooding of the Muʿallā Canal, he moved to the Archway Gate, settling in Dīwān Street in al-Ruṣāfah and teaching in the mosque there as well as the mosque of al-Mahdī. He also convened sessions where speculative discussions took place. 100.46

When Judge Abū Yaʿlā was on his deathbed he asked ʿAbd al-Khāliq to wash his corpse. Later, when the Caliph al-Qāʾim bi-Amr Allāh was on his deathbed, he made the same request. ʿAbd al-Khāliq did as he was asked but took nothing from the palace. He was told that the caliph had made him numerous bequests, but he refused to take anything. Finally they offered him the caliph's shirt, saying he could gain a blessing from it. In response, he took his own waist-cloth, dried the body with it, and said, "Now I've got the caliph's blessing." He was then summoned by al-Muqtadī to offer the oath of allegiance on the spot. ʿAbd al-Khāliq tendered his oath alone.[549] 100.47

When al-Qushayrī's boy came to Baghdad and unrest broke out, ʿAbd al-Khāliq, who was severe in his treatment of innovators, 100.48

fought to keep them down, and succeeded, though he was arrested and jailed.[550] Hearing that he was in jail, the people raised an outcry. ʿAbd al-Khāliq was removed to the Harem of Ṭāhir on the West Side and died there on Thursday, the fifteenth of Ṣafar 470 [September 7, 1077], a day long remembered. He was buried in a grave next to Aḥmad's. People spent days and nights by the gravesite. It is said that within months the Qur'an had been read there in its entirety more than ten thousand times.

Someone saw ʿAbd al-Khāliq in a dream and asked how he had fared. "When they buried me," he replied, "I saw a dome of white pearl with three doors, and I head a voice say, 'This is yours; enter by whichever door you wish!'"

Another dreamer who saw him asked the same question and was told, "I met Aḥmad ibn Ḥanbal, and he told me, 'You've fought the good fight for God, and He's pleased with you.'"

100.55 *Abū Bakr Aḥmad ibn ʿAlī ibn Aḥmad al-ʿUlabī.* Among those renowned for righteousness and renunciation. He heard Hadith and studied some of our jurisprudence with Judge Abū Yaʿlā. He worked for a time plastering walls with his own two hands before giving that up and staying permanently at the mosque, teaching others to read the Qur'an and leading worshippers in prayer. He guarded his person and would accept nothing from anyone. Every night he would go by himself to the Tigris and fill a pitcher with water for his breakfast. He would run all his own errands rather than send someone else.

Whenever he went on the pilgrimage, he would visit the graves in Mecca. At the grave of al-Fuḍayl ibn ʿIyāḍ, he would draw his stick across the ground and say, "Here, Lord! Here!" In 503 [1109–10] he went out to perform the pilgrimage. On the way, he had twice fallen off his camel. He lived long enough to stand at ʿArafah in his pilgrim's garb, but died that evening[551] in ʿArafāt. His body was taken to Mecca and carried around the Kaʿbah, then buried on the Day of Sacrifice next to the tomb of al-Fuḍayl ibn ʿIyāḍ.

Abū l-Wafā' 'Alī ibn 'Aqīl ibn Muḥammad ibn 'Aqīl al-Baghdādī. Heir of the school's expertise in both the principles and the applications of jurisprudence. He was possessed of a piquant turn of mind, a penetrating intelligence, and the sharp eyes and sharp wits that Baghdadis are famous for. Anyone who peruses his compilations or reads the reflections and experiences he describes in his book *Varieties*, in two hundred bound sections, will second my appreciation of the man. I have so far managed to get a hold of some 150 volumes. He heard Hadith from Abū Bakr ibn Bishrān, Abū l-Fatḥ ibn Shīṭā, Abū Muḥammad al-Jawharī, Judge Abū Ya'lā, and others. He was born in 430 [1038–39], or according to some others, 431 [1039–40], and died in 513 [1119–20]. 100.57

Selected Members of the Seventh Generation

Muḥammad ibn Abī Ṭāhir ibn 'Abd al-Bāqī ibn Muḥammad ibn 'Abd Allāh ibn Muḥammad ibn 'Abd al-Raḥmān ibn al-Rabī' ibn Thābit ibn Wahb ibn Mashja'ah ibn al-Ḥārith ibn 'Abd Allāh ibn Ka'b ibn Mālik al-Anṣārī (one of the three Helpers who stayed behind).[552] Born in Safar of '42 [June–July 1050] in al-Karkh. He used to say, "When I was born my father brought in one astrologer and my mother brought in another. They took my horoscope and agreed that I would live for fifty-two years. But here I am in my tenth decade!" 100.60

He is the last to have transmitted Hadith citing Abū Isḥāq al-Barmakī, Abū l-Ṭayyib al-Ṭabarī, Abū Ṭālib al-'Ushārī, Abū l-Ḥasan al-Bāqillānī, Abū Muḥammad al-Jawharī, and others. He used to say, "I memorized the Qur'an at the age of seven, and there's no branch of learning I haven't studied, either completely or in part. I don't think I've wasted a single hour of my life with distractions or diversions."

He was unique in his mastery of mathematics and inheritance calculation. I went to see him when he was ninety-three, and he hadn't lost any of his faculties. He died before noon on Wednesday, the second of Rajab 535 [February 11–12, 1141], and was buried near

Bishr al-Ḥāfī. He spent the last three days of his life tirelessly reciting the Qur'an.

Selected Figures from the Eighth Generation

100.63 *Abū l-Barakāt ʿAbd al-Wahhāb ibn al-Mubārak al-Anmāṭī.* Of all the Hadith teachers I have seen, he had heard the most reports and copied the most despite knowing them by heart. I never had a teacher who corrected our reading more patiently, or one more likely to be moved to tears despite his customary cheerfulness and the warm welcome he extended. He was born in Rajab '62 [April–May 1070] and died in Muḥarram 538 [July–August 1143]. He is buried in al-Shūnīziyyah.

100.64 *Abū Bakr Aḥmad ibn Muḥammad ibn Aḥmad al-Dīnawarī.* Studied jurisprudence with Abū l-Khaṭṭāb al-Kalwadhānī and excelled in it. He also outdid his fellows in disputation to the point that Asʿad al-Mīhanī said of him, "Abū Bakr al-Dīnawarī never saw an argument he couldn't poke a hole in." Whenever the righteous were mentioned, he would break down and weep, saying "Learned men have some standing with God, and perhaps . . ."[553] I began attending his lectures after the death of my teacher Abū l-Ḥasan al-Zāghūnī and continued with him for some four years. He once recited to me:

The things a scholar needs are six.
  Here's a list of them in rhyme:
Brains, drive, ripe age, poverty,
  His teacher's help, and time.[554]

100.65 He also recited to me:

You want to be well versed in law
  And a whiz at disputation,
But without much work, or pain, or toil:
  Now there's a mental aberration!
To make a dirham, as you know,
  Means work and toil and pain;

Why should the learning that you seek
Be an easier thing to gain?[555]

He died in 532 [1137–38] and was buried near Aḥmad's grave.

Abū Muḥammad ʿAbd Allāh ibn ʿAlī ibn Aḥmad al-Muqriʾ. Heard much Hadith and could read the Qur'an in many variant readings, on which he authored well-executed compilations. He had some knowledge in the sciences of the Arabic language. I never heard anyone recite more beautifully, perfectly, or correctly. He was a strong Sunni who spent his whole life alone in his mosque. He was born in Shaʿbān '64 [April–May 1072] and died Monday, the twenty-eighth of Rabīʿ II 541 [October 7, 1146]. Countless people attended his funeral—more than I have ever seen attend for anyone. 100.67

Abū l-Faḍl Muḥammad ibn Nāṣir ibn Muḥammad ibn ʿAlī. He was born in Shaʿbān of '67 [March–April 1075]. He heard much Hadith and was gifted with a good deal of knowledge in that field. He also studied linguistics with Abū Zakariyyā. It is through him that God guided me toward a life of learning. When I was young he worked hard to bring me with him to the study circles. I first heard Aḥmad's *Authenticated Reports*, as well as collections of prized Hadith with short transmission chains,[556] when he read them aloud for Ibn al-Ḥuṣayn. At the time I had no idea what it meant to be involved in learning from a young age. He would check to make sure I understood everything I heard. I studied with him for thirty years and never learned as much from anyone else. He died in Shaʿbān of 550 [September–October 1155]. God be pleased with him! 100.68

Selected Figures from the Ninth Generation

Abū Ḥakīm Ibrāhīm ibn Dīnār al-Nahrawānī. Met Abū l-Khaṭṭāb al-Kalwādhānī and other teachers. Studied jurisprudence, engaged in disputation, and heard much Hadith. He was deft at calculating inheritances. He was a learned man who put what he knew into effect. He was given to fasting and worship, and he was extremely humble, preferring to be ignored. His forbearance and 100.71

self-deprecation became proverbial; indeed I never saw anyone like him in that respect. He died Tuesday, the twenty-third of Jumādā II 556 [June 19–20, 1161], and was buried on Wednesday morning near Bishr al-Ḥāfī.

100.72 If we had mentioned all the figures in each generation, or written complete biographies of the men we have listed, the book would have grown much longer. We have therefore confined ourself to mentioning only the most prominent figures in each generation and saying a few words about the sort of people they were. We give God our thanks and to Him direct our pleas for help.

Here ends the book. We give praise to God always, and ask Him to bless and save Muḥammad, the unlettered[557] Prophet and the best of His creation, and his family and Companions.

[Colophons]

[Colophon of H:] Copying completed by Maḥfūẓ ibn ʿIsā ibn Maḥfūẓ al-Zamlakānī, who read aloud for correction by the elder exemplar and jurisprudent Abū Muḥammad ʿAbd al-Raḥmān ibn ʿAbd Allāh from a copy of the original written by the author, the elder, exemplar, unique scholar, and pillar of the *sunnah*, Jamāl al-Dīn Abū l-Faraj ʿAbd al-Raḥmān ibn ʿAlī ibn Muḥammad ibn ʿAlī ibn al-Jawzī, on Tuesday, the nineteenth of Shaʿbān 566 [April 27, 1171]. May God bless Muḥammad, the Seal of the Prophets, and his noble family and Companions. 101.1

[Colophon of D:] Completed before noon on Monday, the third of Dhu l-Qaʿdah 599 [July 14, 1203]. May God bless our master, the Prophet Muḥammad, and his pristine family and Companions. 101.2

[Colophon of SH:] Completed on Saturday, the twentieth of the holy month of Ramadan 850 [December 9, 1446], by Maḥmūd ibn Muḥammad ibn ʿUmar al-Shishīnī, a Shāfiʿī in law, and an inadequate, unworthy, and supplicant servant of God needful of the mercy of his great and mighty Lord. May God forgive him, his parents, and anyone who reads any of this work and prays that God forgive him and be merciful unto him, whether he be living or dead. This work was completed in Mecca, at the Salām Gate under the porticos facing the Holy Mosque. Praise is God's alone. May God bless and keep our master, the Prophet Muḥammad, and his family and Companions. 101.3

NOTES

1 On Ibn Ḥanbal as “an indispensable authority and resource for the fashioning of authentically Muslim selves,” see Sizgorich, *Violence and Belief*, 231–71 (quote at 237).

2 This is the most common voweling (al-Dhahabī, *Al-Mushtabih*, 491) though al-Muʿaddil is also possible (Ibn Ḥajar, *Tabṣīr*, 1299). For the meanings of this root and its derivatives, see Tyan, “*ʿAdl*” and sources cited.

3 The beginning of a new chain of transmitters that will intersect with the previous one is sometimes indicated by the letter *ḥāʾ*. As the usage is inconsistent, I have not duplicated it.

4 Not otherwise attested but possibly a variant of Mihrāwī, “of Mihrawān,” a region near Hamadhān (al-Samʿānī, *Al-Ansāb*, 5:415). Al-Turkī emends to the more common al-Harawī (of Herat).

5 The capital of what was then the province of Khurasan. Marv, now called Mary, is today a city in west-central Turkmenistan.

6 “Full-blooded” means that he was born into the tribe, as opposed to joining it by entering into a patronage relationship with one of its members, as non-Arab converts to Islam sometimes did (though far less commonly than previously thought). See Bernards and Nawas, eds., *Patronate*, esp. Bulliet, “Conversion-Based Patronage,” 246–62.

7 Ibn Ḥanbal’s ancestors had come from Arabia and settled in the newly founded city of Basra, then moved east with the Arab conquests and settled in Marv.

8 A major province of the Abbasid Empire. It included the regions today called northeastern Iran, northern Afghanistan, southern Turkmenistan, and southern Uzbekistan.

9 A town that lay on what is today the border between Iran and Turkmenistan. The modern town is on the Iranian side.

10 The revolution that brought the Abbasid dynasty to power began in the 740s in Khurasan. Those who joined it, and their descendants, enjoyed particular privileges under the new regime. Though Ibn Ḥanbal's uncle Isḥāq was later to invoke this connection, it evidently "meant nothing to Ibn Ḥanbal himself" (Cook, *Commanding Right*, 111).

11 Dhū l-Qarnayn is a figure in the Qur'an (Q Kahf 18:83ff.) sometimes identified with Alexander the Great. Hadith reports in which the Prophet Muḥammad gives personal advice based on detailed knowledge of future events are generally agreed to be later fabrications; see al-Turkī, *Manāqib*, 2nd ed., 15n4.

12 For discussion of Ibn Ḥanbal's lineage and its social meanings, see Hurvitz, *Formation*, 27ff., and Cook, *Commanding Right*, 110–11. Another source, Ibn al-Dāʿī, gives a different lineage for Ibn Ḥanbal, calling him a member of the clan of Zuhayr ibn Ḥurqūṣ. This ancestry would appear to link him with the Khārijī Ḥurqūṣ ibn Zuhayr, as well as with an obscure group of sectarians called the Hurqūṣiyyah, who seem to have held a view of God denounced by critics as anthropomorphic (van Ess, *Theologie*, 3:449–51).

13 This is the prophet Abraham.

14 Al-Turkī takes the subject here to be ʿAbd al-Malik and emends the text to *ʿalayhi* and *yuḍīfuhum*: "He would show them hospitality." Although this reading does seem more plausible, I have retained the feminine forms that appear in SH and D and translated accordingly.

15 The "One-Eyed Tigris" (*dijlah al-ʿawrāʾ*) is an old name for the waterway now called Shatt al-Arab, where the Tigris and Euphrates converge and empty into the Persian Gulf. But the Shatt al-Arab flows past Basra, not Baghdad. The reference may therefore be to the

family's ancestral home in Basra. Yet the context suggests that what is meant is a place in Baghdad, perhaps the Upper Harbor, where the Trench of Ṭāhir joined the Tigris (Cook, *Commanding Right*, 108n96, and Le Strange, *Baghdad*, map 5). A place in the southeastern Iraqi province of Maysān was called Rijlat al-ʿAwrāʾ (Ibn Manẓūr, *Lisān*, *ʿ-W-R*).

16 Or possibly "how well he carries himself when he goes out."

17 Literally, "I began frequenting the *dīwān*," perhaps the courier and intelligence service, which was headed by his paternal uncle. The following reports may represent memories of his unwillingness to work there (Hurvitz, *Formation*, 30, and Melchert, *Ahmad*, 3). *Dīwān* can also mean registry of persons entitled to a pension, which Ibn Ḥanbal might have been, given his grandfather's service to the state (Hurvitz, *Formation*, 27 and 170n12).

18 *Ṭāq*: usually "arch," but here evidently an arched recess with a shelf in it; see Anvarī, *Farhang*, under *ṭāqche* and *ṭāq* (2), definition 3.

19 Evidently the uniform worn by official couriers.

20 In later life, Ibn Ḥanbal shunned representatives of the state, either because he considered the Abbasid dynasty illegitimate, or because he questioned their use of public funds, or both. It seems odd for him to have held this view as a child (Hurvitz, *Formation*, 42).

21 To judge by his punctuation, al-Turkī takes this to mean "As if I would do that!"

22 Q Baqarah 2:156, which describes the long-suffering as "those who, when affliction strikes them, say, 'We are of God and to Him we return.'"

23 *Tawarraʿ*, translated here as "to have scruples," more specifically means to refrain from acts permitted in themselves but which might accidentally entail a violation of God's commandments. Perhaps Ibn Ḥanbal does not want to deliver the dispatches because he does not know what is in them, or perhaps he had already come to believe that contact with representatives of the Abbasid regime for any reason was bad. See chapter 49 of this book, and further Ibn Ḥanbal, *Kitāb al-Waraʿ*; Kinberg, "What is Meant by *Zuhd*"; Cooperson, *Classical*, 112–17.

24 Ibn Ḥanbal, like present-day speakers of Arabic, counted his age from one instead of zero as one does in English. Here, then, he would be nineteen in English rather than twenty. I thank Omar Issa Attar for pointing this out to me.

25 This and several subsequent chapters contain a great many personal names. In most cases, they are the names of Ibn Ḥanbal's fellow Hadith-men. Recurring names of particular importance are listed in the key figures section at the end of the book. Background information essential to understanding a particular story is included in the notes.

26 The jurist Abū Yūsuf (d. 182/798), a disciple of Abū Ḥanīfah, based his verdicts on *ra'y* (reason, judgment, opinion) rather than Hadith and served as judge under al-Rashīd. In both these respects—use of *ra'y* and service to the state—Abū Yūsuf took positions entirely opposed to those later advocated by Ibn Ḥanbal. Ibn Ḥanbal thus appears to have been rather more open-minded in his youth than he was to become in later life, when he evidently tried to downplay his association with Abū Yūsuf (Hurvitz, *Formation*, 44–49).

27 As in English, speakers often abbreviate dates. In this chapter, the missing element is always 100.

28 Here Ibn Ḥanbal is using the death dates of well-known Hadith transmitters to date the events of his life. Death dates were important because they helped establish whether Transmitter A could have heard reports from Transmitter B.

29 These titles refer to collections of Hadith reports on particular topics, in this case the proper conduct of funerals and the correct performance of the pilgrimage rites. Hushaym may have been unusual in his practice of teaching Hadith by category (Melchert, *Ahmad*, 33). On funerals as occasions for the negotiation of boundaries between faith communities, see Sizgorich, *Violence and Belief*, 238–62.

30 A town near the Mediterranean coast in what is today southeastern Turkey. In this period, it lay on or near the Byzantine frontier, and thus attracted ascetics (such as Ibn al-Mubārak) and other Muslims who wished to prove themselves against the Byzantines.

31 The years referred to here correspond to 795–808 of the Gregorian calendar.

32 At the end of the prayer, most Muslims turn to the right and then to the left, each time pronouncing the greeting *al-salāmu ʿalaykum wa-raḥmatu l-lāh* ("peace be upon you and the mercy of God"). Some, however, say it only once, to the right, a practice that Ibn Ḥanbal finds unusual.

33 Practicing *kalām* (literally, "talking"), or speculative theology. Ibn Ḥanbal, at least in his mature years, roundly rejected the practice (see chapter 13 of this book), though he may have been more accepting of it early in his career (Hurvitz, *Formation*, 45ff.).

34 A name of Hudbah ibn Khālid al-Qaysī (Ibn Ḥajar, *Tabṣīr*, 1451).

35 Here a variant text adds "And I went in '95"; see al-Turkī, *Manāqib*, 2nd ed., 31n4.

36 These years correspond to the period AD 802 to 815 or 816.

37 A distance of approximately 950 kilometers or 590 miles (http://www.mapcrow.info).

38 This report is an unusually transparent invention. There is no other reference to Ibn Ḥanbal's traveling by sea, much less being shipwrecked. The topos of the gnomic graffito, often translated from an ancient language, is common in premodern Arabic tales (Crone and Moreh, *Book of Strangers*).

39 Two *rakʿah*s or sequences of movements and recitations. Ritual prayers consist of specified numbers of cycles (Toorawa, "Prayer").

40 The "station of Abraham," a place near the eastern wall of the Kaaba in Mecca. According to tradition, Abraham prayed there after building the shrine, leaving the rock he had been using as a step-stool to reach the upper part of the walls. Today the rock that stands on the spot is enclosed by a cupola.

41 Making a resolution (*niyyah*) is a legally meaningful act, as when, for example, one declares (mentally) one's intention to pray.

42 That is, Ibn Sinān sold the fur on Ibn Ḥanbal's behalf and gave him the proceeds to use as spending money.

43 Al-Raqqah is a town on the upper Euphrates, located in what is now eastern Syria.

44 *Jubbah* is defined as "a coat-like outer garment worn by both sexes" and translated "tunic" (Y.K. Stillman, "Libās"). A *jubbah* of felt would presumably have been scratchy and uncomfortable. As the next line suggests, some *jubab* were evidently padded.

45 This name, though given fully voweled in H, is not otherwise attested. It may be a variant of al-ʿIrfī, which is attested; see al-Samʿānī, *Al-Ansāb* 4:180; cf. al-Dhahabī, *Al-Mushtabih*, 357.

46 *Mudhākarah*: the practice of "instructive conversation ... in which the parties ... exchanged their knowledge to their mutual benefit, as well as to that of the audience, if any." A *mudhākarah* could also become a contest in which speakers would respond to challenges from the audience or from each other (Makdisi, "Rise of Humanism," 208–9; Schoeler, *Genesis*, 42).

47 Sulaymān ibn Dāwūd al-Shādhakūnī, also called Ibn al-Shādhakūnī, a name apparently meaning "maker of Yemenī quilts" (see 45.4).

48 It seems that Khalaf was sitting on a platform, bench, or stoop, and Ibn Ḥanbal could have joined him there, or on some corresponding item of masonry or furniture, but chose to sit on the ground.

49 The first part of this sentence may also mean "I named Hadith reports to him and he supplied them with alternative *isnād*s." I thank Christopher Melchert and Geert Jan van Gelder for their help with this passage.

50 That is, Ibn Ḥanbal could provide the *isnād* of each report when he heard it, but al-Muʿayṭī was afraid to try for fear of making a mistake. I thank Christopher Melchert for improving my translation of this passage.

51 A quire is "any gathering or set of sheets forming part of a complete manuscript or printed book" (*OED*), which seems a reasonable equivalent of *juzʾ*, literally "part," here evidently meaning a list of reports that might later be sewn up with other similar lists to form a volume.

52 Very conjecturally taking one *ḥiml* to be 266 kilograms; see Ashtor, "Mawāzīn (1)." Ibn Ḥanbal would have left 3225 kilograms (7330 pounds) of paper.

53 I thank Christopher Melchert for checking my reading of this passage.

54 Ibn Ḥanbal here uses *kalām* ("speech, talking, what someone says") to refer to the content of a report. The (apparently later) technical term is *matn*.

55 That is, one whose hair had not yet turned white.

56 On how Ibn Ḥanbal served to police the boundary between Muslims and non-Muslims, see Sizgorich, *Violence and Belief*, 242–55.

57 My translation of this passage is based on a personal communication from Devin Stewart.

58 Ibn ʿAqīl (d. 513/1119) was a famous jurist and theologian of the Ḥanbalī school. The remainder of this chapter consists of remarks attributed to him, evidently copied by Ibn al-Jawzī from an unidentified written work.

59 This paragraph was kindly translated for me by Joseph Lowry.

60 Ibn Ḥanbal reasons that two circumambulations on foot are equivalent to one performed on all fours.

61 That is, he would not be liable for that amount of her value added because of her ability to sing. Having established this principle by referring to cases of usurpation, Ibn Ḥanbal applies it to a case of inheritance. The translation and explanation of this passage are based on personal communications from Devin Stewart and Joseph Lowry.

62 In assessments of merit, *ghaḍḍa min* normally means "to disparage," but if this meaning is adopted the sentence would mean the opposite of what Ibn al-Jawzī clearly intends to say. The copyists also seem to have been unsure of the sense. Al-Turkī tries to solve the problem by using punctuation to indicate a rhetorical question. Technically, however, this would require an interrogative particle of some kind. I am grateful to Tahera Qutbuddin for suggesting that the verb be understood in the literal sense of "avert one's eyes."

63 Yazīd, following Ḥajjāj, evidently thinks that the lender, by giving up his property without expectation of profit (as would be the case if he

had sold or lent it) has no right to be compensated if the item is lost or destroyed. Ibn Ḥanbal does not respond to the implied argument but instead cites a Hadith attributing to the Prophet a different view. The translation and explanation of this passage are based on a personal communication from Joseph Lowry.

64 *Al-ʿirq al-madīnī*: a parasitic infection known since antiquity and still endemic in a few countries in Africa. The guinea worm, whose larvae enter the body through contaminated water, causes a painful blister as it emerges from the leg or foot (*Wikipedia*, "Dracunculiasis," accessed May 5, 2013, http://en.wikipedia.org/wiki/Dracunculiasis).

65 These telegraphic phrases suggest that Yazīd came to visit Ibn Ḥanbal after the latter had moved from Wāsiṭ back to Baghdad. By "outside," Ibn Ḥanbal may mean outside Ḥarbiyyah, the northwest Baghdad district where his family was based.

66 *Arwaʿ*: more careful in avoiding *shubuhāt*, that is, things or actions permissible in themselves, but dubious by association with a suspected source of illegality or pollution, for example, a gift of food or money from someone whose source of income is unknown (Cooperson, *Classical*, 112–17).

67 "The restorer of religion and justice who, according to a widely held Muslim belief, will rule before the end of the world" (Madelung, "Mahdī").

68 The sea is apparently the proverbial sea of knowledge. Ibn Ḥanbal is therefore a sea creature, albeit one who walks on land. In the other version, he is a land animal that may as well be a fish.

69 An obscure figure, possibly believed to exist only because of a confusion of names, evidently cited here because he is credited for having said "I fought beside the Prophet and killed ninety-nine pagans, but I am not pleased to have killed them, or to have exposed any Muslim." See Ibn al-Athīr, *Usd al-ghābah*, 1:186.

70 The narrator seems to have forgotten that he was supposed to be presenting the paper, or perhaps he refused to do so and has omitted to say so. Alternatively, the preceding "give" (*aʿṭihi*) might be read as a

first-person jussive (*uʿṭihi*) "let me give," though such a form would be unusual here.

71 The Arabic is a general word meaning (among other things) "cover." More specifically it can be a lid (e.g., of an inkpot; see Gacek, *Arabic Manuscripts*, 135) and a wrapper for musical instruments (Dwight Reynolds, personal communication). Here it may refer to a folder or envelope for carrying documents (Nuha Khoury, personal communication). It may, however, also refer to a stack of paper of a certain size (Gacek, *Arabic Manuscripts*, 35; cf. the modern term *ṭabqat waraq* in Clarity et al., *Dictionary of Iraqi Arabic*). Given the various possibilities, I have chosen the vague term "sheaf" in the sense of a "cluster or bundle of things tied up together; a quantity of things set thick together" (*OED*). Cf. also the *kharīṭah* in which Ibn Ḥanbal carries his *kutub* (4.20).

72 Among proto-Sunnis, to support the community (*al-jamāʿah*) meant preferring unity over schism, meaning (for example) that one should accept all past caliphs as legitimate rulers. This position distinguished the proto-Sunnis from groups such as the Shiʿa and the Khawārij.

73 Most of the reports in this chapter are intended to show that Ibn Ḥanbal transmitted certain Hadith-reports, many of them reports of special significance to the early Sunni movement. As the points at issue are explained elsewhere in this book, I have retained only those reports that describe Ibn Ḥanbal directly.

74 There are several versions of this report as told by these transmitters. All say that the Prophet saw his Lord in the form of a young, beardless boy. Some commentators explain "seeing" figuratively rather than literally. See al-Turkī, *Manāqib*, 2nd ed., 110n1, and Williams, "Aspects of the Creed."

75 This chapter is simply a list of names and I have omitted all of it except for the last section, which names several of the women in Ibn Ḥanbal's circle.

76 *Atqā*: having more *taqwā*, or what in this period seems to have been a kind of intense anxiety intended to prevent complacency (Melchert, "Exaggerated Fear").

77 On writing Hadith, see Cook, "Opponents," Melchert, *Ahmad*, 24–33, and Schoeler, *Genesis*, 47–50.

78 The Apostasy was the abandonment of Islam by certain Arab tribes after the death of the Prophet; Abū Bakr brought them back into the fold by force. For more on this theme, see Sizgorich, *Violence and Belief*, 23–38.

79 ʿAlī was condemned for giving in to the Inquisition.

80 An odd thing to say. The gold would not go into the bellows (*kīr*), which supplies air, but into or onto the furnace, where it is extracted, or the forge, where it is heated in order to be worked. In premodern times, gold would often acquire a reddish color because of impurities in the smelting process (*Wikipedia*, "Colored Gold," accessed April 5, 2013, http://en.wikipedia.org/wiki/Colored_gold), though Bishr may be thinking of red-hot gold.

81 A reference to the various prophets who speak truth to power (e.g., Mūsā/Moses before Pharaoh, Q Aʿrāf 7:103ff., Yūnus 10:75ff., Ṭā Hā 20:24ff.).

82 *Mutaʿabbid* (also *ʿābid*): a term used by the Hadith-men to refer to those who were not necessarily fellow scholars but practiced austerities and associated with renunciants like Bishr. By using this term to identify certain figures, Ibn Ḥanbal's biographers seem to be arguing indirectly that even the renunciants of Baghdad acknowledged Ibn Ḥanbal's superiority.

83 The point at issue here is "whether to raise the hands at saying *Allāh akbar*, an issue that separated the Ḥanabilah from the Ḥanafiyyah," the followers of Abū Ḥanīfah (Melchert, review of *Virtues*, 355).

84 Q Nūr 24:63.

85 *Izār*: "unsewn close-fitting garment wrapped round the waist and legs and extending upwards as far as the navel, and downwards as far as the middle of the leg or beyond" (Ahsan, *Social Life*, 34); "a large sheet-like wrap worn both as a mantle and a long loin cloth or waist cloth" (Stillman, "Libās").

86 A difficult and dubious passage. The manuscripts cannot be reconciled and none gives an entirely satisfactory reading. I have chosen

ḥaṭṭihā, "their bringing him low," that is, his being humiliated by the blows of the whip, because it can be read as antithetical to *ṭāra*, "he flew"; I have chosen *ʿināʾihā* "the suffering they caused him" because it plausibly completes the idea. Al-Turkī has *bi-ḥaẓẓihā wa-ghināʾihā*, by which he seems to understand "by the good fortune they brought him, and their obviating the need for any further accomplishment." I am not entirely satisfied with either of our suggestions.

87 The significance of having a twisted or rolled-up breechclout is unclear. It may have suggested austerity or lack of pretense. Ibn Ḥajar, *Fatḥ al-bārī*, no. 5456, mentions that a fringed breechclout might be rolled up to protect the fringe.

88 See Picken, "Ibn Ḥanbal and al-Muḥāsibī."

89 *Al-ʿaskar*, literally "the army camp," here referring to the Iraqi town that served as the Abbasid capital from 221/836 to 279/892. Ibn Ḥanbal and his family were brought there after the end of the Inquisition.

90 "Those people": the Abbasid officials carrying out the Inquisition, on which see chapter 66ff.

91 Abū Zurʿah (d. 264/877–88) died some twenty years after Ibn Ḥanbal, so I have put his recollections in the past tense, but the Arabic is ambiguous: he could have said all of this while Ibn Ḥanbal was still alive.

92 A likelier comment, though unattested here, is "The greatest champions of Islam have been Aḥmad ibn Ḥanbal during the Inquisition, Abū Bakr during the Apostasy," etc.

93 The Porch was the place where ʿUmar pushed through the nomination of Abū Bakr as caliph over the objections of the Medinans. ʿUthman, the third caliph, died fighting rebels who had besieged his house. Ṣiffīn was the site of the battle between ʿAlī and Muʿawiyah over the succession.

94 *Fāsiq*: that is, one who knows, or should know, the right thing to do, and does something else; sometimes rendered as "grave sinner."

95 Or, to take the variant reading: "He would confront the offender, having turned people against him."

96 Ibn Ḥajar, *Tahdhīb*, 1:343.

97 Apparently Ibn Ḥātim recited the reports from memory the first time, and read them from his notes the second time.

98 The point is that not praying for Ibn Ḥanbal is as bad as not joining Muslim fighters on the frontiers.

99 Ibrāhīm has evidently been asked a legal question, and Ibn al-Jawzī cites the answer in full since it contains a reference to Ibn Ḥanbal.

100 Instead of in front, as is normally done.

101 An allusion to two verses that describe those who believe in the Revelation (Q Āl ʿImrān 3:7 and Nisāʾ 4:162).

102 A reference to the Inquisition (see chapter 66ff.).

103 Q Āl ʿImrān 3:173; Māʾidah 5:104; Tawbah 9:59.

104 Al-Turkī declares this, along with the stories that appear in the following chapters, as absurd inventions unworthy of Ibn Ḥanbal, "who stuck close to his texts and rejected fictions and dream-stories," adding that "those who write his biography would do well to follow his lead" (*Manāqib*, 2nd ed., 190n2).

105 One of (usually) four figures, each associated with one of the cardinal points, occupying (in some accounts) the third rank in the hierarchy of secret Sufi saints (Goldziher, "Awtād"). Stories of this type appear to have been constructed in order to reconcile the sometimes conflicting claims of those Muslims who (like Ibn Ḥanbal) favored outward conformance to the law based on the literal reading of texts and those who (like the Sufis) privileged experience and encouraged the allegorical reading of texts. This story doubtless dates to a period later than that of al-Shāfiʿī, Ibn Ḥanbal, or Bishr ibn al-Ḥārith, in whose time Sufism was only beginning to emerge as a distinct tradition.

106 See Rippin, "Ṣiddīq."

107 Q Rūm 30:60.

108 *Abdāl* or *budalāʾ*: "one of the degrees in the *ṣūfī* hierarchical order of saints, who, unknown by the masses . . . participate by means of their powerful influence in the preservation of the order of the universe." Their name comes from the fact that "vacancies which occur in each of the classes are filled by the promotion to that class of a member

of the class immediately below it" (Goldziher and Kissling, "Abdāl"); cf. the Jewish legend of the thirty-six righteous men whose number must remain constant lest the world be destroyed (*Encyclopaedia Judaica*, "Lamed Vav Ẓaddikim"). I thank Jay Cooperson for this explanation. In Sufi thought, which was still nascent in Ibn Ḥanbal's time, there are different accounts of the number and ranking of the *abdāl*. Ḥanbalī biographers appear to have taken over the term—without troubling themselves about the technicalities—as a way of praising their heroes. On the relationship between early Ḥanbalism and early Sufism, see Melchert, "Ḥanābila."

109 That is, you need not fear that it has been wrongly taken from its source and thereby tainted—an important concern for practitioners of *wara'* (scrupulosity).

110 *Kāmakh*: a fermented grain condiment. Charles Perry has identified two basic varieties: "*kāmakh rijāl*, also called *kāmakh Baghdād*, which was semiliquid and tasted rather like Cheddar cheese, and *kāmakh aḥmar*, which was much the same but with a flavor like blue cheese" (personal communication).

111 Meter: *sarī'*.

112 A mangonel is a device for hurling large projectiles (Kennedy, *Armies*, index).

113 The word *'ilj*: a word that carries the connotations of being non-Arab, non-Muslim, physically formidable, and subordinate to, or fighting against, Muslims.

114 The idea is that praying for Ibn Ḥanbal would make the shot hit its target.

115 Apparently meaning to recite the Qur'an.

116 On arbitration as an alternative to consulting a *qāḍī*, or government-appointed judge, see Tillier, *Cadis d'Iraq*, 301–18.

117 On the problem of utterance, see below, chapter 20.

118 Ar. *murji'ah*: those who hold that latter-day Muslims cannot judge the Companions or resolve the disputes that divided them, and that any such resolution must be postponed until Judgment Day. They also argue (or are accused of arguing) that all believers have the same

amount of faith, making it possible for an ordinary Muslim to say that he is as faithful as the angel Gabriel. The standard Sunni position is that faith can increase or decrease, making it possible for some people to have more faith than others.

119 *Kāfir*: one who commits *kufr*, originally "ingratitude," and by extension refusal to believe in, or declare a belief in, God (see further Björkman, "Kāfir" and Adang, "Belief and Unbelief"). *Kāfir* is often translated as "unbeliever," but since that term has no particular resonance in modern English, I have decided in most cases to use "Ingrate," capitalized to indicate that the word is being used to enact a kind of formal condemnation. I have nevertheless retained "unbelief" for *kufr*, since "ingratitude," unlike "ingrate," is commonly used in English to condemn social rather than creedal faults. On the uses of this term to render "a complicated and confusing world considerably simpler," see Sizgorich, *Violence and Belief*, 241.

120 Both manuscripts read *kāfir wa-fataḥ al-kāf*. Since the latter expression usually means to pronounce a consonant with a short *a*, al-Turkī emends the first word to read *kafar*, "he committed unbelief." Given the preceding report, however, and in light of the facts that (1) Arabic linguistic terminology was not yet standardized and (2) Hadith scholars were not yet expected to study such linguistics as existed, I think it entirely possible that al-Baghawī meant to say that Ibn Ḥanbal said the word *kāfir* with a long *ā*, thereby calling the offenders Ingrates. Either way, the point is that Ibn Ḥanbal did *not* use the noun *kufr* "unbelief," a term that would condemn the sin rather than the sinner.

121 Jahm ibn Ṣafwān, d. 128/745, to whom are attributed a number of teachings hateful to Ibn Ḥanbal and his associates, particularly the claim that the prototype of the Qur'an began to exist only at a particular point in time (van Ess, *Theologie und Gesellschaft*, 2:493–508, 4:625–30; Martin, "Createdness of the Qur'ān"). The people Ibn Ḥanbal associates most strongly with the createdness doctrine are the followers of Jahm, not the Muʿtazilah (Melchert, "Adversaries").

122 This way of putting it emphasizes that the Qur'an, being known to God, was inseparable from Him, and thus not an object created by Him at a particular moment in time (Madelung, "Controversy").

123 Ibn Ḥanbal's associate Abū Muḥammad ʿAbd Allāh ibn Muḥammad ibn al-Muhājir. His name is also given as Būrān (see al-Turkī, *Manāqib*, 2nd ed., 208n4) and Fawzān (al-Khaṭīb al-Baghdādī, *Ta'rīkh Baghdād*, 10:78 [no. 5190]).

124 Q Ikhlāṣ 112:1.

125 This section addresses the problem of how to understand verses and reports that speak of God as if He possesses attributes such as motion and visibility. Some thinkers, including the so-called followers of Jahm, interpreted such passages metaphorically in order to avoid asserting a likeness between God and His creatures. In the remarks cited here, Ibn Ḥanbal insists that one should not try to explain the passages at all. Some later Ḥanbalīs insisted that a faithful understanding of the texts requires us to believe that God has a physical body. In support of this view they cite arguments reportedly made by Ibn Ḥanbal himself (Ibn Ḥanbal, attr., *Radd*).

126 Hadith reports like this one, as well as Q Qiyāmah 75:22–23, say that the saved will see God in the afterlife. Sunnis like Ibn Ḥanbal understood this claim literally, while the Muʿtazilah (among others) did not. See Omari, "Beatific Vision," with further references.

127 *Kalām*: that is, speculative theology, or dialectic concerning religion. The Arabic term is also the ordinary word for "talking." On the history of the word, see Cook, "Origins."

128 Despite Ibn Ḥanbal's warning to avoid Disputation, some of his followers did engage in *kalām*, especially when they could do so anonymously (Omari, "*Kitāb al-Ḥayda*"). On Ibn Ḥanbal's role in "making the boundaries of the Muslim community a component of the social reality of life within the *dār al-Islām*," see Sizgorich, *Violence and Belief*, 255ff (quotation at 256–57).

129 The doctrines of these groups are explained in the reports that follow.

130 I.e., and does not go on to say "uncreated." These are the Stoppers. Melchert describes them, along with the Proponents of the Created

Utterance (my translation of *lafẓiyyah*) as "semi-rationalists" who tried to stake out a position between the "traditionalists" (people who, like Ibn Ḥanbal, insisted on citing texts rather than using reason) and the rationalist Secessionists and followers of Jahm (Melchert, "Adversaries").

131 I.e., if spoken aloud by humans, while the Qur'an as known to God is uncreated. Those who held this view are the Proponents of Created Utterance.

132 A theologian condemned as a follower of Jahm, d. 218/833; on him, see van Ess, *Theologie*, 3:175–88.

133 The Muʿtazilah, literally "those who sent themselves apart": the name applied to scholars who were, broadly speaking, rationalist in their approach. For example, they favored metaphorical explanations for the apparently physical attributes of God. See Omari, "Muʿtazilah," with further references.

134 Ar. *zanādiqah*: a term originally applied to Manichean dualists, and later to anyone suspected of secretly adhering to a creed incompatible with Islam.

135 Ar. *rāfiḍī*: a disparaging term of reference to Shiʿa, referring to their rejection of Abū Bakr, ʿUmar, ʿUthmān, and Muʿāwiyah as legitimate caliphs.

136 The issue here was one of political legitimacy. According to Shiʿi Muslims, the Prophet's cousin ʿAlī should have been chosen as caliph over Abū Bakr, ʿUmar, or ʿUthmān. In response, Muslims who disagreed were forced to argue that the three actually chosen were more meritorious than ʿAlī. (A third position was that judgment on the matter should be suspended.) There were religious implications too, since the Shiʿa accepted only ʿAlī and his descendants as exemplars and rejected reports transmitted by other Companions. On the development of these positions, see Crone, *God's Rule*, 3–141.

137 For this report, see 20.28 below, and for references, see al-Turkī, *Manāqib*, 2nd ed., 214–15n2.

138 *Mubtadiʿ*, often translated as "innovator," a word which—in contrast to the Arabic—is a positive one in English. I have used different

translations of *bid'ah* (belief or practice condemned as new and contrary to that of the first Muslims) and its derivatives depending on context. I thank James Mongtomery for suggesting "novelty" as one possibility.

139 That is, the Companions who chose the first four caliphs.

140 Many Muslims ascribed special sanctity to 'Alī and his family, with some—the Imami Shi'a—claiming that anyone who did not take certain members of the family as guides and exemplars would not be saved. Ibn Ḥanbal and his associates rejected this view, holding instead that salvation might be attained by following the Qur'an and the *sunnah*. At the same time, they did not want to disparage 'Alī and his family, all of whom belonged to the Prophet's household.

141 This is the report cited in 20.24.

142 Q Fatḥ 48:29.

143 Q Baqarah 2:141.

144 A term applied to Shi'a by those who disagreed with them.

145 The remainder of this chapter consists of several very long, itemized accounts of the Sunni creed. Unlike the short statements that take up the beginning of the chapter, these are too explicitly polemical, and too obviously cobbled together, to seem authentic. Michael Cook has expressed doubts about one creed (*Commanding Right*, 110–11n232), and Saud AlSarhan has convincingly attributed it and five others to later sources (*Early Muslim Traditionalism*, 29–48). AlSarhan concludes that "these creeds are more likely to present traditionalist theology in the third and the fourth/ninth and tenth centuries than Ibn Ḥanbal's own beliefs," adding that they nevertheless served to place Ibn Ḥanbal on a par with the pious early Muslims as an authoritative source for right doctrine (ibid., 53). As this abridged edition focuses on the historical Ibn Ḥanbal, I have omitted the long creeds.

146 *Muḥdath*, or possibly *muḥaddith*, "Hadith scholar."

147 Cupping is an operation performed by using a flame to create a vacuum inside a glass vessel and then applying the vessel to the body, sometimes after (or before) making an incision in the skin. According to the principles of Greco-Islamicate medicine, this operation

was supposed to draw noxious vapors out of the body. Cupping was not a respected profession (the poet Abū l-ʿAtāhiyah tried to work as a cupper to mortify himself; see Iṣfahānī, *Aghānī*, 4:107–9), and a dinar—a whole gold coin—was too much to pay for the operation. In chapter 63, Ibn Ḥanbal's slave Ḥusn pays a cupper one dirham.

148 Al-Ḥiẓāmī is not otherwise identified. Ibn Abī Du'ād was adviser to the caliph al-Ma'mūn and chief judge under the caliph al-Muʿtaṣim. He was disgraced under al-Mutawakkil and died in 240/854. He is decried in Sunni sources as the force behind the Inquisition. See van Ess, *Theologie*, 3:481–502; Tillier, *Cadis*, index; Turner, "Aḥmad b. Abī Du'ād."

149 His *wird*: that is, a voluntary prayer regularly performed in addition to the regular ritual prayers.

150 That is, spiritual experience, as opposed to studying the Law, which is what Ibn Ḥanbal does.

151 This report seems an invention intended to legitimate al-Muḥāsibī's teachings using Ibn Ḥanbal as a foil, with the last remark being a counter-invention by a skeptical Ḥanbalī transmitter. Al-Dhahabī and Melchert agree that the story "simply does not sound right" ("Adversaries," 244, with a reference to al-Dhahabī, *Mīzān al-iʿtidāl*, 1:430).

152 A well that forms part of the mosque complex in Mecca. See J. Chabbi, "Zamzam."

153 In al-Minā, in Mecca. Ibn Ḥanbal was evidently on pilgrimage, making the year 814 rather than 813 (the other possibility given the *hijrī* date).

154 This last expression is unfamiliar and the translation is conjectural.

155 *Kitāb al-Fawā'id*, a vague title used in many fields. Schacht translates the term as it appears in the title of a later *fiqh* work as "difficult details" ("Ibn Nujaym").

156 As several reports in the *Manāqib* indicate, Ibn Ḥanbal's house opened onto a place of prayer commonly referred to as his mosque.

157 Perhaps *Kitāb al-Waraʿ wa l-īmān* [Book of scrupulousness and faith] (Sezgin, *GAS*, 1:506), though the published *Kitāb al-Waraʿ* contains

Ibn Ḥanbal's answers to questions about permissible food and the like, and nothing about faith.

158 Sezgin credits Ibn Ḥanbal with a *Kitāb al-Ashribah al-ṣaghīr* [Smaller book on drinks] (ibid.). This was probably a collection of Hadith reports or of Ibn Ḥanbal's responsa regarding the permissibility of various drinks.

159 Melchert takes this report as evidence of Ibn Ḥanbal's experimentation with arranging Hadith by topic; see *Ahmad*, 39–40.

160 It is not clear whose servant he was, but he may have been the attendant of some exalted personage, as the point of the story seems to be that Ibn Ḥanbal dismissed him in order to teach the ragged stranger some Hadith reports.

161 *Mushammir* can also mean "bustling" or "worldly-wise."

162 A modern (as of 1967) list of his works, whether printed or in manuscript, as well as secondary studies of them, appears in Sezgin, *GAS*, 1:502–9.

163 On the arguments made in this period for and against writing down "knowledge" (i.e., knowledge of Hadith and related matters), see Cook, "Opponents."

164 Extant and much published, and containing, in modern printings, at least 26,000 reports. See Sezgin, *GAS*, 1:504–6; Melchert, *Aḥmad*, 39–48; Melchert, "*Musnad*."

165 Such a work would have listed Hadith reports that clarify particular verses. However, Sezgin finds no such work attributed to Aḥmad. Melchert cites the biographer al-Dhahabī (d. 748/1348) as doubting that it ever existed, arguing that if it did, it would have left some traces in the literature (*Siyar*, 13:522). Melchert suggests that tenth-century Ḥanbalīs might have attributed a commentary to their exemplar out of "anxiety not to be outdone by al-Ṭabarī," compiler of the enormous *Jāmiʿ al-bayān* (Melchert, "Aḥmad ibn Ḥanbal and the Qur'ān," 24).

166 These are the verses whose legal implications override, or are overridden by, other verses. This work, if it existed, has apparently not survived; Sezgin does not mention it.

167 Not in Sezgin and apparently lost; the translation is conjectural. A work by the same title by Ibn Ḥanbal's contemporary al-Bukhārī is an alphabetical list of Hadith transmitters and their dates of death.

168 Presumably Shuʿbah ibn al-Ḥajjāj (d. 160/776?) a Basran transmitter credited with pioneering the evaluation of other transmitters for their reliability; see Juynboll, "Shuʿbah ibn al-Ḥadjdjādj." The work is not in Sezgin and is apparently lost.

169 The last four items listed seem not to have survived. Sezgin (*GAS*, 1:506–9) attributes several more works to him, of which the most important are *Kitāb al-Sunnah* [On the Prophet's exemplary way of life], *Kitāb al-Zuhd* [On renunciation], *Kitāb* (or *Risālat*) *al-Ṣalāh* [On prayer], *Kitāb al-Waraʿ wa l-īmān* [Scrupulousness and faith], *Kitāb al-Radd ʿalā l-zanādiqah wa l-jahmiyyah* [Rebuttal of the heretics and the followers of Jahm] (a book that, being full of *kalām*, was doubtless written by someone else; see al-Dhahabī, *Siyar*, 11:286–87, and Omari, "*Kitāb al-Ḥayda*," 442–46), *Kitāb ʿIlal al-ḥadīth* [Defects in hadith] (mentioned in chapter 98), *Al-Masāʾil* [Responsa], and *Al-ʿAqīdah* [The creed].

170 I thank Joseph Lowry for help with this passage. Presumably Ibn Ḥanbal would have found Mālik's compilation of Hadith reports acceptable but would have objected to Sufyān's rationalist inclinations (see Raddatz, "Sufyān al-Thawrī").

171 The original adds "and his aversion thereto," which is not part of the title as given in the table of contents.

172 This passage appears to be the author's indirect excuse for doing exactly what Ibn Ḥanbal forbade people to do. It is not entirely clear where Ibn al-Jawzī begins speaking; the paragraph break is my best guess.

173 Inkpots during this period were evidently round and made of glass. Examples from later periods were decorated with copper, silver, and gold, and scholars are described as showing them off. Ibn Ḥanbal may also be referring to boxes used to carry inkpots and pens (Baer, "Dawāt").

174 "His people" (*al-qawm*) could also be translated "any given group," but the question seems to be about the proto-Sunni Hadith scholars and renunciants.

175 Scholarly and pious works alike contain many imaginative translations of *raqāʾiq*. The most concrete meaning of the word is "thin places" or "tender spots." Given the subjects discussed in this chapter, I am inclined to think it refers to points where the spiritual seeker is likely to commit an error of omission. Note also the expression *raqīq al-dīn* ("weak in respect of religion") (Lane, *Lexicon*, s.v. *R-Q-Q*).

176 Q Raʿd 13:28.

177 People would carry objects in their sleeves, which served as pockets do today; see Goitein, *Mediterranean Society*, 4:161.

178 The reference here is to the exegesis of Q 69, Sūrat al-Ḥāqqah. Threatened with death, Abraham reportedly refused to ask for help from the angel Gabriel, trusting instead in God alone; see al-Turkī, *Manāqib*, 2nd ed., 271–72n4.

179 That is, in an attitude of ritual prayer.

180 "To be fearful" (*yattaqī*) can mean both "to be fearful of God" and "to guard against forbidden objects and actions."

181 "The heart" (*al-qalb*) often corresponds to what we might call "consciousness" or "the self." It should be distinguished from *nafs*, which is often translated "soul," but for renunciants usually means the place where base urges and unworthy desires come from.

182 Sickly and powerless Abbasid caliph, reigned 334–63/946–74.

183 *Lawzīnaj*: ground nuts spread on extremely thin bread then rolled and drenched in syrup (Perry, *Baghdad Cookery*, 99–100).

184 The point seems to be that the present world is as trivial a pleasure as a bite of dessert.

185 That is, to find the living transmitter closest to the source of the report and ask him to recite it, rather than getting it from one of his auditors.

186 Meter: *ṭawīl*.

187 Literally, "it was as if fire [or Hell] was burning between his eyes," which might also mean that he had a burning gaze.

188 Meter: *ṭawīl*.

189 Meter: *basīṭ*.

190 "Riches": literally, "a female camel and her offspring."

191 Meter: *kāmil.* Other citations of this poem do not credit it to Ibn Ḥanbal. See al-Turkī, *Manāqib*, 2nd ed., 282n2.

192 *Ilā* means "to" in the sense of "toward," while *li-* means "of," "for," or "belonging to," though it can also mean "to" when a pronoun suffix is attached (as in *qultu lahu*, "I said to him"). *Li-* is still used for *ilā* in many varieties of Arabic.

193 It is not clear here who the various verbs and pronouns refer to, and some words may be missing or assumed. One possibility is that Abū Bakr told the boy where to find the narrator, who then asked Ibn Ḥanbal's permission to bring him inside.

194 The speaker here may be Ibn al-Jawzī or one of the transmitters in the chain.

195 Hair removal was a matter of *sunnah*; see Reinhart, "Sha'r (2)." The glove may have been similar to the *kāsah* used in traditional bathhouses: "The friction-glove is made of a mixture of woollen and goat's hair threads sewn together and arranged so as to form a rough surface. This vigorous friction enables the top layer of skin, together with the dirt . . . accumulated in the pores, to be rubbed off in greyish rolls" (Sourdel-Thomine, "*Ḥammām*").

196 On the contrast between Ibn Ḥanbal's reported kindness and the rigidity of the doctrines attributed to him, see Sizgorich, *Violence and Belief*, 271.

197 Or, counting from one instead of zero, "I was about seven years old the first time. I was nine when he died."

198 On consumption of fruits and nuts, see Goitein, *Mediterranean Society*, 4:246.

199 Al-Turkī gives Sakānah, a place name, but SH has *sukkānihi*, "his tenants," which seems more likely, as Ibn Ḥanbal was a landlord (see chapter 40).

200 *Maṣliyyah*, for which al-Baghdādī gives the following recipe: "The way to make it is to cut up fat meat and boil it as usual, and remove the scum. When it is done, throw on a handful of chopped onion, a little salt, ground dry coriander, cumin, pepper, sticks of cinnamon

and mastic. When its liquid has dried up and the fat appears, take dried whey, pound it fine, throw hot water on it and macerate it well by hand until it becomes like sour yogurt [in appearance] and of the same consistency, then throw it in the pot. Grind a little garlic and throw it in the pot with bunches of fresh mint. Sprinkle some finely ground cinnamon on the surface. Then wipe the sides of the pot with a clean cloth, leave it on the fire awhile to grow quiet and take it up" (Perry, *Baghdad Cookery*, 44).

201 *Khabīṣ*: a pudding made of the pith of a semolina loaf torn up and then breaded, fried in sesame oil, and stirred with refined sugar. Different varieties might include saffron, rosewater, honey, poppy seeds, pistachios, camphor, molasses, gourd, and carrots (Perry, *Baghdad Cookery*, 95–97).

202 A roundabout way of saying "That's enough!"

203 Literally, "That is a scrupulosity that makes things dark," apparently from *aẓlama ʿalaynā l-bayt*, "he darkened our house," meaning "he said things we didn't want to hear" (Ibn Manẓūr, *Lisān*, s.v. *Ẓ-L-M*). One of the principles of *waraʿ* was refusal to use anything without the owner's permission.

204 That is, he could then say "He isn't here," meaning "He isn't in my hand," and thus avoid lying outright. I thank Tahera Qutbuddin for this explanation.

205 This story refers to an incident (covered in chapter 73) in which Ibn Ḥanbal was denounced to the authorities for allegedly harboring a member of the family of ʿAlī who had been active against the Abbasid regime.

206 *Salām ʿalaykum*, perhaps a reference to Q Furqān 25:63: «The true servants of the Gracious One are those who walk upon the earth with humility and when they are addressed by the ignorant ones, their response is, "Peace"» (*salām*).

207 The question seems to be coming from an official charged with rooting out crypto-Manicheans, as was done under the caliph al-Mahdī. In any case, the questioner seems to have no idea who he's talking to.

208 For a detailed account of the difficulties of being a landlord in ninth-century Iraq, see al-Jāḥiẓ, *Al-Bukhalāʾ*, 81–90; trans. Serjeant, *Misers*, 67–75. For a discussion of renting based on the Cairo Geniza, see Goitein, *Mediterranean Society*, 4:91–97.

209 The Black Land is the alluvial plain on the Tigris and Euphrates rivers. When it was conquered, ʿUmar reportedly ordered that it remain in the hands of those who cultivated it, with the tax revenues going to the Muslim treasury (al-Turkī, *Manāqib*, 2nd ed., 306n3). Ibn Ḥanbal is evidently trying to apply this command by paying *zakāt* on the house.

210 This passage is obscure. Among other things, the pronouns do not agree properly for gender. The reading is my best guess.

211 That is, collect the ears of grain missed by the sickle at harvest time. He seems to have done this while traveling to Tarsus to be interrogated by al-Maʾmūn (see chapter 67).

212 Or "a good number of dirhams."

213 In the Cairo Geniza, cheap shoes are often described as costing a quarter of a dinar (Goitein, *Mediterranean Society*, 4:164).

214 Ibn Ḥanbal's concubine; see chapter 63.

215 None of the manuscripts gives a satisfactory reading of this word. Al-Turkī gives it as *yarubbuhā*, although no dictionary definition of this word seems to fit.

216 References exist to numerous devices for raising water, conveying it from one place to another, and dispensing it; see, e.g., Hill, "*Māʾ*" and "*Nāʿūra*"; Guthrie, *Arab Social Life*, 136–39; Cooperson, *Classical*, 170n97. It being impossible to tell from this brief allusion exactly what is meant, I have used the vaguest possible English word, "conduit," meaning "a structure from which water is distributed or made to issue" (*OED*).

217 *Dusūt*: not explained in the works I have consulted; I have translated based on context.

218 This passage is unclear to me. It may be an expression of a theme common in renunciant writings, namely that a relaxation of standards,

even for what seems to be good cause, sends one down a slippery slope toward wastefulness and corruption.

219 It is unclear whether *miqrāḍ* here means scissors, shears, or (as in modern Arabic) nail clippers.

220 That is, 1/12 of a dirham.

221 For rental amounts paid for dwellings and commercial premises in Egypt between 1040 and 1250, see Goitein, *Mediterranean Society*, 4:93–97, 291–96.

222 That a tree trunk is meant becomes clear in the next section.

223 That is, 9 and 1/3 dirhams.

224 Namely to acquire blessings from an object that had belonged to Aḥmad.

225 To explain his kindness Ibn Ḥanbal makes the excuse that the dog "might retaliate by the evil eye" (Melchert, *Ibn Ḥanbal*, 5).

226 The son of his slave Ḥusn; see chapter 64.

227 Apparently the Persian name Chobin.

228 Kinberg explains renunciation as the result of scrupulous avoidance (*wara*ʿ) of anything possibly against the Law (Kinberg, "What is Meant by *Zuhd*"). Melchert, by contrast, argues that "right religion in the *zuhd* tradition was not mainly about precisely following a lot of rules, although renunciants usually did precisely follow a lot of rules; rather, it was about an attitude, above all this unremitting seriousness about life. The threat of death and judgment was to be taken seriously. Time was not to be wasted on frivolous entertainments but directed to the performance of duties" (Melchert, "Aḥmad ibn Ḥanbal and the Qur'ān," 72).

229 The meanings of *qindīl* and *sirāj* as reconstructed by Goitein from the Cairo Geniza seem to make sense here (*Mediterranean Society*, 4:135–36).

230 *Khalūq* is described as a thick yellow perfume. It may be based on saffron, which can also be used to make incense.

231 Q Ṭā Hā 20:131. The whole verse reads «Do not regard the worldly benefits We have given some of them, for with these We seek only to test them. The provision of your Lord is better and more lasting.»

232 A unit of weight with various definitions. One early definition sets it equal to sixty grains of barley; see Ashtor, "*Mawāzīn* (1)," and Ibn Manẓūr, *Lisān*, s.v. *M-K-K*.

233 None of the manuscripts agree on what was painted, and none gives a word that makes sense. Following the parallel text in Ibn Ḥanbal, *Zuhd*, 191, I have emended to *saqā'if*, plural of *saqīfah*, "any broad piece of wood . . . with which one may form a roof" (Lane, *Lexicon*, s.v. *S-Q-F*).

234 This passage is very terse and the pronoun references are ambiguous. The translation is therefore conjectural.

235 This story refers to the period after the end of the Inquisition, when the caliph al-Mutawakkil welcomed Hadith scholars to the palace. Al-Miṣrī and his companions thought it acceptable to enjoy whatever privileges the caliph offered, but Aḥmad, whose objections to Abbasid rule went beyond matters of dogma, did not. He was also old and ill at the time, which seems to be why he was lying down.

236 *Umm walad*: a concubine who has borne her master a child.

237 This incident evidently took place after Ibn Ḥanbal was stricken with paralysis.

238 The point seems to be that Ibn Ḥanbal did not realize that his life of austerity was undermining his health.

239 That is, the slave who had borne one of his sons.

240 Literally "a grain," a coin or measure of weight equivalent to 1/48 of a dirham (Ibn Manẓūr, *Lisān*, s.v. *M-K-K*). It and the *qiṭʿah* ("scrap") seem to be the smallest units mentioned in the *Virtues*.

241 The custom seems to have been to visit the bathhouse once a week. Ibn Ḥanbal may have shunned bathing because it was a pleasurable activity, usually undertaken with friends; "a vow to forego this amenity was a severe means of self-castigation" (Goitein, *Mediterranean Society*, 5:96–97).

242 "Ibn Ḥanbal is perhaps the only ordinary citizen of third/ninth century Baghdad whose life we can place in its concrete surroundings" (Cook, *Commanding Right*, 108); Cook provides an evocative summary of what the *Virtues* and other sources tell us about Ibn Ḥanbal's

home and neighborhood (108–10). Beyond Baghdad, a great deal of detailed information on houses and furnishings appears in Goitein, *Mediterranean Society*, 4:105–50; although Goitein's documents are Egyptian and date almost entirely from a later period, the Geniza Jews' attitudes toward comfort, luxury, and abstinence provide an instructive background to this chapter.

243 It was a common Iraqi custom to sleep on the roof in the summer.

244 References to the *shādhikūnah* (so voweled in SH) or *shādhakūnah* (Maṭlūb, *Muʿjam*, 76) indicate that it was made in Yemen, that people sat on it, that it was large, and that it was stitched (*muḍarrabah*; see al-Samʿānī, *Al-Ansāb*, 3:371). "Quilt" is my best guess.

245 The *bardaʿah* or *bardhaʿah* is variously described as a a saddle-cloth, a pad stuffed with straw, a mattress, or a pad placed atop a mattress (Lane, *Lexicon*, s. v. *B-R-Dh*; Sadan, "Mafrūshāt"; Goitein, *Mediterranean Society*, 4:115).

246 On hangings, curtains, and drapes, see Goitein, *Mediterranean Society*, 4:119–22.

247 Two of the MSS, and following them al-Turkī, read *yuʿazzīnī*, evidently meaning that Ibn Ḥanbal tried to console al-Zuhrī by saying that he had borrowed money to build the door (or gate). But *ʿazzā* usually means to offer condolences to the bereaved; I therefore follow SH in reading *yuʿaddīnī*. I also read *bi l-dayn* over SH's plausible *bil-labin* "in brick," because Ibn Ḥanbal later says, apparently speaking of the same structure, that he had to go into debt to build it because he refused to take money from his son (49.12).

248 On the *kānūn*, see Goitein, *Mediterranean Society*, 4:136.

249 This incident took place during Ibn Ḥanbal's confinement at the house of Isḥāq ibn Ibrāhīm, the emir or governor of Baghdad. Ibn Ḥanbal's family was evidently responsible for his upkeep, perhaps because he refused to eat food provided by anyone else. The meal described here was Ibn Ḥanbal's *ifṭār*, or fast-breaking meal during Ramadan.

250 Normally one would eat meat during the festival. Al-Turkī reads this as a question meaning something like "But what good were they?"

From other passages (49.17 and 49.22), however, it seems that Ibn Ḥanbal was fond of beans.

251 On this spread (*kāmakh*), see 18.3.

252 Made by boiling almonds and crushing them.

253 The translation of clothing terms in this chapter must be taken as conjectural. We have some idea what Iraqi dress may have looked like, at least in later periods, from the illustrations for al-Ḥarīrī's *Maqāmāt* (see Grabar, *Illustrations* and Guthrie, *Arab Social Life*). We have some actual garments (or parts of garments) from this period, though not from Iraq (see e.g., Fluck, "Dress Styles"; Colburn, "Materials"; Evans, *Byzantium and Islam*, 164–71), and we have many attested words for items of clothing, both from dictionaries (see, e.g., Maṭlūb, *Muʿjam*) and from documentary sources (Goitein, *Mediterranean Society*, 4:150–200). Unfortunately it is only occasionally possible to match a word with a particular garment, or depiction of one. For many items, finally, there do not seem to be precisely equivalent items in English.

254 *Bayn al-thawbayn*, apparently meaning of a length between that of the usual inner and the usual outer garment.

255 Goitein translates *milḥafah* or *malḥafah* as "wrap" (*Mediterranean Society*, 4:157).

256 Goitein insists that a *qamīṣ* is a robe (ibid, 4:156). The *OED*, however, calls a robe "an outer garment," which this object is clearly not. I have chosen "tunic," which means "a garment resembling a shirt or gown . . . over which a loose mantle or cloak was worn" (*OED*), and is the term used by historians of material culture to describe the shirt-like garments that have survived from early Islamic times (see, e.g., Evans, *Byzantium and Islam*, 168–69).

257 *Qalansuwwah*: "the cap worn under the turban, equivalent to the modern *ṭarbūsh*" (Dozy, *Noms*, 366).

258 The word *muʿaqqad*, literally "many-knotted," is explained as "a kind of striped garment from Hajar"; see Ibn Manẓūr, *Lisān*, s.v. *ʿ-Q-D*.

259 Goitein translates *ridāʾ* as "coat" (*Mediterranean Society*, 4:116). "Coat," however, suggests something worn to keep warm, and Ibn

Ḥanbal wore his in the summer (48.5). Guthrie describes the *ridāʾ* as worn over the shoulder (*Arab Social Life*, 49). "Mantle," meaning "a loose sleeveless cloak" (*OED*), seems a reasonable guess.

260 On the *ṭaylasān*, see Dozy, *Noms*, 278–80, and Guthrie, *Social Life*, 77–78 and plate 8.

261 Approximately three meters, or almost ten feet; see W. Hinz, "Dhirāʿ."

262 From the city of Marv; see Ibn Manẓūr, *Lisān*, s.v. *M-R-W*.

263 *Murabbaʿ* means either "square" or "checked." A *kisāʾ* "was evidently a simple oblong piece of cloth" (Lane, *Lexicon*, s.v. *K-S-W*) and in this case may have been square. The dictionaries also mention *washy murabbaʿ*, a pattern of checks printed or embroidered on a garment (Ibn Manẓūr, *Lisān*, s.v. *K-ʿ-B*).

264 The point seems to be that he did not want to take money from anyone else because he could not be sure of its acceptability.

265 It is unclear what a *kaylajah* is a fourth of, but it may be possible to derive an answer from the bewildering list of equivalences in Ibn Manẓūr, "Lisān", s.v. *M-K-K*.

266 See note at the first appearance of this report in chapter 40.

267 Literally, an aromatic paste made of dried musk, and a red dye used in preparing kidskin shoes.

268 The conversation is apparently about repairing or installing a gate or door on the property where Ibn Ḥanbal rented out rooms. The revenue was apparently divided among the members of the family, among them ʿAbd Allāh. Since he does not approve of the latter's other sources of income, however, Ibn Ḥanbal cannot allow him to contribute to the upkeep of the property.

269 Since Ṣāliḥ had accepted gifts from the caliph, anything that came from his house was tainted.

270 Q Ibrāhīm 14:45. This is one of the reproaches the damned will hear in the afterlife.

271 The precise nature of the financial arrangement described here is not clear to me.

272 In Egypt banana leaves were used for wrapping purchases (Goitein, *Mediterranean Society*, 4:246).

273 Al-Turkī takes *ḍubnah* (or *ḍabnah* or *ḍibnah*) to mean "dependents" (*Manāqib*, 2nd ed., 352n1), but since Yaḥyā was chief judge under al-Maʾmūn, "entourage" (Ibn Manẓūr, *Lisān*, s.v. *Ḍ-B-N*) seems more likely.

274 Ibn Ḥanbal did not believe in accepting payment for teaching and so refused to accept the gift. I thank Tahera Qutbuddin for correcting an earlier translation of this passage.

275 Ibn Ḥanbal seems to be applying the principle that Muslims should not create a nuisance or impediment in a public thoroughfare.

276 Assuming that the text and translation are accurate here, "S" (the letter *sīn*) may have needed correction because its abbreviated form is a simple line that is not always readily legible as a distinct letter. I thank Devin Stewart for discussing this passage with me.

277 This was a much-discussed problem, and Ibn Ḥanbal apparently thought it better not to answer for fear of being wrong. See al-Turkī, *Manāqib*, 2nd ed., 358n2.

278 The point seems to be that there was only one.

279 Ibn Ḥanbal's disapproval of figured fabrics (Ibn Ḥanbal, *Waraʿ*, 141–43) suggests that he would have objected to the floral and vegetal patterns extremely common in surviving examples of plaster decoration from this period (see, e.g., Mietke, "Vine Rinceaux"). The palace may also have been decorated with paintings of hunting scenes, drinking parties, musicians, dancers, and the like (see, e.g., Ballian, "Country Estates").

280 The reluctance of pious scholars to assume judgeships is a common topos of biography. Tillier, *Cadis d'Iraq*, 652ff., offers, in addition to references to the older literature, a striking new interpretation of these refusals as ritual exchanges between learned men and the authorities.

281 This story gives the impression of being invented to praise Ibn Ḥanbal at al-Shāfiʿī's expense; see Cooperson, *Classical*, 149–51.

282 Al-Amīn took office in 809/193, when Ibn Ḥanbal would have been thirty or thirty-one.

283 The proper name of the caliph al-Amīn. During this period, pious Hadith-men seem to have avoided calling the Abbasid caliphs by their titles, since many of them considered the dynasty illegitimate.

284 Al-Ribāṭī must have accepted the patronage of ʿAbd Allāh ibn Ṭāhir, governor of Khurasan, which to Ibn Ḥanbal's way of thinking meant compromising himself as a Muslim and as a scholar.

285 The speaker is surprised that an Arab—that is, a descendant of the original Muslim conquerors—is poor. Indeed, Ibn Ḥanbal belonged to a prestigious tribe and his relatives occupied positions in the Abbasid administration (see chapters 1–3).

286 The problem was not the chair itself but the fact that it was decorated with silver, as becomes clear in the next report. I thank Hossein Modarressi for clarifying this point.

287 Al-Sawwāq seems to mean a banquet (apparently known to his audience) held in a house near the Bāb al-Muqayyir, which may mean "Pitch-Worker's Gate" but not "Pitched Gate," pace Le Strange, *Baghdad*, 224–26. The gate was located in al-Mukharrim, a quarter of northeast Baghdad.

288 Ibn Ḥanbal's ascetic contemporary Bishr ibn al-Ḥārith the Barefoot (see Glossary).

289 Identified by al-Turkī as Ibn ʿAbd al-Ḥakam ibn Nāfiʿ al-Warrāq (d. 251/865–66).

290 *Akhāfu an takraha l-rijl*, so voweled in H, which al-Turkī evidently understands to mean "I'm afraid you don't like crowds." For this unusual meaning of *rijl*, see Ibn Manẓūr, *Lisān*, *R-J-L*.

291 The rest of the thought apparently being "even when he's alone."

292 The various political interpretations of this term (discussed in Nagel, "Qurrāʾ," and Shah, "Quest") are based on references to earlier periods and none makes obvious sense here. From the passage itself it is clear that the *qurrāʾ*, whatever else they may have been, were associated, in Ibn Ḥanbal's milieu, with pious shabbiness.

293 The manuscripts read *asmārjūn*, the Arabic pronunciation of *āsemāngūn*, meaning "sky-colored" in Persian. Al-Turkī emends to *asmān jūn*, which is closer to the Persian but not attested in the manuscripts.

294 "They" would appear to be the Abbasid authorities, who tried to court his favor after the Inquisition.

295 Reportedly what ʿUmar ibn al-Khaṭṭāb said about having served as caliph. Here Ibn Ḥanbal seems to be talking about the Inquisition.

296 Sahl ibn Salāmah was a leader of the vigilante movement that sought to restore law and order in Baghdad after the siege of 813. See al-Ṭabarī, *Taʾrīkh*, 8:552/3:1009–10, 572–73/3:1035–36; van Ess, *Theologie*, 3:173–75.

297 The term *ṭunbūr*, "long-necked lute," is sometimes translated using the cognate term "pandore," which, however, is also used to describe many different forms of medium- and long-necked lutes, as well as certain unrelated European instruments. I thank Dwight Reynolds for explaining these terms. On the pious smashing of musical instruments, see Cook, *Commanding Right*, 79, 90–91, 98, 100 (where this incident is discussed), 121, 149, 238, 300, 309, 383, 384, and 481.

298 Q Mulk 67:30.

299 Al-Shāfiʿī was a foundational Sunni legal theorist (see Glossary). Supplications at dawn were thought to be especially effective. This report, though not impossible in itself, is the sort of story that was circulated to paper over the differences between jurists who followed al-Shāfiʿī's approach and those who favored Ibn Ḥanbal's.

300 This story was clearly invented to make Ibn Ḥanbal look good, to argue that prayer is more important than scholarship, or both. But only the first half of the story makes the point effectively; the second part may have been added to avoid giving offense.

301 The word *ṣabr* (fortitude, patience) and its various derivatives appear ninety-six times (searched on tanzil.net).

302 Q 18, Sūrat al-Kahf. This chapter deals with the themes of ingratitude, quarrelsomeness, and impatience. It tells several well-known stories. One is that of the People of the Cave, fugitive believers whom God

cast into a deep sleep and revived 309 years later as a sign and a test to humankind. Another is that of the ungrateful grower who comes to understand his absolute dependence on God when his crops fail. Yet another is that of Moses's travels with an unnamed servant of God who commits a series of apparently wicked actions, which are later explained as benevolent. It also contains the story of "the horned one," often identified as Alexander the Great, and his encounters with various peoples. It ends with a description of the Day of Judgment and a exhortation to the Prophet to proclaim that God is one and to urge humankind to good deeds.

303 The salutation, which ends the prayer, is "Peace be upon you, and the blessing of God."

304 One should not interrupt someone who is praying, or pass directly in front of him or her.

305 It is not clear who was keeping whom busy, though the preference should perhaps be given to Ibn Ḥanbal as the subject.

306 "The rest": the *nawāfil*, or "supererogatory prayers," that is, optional observances performed in addition to the ritual devotions.

307 Worshippers may choose which chapters to read during their prayers. Several reports say that Ibn Ḥanbal preferred this one. On the chapter itself, see 58.7.

308 That is, transported supernaturally to Mecca. In Sufi biography, the Allies of God can cross great distances instantly and can carry others with them.

309 This awkwardly constructed story was apparently intended to establish cordiality between exemplars of the religious sciences and exemplars of the mystical tradition. See Cooperson, *Classical*, 138–51, 178–84.

310 Q Sharḥ 94:5–6.

311 Q Fuṣṣilat 41:11.

312 H and SH have *mā yaṣnaʿu*, "what He does," though the *fatḥah* in H may also be a *ḍammah*, giving *mā yuṣnaʿu*, "what is done" (thus al-Turkī). Though odd, "what He does" makes sense if Ibn Ḥanbal believed that God has predestined all our actions (see 20.49). Since H

and SH represent independent manuscript traditions, I have adopted *mā yaṣnaʿu* and translated accordingly. But theodicy aside, D's *mā naṣnaʿu*, "what we do," is the most natural reading.

313 H and D have *ṭibb*, commonly "medicine," and not attested as a plural of *ṭabīb*, "physician," but apparently being used in that sense here.

314 The child's family seems to have been using a preparation made of *fatl*, the blossoms of the *samur* or acacia, to stop the bleeding. For a modern description of how the acacia is used medicinally, see http://www.cloverleaffarmherbs.com/acacia/. I thank Kyle Gamble for suggesting this possibility, which is far likelier than the "twisted cord" of the first edition.

315 "Thirty years" appears to be wrong; see 62.8.

316 Rayḥāna is also identified (see 63.5) as Ibn Ḥanbal's concubine, though this claim seems less well documented.

317 Literally something cut off or cut out. Here it obviously refers to some kind of footwear but I have not found it attested in other sources.

318 Probably the head of a sheep.

319 This seems to mean that he has just spent the last dirham they have, and that she should not count on him to throw any more celebrations for her. Another possible reading is: "This is all you'll get from me today."

320 A dry measure whose value varied greatly by region, from approximately 926.7 grams to 1.6 kilograms (Ashtor, "*Mawāzīn*, 1").

321 It is unclear to me whether Ḥusn paid for the fabric or was paid for the work she did when she made the garment. *Kirā* usually means the rent, but here it seems to mean the fee paid for a service. I thank Isam Eido, Saud AlSarhan, and Julia Bray for discussing this problem with me. It is also unclear exactly why Ibn Ḥanbal did not want the garment. He may have disliked its being finely woven, or he may have disapproved of the transaction Ḥusn mentions (the *ghallah* being the money he collected from his tenants).

322 Ibn Ḥanbal decided immediately to use the cloth as a shroud and therefore asked Ḥusn not to cut it, as a shroud is simply a wrapper. At the end, though, she seems to be saying that he cut the cloth in order to use only the coarser part for the shroud.

323 Evidently a now-lost biography of Ibn Ḥanbal.

324 Since Rayḥānah is also given as the name of Ibn Ḥanbal's second wife (62.4) the most economical explanation of the discrepancy is that al-Munādī mistakenly applied the name to Ḥusn. The details about asking his wife's permission and following the *sunnah* may be pious embellishments.

325 Ibn Ḥanbal is referring to Q Aʿrāf 7:172, where God summons the souls of all those yet unborn and has them acknowledge Him as their Lord. Here, then, he is apologizing to his older son for fathering the younger ones. He leaves out the younger al-Ḥasan and al-Ḥusayn, who died young (see 63.2), though why he should leave out Muḥammad, the fourth of his young sons, is not clear. Following this understanding of the passage, I have translated based on the text of H, which reads "al-Ḥasan." For their part, D and SH both read Ḥusn (Ibn Ḥanbal's concubine) instead of Ḥasan. If this reading is adopted, the report means that Ibn Ḥanbal is apologizing for buying Ḥusn and fathering Saʿīd.

326 A *qanṭarah* is a masonry bridge as opposed to one supported by boats or inflated skins. Fūrān is using local shorthand to refer to a market near one such bridge. For a list of the possibilities, see Le Strange, *Baghdad*, 368, left column.

327 "The gate leading out from the [northwest] suburbs to the shrine of the Kâẓimayn," and for legal purposes "the northern limit of Western Baghdad." Le Strange, *Baghdad*, 115 and map 5.

328 One who measures cloth or plots of land (al-Samʿāni, *al-Ansāb*, 3:5).

329 Al-Turkī, drawing on a parallel text, emends *Aḥmad* to *aḥmadu l-Lāh*, but the original, which appears in all the manuscripts, strikes me as much more plausible.

330 To judge by third/ninth-century works intended to correct writing errors, "bad Arabic" (*laḥn*) in this period probably did not mean making errors in inflection (*iʿrāb*), as in the (probably contrived) stories told of early Islamic figures. Rather, it meant making errors such as mixing up Form I and Form IV verbs, or using *yāʾ* instead of the

glottal stop. For examples, see Ibn Qutaybah, *Adab al-kātib*, passim. For "bad Arabic" as a matter of word choice, see 98.23.

331 *Qarāmil*: "twisted strips of hair, wool, or silk, used by women to pull back their hair" (*Lisān*, s.v. *Q-R-M-L*).

332 Ibn al-Jawzī's claim that the early Muslims held the Revelation to be uncreated is tendentious. Elsewhere in this volume (72.9–10, 72.13–14) his sources will argue that the subject is off limits precisely because the early Muslims announced no position on the matter.

333 Ibn al-Jawzī sees the Secessionists (Muʿtazilah) as the villains behind the Inquisition, and this is a commonly repeated view, but Ibn Ḥanbal himself casts the Jahmists in that role. See Jadʿān, *Miḥnah*, 47–109, and Melchert, "Adversaries."

334 It is unlikely that Ibn Nūḥ, an obscure student of Hadith (see chapter 67), would have been in a position to overhear the caliph say anything. This series of reports was probably invented in the course of the post-Inquisition rapprochement between the Hadith community and the Abbasid regime. The point was to show that, except for two bad eggs—al-Maʾmūn and al-Wāthiq—the caliphs had always held the correct (that is, the Sunni) view of the Qurʾan: that it was not created.

335 Modern scholarship has explained the Inquisition as al-Maʾmūn's attempt to make the caliphate the source of all guidance in matters of belief and law. This attempt can broadly be characterized as a Shiʿi one. Al-Maʾmūn adopted several other pro-Shiʿa positions, including the nomination of a descendant of ʿAlī as his heir apparent. He did not, however, limit exemplary leadership to ʿAlī's family. He included his own family, the Abbasids, among the potential imams or guides, and of course believed himself to be the imam in his own time. He seems to have developed these ideas in the course of the civil war between himself and his predecessor, the caliph al-Amīn. Intentionally or not, al-Maʾmūn's Shiʿi self-positioning brought him into conflict with people like Ibn Ḥanbal, who believed that the Law was to be found in the *sunnah* rather than in the declarations of individuals. To force the Hadith-men and like-minded jurists to acknowledge his authority,

al-Ma'mūn craftily decided to ask them about the createdness of the Qur'an. Unlike other points of contention between the two parties, this issue is not mentioned in the Book itself or in the Hadith. The caliph's plan was thus to force his opponents to engage in the kind of theological argument he was sure he could win. For discussions of the *miḥnah* and further references, see Patton, *Aḥmed ibn Ḥanbal*; Sourdel, "Politique religieuse"; Nagel, *Rechtleitung*, esp. 116–54, 430–46; Lapidus, "Separation"; Crone and Hinds, *God's Caliph*, esp. 80–96; Jad'ān, *Miḥnah*, 47–109; Steppat, "From *'Ahd Ardeshir*"; Nawas, "The Mihna"; van Ess, *Theologie*, 3:446–508; Nawas, *Al-Ma'mûn*, 25–78; Zaman, *Religion*, 106–18; Cooperson, *Classical*, 117–38; Hurwitz, *Formation*, 113–44; Cooperson, *Al-Ma'mun*, 107–28; Winkelmann-Liebert, "Die *miḥna*"; Yücesoy, *Messianic Beliefs*, 128–35; Turner, *Inquisition*; de Gifis, *Shaping*, 91–115.

336 Although Yaḥyā served as chief judge under al-Ma'mūn, he argued consistently for proto-Sunni positions. Ḥanbalī biographers therefore tend to treat him as a reliable source.

337 A parallel account by Aḥmad ibn Ḥanbal's cousin Ḥanbal ibn Isḥāq sheds additional light on Aḥmad's first encounter with the Inquisition. It begins with a list of the scholars summoned to meet with the caliph in al-Raqqah. (Here Ḥanbal seems to have confused the initial dispatch of scholars to al-Raqqah with the later transport of Ibn Ḥanbal and Ibn Nūḥ to the Byzantine front. As it stands, his account includes Ibn Ḥanbal among those who made the initial trip and proclaimed the Qur'an created: see Ḥanbal, *Dhikr*, 34-36. Van Ess, *Theologie*, 3:455n23, thinks the editor is wrong to supply Ibn Ḥanbal's name to complete the text here, though the mistake seems to be Ḥanbal's, not the editor's, as the claim is repeated, the second time without emendation. As Ḥanbal's account continues, in any event, it comes into agreement with our other sources, which say that Ibn Ḥanbal was first questioned in Baghdad.) Ḥanbal's report quotes his father Isḥāq, who was also Aḥmad ibn Ḥanbal's uncle, as saying:

> At sunset a messenger arrived from the captain of the ward (*ṣāḥib al-rab'*) and took Aḥmad away. I went out

with them. The ward captain said: "The chief wants to see you at his place tomorrow." After we left [the ward captain's house] I said to Aḥmad: "Why not go into hiding?"

"How could I do that?" he replied. "If I did, I'd worry that something might happen to you, or to my children, your children, or the neighbors. I wouldn't want anyone to suffer on my account. Let's just see what happens" (Ḥanbal, *Dhikr*, 36).

338 Al-Ma'mūn was in al-Raqqah, having stopped there on his way to the Byzantine front. During his visit to Syria, the caliph may have realized the extent of anti-regime sentiment there, and the extent to which such sentiment correlated with what were to him heretical religious ideas. The trigger may have been his meeting with the Hadith scholar Abū Mushir al-Ghassānī, who at first refused to describe the Qur'an as created (see 78.19, and van Ess, *Theologie*, 3:452–53).

339 Ibn Ḥanbal and his circle avoided referring to the Abbasid caliphs by their regnal titles, evidently because they rejected their Shiʿi-millenarian implications. *Al-ma'mūn* means "the trustworthy" and was a common form of reference to the Prophet.

340 Q Shūrā 42:11.

341 Q Anʿām 6:102; Raʿd 13:16; Zumar 39:62; Ghāfir 40:62. Here al-Ma'mūn puts together parts of different Qur'anic verses to emphasize that God is fundamentally different from His creations, including the Qur'an. In this first letter, the full text of which we have from other sources, the caliph also emphasizes his duty to guide the community and protect Islam from the false teachings of the self-proclaimed people of the *sunnah* (al-Ṭabarī, *Ta'rīkh*, 3:1112–32/8:631–44, and van Ess, *Theologie*, 3:452–56).

342 That is, Ibn Ḥanbal completed the citation of Q Shūrā 42:11, of which the interrogators recited only the part given above. He thus reminded those present that one cannot simply ignore the passages that seem to describe God as if He has a physical body. He may have believed that God did have a physical body, all of whose attributes, including the voice that had spoken the Qur'an, were uncreated. Alternatively,

he may have been trying to make the point that the problem of attributes could not be resolved by human reason. In any case, Ibn al-Jawzī might not be giving us an entirely reliable account, as he himself was opposed to anthropomorphist interpretations of the Qur'an (Swartz, "Ḥanbalī Critique").

343 Called Raḥbat Ṭawq in another telling (see below). Perhaps the same as the place today called al-Raḥbah, which lies on the Euphrates between Baghdad and al-Raqqah.

344 That is, al-Ma'mūn. Some chroniclers state that he contracted a fever after being splashed with cold water, while others say he fell ill after dangling his feet in cold water while eating freshly delivered dates (that is, he presumably caused an imbalance in his humours, according to the Greco-Islamic medical theories of the day). See al-Ṭabarī, *Ta'rīkh*, 3:1134–41/8:646–651.

345 Or al-Mutawakkil, as the storyteller has forgotten to add. The third request—the one not granted—was presumably not to meet al-Muʿtaṣim. The story switches from first to third-person narration in mid-sentence and thus seems to have been garbled in transmission.

346 A town, also known as ʿĀnāh (67.14), on the Tigris in what is now northeastern Iraq, near the Syrian border (Longrigg, "ʿĀna").

347 An earlier report says that Ibn Ḥanbal got as far as Adana, which is plausible enough given that the news of al-Ma'mūn's death would not have reached al-Raqqah immediately.

348 A western suburb of Baghdad, located approximately two miles west of the Round City just northeast of the ʿĪsā Canal (Le Strange, *Baghdad*, index and map 6).

349 ʿUmārah ibn Ḥamzah was a freedman of the Caliph al-Manṣūr. His palace was located on the Trench of Ṭāhir just west of the Upper Harbor on the Tigris (Le Strange, *Baghdad*, 117 and map 5).

350 There were at least two prisons in use in Baghdad at this time: the Muṭbaq (Le Strange, *Baghdad*, 27 and map 5) and the Prison of the Syrian Gate (ibid., 130–31 and maps 2, 5, and 6). It is not clear whether the "Commoners' Prison" was one of these, or another place altogether.

351 I have not been able to identify this street. In any case it seems that the authorities first intended to keep Ibn Ḥanbal confined inside a house, as seems to have been customary with high-profile figures, but then decided to put him in a prison for common criminals.

352 According to Ḥanbal, Ibn Ḥanbal's fetters were loose enough that he could slip them off, which he did in order to perform his prayers properly (Ḥanbal, *Dhikr*, 38–39).

353 According to the account (ignored by Ibn al-Jawzī) by Aḥmad ibn Ḥanbal's cousin Ḥanbal, it was Ḥanbal's father Isḥāq—Aḥmad's uncle—who persuaded the authorities to put Aḥmad on trial. The report runs as follows:

> With Aḥmad still in prison, my father, Isḥāq ibn Ḥanbal, made the rounds of the commanders and regime figures on his behalf, hoping to get him released. Eventually, seeing that his efforts were leading nowhere, he went directly to Isḥāq ibn Ibrāhīm. "Commander," he said, "our families are bound together in a way I'm sure you appreciate. We were neighbors in Marv and my father Ḥanbal was with your grandfather al-Ḥusayn ibn Muṣʿab."
>
> "So I've heard."
>
> [My father continued:] I said: "So would the Commander not do something to honor that bond? Your position is one my nephew approves of. He has not denied Revelation; the only disagreement concerns its interpretation. Even so, you have deemed it lawful to keep him confined for a long time. Commander: put him together with some jurists and scholars." I didn't say anything to him about Hadith-men and transmitters of reports.
>
> "Would you accept the outcome, whatever it was?"
>
> "Yes!" I said. "Let the best argument win."
>
> [My father continued:] "[Later, when I told] Ibn Abī Rabʿī, he said, 'What have you done? You want to gather your nephew's opponents—whatever Debaters and

squabblers Ibn Abī Du'ād can find--and let them beat him in a debate? Why didn't you consult with me first?'"

[...]

Escorted by [Isḥāq ibn Ibrāhīm's] chamberlain, I went in to see Aḥmad.

"Your companions have surrendered," I told him. "You've discharged your responsibility before God. Everyone else has given in, and here you are, still locked up!"

"Uncle," he replied, "if those who know remain silent out of fear, and the ignorant remain silent out of ignorance, then when does the truth come out?"

Hearing this I stopped trying to change his mind (Ḥanbal, *Dhikr*, 41).

The failure of Isḥāq's plan, along with his later attempt to talk Ibn Ḥanbal down (Ḥanbal, *Dhikr*, 49), not to mention his alleged complicity in persuading the crowd that Ibn Ḥanbal was unharmed after the flogging (see 69.57), may have made him a *persona non grata* and his reports distasteful (van Ess, *Theologie*, 3:461–62).

354 The relevant part of the report reads: "You must know that, when I'm gone, princes will arise. Anyone who seeks them out, believes their lies, and abets their tyranny is not part of my community nor am I of his." See al-Turkī, 431n2.

355 Ḥanbal's account includes a tantalizing detail regarding this episode. The interrogators, he says, came to see Ibn Ḥanbal, carrying with them "a picture of the heavens and the earth, and other things" (*ṣūratu al-samawāti wa-l-arḍi wa-ghayru dhālika*). Then, Ibn Ḥanbal is quoted as saying, "They asked me something I knew nothing about" (Ḥanbal, *Dhikr*, 42). Al-Ma'mūn is known to have sponsored the drawing of world maps and star charts (Sezgin, *GAS*, 10:73–149) so the claim is believable, but one can only speculate about why the interrogators would show those items to Ibn Ḥanbal. Perhaps they hoped to persuade him that the caliph had access to knowledge that could not be derived from the Hadith (Cooperson, *Al-Ma'mun*, 105).

356 The line of argument implied here runs as follows: If God is not created, none of His attributes, including knowledge, can be created either. Since it is encompassed by God's knowledge and spoken in His voice, the Qur'an must also be uncreated.

357 Q Zukhruf 43:3.

358 Q Fīl 105:5. In this verse and the one cited just before, the verb *ja'ala*, as Ibn Ḥanbal points out, means "to make" in the sense of "cause to have a certain attribute." It does not mean "to create."

359 Perhaps the Orchard Gate (or Garden Gate) located on the east side of the Tigris, near the palace of al-Muʿtaṣim (Le Strange, *Baghdad*, 221, 276, maps 5 and 8). Ibn Ḥanbal seems to have been taken there by boat.

360 That is, on the permissibility of performing one's ablutions by wiping one's shoes instead of removing them and washing the feet. This was a distinctively Sunni position. The story itself is obviously contrived. For one thing, protocol did not permit speaking without first being addressed by the caliph.

361 A longer version of this report appears in 69.30. Both reports overlook the twenty-eight months Ibn Ḥanbal spent in prison (69.28) and thus give an incorrect date for his trial, which took place in Ramadan 220/September 835 (van Ess, *Theologie*, 3:460).

362 According to Ḥanbal's account, the caliph was surprised that Ibn Ḥanbal was middle-aged: "You told me he was a young man!" (*a-laysa zaʿamtum li-annahu ḥadathun*). See Ḥanbal, *Dhikr*, 43.

363 Ibn Ḥanbal (or more likely one of his biographers) is using a report transmitted by Ibn ʿAbbās, the ancestor of the Abbasid caliphs, to argue by implication that the authorities have no business questioning Muslims who profess faith by the definition given here.

364 Q Anʿām 6:120; Raʿd 13:16; Zumar 39:62; Ghāfir 40:62.

365 Q Aḥqāf 46:24–25.

366 The point is that the expression "everything" is not always categorical.

367 Q Anbiyā' 21:2.

368 Q Ṣād 38:1. This verse, like several others, begins with the name of an Arabic letter or letters, in this case *ṣād*.

369 That is, you should seek nearness to God by reciting the Qur'an. The disputant understands this to imply that God and His word are two distinct entities.

370 I thank Tahera Qutbuddin for suggesting this interpretation of a puzzling passage. After the first hundred thousand I expected *mi'atay alf*, "two hundred thousand," which is written almost indistinguishably from *mi'at alf*, but the manuscripts agree on the latter.

371 Ḥanbal's account sets this remark in a different light. In his telling, Ibn Abī Du'ād says to Ibn Ḥanbal: "I hear you like to be a leader" (*balaghanī annaka tuḥibbu r-ri'āsah*; *Dhikr*, 51), and then the caliph makes his offer to parade Ibn Ḥanbal around as a hero. This question of Ibn Ḥanbal's popular following is a tantalizing one. Steppat ("From *Ahd Ardašīr*") notes that a Persian work on statecraft known to al-Ma'mūn urges rulers to crush any manifestations of religious leadership among the people, and may have inspired the Inquisition. Ḥanbal claims that during the Ibn Ḥanbal's flogging "people had gathered in the square, the lanes, and elsewhere; the markets had closed and crowds had gathered" (*Dhikr*, 60). Later Ḥanbalī accounts make much of the crowd, though these accounts are not very persuasive (Winkelmann-Liebert, "Die *miḥna*," 246). On the other hand, sources hostile to Ibn Ḥanbal and his followers speak fearfully of their supposed power to command the rabble (Qāḍī, "Earliest *Nābita*" and Cooperson, "Al-Jāḥiẓ").

372 This passage is puzzling, as the fast should already have ended after the sunset prayer mentioned just above.

373 That is, the scholars summoned to al-Raqqah at the beginning of the Inquisition (in 212/827–28) to be questioned regarding the Qur'an (see chapter 76). All of them reportedly agreed to say that it was created.

374 This list is an interpolation by a transmitter or by the author. Only three of these names agree with those listed by al-Ṭabarī, *Ta'rīkh*, 1116–67/8:634; cf. Ḥanbal, *Dhikr*, 34–36. The descendants of the men involved doubtless tried to get their names off such an infamous list (van Ess, *Theologie* 3:455n23).

375 Q Nisāʾ 4:11.

376 The point is that one needs Hadith in order to understand the Qurʾan properly. This was Ibn Ḥanbal's reply to those who sought to dismiss Hadith as a source of knowledge.

377 The day began at sunset, so for Ibn Ḥanbal the third night would be followed by the third day.

378 Literally, "my voice became louder than theirs." The text may indeed mean this, though it seems implausible for him to be depicted as shouting at his opponents.

379 At roughly this point in the parallel account by Ḥanbal, there is mention of an argument that the editor has omitted on the grounds that it contradicts what is known of Ibn Ḥanbal's opinions (Ḥanbal, *Dhikr*, 55, note 1). As the passage is of some interest, I reproduce it here from the Dār al-kutub manuscript (Taʾrīkh Taymūr no. 2000, microfilm no. 11159, folio no. 16). After *wa-kān min amrihi mā kan*, which appears in the printed edition (p. 55), the account continues:

> . . . *wa-samiʿtu Abā ʿAbda l-Lāhi yaqūlu wa-ḥtajjū ʿalayya yawmaʾidin qāla tajīʾu l-baqaratu yawma l-qiyāmati wa-tajīʾu tabāraka fa-qultu lahum innamā hādhā th-thawābu qāla l-Lāhu wa-jāʾa rabbuka wa l-malāku ṣaffan ṣaffan innamā taʾtī qudratuhu innamā l-Qurʾānu amthālun wa-mawāʿiẓu wa-amrun wa-kadhā* [sc. *wa-hādhā*?] *fa-kadhā* [print edition resumes] *wa-qultu l-ʿAbdi r-Raḥmāni . . .*
>
> I heard Abu ʿAbd Allāh [Ibn Ḥanbal] say: "They argued against me that day by saying: '[Don't you say that the chapter called] the Cow and the [chapter called] Tabārak will come on the Day of Resurrection?'
>
> "I told them: 'This [sc. the thing that will come] is only the reward [for reading the Qurʾan]. God [also] says: "Your Lord will come, with the angels arrayed in rows" [Q Fajr 89:22]. [By this is meant] only [that] His power comes. The Qurʾan is only similitudes, exhortations, and commandment; and this [expression] is like that.'"

Here ʿAbd al-Raḥmān is accusing Ibn Ḥanbal of holding the anthropomorphist view that the chapters of the Qurʾan would come to life on the Day of Resurrection. The chapters in question (Baqarah and Tabārak or Mulk) seem to have figured as part of the accusation because they mention creatures (cows and birds respectively) that were supposed to take on physical reality. The argument was that if God had literal, physical eyes and ears, as the Qurʾan seems to say, then the cows and birds (for example) must have a real existence too. In this passage Ibn Ḥanbal rejects the *reductio ad absurdem* but as a consequence is forced to say that the Qurʾan need not always be taken literally. This is the view that Naghsh, the editor, finds contradictory with Ibn Ḥanbal's known opinions. (I thank Josef van Ess for helping me understand this passage; any errors are of course mine.)

380 The copyists of D and SH appear not to have understood this passage, but H has a fairly clear *nābayi l-khashabatayn*, meaning literally "the two tusks" or "eye-teeth" of the posts. Al-Turkī reads *nātiʾ*, "the part sticking out," which is plausible in itself but requires emending H. Although I have not found either term attested as the name for part of a whipping apparatus, the instructions seem clear enough. The person being flogged was suspended from ropes or straps (the latter suggested by Winkelmann-Liebert, "Die *miḥnah*," 255) tied around the wrists and attached to the posts by a horizontal peg or bar. Ibn Ḥanbal is being told to hold on to this horizontal element, or the ropes, and pull himself up to ease the tension on his wrists.

381 Cooperson ("Two Abbasid Trials") argues that al-Muʿtaṣim may here be calling for the unbarbed whips mentioned in the hostile account by al-Jāḥiẓ (*Rasāʾil*, 3:295–96), in order to minimize Ibn Ḥanbal's injuries. Winkelmann-Liebert, by contrast, thinks the references to al-Muʿtaṣim's soft-heartedness are much exaggerated ("Die *miḥnah*," 253ff.).

382 Lictors were ancient Roman officials who did many jobs besides flogging, but English does not have another common word for flogger, and "lictor" has the sanction of having been used by Patton in his 1897 rendering of this episode (*Aḥmed*, 108).

383 On the face of it, this curse suggests that the caliph was angry that the lictors were not striking more forcefully. Winkelmann-Liebert, however, suggests that the caliph was upset about having to flog Ibn Ḥanbal—or at least that the Ḥanbalī biographers wanted to depict him that way ("Die *miḥnah*," 255).

384 This account places the trial in a courtyard. Extant examples of Abbasid-era buildings indicate that they consisted of rooms, or complexes of rooms, arranged around a central courtyard (see, for example, Northedge, *Historical Topography*). Literary sources indicate that the yard was used for formal events and the rooms for intimate gatherings. Al-Muʿtaṣim would have been sitting under a shade; when he got up to address Ibn Ḥanbal, he would have been exposing himself to the sun.

385 Or "I didn't know what I was doing." Ḥanbal's account says: "I passed out and came to more than once [*rubbamā lam aʿqil wa-rubbamā ʿaqaltu*]. When they hit me again I would pass out and not know [anything], and they would stop hitting me" (Ḥanbal, *Dhikr*, 57). Van Ess has argued that this way of putting things is intended to cover up some act of capitulation on Ibn Ḥanbal's part, without which he would never have been released (*Theologie*, 3:465). Three sources (al-Jāḥiẓ, *Rasāʾil*, 3:295–96; al-Yaʿqūbī, *Taʾrīkh*, 2:576–77; Ibn al-Murtaḍā, *Tabaqāt*, 122–25) agree that he capitulated. One (al-Jāḥiẓ) even refers to the event as if to a matter of common knowledge (see further Hinds, "Miḥna" and Winkelmann-Liebert, "Die *miḥnah*," 267). References to *taqiyyah*, or dissimulation justified by circumstance (e.g., 69.28, and Ḥanbal, *Dhikr*, 37–38), indeed suggest that the principle was invoked by Ibn Ḥanbal's partisans to justify a lapse on his part during the trial. And the proliferation of fantastic reports exonerating him (Abū l-ʿArab, *Miḥan*, 438–44; Abū Nuʿaym, *Ḥilyah*, 9:204–5; Ibn Abī Yaʿlā, *Ṭabaqāt*, 1:437–43 [the entry on Sulaymān ibn ʿAbd Allāh al-Sijzī of the first *ṭabaqah*]; al-Maqdisī, *Miḥnah*, 109) implies there was indeed a scandal that needed to be narrated away (Cooperson, *Classical*, 129–38). However one chooses to evaluate the evidence, three points are worth bearing in mind. First, the circumstances of

the trial—its being held inside the palace, the use of torture, and the lack of sympathetic witnesses—made the facts of the matter almost immediately irretrievable (a point some of the participants seem to have realized; see 69.56). Second, Ibn Ḥanbal made his opposition to rationalist theology and imamic pretentions clear enough on numerous occasions, such that there need be little doubt of his actual views, regardless of what happened at the trial. Finally, Sunni tradition is unanimous in its conviction that he did not capitulate, so that, even if he did, his having done so has effectively been abolished from history.

386 Ḥanbal gives a more detailed report of Ibn Ḥanbal's departure:

> At sunset, Aḥmad was led out of the house on a mount belonging to Isḥāq ibn Ibrāhīm and rode to his own house surrounded by the caliph's officials and his own people. When he reached the gate, I heard ʿAyyāsh, the Master of the Bridge, say, when he saw Aḥmad approaching—I heard ʿAyyāsh say to Isḥāq's man, with everyone standing there—"*Tāzīh tāzīh*," which means "Arab! Arab!" (Ḥanbal, *Dhikr*, 60).

The Persian word *tāzīh* means "Arab," and apparently in this case "Arab's son reared in Persia" (Steingass, *Persian-English Dictionary*, s.v. *tāzīk*); I thank John Patrick Flanagan for this reference. Beyond that, though, ʿAyyāsh seems to have meant something else: namely, that he was a rigid, legalistic scholar. This interpretation was suggested to me by Patricia Crone, who notes that Bābak referred to Muslims as *yahūd* for the same reason: both (he thought) believed in a distant God who issued "an endless stream of restrictive rules" (Crone, *Nativist Prophets*, 273).

387 Since Ibn Ḥanbal had been fasting all day, he could have eaten, though he is depicted as refusing to consume anything provided for him by the caliph. The second point regards *taqiyyah*, or "prudential dissimulation," according to which a Muslim may conceal his beliefs to protect himself from harm. Ibn Ḥanbal is depicted as rejecting this option.

388 *Al-hanbāzān*: perhaps from Persian *hambāz*, "companion" or "partner," here Arabized to mean the two parallel supports of the scaffold.

389 Q Nisā' 4:30.

390 This is the first of many reports invented to make Ibn Ḥanbal's ordeal into a test of the rightness of the Sunni creed.

391 Bilāl ibn Abī Rabāḥ, a slave who was one of the first to accept Islam, is described as suffering tortures at the hands of his masters but nevertheless refusing to recant.

392 Q Tawbah 9:51.

393 The sharply critical biographer Shams al-Din al-Dhahabī (d. 748/1348) denounces this report as "wrong" and condemns Abū Nuʿaym al-Iṣfahānī (but not Ibn al-Jawzī) for repeating "abominable fantastications" (*khurāfāt samijah*) about Ibn Ḥanbal's ordeal (al-Dhahabī, *Siyar*, 11:255). See al-Turkī, 488n3, and Cooperson, "Probability."

394 The most natural reading makes Ibn Ḥanbal the one who would have died. The day was still momentous for the caliph because killing Ibn Ḥanbal would entail being punished in the afterlife. The Arabic sentence can also mean that the caliph is the one who would have died—a possibility worth considering only because of the fantastic nature of these accounts. See also 69.58.

395 As used here, the verb *baṭṭala* (so voweled in H and D) seems to mean that Ibn Ḥanbal has given the lie to the bandits' claims to toughness. On this trope, see Cooperson, *Classical*, 138–41.

396 This sentence displays unusual pronoun agreement: the *-hu* suffix on *ḍarabtu* refers to the masculine singular *sawṭ*, but the verb *haddat* is feminine singular as if referring to the set of eighty blows.

397 This is the philologist Nifṭawayh (d. 323/935); his *History* is lost (Bencheikh, "Nifṭawayh").

398 This (probably invented) story is set in the period after the Inquisition.

399 Apparently meaning: join him in protesting to the caliph over what was being done to Ibn Ḥanbal.

400 Bishr's extreme asceticism and refusal to teach Hadith distinguished him from Ibn Ḥanbal. Stories like this were invented to help negotiate

the conflict between the two visions of piety (Cooperson, *Classical*, 178–84).

401 Ibn al-Jawzī may have in mind reports claiming that Ibn Ḥanbal did capitulate (see 69.26). Conversely, he may be thinking of certain pro-Ḥanbalī fictions even less likely than the ones cited here (Cooperson, *Classical*, 129–38).

402 It is not clear which of the above-named transmitters is speaking here.

403 Catacombers: warriors based in, or near, the *maṭāmīr*, that is, the underground complexes of Cappadocia, on the Byzantine frontier (Honignmann, *Ostgrenze*, 46; cf. Eger, *Islamic-Byzantine Frontier*, 252).

404 A parallel text (al-Dhahabī, *Siyar*, 11:259; added in brackets by al-Turkī, 459) has here "Some will say he did give in," which is a plausible addition but not present in our manuscripts.

405 This speech provides a convenient explanation for Ibn Ḥanbal's release—so convenient, in fact, that it is likely to have been fabricated by one of his partisans.

406 "He" most likely refers to the Caliph al-Muʿtaṣim, though it might also refer to Isḥāq, Ibn Ḥanbal's uncle, who apparently went along with the trick.

407 The rough cloak would shrink painfully after being drenched.

408 "Rejoice!" may mean "Rejoice in the prospect of entering Paradise," to which the pious caliph replies that the innocent man would testify against him on the Day of Judgment.

409 A marginal note in D, partially cut off on the left, reads: "These [men] were not beaten under the same circumstances as Aḥmad. Had Aḥmad not stood firm, people would have strayed from right belief. The trials [of these men] are therefore not to be compared to his." A second marginal comment adds that Ibn Ḥanbal's trial can be compared only to that of ʿUmar, the second caliph. Ibn Ḥanbal's achievement is still greater, though, because he, unlike ʿUmar, had no one fighting with him.

410 This seems to be a (rather harsh) reference to al-Muʿtaṣim.

411 Q Shūrā 42:40.

412 Q Shūrā 42:40.

413 Ḥanbal tells us that his name was Abū Ṣubḥ (*Dhikr*, 61).

414 A reference to the Prophet's concealing himself in a cave during his flight from Mecca to Medina.

415 Abū Zurʿah seems to be asking "Why did al-Muʿtaṣim flog you instead of beheading you, and why didn't al-Wāthiq hurt you at all?" Ibn Ḥanbal appears to give him the answer to a different question, namely: "How did you survive the flogging?"

416 This apocryphal story, in its two variants, has a character very much like Ibn Ḥanbal make all of the arguments that Ibn Ḥanbal himself was unable or unwilling to make at his trial. See further van Ess, *Theologie*, 3:502–4. For much more elaborate fiction, in which al-Maʾmūn himself is bested, see van Ess, *Theologie*, 3:504–8, and Omari, "Kitāb al-Ḥayda."

417 Q Nisāʾ 4:86.

418 This putative recording of an insignificant variant seems to be an attempt on the part of the storyteller to give the impression that he is upholding the strictest standards of accurate transmission.

419 All the manuscripts have *yaṣbaʾ*, "to go from one religion to another." Al-Turkī, drawing on a parallel text, emends to *yaṣbū*, "to suffer from youthful ignorance." This is a plausible reading but has no support in the manuscripts.

420 Addressing a stranger by his name instead of his *kunyah* (Ibn Abī Duʾād) was rude and dismissive.

421 Q Māʾidah 5:3.

422 What Ibn al-Jawzī does not tell us is that Ibn Ḥanbal was reportedly asked to join a rebellion against al-Wāthiq. During al-Wāthiq's reign, teachers were ordered to tell their pupils that the Qurʾan was created, and scholars who did not accept the caliph's teaching were separated from their wives. A number of Baghdad jurisprudents came to Ibn Ḥanbal saying that they no longer acknowledged al-Wāthiq as caliph. Ibn Ḥanbal reportedly urged them not to make a bad situation worse by rejecting their obligation to obey the authorities. It was at this juncture that al-Wāthiq ordered him to make himself scarce (Ḥanbal, *Dhikr*, 69–73).

423 On the end of the Inquisition, see Melchert, "Religious Policies." The "reports on seeing God" were among those interpreted literally by the Sunnis and figuratively by their rivals; see further Omari, "Beatific Vision."

424 Meter: *kāmil.*

425 Q Aʿrāf 7:54.

426 The partisans of ʿAlī—that is, the Shiʿa—believed that the only legitimate religious exemplar, and by extension the ideal leader of the community, was a descendant of ʿAlī ibn Abī Ṭālib. During the civil war between al-Amīn and al-Maʾmūn, Shiʿi claimants had rebelled in Kufa, Yemen, and the Hijaz.

427 Here Ibn Ḥanbal seems to be saying that he has not disappeared from public life in order to signal disapproval of the regime, but rather because al-Muʿtaṣim and al-Wāthiq had forbidden him to appear in public.

428 Jadʿān, who thinks of Ibn Ḥanbal as willing to countenance rebellion against the Abbasid regime, suggests that the accusation may have been true (Jadʿān, *Miḥnah*, 285–90).

429 This is presumably an error for Abū ʿAlī Yaḥyā (al-Turkī, 488n5).

430 The word *ijjānah* usually means a large shallow drinking bowl, but since it is used here to cover a sizable bag of coins I have chosen the secondary meaning of washtub. It may have been green because it was made of oxidized copper. I thank Paul Cobb, Nancy Khalek, and Noura Elkoussy for their thoughts on this point.

431 Apparently Ibn Ḥanbal did not want to use the light without paying for it, a problem he addresses elsewhere; see Cooperson, *Classical*, 176.

432 The Arabic says only "after he passed Yaḥyā ibn Harthamah," leaving it unclear who passed Yaḥyā (a military commander), and what it meant to pass him. The translation is my best guess.

433 Ibn Abī Duʾād, who by this time had fallen out of favor, had pushed for broad adoption of the dogma of the created Qurʾan. Al-Mutawakkil seems to be asking Ibn Ḥanbal to preach in favor of the opposite view and thus make up for the Abbasid adoption of a now-heretical creed.

434 I take this to be the horse's name. The dictionaries define the word as "the horse that places second in a race," here perhaps meaning a horse of good but not superior quality. It may be that Yaḥyā is making a joke: *muṣallī* also happens to mean "engaged in prayer," which may have struck him as an appropriate name for an animal ridden by Ibn Ḥanbal.

435 Q Ṭā Hā 20:55.

436 Ḥanbal gives a more detailed account of this meeting. Upon seeing Ibn Ḥanbal, the caliph's mother says to her son: "I beg you: fear God in your dealings with that man. There's nothing you can offer him to tempt him, and it's no good trying to keep him here away from his home. So let him go: don't try and hold him!" Ibn Ḥanbal then enters the presence of the heir apparent, al-Muʿtazz, but fails to address him as "emir." Isḥāq ibn Ibrāhīm was reportedly minded to strike Ibn Ḥanbal with his sword, but the prince's tutor, Ibn Ḥanbal's former interrogator ʿAbd al-Raḥmān al-Ḍabbī, merely tells the boy, "This is the tutor your father has sent you." Ibn Ḥanbal then reports: "The boy replied that he would learn whatever I taught him. I was impressed with his clever answer given how little he was" (Ḥanbal, *Dhikr*, 90).

437 *Khayshah*: a strip of wet cloth suspended from the ceiling and moved back and forth by a servant to cool a room. The only English word for this seems to be punkah, which comes from Hindi.

438 Yaʿqūb's request seems to have been a trick intended to find out whether Ibn Ḥanbal indeed refused to teach anyone or just the caliph's sons.

439 Q Māʾidah 5:1.

440 Q Baqarah 2:156–7: «Those who say, when afflicted with a calamity, "We belong to God and to Him we shall return," are the ones who will have blessings and mercy from their Lord.»

441 Apparently the stipend granted by al-Mutawakkil.

442 Literally "some knots have slipped off me." Ibn Ḥanbal may be alluding to a report in which ʿUmar used the word "knots" to mean "appointments to positions of power." See Ibn Manẓūr, *Lisān*, s.v. *ʿ-Q-D*.

443 I am not entirely satisfied that I understand what *huwa muṣaddaq* means here, but al-Turkī's voweling imposes this reading. Other

possibilities, e.g., *muṣaddiq* and *muṣṣaddiq*, mean payer or collector of the alms-tax, but neither fits the sense or the syntax of the passage.

444 Following the parallel text in Ṣāliḥ, *Sīrat al-imām*, al-Turkī has "the children of Sāliḥ and ʿAbd Allāh, the two sons of Aḥmad ibn Muḥammad ibn Ḥanbal."

445 This description is not entirely clear to me, but it seems to refer to the sunken-eyed look that accompanies starvation.

446 That is, to exhort and admonish him. On this tradition, see Cook, *Commanding Right*.

447 Ibn Ḥanbal apparently means that he would remind the caliph of his duty to care for the descendants of the first Muslims.

448 The elaborate courtly style of the first paragraph, the omission of important details, and the direct reference to Ibn Ḥanbal's view of Disputation all suggest that this letter is a forgery intended to make his doctrine palatable to outsiders.

449 Q Tawbah 9:6.

450 Q Aʿrāf 7:54.

451 A reference to Q Furqān 25:63: «The true servants of the Gracious One are those who walk upon the earth with humility and when they are addressed by the ignorant ones, their response is, "Peace"» (or "Goodbye," *salāman*).

452 A less elaborate telling of this story is dismissed as a fabrication by al-Dhahabī, *Siyar*, 11:321; see Cooperson, "Probability," 71. The point of the fiction may be to rehabilitate Ibn Rāhawayh, of whom Ibn Ḥanbal disapproved.

453 That is, the property he coveted would appear to testify against him.

454 All the manuscripts read *ilā mā d.w.r.nā*, which makes no evident sense. Al-Turkī instead gives *balaghahu*, "and it reached him" (that is, the news reached Ibn Ḥanbal), from a parallel account.

455 Ibn Ḥanbal's two youngest children.

456 Leading the Muslims into battle, defending the frontier, and dividing up the spoils were among the duties of the imam or head of the community. Since al-Mutawakkil, in Ibn Ḥanbal's view, was not carrying out these tasks, the money he collected through taxation was

misappropriated. Consequently, any gift of money from the treasury was unacceptable to the scrupulous.

457 Ibn ʿUlayyah reportedly died before the Inquisition; see al-Turkī, 519n1.

458 Q Baqarah 2:156, recited when affliction strikes.

459 The passage in context runs as follows: "God will not guide those who will not believe in the signs of God, and theirs will be a painful punishment. Only those fabricate lies concerning God who do not believe in the signs of God, and these are the liars. As for one who denies God after he has believed—not one who is forced to do it while his heart rests securely in faith, but one who opens his heart to a denial of truth—such as these will have a terrible punishment" (Q Naḥl 16:104–06).

460 In the report, the pagans force ʿAmmār ibn Yāsir to curse the Prophet and praise their deities. He later confesses his misdeed to the Prophet, who tells him that as long as he remained a believer in his heart then no harm was done. The Hadith does not appear in the collections in the form cited here; see al-Turkī, 524n2.

461 Part of a report in which believers are told to act on the parts of the Qurʾan they do understand and to leave the rest for God to clarify. See al-Turkī, 326n1.

462 ʿAlī seems to be trying to protect his shoes and clothing from getting dirty, a matter of concern if one were attending the state-sponsored prayer but presumably not an issue for Ibn Ḥanbal and his ascetic circle.

463 Q Ikhlāṣ 112:1–2. *Ṣamad* may once have meant "with no hollow" (Gardet, "Allāh") or "impenetrable," "dense to the absolute degree" (Böwering, "God"). English translations of the verse vary significantly, rendering *ṣamad* as, e.g., "the Self-sufficient One" (Wahiduddin Khan), "the Everlasting Refuge" (Arberry), "the eternally besought of all" (Pickthall), "immanently indispensable" (Ahmed Ali), "the Eternal, Absolute" (Yusuf Ali) (all translations at tanzil.net). Chapter 112 as a whole denies trinitarianism, so *ṣamad* may (also) carry the sense that God does not consist of distinct persons. In view of the divergent possibilities I have not ventured a translation.

464 Q Dhāriyāt 51:22.

465 Q Dhāriyāt 51:22.

466 It is unclear precisely who is meant.

467 Forty *raṭls* times four hundred grams, the approximate value of a Baghdad *raṭl* (Ashtor, "*Mawāzīn*").

468 Q Shuʿarāʾ 26:2.

469 An allusion to Q Ikhlāṣ 112:31; Dukhān 44:53.

470 *Laylat al-arbiʿāʾ*: in the Islamic calendar, the day begins at sunset, so "Wednesday night" in Arabic is Tuesday night in English. But the date seems wrong anyway, as the first of Rabīʿ I 241 [July 20, 855] was a Saturday.

471 It seems to have been ʿAlī ibn al-Jaʿd's son who came: ʿAlī himself was already dead by this time, and a parallel text has *ibn*. See al-Turkī, 541n2.

472 The manuscripts insist on *uʿṭiyat*, which provides the basis for my translation, though I am not certain it is right.

473 According to the common understanding of Q Anfāl 8:59, one who swears an oath and does not fulfill it may make expiation by (among other things) feeding ten destitute persons. See further Lange, "Expiation." Presumably Ṣāliḥ gave the dates away to the poor. Neither Ibn Ḥanbal nor his biographers tell us what vow it was he broke.

474 Al-Faḍl ibn al-Rabīʿ had been vizier to al-Rashīd and al-Amīn. He survived the civil war during which al-Maʾmūn overthrew al-Amīn, but was thereafter disgraced. His son's visit to Ibn Ḥanbal in prison shows that the old Abbasid order disapproved of the Inquisition. Like many of al-Maʾmūn's other initiatives, it undermined the legitimacy of the dynasty by suggesting that only some of its members—specifically, those that behaved like Shiʿi imams—could serve as rulers.

475 *Al-rukhaṣ* are cases of replacing a commandment "with a less onerous alternative in cases of need or duress" (Katz, "*ʿAzīmah* and *Rukhṣah*"). Presumably Ibn Ḥanbal was worried about having failed to complete all his religious duties during his illness and wanted reassurance that he had a good excuse.

476 For an analysis of this story, see Cooperson, "Probability," 78–81.

477 Unfortunately, this date, which corresponds to July 31, 855, was a Wednesday.

478 Muslim funeral practice requires that a man's body be wrapped in three pieces of cloth, each of which covers it entirely.

479 The Amānūs or Nur Dağları mountain range in what is today Turkey, just across the northwest border with Syria. God has given the visitors the power to travel instantly from there in time for the funeral.

480 For a caustic denunciation of this unlikely story, see al-Dhahabī, *Siyar*, 11:343, and Cooperson, "Probability," 74–75.

481 The passage in H and SH is garbled. Al-Turkī supplies *al-ḥuzn*, "sorrow," giving the more likely meaning that all virtuous households were in mourning. Here I have rendered what is in the manuscripts, garbled though it may be.

482 Or: "We keep them here so people can copy them." The point, in any case, seems to be that he knows these reports to have been properly transmitted. If they leave his hands, he cannot guarantee their authenticity should others someday wish to copy them.

483 This chapter contains ten poems, some of them very long. Hadith-scholars and their friends are not usually admired for their poetic talents, and these verses are not particularly distinguished. But I have included two examples to give the curious reader a sense of the original chapter.

484 "Aḥmad" means "most praiseworthy."

485 Meter: *sarīʿ*.

486 Meter: *kāmil*.

487 Biographies of exceptional Muslims often describe their posthumous appearances in the dreams of others. The more different people claimed to have had the same dream, the likelier it seemed that it contained a true communication from the deceased. For this reason, this chapter contains many nearly identical accounts of the same dream as reported by different speakers. I have removed as many of these near-duplicates as possible.

488 The original sentence seems patched together here, probably because a transmitter omitted the curse that appears in the version immediately following.

489 Q Zumar 39:74. This is what the blessed say after being admitted to the Garden.

490 The first person singular here and in the corresponding place in the parallel reports could be Ibn Ḥanbal and the one answering could be Sufyān. In 92.12, though, the questioner asks about Miskīnah, who says "If only you knew!" This means that the questioner must still be alive and dreaming rather than dead and in the Garden.

491 The storyteller has God refer to Himself in the third person, as in the Qur'an. The transmitters of this report evidently thought that hating ʿAlī was a grave fault in a Sunni. The transmitters of the variant immediately preceding either thought otherwise or simply did not wish to repeat God's supposed cursing of Jarīr.

492 Q Zumar 39:74.

493 Q Anʿām 6:89.

494 Q Anʿām 6:89–90.

495 Q Anʿām 6:89.

496 From Q Baqarah 2:137: «If they believe as you have believed, then are they rightly guided; but if they turn back, then know that they are entrenched in hostility. God will surely suffice to defend you against them, for He is All Hearing, All Knowing.»

497 The text seems garbled here and the variant does not help. The likeliest way for the story to go is: "I noticed that many of them were carrying spears. The Prophet looked out, as if intending to dispatch an expedition, and saw a spear taller than any of the others."

498 Or: those whom Ibn Ḥanbal loves.

499 Evidently Yaḥyā ibn Maʿīn.

500 "Pelting" is explained as being struck by stones flung from the skies, and "disfigurement" as being changed into an uglier form, such as that of an animal. The report is described as referring to the punishments that will befall Muslims who commit certain transgressions.

501 Apparently Isḥāq ibn Rāhawayh.

502 That is, he was a Ḥanafī or a Shiʿi.

503 The niche is the feature in a mosque that indicates the direction to Mecca. Ibn Ḥanbal seems to be saying, "Keep praying until you die."

504 A *sāq* is normally a leg or stalk. Here it is being used as a measure of length but I have not been able to pin down the meaning any more precisely.

505 In this chapter, as in the one preceding, I have omitted nearly identical retellings of the same dream.

506 For the story, see the second report following.

507 Q Baqarah 2:156.

508 The original story may have specified the caliph or governor involved, but later Sunni transmitters seem to have suppressed the name to protect his reputation.

509 The verb used means literally "to grasp someone's forearm." The gesture was used (among other things) to show allegiance to a newly appointed caliph.

510 That is, al-Khaḍir appeared to him in a dream.

511 A name for Baghdad, reportedly given because its first mosque was imperfectly aligned toward Mecca.

512 An expression of great esteem, based in the pre-Islamic practice of capturing members of rival tribes and releasing them in exchange for something valuable.

513 A reference to Q Nisāʾ 4:164, where God speaks directly to Moses.

514 A reference to Q Muṭaffifīn 83:18–21: «But, the record of the righteous is [preserved] in the ʿIlliyyīn. And what will make you understand what the ʿIlliyyīn is? A written record, which those angels closest to God will bear witness to.» Some exegetes also explain the word as referring to a high place in the Garden.

515 This seems to be an error for Aḥmad, as Ibn al-Jawzī points out.

516 That is, adopt his positions on law and the like.

517 A respected transmitter of reports from his father, ʿUmar, the second caliph.

518 This report offers a puzzling chronology. Aḥmad ibn Naṣr al-Khuzāʿī, who is sitting with the Prophet, was executed during the reign of

al-Wāthiq—that is, long after al-Qawārīrī's forced capitulation to the Inquisition.

519 A quarter called Dār al-Quṭn (with the article) existed between the ʿĪsā Canal in al-Karkh (Le Strange, *Baghdad*, 84, and map 4, no. 32).

520 The word *ṭūbā* appears in Q Raʿd 13:29. Some exegetes explain it as the name of a tree in Paradise while others say that it means simply "bliss." See Waines, "Tree(s)" and Kinberg, "Paradise."

521 Q Kahf 18:63ff, where an unnamed servant of God teaches Moses about patience.

522 A reference to two nearly identical verses of the Qur'an: «Before you also the messengers We sent were but [mortal] men to whom We vouchsafed revelation. Ask the People of the *dhikr*, if you do not know» (Q Naḥl 16:43 and Anbiyāʾ 21:7). The term *ahl al-dhikr* in this verse has been explained as "the recipients of previous scriptures." More generally it can also mean people mindful of God.

523 So says the one manuscript that contains the story, though "he was wearing fine clothes" seems a likelier thing to say here.

524 Ar. *mukhannath*, originally a man, usually a musician, who dressed and acted like a woman for entertainment. In Ibn Ḥanbal's time, *mukhannathūn* associated with the court were famous for "savage mockery, extravagant burlesque, and low sexual humor" (Rowson, "Effeminates," quotation at 693). The word can also mean "hermaphrodite," but being a hermaphrodite was not a sin or a crime, so the speaker in this story would not need to be forgiven (at least, not for that).

525 Q Hūd 11:105.

526 In Arab folklore, every human being has a jinni counterpart of the opposite sex.

527 Based on the account in Lane, s.v. *T-N-R*, it seems we must imagine an oven open at the top which had to be turned over to create a closed space. It must also have had a door on the side for inserting the clover, which apparently served as a fireproof sort of bedding.

528 The historical Harthamah took part in the siege of Baghdad, which ended in the death of the Caliph al-Amīn. But he was himself executed shortly thereafter, during the reign of al-Maʾmūn: that is,

several decades before al-Mutawakkil became caliph. Ḥanbalī storytellers seem to have had a confused idea of Abbasid prosopography.

529 Meter: *kāmil.*

530 This seems to mean that he did not send his son to school or hire a tutor for him but instead preferred to instruct him himself.

531 Unassimilated, this word would be *iʾtakhadhtum,* which as far as I know is not actually used.

532 For more on Ibn Ḥanbal's views on recitation, see Melchert, "Aḥmad ibn Ḥanbal and the Qurʾān," 25–26.

533 The speaker, al-Shāfiʿī, will defend Mālik ibn Anas, and the challenger will defend Abū Ḥanīfah.

534 The book written in Baghdad is apparently (the first draft of) the *Risālah* (*Epistle,* trans. Lowry) and the one written in Egypt is the *Umm.*

535 That is, one to clean the face and another to clean the arms as far as the elbows.

536 The Prophet is described as "striking his palms on the ground, blowing on them, and wiping his face and hands" (see references in al-Turkī, 666n1).

537 That is, if having met the Companions necessarily confers precedence, Saʿīd and others should outrank Abū Ḥanīfah.

538 That is, if certain Successors thought more highly of Mālik than they did of the Prophet's Companions then the premise that one gains precedence simply by having met the Companions cannot be valid.

539 That is, people preferred the word of transmitters more distantly related to the Prophet than Ibn ʿAbbās.

540 Q Nisāʾ 4:3.

541 That is, the person to whom I owe everything in my books is Ibn Ḥanbal. Al-Turkī, 668n5, inserts this phrase for clarity, but it is not there in the manuscripts. The original audience doubtless knew what was meant.

542 In this abridgement I have cut down the number of biographies even further, retaining only those of particular historical or literary importance.

543 To take something from someone *min taḥt yadihi* ("from under his hand") elsewhere means to take what one is owed from another party without his knowledge or permission. As that is hardly likely here, I am guessing that a more literal meaning is intended. Possibly, too, the phrase is *man taḥt yadihi*, "those dependent on him," but then an additional word would be needed to complete the sentence.

544 I thank Christopher Melchert for suggesting an explanation for this passage.

545 I thank Peter Pormann for explaining the term *qiyām al-dam*.

546 The "City of Salvation" is Baghdad, so named (in my view) because its Abbasid founders and rulers considered themselves imams, meaning that allegiance to them implied salvation. Commonly, however, the title is translated as "City of Peace."

547 A question motivated by *wara'* (scrupulosity): if, for example, the man had taken the water from someone else without permission, it would be wrong to drink it.

548 *Muballighūn*: people who repeat the words of the prayer leader or lecturer when the crowd is too large for everyone to hear him.

549 This is the oath of assent that formalized the accession of a new caliph. Normally a crowd of dignitaries would be involved.

550 In 469/1077, the Shāfi'ī jurist Abū l-Naṣr 'Abd al-Raḥīm (d. 514/1120), son of the mystic and theologian 'Abd al-Karīm al-Qushayrī, came to Baghdad to teach the speculative theology of al-Ash'arī. Although the Ash'arite system was intended to defend the texts and conclusions favored by the Ḥanbalīs, the latter were having none of it, and rioted. Eventually Abū l-Naṣr was sent back to Isfahan. See Halm, "al-Qushayrī."

551 The ninth of Dhu l-Hijjah 503 [June 29, 1110].

552 Ka'b ibn Mālik was one of three Helpers reportedly condemned and later forgiven for staying behind during the Prophet's raid on Tabūk.

553 ". . . God will make me one of them." The rest of the sentence does not appear in the manuscripts, perhaps because al-Dīnawarī was too modest to say it, but it does appear in a parallel text from *Shadharāt al-dhahab*, whence it is supplied by al-Turkī (see 705n1).

554 Meter: *ṭawīl.*

555 Meter: *ṭawīl.*

556 Such collections contained reports that not only had short chains of transmitters but also one transmitter, or some other distinctive feature, in common. I thank Devin Stewart for explaining this point.

557 There is some debate about what *ummī* may have meant in the Qur'an (for which see Sebastian Günther, "Ummī"). By Ibn al-Jawzī's time, though, it was understood to mean "illiterate," meaning that Muḥammad could not have been inspired by reading older scriptures.

Glossary of Names and Terms

ʿAbbādān town at the head of the Persian Gulf, in the southwest of what is now Iran; in early Abbasid times a gathering place for renunciants (q.v.).

ʿAbbāsah bint al-Faḍl Ibn Ḥanbal's first wife, and mother of his son Ṣāliḥ.

Abbasid (caliphate) the line of caliphs (q.v.) descended from the Prophet's uncle al-ʿAbbās, established in 132/749 after the overthrow of the Umayyad dynasty and essentially Shiʿi (q.v.) until 237/851; thereafter the nominal dynasts of Sunni (q.v.) Islam until the fall of Baghdad to the Mongols in 656/1258.

ʿAbd Allāh ibn Aḥmad ibn Ḥanbal (d. 290/903) one of Ibn Ḥanbal's sons, and a major transmitter of his Hadith reports.

ʿAbd Allāh ibn al-Mubārak (d. 181/797) a famously pious and ascetic Hadith scholar.

ʿAbd al-Raḥmān al-Shāfiʿī see Abū ʿAbd al-Raḥmān al-Shāfiʿī.

ʿAbd al-Razzāq ibn Hammām al-Ṣanʿānī (d. 211/827) a Yemeni Hadith scholar.

ʿAbd al-Wahhāb al-Warrāq (251/865 or 866) Ibn Ḥanbal's close friend, described as right-minded and pious.

Abū ʿAbd al-Raḥmān al-Shāfiʿī (d. ca. 230/845) jurist and theologian who debated with Ibn Ḥanbal during his trial.

Abū Bakr (al-Ṣiddīq) (r. 11–13/632–4) a Companion of the Prophet and first caliph.

Abū Bakr Ahmad ibn Muḥammad al-Marrūdhī (d. 275/888) a close associate of Ibn Ḥanbal and a transmitter of his reports.

Abū Bakr al-Khallāl (d. 311/923) a disciple of al-Marrūdhī and author of the formative compilations of the Ḥanbalī school.

Abū Ḥanifah (d. 150/767) early legal authority who favored judgment (*ra'y*) over *sunnah* (q.v.).

Abū Khaythamah Zuhayr ibn Ḥarb (d. 243/847) a Hadith scholar and compiler of reports.

Abū Mushir al-Ghassānī (d. 218/833) Syrian Hadith scholar persecuted by al-Ma'mūn (q.v.) for his unwillingness to declare the Qur'an created; his resistance may have provoked al-Ma'mūn to pursue the Inquisition (q.v.) .

Abū 'Ubayd see al-Qāsim ibn Sallām.

Abū Zur'ah al-Rāzī (d. 264/878) major Hadith scholar known for his critical examination of isnāds and his disapproval of Disputation.

Aḥmad ibn Naṣr al-Khuzā'ī (d. 231/845) leader of a failed rebellion against the Caliph al-Wāthiq (q.v.) and much admired by the Sunnis (q.v.).

'Alī ibn Abī Ṭālib (r. 35–40/656–60) the Prophet's son-in-law and the fourth caliph (q.v.) according to the Sunni count or the first imam (q.v.) according to several Shi'i groups.

'Alī ibn al-Ja'd (d. 230/845) Hadith scholar condemned by Ibn Ḥanbal for capitulating to the Inquisition.

'Alī ibn al-Jahm an official at the court of al-Mutawakkil (q.v.).

'Alī ibn al-Madīnī (d. 239/853) major Hadith scholar, reportedly criticized by Ibn Ḥanbal for accepting the createdness (q.v.) of the Qur'an.

al-Amīn (r. 193–8/809–13) sixth Abbasid caliph.

Antichrist (al-Dajjāl) in Islamic tradition, a figure who will arise to battle Jesus at the end of the world.

Ascalon (modern Ashkelon) a town on the southeast Mediterranean coast in what is now Israel.

Authenticated Reports Listed By Transmitter (al-Musnad) a book of Hadith reports compiled by Ṣāliḥ, 'Abd Allāh, and Ḥanbal ibn Isḥaq (qq.v.) at Ibn Ḥanbal's direction. The work has been published in many modern editions.

Basra a port city in southern Iraq, near the head of the Persian Gulf; a major intellectual center in early Islamic times.

Bishr ibn al-Ḥārith (the Barefoot) (d. 227/841–42) famous ascetic who was suspicious of Hadith study but admired Ibn Ḥanbal.

Bishr al-Marīsī (d. 218/833) a Ḥanafī and Postponer influential during the reign of al-Ma'mūn (q.v.); he was hated by Ibn Ḥanbal and his followers for his belief that the Qur'an is created.

Bughā the Elder a Turkish general who served several Abbasid caliphs (d. 248/862).

caliph the head of the Muslim community, understood by Sunni Muslims to be any qualified Muslim appointed by his fellows, but in practice Muhammad's first four successors, followed by the rulers of the Umayyad dynasty and then those of the Abbasid dynasty (who were accepted only grudgingly until they adopted Sunnism in the mid-third/ninth century).

Commander of Believers the title of the caliph (q.v.).

Commander of the Faithful the title of the caliph (q.v.).

community (al-jamā'ah) for Sunnis, the historically continuous group of right-minded believers, and more broadly, the principle that all positions taken by this group were correct and remain binding.

Companions Muslims whose lives overlapped with that of the Prophet Muḥammad.

createdness (of the Qur'an) the belief that God's revelation to the Prophet Muḥammad is a created thing, as opposed to being eternal by virtue of its divine origin.

cupping the application of a vacuum (created by placing a flame under an inverted glass) to the skin, with the aim of removing harmful substances from the body.

cycle (rak'ah) any of the rounds of standing, kneeling, and prostration that make up the Muslim ritual prayer.

dāniq (also dānaq) a coin equal in value to one-sixth of a dirham (q.v.).

al-Dāraquṭnī (d. 385/995) a Hadith scholar and Shāfi'ī (q.v.) jurist fiercely opposed to Disputation (q.v.).

Day of Resurrection according to the Qur'an, the day when the dead are brought back to life before being judged and sent to the Garden (q.v.) or the Fire (q.v.).

dinar a gold coin originally weighing 4.25 grams, and the most valuable coin in use during the early Abbasid period.

dirham a silver coin, until the mid-third/ninth century weighing between 2.91 and 2.96 grams.

Disputation (kalām; literally, "talking") a discourse on physical or spiritual matters that employs syllogistic reasoning; theological or dogmatic speculation.

Dissident (khārijī) sectarians who refused to support either ʿAlī (q.v.) or Muʿāwiyah in the battle for the caliphate and who believed themselves to be the only true Muslims.

Emigrants followers of the Prophet Muḥammad who joined him when he left Mecca for Medina in 1/622.

Emissary of God a title of the Prophet Muḥammad.

fatā see *futuwwa*.

al-Fatḥ ibn Khāqān (d. 247/861–62) an administrator and scholar who served al-Mutawakkil (q.v.).

Fāṭimah Ibn Ḥanbal's daughter; possibly the same as Zaynab (q.v.).

festival either the Feast of Sacrifice, when animals are slaughtered during the pilgrimage, or the Feast of Fastbreaking, celebrated at the end of the Ramadan fast.

Fire (al-nār) according to the Qur'an, the place where the wicked spend eternity after death.

Fūrān, ʿAbd Allāh ibn Muḥammad (d. 265/879) a Hadith scholar and close associate of Ibn Ḥanbal.

futuwwah the virtues associated with brave young men; in religious contexts, the admirable qualities of one who fulfills his duties to God and to his fellows.

Garden (al-jannah) according to the Qur'an, the place where the blessed spend eternity after death.

ḥabbah literally "a grain"; a coin or measure of weight equivalent to 1/48 of a dirham (q.v.).

Hadith the entire corpus of hadiths (q.v.), used to determine the *sunnah* (q.v.).

hadith a report of something the Prophet Muḥammad said or did, including tacit expressions of approval or disapproval, consisting of the report itself as well as a list of those who transmitted it.

Ḥanafī a follower of the legal school named after Abū Ḥanīfah (q.v.).

Ḥanbal ibn Isḥāq (d. 273/886) Ibn Ḥanbal's cousin, and author of an account of the Inquisition; less often cited than other sources, perhaps because of his father Isḥāq ibn Ḥanbal's (q.v.) role in the episode.

al-Ḥārith al-Muḥāsibī (d. 243/857) mystical theologian.

Harthamah ibn Aʿyan (d. 200/816) Abbasid general anachronistically used as a character in a story (96.9) about al-Mutawakkil and his court.

Ḥasan ibn Aḥmad either of two sons by this name born to Ibn Ḥanbal's concubine Ḥusn.

Hāshim the clan of the tribe of Quraysh into which the Prophet was born.

Hāshimī a member of the clan to which the Prophet Muḥammad belonged.

Helpers (anṣār) those citizens of Medina who accepted Islam after the Prophet moved there from Mecca in 1/622.

heretic (zindīq) originally a Manichean dualist, and later anyone suspected of secretly adhering to a creed incompatible with Islam.

Hims (or Homs) a town in the west-central part of what is today Syria.

Hushaym ibn Bashīr (183/799) a Hadith scholar who transmitted to Ibn Ḥanbal.

Ḥusn Ibn Ḥanbal's concubine and mother of six of his children.

Ibn ʿAbbās (d. ca. 68/687–88) a cousin of the Prophet and the nominal ancestor of the Abbasid line; later generations of Sunnis (q.v.) credited him with vast knowledge of the Qur'an and the *sunnah* (q.v.).

Ibn Abī Du'ād (d. 240/854) a Secessionist (q.v.) and advisor to the caliphs al-Ma'mūn, al-Muʿtaṣim, al-Wāthiq, and al-Mutawakkil; hated by Ibn Ḥanbal and his followers for his role in the Inquisition.

Ibn Māsawayh (d. 243/857) physician to several Abbasid caliphs.

Ibn Rāhawayh see Isḥāq ibn Rāhawayh.

Ibn Ṭāhir see Muḥammad ibn ʿAbd Allāh ibn Ṭāhir.

Ibn al-Zayyāt (d. 233/847) vizier under al-Muʿtaṣim, al-Wāthiq, and al-Mutawakkil (q.q.v.).

Ibrāhīm (ibn Isḥaq) al-Ḥarbī (d. 285/898–99) Hadith scholar, renunciant (q.v.), and polymath.

Ibrāhīm al-Nakhaʿī (d. ca. 96/717) Kufan Hadith-transmitter and *faqīh* known for his exercise of independent judgment.

imam one who in his capacity as a Muslim leads other Muslims, whether in group prayer, in pursuing a particular path in interpretation, or as head of state; among Sunnis (q.v.), an exemplary scholar; among Shiʿa, a member of the Prophet's family entitled to lead the community, usually by virtue of special knowledge of the law.

Ingrate (kāfir) one who refuses to believe in, or declare a belief in, God.

innovator a term used by Ibn Ḥanbal and his followers to condemn persons they believed responsible for introducing beliefs and practices not present in the *sunnah* (q.v.) and therefore bad.

Inquisition the interrogation of judges, notary witnesses, Hadith scholars, and miscellaneous other persons, to determine their assent to the doctrine that the Qur'an is created, and by extension, their acknowledgement that the Abbasid caliph had the final word in matters of belief and practice; introduced by the caliph al-Ma'mūn in 218/833 and intermittently enforced until ended by al-Mutawakkil in 237/851.

Isḥāq ibn Ḥanbal Ibn Ḥanbal's uncle; reportedly responsible for having him put in trial, and described as urging him to compromise with the Inquisition.

Isḥāq ibn Ibrāhīm (d. 235/849) governor of Baghdad under al-Ma'mūn, al-Muʿtaṣim, al-Wāthiq, and al-Mutawakkil (q.q.v.).

Isḥāq ibn Rāhawayh (d. 238/853) respected Hadith scholar who transmitted to Ibn Ḥanbal.

Ismāʿīl ibn ʿUlayyah (d. 193/809) Hadith scholar who transmitted to Ibn Ḥanbal.

Ītākh (d. 235/849) Khazar military commander under the Abbasid caliphs al-Muʿtaṣim, al-Wāthiq, and al-Mutawakkil (q.v.).

Jahm ibn Ṣafwān (d. 128/745) early Muslim thinker to whom are attributed a number of teachings hateful to Ibn Ḥanbal and his associates, particularly the claim that the prototype of the Qur'an began to exist only at a particular point in time.

jinni a sentient creature made of fire, often described as interfering in human affairs.

jurisprudence (fiqh) most broadly, the ability to discern the right course of action in ritual, legal, and ethical matters; more narrowly, formal text-based legal reasoning.

al-Karābīsī (d. 245/859 or 248/862) a jurist and theologian who argued that God's speech (including the Qur'an) is uncreated but human utterance of it is not.

al-Karkh the general name for the region of Baghdad south of the caliphal compound in the Round City.

al-Khaḍir (also called al-Khiḍr) a figure who appears in the Qur'an (Q Kahf 18:60–82) and guides Moses; in popular belief, a perennially recurrent figure who provides guidance to Muslims in time of need.

al-Khallāl see Abū Bakr al-Khallāl.

Khurasan a region that includes what is today northeastern Iran, Afghanistan, and parts of Central Asia.

al-Khuzāʿī see Aḥmad ibn Naṣr al-Khuzāʿī.

Kufa city in central Iraq, on the Tigris River; an important center of learning in early Islamic times.

kunyah a form of address consisting of Abū ("father of") or Umm ("mother of") followed by the name of that person's child or other figure closely associated with them. The use of a *kunyah* can convey intimacy, respect, or both.

Magians (majūs) a term used by outsiders to refer to Zoroastrians.

Mālik ibn Anas (d. 179/795) early legal thinker associated with the doctrine that the practice of the people of Medina constituted the best precedent.

al-Ma'mūn (r. 198–218/813–33) seventh Abbasid caliph.

manifestations of grace see signs of grace.

al-Manṣūr, mosque of the mosque built by the second Abbasid caliph (r. 136–58/754–75). The mosque continued to serve as a center for Friday worship even after the caliphs moved out of the purpose-built Round City.

al-Marīsī see Bishr al-Marīsī.

al-Marrūdhī see Abū Bakr al-Marrūdhī.

Maʿrūf al-Karkhī (d. 200/815–16) a Baghdadi ascetic prominent in Sufi (mystical) traditions.

Marv city in what is now Turkmenistan; in early Islamic times, the capital of Khurasan (q.v.).

al-Miṣṣīṣah town near the northeast Mediterranean coast in what is today Turkey, and in early Abbasid times on the frontier with the Byzantines.

mithqāl a unit of weight equal to sixty grains of barley (among other definitions).

Muḥammad ibn ʿAbd Allāh ibn Ṭāhir military commander in Baghdad and representative of al-Muʿtaṣim (q.v.) at Ibn Ḥanbal's funeral.

Muḥammad ibn Idrīs see al-Shāfiʿī.

Muḥammad ibn Nūḥ (218/833) a young man of little Hadith-learning who joined Ibn Ḥanbal in refusing to declare the Qur'an created.

Muḥammad ibn Zubaydah see al-Amīn.

al-Muḥāsibī see al-Ḥārith.

al-Muhtadī (r. 255–56/868–70) fourteenth Abbasid caliph.

Munkar one of the two angels said to interrogate the dead in their graves.

Musaddad ibn Musarhad (d. 228/842–43) well-respected Basran Hadith transmitter.

al-Musnad see *Authenticated Reports Listed By Transmitter*.

al-Muʿtaṣim (r. 218–27/833–42) eighth Abbasid caliph.

al-Mutawakkil (r. 232–247/847–61) tenth Abbasid caliph.

Nakīr one of the two angels said to interrogate the dead in their graves.

Nishapur a town in northeastern Iran near present-day Mashhad.

notary-witness a person engaged by a judge to serve as a regular witness to the undertaking of contractual obligations or to the character of persons who appear in court.

Nuʿaym ibn Ḥammād (d. 228/843?) a Hadith scholar imprisoned for refusing to declare the Qur'an created; also famous as a compiler of apocalyptic traditions.

Pegs (awtād) one of four figures associated with the cardinal points of the compass and occupying the third rank in the hierarchy of Sufi masters.

Postponers (murji'ah) those who hold that latter-day Muslims cannot judge the Companions or resolve the disputes that divided them, and that any such resolution must be postponed until Judgment Day.

Proponent of Created Utterance one who believes that, while the Qur'an as known to God is uncreated, the Qur'an as spoken aloud by humans is a created thing.

al-Qā'im bi-Amr Allāh (r. 422–67/1031–75) twenty-sixth Abbasid caliph.

al-Qāsim ibn Sallām (d. 224/838) compiler of works on legal and linguistic issues.

Qaṭī'at al-Rabī' a district of Baghdad, located southwest of the Round City in al-Karkh (q.v.).

al-Qawārīrī (d. 235/850) Baghdadi Hadith scholar who at first refused, then agreed under duress, that the Qur'an is created.

Qazwīn a town in north-central Iran west of present-day Tehran.

qīrāṭ a coin worth one-twelfth of a dirham (q.v.).

qiṭ'ah a coin, or a scrap or shard made by cutting or trimming a silver coin.

quire (juz') a grouping of sheets that makes up part of a manuscript or book.

Quraysh the tribe to which the Prophet Muḥammad belonged.

rak'ah see cycle.

al-Raqqah a town located on the Euphrates River in north-central Syria; a common stopping point on the journey between Baghdad and the Byzantine frontier.

al-Rashīd (r. 170–93/786–809) fifth Abbasid caliph.

Rayḥanah Ibn Ḥanbal's second wife and mother of his son 'Abd Allāh.

Rejection (rafḍ) a disparaging term of reference to Shi'ism, referring to its rejection of Abū Bakr, 'Umar, 'Uthmān, and Mu'āwiyah as legitimate caliphs.

Rejectionist (rāfiḍi) a term of disparaging reference to a Shi'i (q.v.).

renunciation (zuhd) disengagement from the present world, usually entailing the shunning of comforts, the suppression of bodily urges, and the avoidance of company; a sign of devotion to God's law.

Rey city in the north-central part of what is now Iran, just south of modern Tehran.

Riḍwān in Muslim tradition, the angel who receives the blessed into the Garden (q.v.).

Righteous Caliphs the Sunni (q.v.) form of reference to Abū Bakr, ʿUmar, ʿUthmān, and ʿAlī (q.v.).

ritual prayer one of Islam's five prescribed daily prayers (as opposed to *duʿāʾ*, "supplication," which may be performed at any time).

al-Ruṣāfah the part of greater Baghdad that lay on the east bank of the Tigris River.

Saʿīd ibn Aḥmad ibn Ḥanbal one of Ibn Ḥanbal's sons, born shortly before his father's death.

Saʿīd ibn al-Musayyab (d. 93/711–12) leading Successor (q.v.) of Medina and noted source of Hadith reports.

Sajjādah, al-Ḥasan ibn Ḥammād (d. 241/855) Baghdadi Hadith scholar who at first refused, then agreed under duress, that the Qur'an is created.

Ṣāliḥ ibn Aḥmad ibn Ḥanbal (d. 265/879) Ibn Ḥanbal's eldest son and a major transmitter of his Hadith reports; served as judge in Isfahan.

Samarqand a city located in what is now Uzbekistan.

Samarra purpose-built city in central Iraq that served as the Abbasid capital from 221/836 to 279/892; the caliph al-Mutawakkil (q.v.) had Ibn Ḥanbal brought here from Baghdad.

Sanaa a town in Yemen.

scrupulosity (waraʿ) the pious practice of shunning not only forbidden objects and activities but also those which are merely suspicious or of unknown legality.

Secessionists (al-muʿtazilah, "those who sent themselves apart") a name applied to scholars who were, broadly speaking, rationalist in their approach. For example, they favored metaphorical explanations for the apparently physical attributes of God.

al-Shāfiʿī, Muḥammad ibn Idrīs (d. 204/820) legal theorist credited with laying the foundation for Sunni jurisprudence by developing methods for deriving law from the Qur'an and *sunnah*.

Shāfiʿī a follower of the legal school named after al-Shāfiʿī (q.v.).

Shiʿi (pl. Shiʿa) one characterized by the belief that certain members of the Prophet's family are the only legitimate leaders of the Muslim community, usually because of their special understanding of God's law.

signs of grace (karāmāt) violations of accustomed causality that serve as evidence that a person enjoys God's special favor. These are generally concealed, and differ from the evidentiary miracles performed by prophets.

Stopper one who, when asked about the Qur'an, says "It is the speech of God," and stops. According to Ibn Ḥanbal, he should add "uncreated."

Substitutes (abdāl) in Sufi thought, one of a limited number of pious servants of God who, when he dies, is replaced by another of equal merit; among Hadith scholars, a term evidently applied to Muslims of great piety whose identity is supposed to be a secret.

Successors the generation of Muslims after the Companions (q.v.).

Sufi originally a Muslim mystic of the Iraqi school, which in Ibn Ḥanbal's time was still in the process of formation; in later usage, any Muslim mystic.

Sufyān, al-Thawrī (d. 161/778) transmitter and jurisprudent admired by Sunnis for his pioneering emphasis on Hadith as well as his pro-Umayyad and anti-Abbasid sentiments.

Sufyān ibn ʿUyaynah (d. 196/811) Meccan Hadith scholar.

sunnah the exemplary practice of the Prophet, preserved in the Hadith (q.v.) and used as a source of law; sometime also includes the practice of the early Muslims (preserved in narratives usually called *akhbār* or *āthār*).

Sunnah (adj. Sunni) the mature form of the movement that began by proclaiming itself "the people of *sunnah* (q.v.) and Community (q.v.)"; it is characterized by solidarity with the historical caliphate, rejection of imamism (see "imam"), and reliance on Hadith (q.v.) rather than Disputation (q.v.).

Tarsus town on the Mediterranean coast of what is today Turkey; a popular destination for pious Muslims seeking to join the frontier wars against the Byzantines.

Tūzūn a Turkish general who siezed control of Baghdad in 331/943.

ʿUbayd Allāh ibn Khāqān (d. 263/877) vizier of al-Mutawakkil (q.v.).

ʿUkbarā town on the east bank of the Tigris north of Baghdad.

ʿUmar ibn ʿAbd al-ʿAzīz (r. 99–101/717–20) Umayyad caliph renowned for his piety and justice.

ʿUmar ibn al-Khaṭṭāb (r. 13–23/634–44) Companion of the Prophet and second caliph; among Sunnis, an exemplar of just rule.

ʿUthmān ibn ʿAffān (r. 23–35/644–56) Companion of the Prophet and third caliph; often praised beyond his merits by Sunnis eager to counter the partisans of ʿAlī ibn Abī Ṭālib (q.v.).

variant readings (of the Qurʾan) In Aḥmad's time, any of several different traditions of reading aloud (and sometimes writing) the text of God's revelation to Muḥammad. The different traditions were partially standardized by Ibn Mujāhid (d. 324/936), though up to fourteen different ones remained acceptable.

Wakīʿ ibn al-Jarrāḥ (d. 197/812) pious Hadith scholar and transmitter to Ibn Ḥanbal.

Waṣīf (d. 253/867) Turkish general who served and subsequently betrayed al-Mutawakkil (q.v.).

Wāsiṭ an agricultural town and administrative center located on the Tigris River in central Iraq. It was founded around 80/700 and seems to have last been inhabited in the tenth/sixteenth century.

al-Wāthiq (r. 227–32/842–47) ninth Abbasid caliph.

witr a voluntary but very meritorious prayer consisting of an odd number of cycles (q.v.) performed at night.

worshipper (ʿābid) any especially pious Muslim who was not a scholar.

Yaḥyā ibn Khāqān an official at the court of al-Muʿtaṣim (q.v.).

Yaḥyā ibn Maʿīn (d. 233/848) famously learned Hadith scholar.

Yazīd ibn Hārūn (d. 206/821) pious Hadith scholar who transmitted to Ibn Ḥanbal; reportedly tried to dissuade al-Maʾmūn (q.v.) from declaring that the Qurʾan is created.

Zaynab Ibn Ḥanbal's daughter.

Zuhayr ibn Ṣāliḥ (d. 303/915–16) Ibn Ḥanbal's grandson and transmitter of some of his reports.

Bibliography

Abbreviations

EI2 *Encyclopaedia of Islam, Second Edition*. Edited by P. Bearman, Th. Bianquis, C. E. Bosworth, E. van Donzel, and W. P. Heinrichs. Leiden: Brill Online, 2012. http://www.brill.com/publications/online-resources/encyclopaedia-islam-online.

EI3 *Encyclopaedia of Islam, Third Edition*. Edited by Gudrun Krämer, Denis Matringe, John Nawas, and Everett Rowson. Leiden: Brill Online, 2014. http://www.brill.com/publications/online-resources/encyclopaedia-islam-online.

Abū l-ʿArab Muḥammad ibn Aḥmad al-Tamīmī. *Kitāb al-Miḥan*. Edited by Yaḥyā Wahīb al-Jubūrī. Beirut: Dār al-Gharb al-Islāmī, 1403/1983.

Abū Nuʿaym al-Iṣfahānī. *Ḥilyat al-awliyāʾ*. Cairo: al-Khānjī, 1932–38. Reprint, Beirut: al-Maktabah al-ʿIlmiyyah, n.d.

Abu Zahra, Nadia. "Adultery and Fornication." In McAuliffe, *Encyclopaedia of the Qurʾān*.

Adang, Camilla. "Belief and Unbelief." In McAuliffe, *Encyclopaedia of the Qurʾān*.

Ahsan, M. M. *Social Life under the Abbasids*. New York: Longman, 1979.

Anvarī, Ḥasan. *Farhang-e bozorg-e sokhan*. 8 vols. Tehran: Intishārāt-e Sokhan, 1381/2002–3.

Ashtor, E. "Mawāzīn." In *EI2*.

ʿAsqalānī, al-. *See* Ibn Ḥajar.

Baer, E. "Dawāt." In *EI2*.

[Baghdādī], Muḥammad ibn al-Ḥasan ibn Muḥammad ibn al-Karīm al-. *A Baghdad Cookery Book*. Translated by Charles Perry. Totnes. UK: Prospect Books, 2005.

Ballian, Anna. "Country Estates, Material Culture, and the Celebration of Princely Life: Islamic Art and the Secular Domain." In Evans with Ratliff, *Byzantium and Islam*, 200–8.

Bencheikh, Omar. "Nifṭawayh." In *EI2*.

Bernards, Monique, and John Nawas, eds. *Patronate and Patronage in Early and Classical Islam*. Leiden: Brill, 2005.

Björkman, W. "Kāfir." In *EI2*.

Böwering, G. "God and His Attributes." In McAuliffe, *Encyclopaedia of the Qur'ān*.

Bukhārī, Muḥammad al-. *Al-Jāmiʿ al-ṣaḥiḥ*. 9 vols. Būlāq: al-Amīriyyah, 1311/1893–94.

Bulliet, Richard. "Conversion-Based Patronage." In Bernards and Nawas, *Patronate and Patronage*, 246–62.

Burton, J. "Muḥṣan." In *EI2*.

Chabbi, Jacqueline. "Zamzam." In *EI2*.

Clarity, Beverly E., Karl Stowasser, Ronald G. Wolfe, D. R. Woodhead, and Wayne Beene. *A Dictionary of Iraqi Arabic*. Washington, DC: Georgetown University Press, 2003.

Colburn, Kathrin. "Materials and Techniques of Late Antique and Early Islamic Textiles Found in Egypt." In Evans with Ratliff, *Byzantium and Islam* , 161–71.

Cook, Michael. *Commanding Right and Forbidding Wrong in Islamic Thought*. Cambridge: Cambridge University Press, 2000.

———. "The Opponents of the Writing of Tradition in Early Islam." *Arabica* 44:4 (October 1997): 437–530.

———. "The Origins of *Kalām*." *Bulletin of the School of Oriental and African Studies* 43, no. 1 (1980): 32–43.

Cooperson, Michael. *Classical Arabic Biography: The Heirs of the Prophet in the Age of al-Ma'mūn*. Cambridge: Cambridge University Press, 2000.

———. "Ibn Ḥanbal and Bishr al-Ḥāfī: A Case Study in Biographical Traditions." *Studia Islamica* 86 (1997): 71–101.

———. "Al-Jāḥiẓ, the Misers, and the Proto-Sunnī Ascetics." In *Al-Jāḥiẓ: A Muslim Humanist for Our Time*, edited by Arnim Heinemann, John L. Meloy, Tarif Khalidi, and Manfred Kropp, 197–219. Beiruter Texte und Studien 119. Beirut: Orient-Institut, 2009.

———. *Al-Ma'mun*. Oxford: Oneworld, 2005.

———. "Probability, Plausibility, and 'Spiritual Communication' in Classical Arabic Biography." In *On Fiction and* Adab *in Medieval Arabic Literature*, edited by Philip F. Kennedy, 69–83. Wiesbaden: Harrasowitz, 2005.

———. "Two Abbasid Trials: Aḥmad Ibn Ḥanbal and Ḥunayn b. Isḥāq." *Al-Qantara. Revista de estudios árabes* 22, no. 2 (2001): 375–93.

Crone, Patricia. *God's Rule: Government and Islam*. New York: Columbia University Press, 2004.

———. *The Nativist Prophets of Early Islamic Iran: Rural Revolt and Local Zoroastrianism*. Cambridge: Cambridge University Press, 2012.

Crone, Patricia, and Martin Hinds. *God's Caliph: Religious Authority in the First Centuries of Islam*. Cambridge: Cambridge University Press, 1986.

Crone, Patricia, and Shmuel Moreh. *The Book of Strangers: Medieval Arabic Graffiti on the Theme of Nostalgia*. Princeton: Markus Wiener, 2000.

De Gifis, Vanessa. *Shaping a Qur'anic Worldview: Scriptural Hermenutics and the Rhetoric of Moral Reform in the Caliphate of al-Ma'mūn*. New York: Routledge, 2014.

Dekhodā, 'Alī Akbar. *Lughatnāmeh-ye Fārsī*. Tehran: University of Tehran, 1982. Online at http://www.loghatnaameh.org/.

Dhahabi, Shams al-Dīn. *Mīzān al-i'tidāl*. Edited by 'Alī Muḥammad al-Bījāwī. 4 vols. Cairo: al-Bābī l-Ḥalabī, 1963.

———. *Al-Mushtabih fī asmā' al-rijāl*. Edited by P. de Jong. Leiden: Brill, 1863.

———. *Siyar a'lām al-nubalā'*. 25 vols. Beirut: Mu'assasat al-Risālah, 1403/1983.

Donner, Frederick M. "Maymūn b. Mihrān, Abū Ayyūb." In *EI2*.

Dozy, Reinhart. *Dictionnaire détaillé des noms de vêtements chez les Arabes*. Amsterdam: Jean Müller, 1845. https://archive.org/details/dictionnairedtaooiiigoog.

Eger, A. Asa. *The Islamic-Byzantine Frontier*. London: I. B. Tauris, 2015.
El Omari: *see* Omari.
[Encyclopaedia Judaica.] "Lamed Vav Ẓaddikim." In *Encyclopaedia Judaica*, 2nd ed., edited by Michael Berenbaum and Fred Skolnik, 12:445–46. Detroit: Macmillan Reference USA, 2007.
Evans, Helen C., ed., with Brandie Ratliff. *Byzantium and Islam: Age of Transition, 7th–9th Century*. New York: Metropolitan Museum of Art, 2012.
Fīrūzābādī, al-. *Al-Qāmūs al-muḥīṭ*. Cairo: Dar al-Ma'mūn, 1938. http://www.baheth.info/.
Fluck, Cäcilia. "Inscribed Textiles." In Evans with Ratliff, *Byzantium and Islam*, 183–85.
Gacek, Adam. *Arabic Manuscripts: A Vademecum for Readers*. Leiden: Brill, 2009.
Goitein, Shelomo Dov. *A Mediterranean Society: The Jewish Communities of the Arab World as Portrayed in the Documents of the Cairo Geniza*. 6 vols. Berkeley: University of California Press, 1967–93.
Goldziher, I. "Awtād." In *EI2*.
Goldziher, I., and H. J. Kissling. "Abdāl." In *EI2*.
Grabar, Oleg. *The Illustrations of the Maqamat*. Chicago: University of Chicago Press, 1984.
Günther, Sebastian. "Ummī." In McAuliffe, *Encyclopaedia of the Qur'ān*.
Guthrie, Shirley. *Arab Social Life in the Middle Ages: An Illustrated Study*. London: Saqi, 1995.
Halm, H. "Al-Qushayrī." In *EI2*.
Ḥanbal ibn Isḥāq ibn Ḥanbal. *Dhikr miḥnat al-Imām Aḥmad ibn Ḥanbal*. Edited by Muḥammad Naghsh. Cairo: Nashr al-Thaqāfah, 1398/1977.
Heller, B. "Lazarus." In *EI2*.
Hill, D. R. "Mā', 3. Hydraulic Machines." In *EI2*.
———. "Na'ūra." In *EI2*.
Hinds, Martin. "Miḥna." In *EI2*.
Hinz, W. "Dhirā'." In *EI2*.
Honigmann, Ernst. *Die Ostgrenze des Byzaninischen Reiches von 363 bis 1071*. Brussels: Institut de philologie et d'histoire orientales, 1935.

Hurvitz, Nimrod. *The Formation of Hanbalism: Piety into Power*. New York: RoutledgeCurzon, 2002.

Ibn Abī Yaʿlā l-Farrāʾ. *Ṭabaqāt al-Ḥanābilah.* Edited by ʿAbd al-Raḥmān ibn Sulaymān al-ʿUthaymīn. 3 vols. Riyad: al-Amānah al-ʿĀmmah li-l-Iḥtifāl bi-Murūr Miʾat ʿĀm, 1419/1999. https://archive.org/details/Tabaqat_Hanabila.

Ibn al-Athīr, ʿIzz al-Dīn. *Usd al-ghābah fī maʿrifat al-ṣaḥābah.* 2nd ed. Edited by ʿAlī Muḥammad Muʿawwaḍ and ʿĀdil Aḥmad ʿAbd al-Mawjūd. Beirut: Dār al-Kutub al-ʿIlmiyyah, 1424/2003.

Ibn Ḥajar al-ʿAsqalānī. *Fatḥ al-bārī bi-sharḥ Ṣaḥīḥ al-Bukhārī.* Edited by Muḥammad Fuʾād ʿAbd al-Bāqī, Muḥibb al-Dīn al-Khaṭīb, and Quṣayy Muḥibb al-Dīn al-Khaṭīb. 13 vols. N.p: Dār al-Rayyān, 1407/1986. http://islamweb.net.

———. *Tabṣīr al-muntabih bi-taḥrīr al-Mushtabih.* Edited by ʿAlī Aḥmad al-Bajāwī and Muḥammad ʿAlī l-Najjār. Beirut: al-Maktabah al-ʿIlmiyyah, 1964. http://www.archive.org/details/TabsirAlmuntabih.

———. *Tahdhīb al-tahdhīb.* Edited by Ibrāhīm al-Zaybaq and ʿĀdil Murshid. 4 vols. Beirut: Muʾassasat al-Risālah, 1416/1995.

Ibn Ḥanbal, Aḥmad. *Al-Jāmiʿ fī l-ʿilāl wa-maʿrifat al-rijāl.* Edited by Muḥammad Ḥuṣām Bayḍūn. Beirut: Muʾassasat al-Kutub al-Thaqāfiyyah, 1410/1990.

———. *Kitāb al-Waraʿ*. Edited by Zaynab Ibrāhīm al-Qārūṭ. Beirut: al-ʿĀlamiyyah, 1403/1983.

———. *Kitāb al-Zuhd.* Edited by Muḥammad Jalāl Sharaf. Beirut: Dār al-Nahḍah, 1981.

——— [attr.]. *Al-Radd ʿalā l-zanādiqah wa-l-jahmiyyah.* Cairo: al-Salafiyyah, 1393/1973–74.

Ibn al-Jawzī, Abū l-Faraj ʿAbd al-Raḥmān ibn ʿAlī. *Kitāb al-Quṣṣāṣ wa-l-mudhakkirīn.* Edited by Merlin L. Swartz. Beirut: Dār al-Mashriq, 1971.

———. *Manāqib al-Imām Aḥmad ibn Ḥanbal.* Edited by Muḥammad Amīn al-Khānjī l-Kutubī. Cairo: Maktabat al-Khānjī, 1349/1931–32.

———. *Manāqib al-Imām Aḥmad ibn Ḥanbal*. Edited by ʿAbd Allāh ibn ʿAbd al-Muḥsin al-Turkī. 2nd rev. ed. Giza: Hajr, 1988. First published in 1399/1979 by Maktabat al-Khānjī in Cairo.
———. *A Medieval Critique of Anthropomorphism: Ibn al-Jawzi's Kitab Akhbar as-Sifat: A Critical Edition of the Arabic Text with Translation, Introduction and Notes*. Edited and translated by Merlin Swartz. Leiden: Brill, 2002.
Ibn Manẓūr. *Lisān al-ʿarab*. Edited by ʿAbd Allāh ʿAlī al-Kabīr, Muḥammad Aḥmad Ḥasab Allāh, and Ḥāshim Muḥammad al-Shādhilī. Cairo: Dār al-Maʿārif, 1981. http://www.baheth.info/.
Ibn al-Murtaḍā, Aḥmad ibn Yaḥyā. *Kitāb Ṭabaqāt al-muʿtazilah. Die Klassen der muʿtaziliten*. Edited by Susanna Diwald-Wilzer. Wiesbaden and Berlin: Franz Steiner, 1961.
Ibn Qutaybah. *Adab al-kātib*. Edited by Muḥammad al-Dālī. Beirut: Mu'assasat al-Risālah, 1402/1982.
Inalcık, H. "Quṭn" (2). In *EI2*.
Iṣfahānī, Abū l-Faraj al-. *Kitāb al-Aghanī*. Edited by Ibrāhīm al-Ibyārī. 33 vols. Cairo: Dār al-Shaʿb, 1969–82.
Iqbal, Muzaffar. Review of *Virtues of the Imām Aḥmad ibn Ḥanbal*. *Islamic Sciences* 13 (2015): 43–44.
Iṣfahānī, Abū Nuʿaym al-: *see* Abū Nuʿaym al-Iṣfahānī.
Jadʿān, Fahmī. *Al-Miḥnah: Baḥth fī jadaliyyat al-dīnī wa-l-siyāsī fī l-Islām*. Amman: Dār al-Shurūq, 1989.
Jāḥiẓ, al-. *The Book of Misers*. Translated by R. B. Serjeant. Reading: Garnet, 1997.
———. *Al-Bukhalā'*. Edited by Ṭāhā l-Ḥājiri. Cairo: Dār al-Kitāb al-Miṣrī, 1948.
———. *Rasā'il*. Edited by ʿAbd al-Salām Hārūn. 4 vols. Beirut: Dār al-Jīl, 1411/1991.
Jeffrey, A. "Āzār." In *EI2*.
Jomier, J. "Dikka." In *EI2*.
Juynboll, J. H. A. "Shuʿba b. al-Ḥadjdjādj." In *EI2*.
Katz, Marion H. "ʿAzīmah and Rukhṣah." In *EI3*.
Keller, Nun Ha Mim. *See* Misri, al-.

Kennedy, Hugh N. *The Armies of the Caliphs: Military and Society in the Early Islamic State*. London: Routledge, 2001.

Khaṭīb al-Baghdādī, al-. *Ta'rīkh Baghdād*. Edited by Muṣṭafā 'Abd al-Qādir 'Aṭā'. 14 vols. Beirut: Dār al-Kutub al-'Ilmiyyah, 1417/1997.

Kilito, Abdelfattah. *The Author and His Doubles*. Translated by Michael Cooperson. Syracuse: Syracuse University Press, 2001.

Kinberg, Leah. "Paradise." In McAuliffe, *Encyclopaedia of the Qur'ān*.

———. "What Is Meant by *Zuhd*." *Studia Islamica* 61 (1985): 27–44.

Lane, Edward William, and Stanley Lane-Poole. *An Arabic-English Lexicon*. London: Williams and Norgate, 1863–93. http://ejtaal.net.

Lange, Christian. "Expiation." In *EI3*.

Lapidus, I. M. "The Separation of State and Religion in the Development of Early Islamic Society." *International Journal of Middle East Studies* 6 (1975): 363–85.

Lassner, J. "Nahr 'Īsā." In *EI2*.

Le Strange, Guy *Baghdad during the Abbasid Caliphate*. Oxford, 1900. Reprint, Westport, CT: Greenwood Press, 1983.

Longrigg, S. H. "'Āna." In *EI2*.

Lucas, Scott C. *Constructive Critics, Hadith Literature, and the Articulation of Sunni Islam: The Legacy of the Generation of Ibn Sa'd, Ibn Ma'īn, and Ibn Ḥanbal*. Leiden: Brill, 2004.

Madelung, Wilferd. "Mahdī." In *EI2*.

———. "The Origins of the Controversy Concerning the Creation of the Qur'ān." In *Religious Schools and Sects in Medieval Islam*, edited by Wilferd Madelung, 504–25. London: Ashgate, 1985.

Makdisi, George. *The Rise of Humanism in Classical Islam and the Christian West*. Edinburgh: Edinburgh University Press, 1990.

Maqdisī, Taqī l-Dīn. *Miḥnat al-Imām Aḥmad ibn Ḥanbal*. Edited by 'Abd Allāh al-Turkī. Giza: Hajr, 1987.

Martin, Richard. "Createdness of the Qur'ān." In McAuliffe, *Encyclopaedia of the Qur'ān*.

Maṭlūb, Aḥmad. *Mu'jam al-malābis fī lisān al-'arab*. Beirut: Maktabat Lubnān, 1995.

McAuliffe, Jane Dammen, ed. *Encyclopaedia of the Qur'ān*. Leiden: Brill Online, 2012. http://www.brill.com/publications/online-resources/encyclopaedia-quran-online.

Melchert, Christopher. "The Adversaries of Aḥmad ibn Ḥanbal." *Arabica* 44 (1997): 234–53.

———. *Ahmad ibn Hanbal*. Makers of the Muslim World. Oxford: Oneworld, 2006.

———. "Ahmad ibn Hanbal and the Qur'an." *Journal of Qur'anic Studies* 6, no. 2 (2004): 22–34.

———. "Aḥmad ibn Ḥanbal's Book of Renunciation." *Der Islam* 85 (2008): 345–59.

———. "Early Renunciants as Hadith Transmitters." *Muslim World* 92 (2002): 407–18.

———. "Exaggerated Fear in the Early Islamic Renunciant Tradition." *Journal of the Royal Asiatic Society* 3, no. 21 (2011): 283–300.

———. *The Formation of the Sunni Schools of Law, 9th–10th Centuries C.E.* Leiden: Brill, 1997.

———. "The Ḥanābila and the Early Sufis." *Arabica* 48 (2001): 352–67.

———. "Hasan al-Basri, al-." In *Dictionary of Literary Biography 311: Arabic Literary Culture, 500–925*, edited by Michael Cooperson and Shawkat M. Toorawa, 121–27. Detroit: Thomson Gale, 2005.

———. "The *Musnad* of Ahmad ibn Hanbal: How It Was Composed and What Distinguishes It from the Six Books." *Der Islam* 82 (2005): 32–51.

———. "The Piety of the Hadith Folk." *International Journal of Middle East Studies* 34 (2002): 425–39.

———. "Religious Policies of the Caliphs from al-Mutawakkil to al-Muqtadir, AH 232–295/AD 847–908." *Islamic Law and Society* 3, no. 3 (1996): 316–42.

———. Review of *Virtues of the Imām Aḥmad Ibn Ḥanbal*, Vol. I. *Journal of Islamic Studies* (2014) 344–55.

Mietke, Gabriele. "Vine Rinceaux." In Evans with Ratliff, *Byzantium and Islam*, 175–82.

Minorsky, V. "Ṣaḥna." In *EI2*.

Misri, Ahmad ibn Naqib al-. *Reliance of the Traveler*. Edited and translated by Nun Ha Mim Keller. Beltsville, MD: Amana, 1999.

Monnot, G. "Ṣalāt." In *EI2*.

Mourad, Sulaiman Ali. *Early Islam between Myth and History: Al-Ḥasan al-Baṣrī (d. 110H/728CE) and the Formation of His Legacy in Classical Islamic Scholarship*. Leiden: Brill, 2005.

Mubārakfūrī, Muḥammad ibn ʿAbd al-Raḥmān al-. *Al-Aḥwadhī bi-sharḥ Jāmiʿ al-Tirmidhī*. Beirut: al-ʿIlmiyyah, 1418/1997. http://islamweb.net.

Nagel, T. "Ḳurrāʾ." In *EI2*.

———. *Rechtleitung und Kalifat. Versuch über eine Grundfrage der islamischen Geschichte*. Studien zum Minderheitenproblem im Islam 2. Bonn: Selbstverlag des Orientalischen Seminars der Universität Bonn, 1975.

Nawas, John A. *Al-Maʾmūn. Miḥna and Caliphate*. Nijmegen, 1992.

———. "The Mihna of 218 A.H./833 A.D. Revisited: An Empirical Study." *Journal of the American Oriental Society* 116 (1996): 698–708.

Northedge, Alistair. *Historical Topography of Samarra*. London: British School of Archaeology in Iraq, 2005.

Omari, Racha El. "Beatific Vision." In *The Oxford Encyclopedia of the Islamic World*, edited by John L. Esposito, 1:331–32. Oxford: Oxford University Press, 2009.

———. "*Kitāb al-Ḥayda*: The Historical Significance of an Apocryphal Text." In *Islamic Philosophy, Science, Culture, and Religion: Studies in Honor of Dimitri Gutas*, edited by Felicitas Opwis and David C. Reisman, 419–51. Leiden: Brill, 2012.

Patton, Walter M. *Aḥmed Ibn Ḥanbal and the Miḥna*. Leiden: Brill, 1897.

Pellat, C. "Al-Masḥ ʿAlā l-Khuffayn." In *EI2*.

Perkins, Tasi. "Hagiography and Hanbalism." *Marginalia*, August 18, 2015. http://marginalia.lareviewofbooks.org/hagiography-and-hanbalism-by-tasi-perkins/

Perry, Charles. *See* Baghdādī, al-.

Pérès, H. "Al-Ramādī." In *EI2*.

Peters, R. "Zinā or Zināʾ." In *EI2*.

Picken, Gavin. "Ibn Ḥanbal and al-Muḥāsibī: A Study of Early Conflicting Scholarly Methodologies." *Arabica* 55 (2008): 337–61.

Qāḍī, Wadād al-. "The Earliest *Nābita* and the Paradigmatic *Nawābit.*" *Studia Islamica* 78 (1993): 27–61.

Qurṭubī, Abū ʿAbd Allāh Muḥammad ibn Aḥmad, al-. *Al-Jāmiʿ li-aḥkām al-Qurʾān.* Edited by ʿAbd Allāh ibn ʿAbd al-Muḥsin al-Turkī. 24 vols. Beirut: Muʾassasat al-Risālah, 2006. http://www.archive.org.

Raddatz, H. P. "Sufyān al-Thawrī." In *EI2.*

Rāghib al-Iṣfahānī, al-. *Muḥāḍarāt al-udabāʾ.* Beirut: Dār Maktabat al-Ḥayāh, 1961.

Reinhart, A. K. "Shaʿr, 2: Legal Aspects Regarding Human Hair." In *EI2.*

Rippin, A. "Al-Ṣiddīḳ." In *EI2.*

Robinson, Neal. "Antichrist." In McAufliffe, *Encyclopaedia of the Qurʾān.*

Rowson, Everett. "The Effeminates of Early Medina." *Journal of the American Oriental Society* 111, no. 4 (1991): 671–93.

Sadan, J. "Mafrūshāt." In *EI2.*

Ṣāliḥ ibn Aḥmad ibn Ḥanbal. *Sīrat al-Imām Aḥmad ibn Ḥanbal.* Edited by Fuʾād ʿAbd al-Munʿim Aḥmad. Alexandria: Muʾassasat al-Jāmiʿah, 1401/1981.

Samʿānī, Abū Saʿd ʿAbd al-Karīm ibn Muḥammad. *Al-Ansāb.* Edited by ʿAbd Allāh ʿUmar al-Bārūdī. 5 vols. Beirut: al-Jinān, 1408/1988. http://www.archive.org.

Sarhan, Saud Al-. "Early Muslim Traditionalism: A Critical Study of the Works and Political Theology of Aḥmad Ibn Ḥanbal." PhD diss., University of Exeter, 2011.

———. "'Patience Is Better Than Sedition': The Political Thought of Ahmad Ibn Hanbal." Paper delivered at the second LIVIT (Legitimate and Illegitimate Violence in Early Islamic Thought) conference, Institute of Arab and Islamic Studies, University of Exeter, UK, September 5–6, 2011.

Schacht, J. "Ibn Nudjaym." In *EI2.*

Schoeler, Gregor. *The Genesis of Oral Literature in Islam. From the Oral to the Read.* In collaboration with and translated by Shawkat Toorawa. Edinburgh: Edinburgh University Press, 2009.

Serjeant: *see* Jāḥiẓ, al-.

Sezgin, Fuat. *Geschichte des arabischen Schrifttums*. 12 vols. Leiden: E.J. Brill, 1967–2010.

Shāfiʿī, Muḥammad ibn Idrīs al-. *The Epistle on Legal Theory*. Edited and translated by Joseph E. Lowry. New York University Press, 2013.

Shah, Mustafa. "The Quest for the Origins of the Qurrāʾ in the Classical Islamic Tradition." *Journal of Qurʾanic Studies* 7, no. 2 (2005): 1-35

Sizgorich, Thomas. *Violence and Belief in Late Antiquity: Militant Devotion in Christianity and Islam*. Philadelphia: University of Pennsylvania Press, 2009.

Sourdel, Dominique. "La politique religieuse du caliph ʿabbaside al-Maʾmūn." *Revue des études islamiques* 20 (1962): 27–48.

Sourdel-Thomine, J. "Ḥammām." In *EI2*.

Steingass, Francis Joseph. *A Comprehensive Persian-English dictionary*. London: Routledge & K. Paul, 1892.

Steppat, Fritz. "From *ʿAhd Ardašīr* to al-Maʾmūn: A Persian Element in the Policy of the Miḥna." In *Studia Arabica et Islamica. Festschrift for Iḥsān ʿAbbās on His Sixtieth Birthday*, edited by Wadād al-Qāḍī, 451–54. Beirut: American University of Beirut, 1981.

Stillman, Y. K. "Libās." In *EI2*.

Swartz, Merlin. *Ibn al-Jawzi, a Study of His Life and Work as Preacher: Including a Critical Edition and Translation of His Kitāb al-Quṣṣāṣ wa ʾl-mudhakkirīn, with Introduction and Notes*. Beirut: Institut de Lettres Orientales, 1971.

———. "A Ḥanbalī Critique of Anthropomorphism." *Proceedings of the Arabic and Islamic Sections of the 35th International Congress of Asian and North African Studies (ICANAS)*, Part Two, edited by A. Fodor, 27–36. Budapest: Csoma de Kőrös Society, 1999.

Ṭabarī, al-. *Taʾrīkh al-rusul wa-l-mulūk*. Edited by M.J. de Goeje. Leiden: E.J. Brill, 1879–1901. Edited by Muḥammad Abū l-Faḍl Ibrāhīm. 10 vols. Cairo: Dār al-Maʿārif, 1979. References in the notes give the page numbers in the Cairo edition, then the Leiden, separated by a slash.

Tillier, Mathieu. *Les cadis d'Iraq et l'État abbasside (132/750-334/945)*. Damascus: Institut français du Proche-Orient, 2009.

Tirmidhī, Abū ʿĪsā Muḥammad al-. *Sunan*. 2nd ed. Edited by Aḥmad Muḥammad Shākir. Cairo: Muṣṭafā l-Bābī l-Ḥalabī, 1398/1978. https://archive.org/details/thermidiosun.

Toorawa, Shawkat M. "Prayer." In *Key Themes for the Study of Islam*, edited by Jamal J. Elias, 263–80. Oxford: Oneworld, 2010.

Turkī, al-. *See* Ibn al-Jawzī, Abū l-Faraj ʿAbd al-Raḥmān.

Turner, John P. "Aḥmad b. Abī Duʾād." In *EI3*.

———. *Inquisition in Early Islam: The Competition for Political and Religious Authority in the Abbasid Empire*. London: I.B. Tauris, 2013.

Tyan, E. "ʿAdl." In *EI2*.

van Ess, Josef. *Theologie und Gesellschaft im 2. und 3. Jahrhundert Hidschra: Eine Geschichte des religiösen Denkens im frühen Islam*. Berlin and New York: Walter de Gruyter, 1991–97.

Waines, David. "Tree(s)." In McAuliffe, *Encyclopaedia of the Qurʾān*.

Wensinck, A. J. "Ḥawḍ." In *EI2*.

———. "Al-Khaḍir (Al-Khiḍr)." In *EI2*.

Williams, Wesley. "Aspects of the Creed of Imam Ahmad ibn Hanbal: A Study of Anthropomorphism in Early Islamic Discourse." *International Journal of Middle Eastern Studies* 34 (2002): 441–63.

Winkelmann-Liebert, Holger. "Die *miḥna* im Kalifat des al-Muʿtaṣim." *Der Islam* 80, no. 1 (2003): 224–83.

Yaʿqūbī, al-. *Taʾrīkh*. . Edited by M. Th. Houtsma. 2 vols. Leiden: Brill, 1883.

Yāqūt al-Ḥamawī. *Muʿjam al-buldān. Jacut's geographisches Wörterbuch*. Edited by Ferdinand Wüstenfeld. 6 vols. Leipzig: Brockhaus, 1866–73.

Yücesoy, Hayrettin. *Messianic Beliefs and Imperial Politics in Medieval Islam. The ʿAbbāsid Caliphate in the Early Ninth Century*. Columbia: University of South Carolina Press, 2009.

Zaman, Muhammad Qasim. *Religion and Politics under the Early ʿAbbāsids: The Emergence of the Proto-Sunnī Elite*. Leiden: Brill, 1997.

Further Reading

Brown, Jonathan A. C. *Hadith: Muhammad's Legacy in the Medieval and Modern World*. Oxford: Oneworld, 2009.

Cook, Michael. *Commanding Right and Forbidding Wrong in Islamic Thought*. Cambridge: Cambridge University Press, 2000.

Cooperson, Michael. *Al-Ma'mun*. Oxford: Oneworld, 2005.

Crone, Patricia. *God's Rule: Government and Islam*. New York: Columbia University Press, 2004.

Goitein, S. D., and Jacob Lassner. *A Mediterranean Society: An Abridgement in One Volume*. Berkeley: University of California Press, 1999.

Katz, Marion Holmes. *Body of Text: The Emergence of the Sunni Law of Ritual Purity*. Albany: SUNY Press, 2002.

Melchert, Christopher. *Ahmad ibn Hanbal*. Makers of the Muslim World. Oxford: Oneworld, 2006.

Shāfiʿī, Muḥammad ibn Idrīs al-. *The Epistle on Legal Theory*. Edited and translated by Joseph E. Lowry. New York: New York University Press, 2013.

Sizgorich, Thomas. *Violence and Belief in Late Antiquity: Militant Devotion in Christianity and Islam*. Philadelphia: University of Pennsylvania Press, 2009.

van Ess, Josef. *The Flowering of Muslim Theology*. Translated by Jane Marie Todd. Cambridge, MA: Harvard University Press, 2006.

Index

About the NYU Abu Dhabi Institute

The Library of Arabic Literature is supported by a grant from the NYU Abu Dhabi Institute, a major hub of intellectual and creative activity and advanced research. The Institute hosts academic conferences, workshops, lectures, film series, performances, and other public programs directed both to audiences within the UAE and to the worldwide academic and research community. It is a center of the scholarly community for Abu Dhabi, bringing together faculty and researchers from institutions of higher learning throughout the region.

NYU Abu Dhabi, through the NYU Abu Dhabi Institute, is a world-class center of cutting-edge research, scholarship, and cultural activity. The Institute creates singular opportunities for leading researchers from across the arts, humanities, social sciences, sciences, engineering, and the professions to carry out creative scholarship and conduct research on issues of major disciplinary, multidisciplinary, and global significance.

About the Translator

Michael Cooperson (PhD Harvard 1994) has taught Arabic language and literature at UCLA since 1995. He has also taught at Dartmouth College, Stanford University, and the Middlebury School of Arabic. His research interests include the cultural history of the early Abbasid caliphate, Maltese language and literature, and time travel as a literary device. His publications include *Classical Arabic Biography*, a study of four ninth-century celebrities and how they have been remembered; and *Al Ma'mūn*, a biography of the caliph. He has translated Abdelfattah Kilito's *The Author and His Doubles*, Khairy Shalabi's *Time Travels of the Man Who Sold Pickles and Sweets*, and Jurji Zaidan's *The Caliph's Heirs: Brothers at War*. He is a co-author, with the RRAALL group, of *Interpreting the Self: Autobiography in the Arabic Literary Tradition*; and co-editor, with Shawkat Toorawa, of *The Dictionary of Literary Biography: Arabic Literary Culture, 500–925*.

The Library of Arabic Literature

For more details on individual titles, visit www.libraryofarabicliterature.org.

Classical Arabic Literature: A Library of Arabic Literature Anthology
Selected and translated by Geert Jan van Gelder

A Treasury of Virtues: Sayings, Sermons and Teachings of ʿAlī, by al-Qāḍī al-Quḍāʿī with the *One Hundred Proverbs* attributed to al-Jāḥiẓ
Edited and translated by Tahera Qutbuddin

The Epistle on Legal Theory, by al-Shāfiʿī
Edited and translated by Joseph E. Lowry

Leg over Leg, by Aḥmad Fāris al-Shidyāq
Edited and translated by Humphrey Davies

Virtues of the Imām Aḥmad ibn Ḥanbal, by Ibn al-Jawzī
Edited and translated by Michael Cooperson

The Epistle of Forgiveness, by Abū l-ʿAlāʾ al-Maʿarrī
Edited and translated by Geert Jan van Gelder and Gregor Schoeler

The Principles of Sufism, by ʿĀʾishah al-Bāʿūniyyah
Edited and translated by Th. Emil Homerin

The Expeditions: An Early Biography of Muḥammad, by Maʿmar ibn Rāshid
Edited and translated by Sean W. Anthony

Two Arabic Travel Books
Accounts of China and India, by Abū Zayd al-Sīrāfī
Edited and translated by Tim Mackintosh-Smith
Mission to the Volga, by Aḥmad ibn Faḍlān
Edited and translated by James Montgomery

Disagreements of the Jurists: A Manual of Islamic Legal Theory, by al-Qāḍī al-Nuʿmān
Edited and translated by Devin J. Stewart

Consorts of the Caliphs: Women and the Court of Baghdad, by Ibn al-Sāʿī
Edited by Shawkat M. Toorawa and translated by the Editors of the Library of Arabic Literature

What ʿĪsā ibn Hishām Told Us, by Muḥammad al-Muwayliḥī
Edited and translated by Roger Allen

The Life and Times of Abū Tammām, by Abū Bakr Muḥammad ibn Yaḥyā al-Ṣūlī
Edited and translated by Beatrice Gruendler

The Sword of Ambition: Bureaucratic Rivalry in Medieval Egypt, by ʿUthmān ibn Ibrāhīm al-Nābulusī
Edited and translated by Luke Yarbrough

Brains Confounded by the Ode of Abū Shādūf Expounded, by Yūsuf al-Shirbīnī
Edited and translated by Humphrey Davies

Light in the Heavens: Sayings of the Prophet Muḥammad, by al-Qāḍī al-Quḍāʿī
Edited and translated by Tahera Qutbuddin

Risible Rhymes, by Muḥammad ibn Maḥfūẓ al-Sanhūrī
Edited and translated by Humphrey Davies

A Hundred and One Nights
Edited and translated by Bruce Fudge

English-only Paperbacks

Leg over Leg: Volumes One and Two, by Aḥmad Fāris al-Shidyāq

Leg over Leg: Volumes Three and Four, by Aḥmad Fāris al-Shidyāq

The Expeditions: An Early Biography of Muḥammad, by Maʿmar ibn Rāshid

The Epistle on Legal Theory: A Translation of al-Shāfiʿī's Risālah, by al-Shāfiʿī

The Epistle of Forgiveness, by Abū l-ʿAlāʾ al-Maʿarrī

The Principles of Sufism, by ʿĀʾishah al-Bāʿūniyyah

A Treasury of Virtues: Sayings, Sermons and Teachings of ʿAlī, by al-Qāḍī al-Quḍāʿī with *The One Hundred Proverbs*, attributed to al-Jāḥiẓ

The Life of Ibn Ḥanbal, by Ibn al-Jawzī